P9-BYR-772

BEST-EVER
BACKYARD
BIRDING TIPS

BACKYARD BIRDING TIPS

Hundreds of Easy Ways to Attract the Birds You Love to Watch

DEBORAH L. MARTIN
and the Editors of RODALE GARDEN BOOKS

Notice

Mention of specific companies, organizations, or authorities in this book does not imply endorsement by the author or publisher, nor does mention of specific companies, organizations, or authorities imply that they endorse this book, its author, or the publisher.

Internet addresses and telephone numbers given in this book were accurate at the time it went to press.

Rodale books may be purchased for business or promotional use or for special sales. For information, please write to: Special Markets Department, Rodale Inc., 733 Third Avenue, New York, NY 10017

Printed in the United States of America

Rodale Inc. makes every effort to use acid-free ♾, recycled paper ♻.

Book design by Christina Gaugler

Illustrations by Michael Gellatly

Library of Congress Cataloging-in-Publication Data

Martin, Deborah L.
Best-ever backyard birding tips : hundreds of easy ways to attract the birds you love to watch / Deborah L. Martin and the editors of Rodale Garden Books.
p. cm.
Includes bibliographical references and index.
ISBN-13 978–1–59486–830–6 direct hardcover
ISBN-10 1–59486–830–1 direct hardcover
ISBN-13 978–1–59486–831–3 trade paperback
ISBN-10 1–59486–831–X trade paperback
1. Bird watching. I. Title.
QL677.5.M37 2008
598.072'34—dc22 2008017681

Distributed to the trade by Macmillan

2 4 6 8 10 9 7 5 3 1 hardcover

2 4 6 8 10 9 7 5 3 1 paperback

To the individuals and organizations that work tirelessly to expand our knowledge and understanding of birds and to promote avian conservation worldwide.

CONTENTS

ACKNOWLEDGMENTS

The editors and writers offer their thanks to the many people who generously shared their ideas, observations, and personal experiences with us, including Bob and Martha Sargent of the Hummer/Bird Study Group; Nancy Newfield; Scott Weidensaul; Laurie Goodrich and Tirah Keal of Hawk Mountain Sanctuary; Gerry Tuning; Ron Rovansek; Frank and Barb Haas; Rudy Keller; Carolyn Reider; Cole Burrell; Joan Silagy; Pat Varner, co-owner of Wild Birds Unlimited store in Allentown, Pennsylvania; and Dr. Daniel Klem Jr., Sarkis Acopian Professor of Ornithology and Conservation Biology at Muhlenberg College, Allentown, Pennsylvania. The following organizations also provided invaluable information and expertise: American Bird Conservancy; American Birding Association; Cornell Lab of Ornithology at Cornell University; Diversity Web, University of Michigan Museum of Zoology; Florida Museum of Natural History; Florida Fish and Wildlife Conservation Commission; Hawk Migration Association of North America; Hinterland Who's Who, Canadian Wildlife Service and Canadian Wildlife Federation; Humane Society of the United States; National Audubon Society; National Wildlife Federation; Newman Library at Virginia Polytechnic Institute and State University; North American Bluebird Society; Pennsylvania Society for Ornithology; University of Florida Institute of Food and Agricultural Sciences Extension; U.S. Fish and Wildlife Service, Office of Migratory Bird Management; U.S. Geological Survey Bird Banding Lab; and Wild Bird Centers of America.

HOW TO USE THIS BOOK

This is a book meant for browsing. You can go from start—"Bird-Attracting Basics"—to finish—"Less-Wanted Guests"—or choose a chapter that interests you—about landscape plants for birds, perhaps, or water features—and dive right in. Or simply open the book to any page and peruse the tips there—you're bound to find something new to add to your own list of best practices for bringing in the birds.

Throughout the book you'll also find opportunities to "Take a Closer Look" at the birds that are most likely to spend some or all of their life cycles in a home landscape setting. Use these features to learn more about your feathered favorites, including which foods they prefer, where and how they raise their young, and what you can do to make them feel at home.

From seeds and feeders to houses and roosting sites, discover page after page of easy, practical, actionable ideas for enjoying maximum bird-watching pleasure. Start with tips that offer almost-immediate results and advance to plans for long-term bird benefits. Find out how to "borrow" bird-friendly elements from beyond your property lines and how to bring birds close for easy window-watching from the comfort of your favorite chair.

The tips that appear in this book have been gathered by and from knowledgeable birders, dedicated gardeners, experts in a variety of subjects, and amateur naturalists. Many of them are people just like you, who began by watching the birds around them and turned that simple pleasure into a passion for bird conservation. There's something for everyone—for every bird lover and for (almost) every bird—among the hundreds of hints ahead. Let's get started: Open this book and let it open your eyes to the wonderful possibilities of surroundings brimming with beautiful birds.

INVITE BIRDS INTO YOUR LIFE!

With very little effort on my part, wild birds have become a feature of my daily life. Over the course of nearly 20 years in my home, I've gone from occasionally noticing a (generic) bird or two to enjoying, identifying, and interacting with several different species almost every single day. From being a gardener who knew the names of a few of the most common birds, I've become a bird-watcher who is acquainted with a few dozen species and who does things on a regular basis to invite more birds into my yard.

This change has been gradual and almost imperceptible. It started with a simple tube feeder, received as a Christmas gift. Filled with seed mix and hung without much thought in our yard, it became a hub of bird activity that couldn't fail to catch my eye when I glanced out the window. Our house cat noticed the action, too, and my family began referring to the feeder scene as "cat TV." Sometimes the cat's interest in what was happening outside would draw my attention to the birds at the feeder, and I found myself lingering at the window, studying their behavior as they dined.

Squirrels play a part in this story, too. Maintaining bird feeders transformed them—in my eyes—from cute woodland creatures to "bushy-tailed rats" that I'd angrily chase away from a fresh supply of seed intended for brilliant cardinals and cheery chickadees. After these terrors in furry disguise chewed up, knocked down, and otherwise destroyed a few feeders, I learned to take defensive measures to keep them from emptying my feeders almost as quickly as I could fill them. Over time we've achieved an uneasy truce—I only put out bird feeders that are built to prevent or, at least, withstand squirrels' efforts to raid their contents. I also offer dried ears of corn on separate squirrel feeders that are designed to entertain me as the greedy bushy-tails engage in amazing acrobatics to get at the treat.

Keeping my feeders filled has taught me which foods my feathered guests prefer and which they fling unceremoniously to the ground. By adapting my seed purchasing habits accordingly, I've been able to reduce the amount of waste and mess beneath the feeders. This cuts down on cleanup work around the feeder—less spoiled seed on the ground and fewer weeds springing up among the plants I've put there.

I've added specialized feeders to my repertoire: a suet cage that invites woodpeckers to fly in for a fatty snack and tubes with tiny holes made to serve shiny black nyjer seed to flocks of busy finches. Tray feeders hold wilted grapes or bits of leftover pasta for jays to feast on; a sturdy nail driven into the post supporting a feeder becomes a holder for an occasional impaled orange half that may bring an oriole into view.

Our household library now contains a small collection of field guides and other bird books to help us identify the birds we see in the yard. My sons have learned along with me, sitting almost patiently by the window to tally birds for a nationwide count of feeder visitors. They get nearly as excited as I do—or at least they feign excitement for my benefit—when an unusual bird appears in the landscape. With their younger eyes and sharper vision, they're quick to spot birds I might miss—like the iridescent dark blue indigo bunting that flits across our backyard now and then or the brilliant tanager perching high in the treetops.

The birds that visit our yard provide punctuation for the passing seasons. Busy male goldfinches wearing feathers newly turned from olive drab to bright yellow reassure me of spring's arrival, while migrating robins are a sign of fall as they arrive en masse to wrest bright red berries from the dogwood's branches. Small flocks of juncos turning up at the feeder tell me that winter weather is near—it's no coincidence that these tidy slate-colored birds are also known as snowbirds. Wild turkeys sometimes troop across our backyard in winter as they search for food, and bluebirds often surprise me in late February when they show up to glean the last lingering berries from pokeweed skeletons sticking up above the snow.

I've stood next to an open window not minding the chill air rushing in as I listen to great horned owls conversing late at night. When I work in my yard, there are always bird sounds to keep me company—the wren's scolding chatter when I pass too near its nest in a hollow gourd, the rustling of thrushes as they hunt for insects in the dry leaves, the startling buzz of a hummingbird zipping past my head on the way to visit a nectar-laden flower. Even when they're quiet, the birds remind me of the goings-on of the natural world—by their silence songbirds often signal the presence of a hawk or other predator nearby.

All this has come about gradually and in small increments, without huge investments of time or money and without major landscape renovations. By installing and maintaining a few feeders, by adding a few fruit- and seed-bearing plants, by hanging a simple gourd birdhouse, I've been able to enjoy the sights and sounds of a diverse and satisfying array of wild birds. When I pause in the course of a busy day to consider a noisy-but-beautiful jay or a soaring raptor, I return to my routine refreshed by this amazing and essential connection to the natural world.

Pull up a chair and browse the pages of this book to discover hundreds of ways to invite birds into your life. I promise you'll be astonished at how easy it is and how little it takes to enjoy their company every single day.

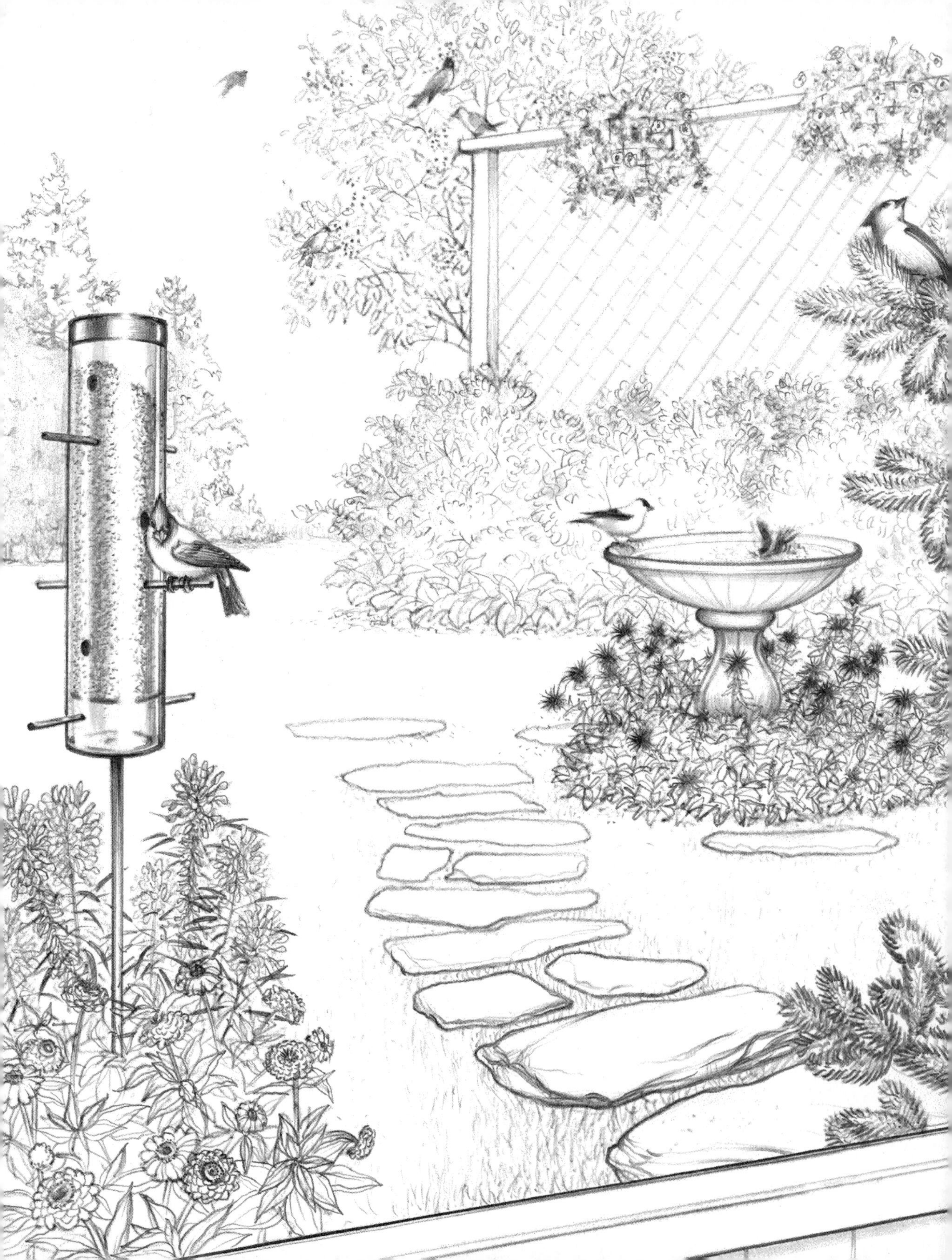

CHAPTER 1

BIRD-ATTRACTING BASICS

Three things have lifted the hearts of humans since the dawn of civilization: birds, butterflies, and flowers. Their beauty and the joy they bring us, without seeking anything in return, have been celebrated by poets, sages, and ordinary people through human history. The reason is simple: When you see a soaring eagle, your heart soars with it. When you see a goldfinch flying through your yard, or a bluebird on the raspberry trellis, or a flock of juncos or pair of cardinals at your feeder, you experience joy. Life is good!

Yes, flowers and butterflies can also inspire us with a love of beauty and a sense of wonder. But birds are special because they sing, they court, they build their homes with care, they carry food to their young, they sometimes mate for life. They remind us of the very best aspects of being human: Sing! Love! Nurture! Live your life to the fullest!

We want birds in our lives. And the good news is we can have them, wherever we live. Whether you live in a high-rise apartment in a concrete jungle like New York or a hacienda in an adobe-dry city like Santa Fe, in icy Alaska or the steamy swampland of the Florida Everglades, it's easy to attract birds—and plenty of them—to brighten your life and your surroundings.

STARTING OUT RIGHT

Let's start with a little myth-busting. Almost every bird-attracting book and article starts by telling you that you need four basic elements to attract birds: food, water, shelter (i.e., birdhouses and other nesting sites), and cover (protection from predators). It is actually much simpler than that. All you really need is a wee bit of outdoor space (balcony, deck, or whole yard) and a bit of enthusiasm. Then just add on from there. A feeder is often enough. A feeder and water are fantastic! And a seed feeder, a hummingbird nectar feeder, a suet or peanut butter-and-seed block in winter, water, and a pot of fiery scarlet annual salvia or a rose-of-Sharon bush is nirvana.

Why? Because you can "borrow" the water, shelter, and cover from neighboring areas if you can't provide them yourself. Birds aren't stupid, and they can fly. If you heard of a café a mile or two from you that set out fabulous *free* coffee and treats for all comers, wouldn't you go there? Likewise, birds will flock to a food source, too.

What *is* true is that you'll attract more birds and more kinds of birds if you can provide an inviting habitat, and you'll keep them hanging around longer. (See "Bird's-Eye View: The Ideal Yard" on page 10 for a vision of bird utopia in a suburban setting.) If you have the space and enthusiasm to create bird housing, water features, and landscaping designed with birds in mind, your yard will become a magnet for everything from hummingbirds to Cooper's hawks (not to mention a vast array of grateful butterflies).

It's also true that once you start making your yard bird-friendly, it's hard to stop. You'll probably find that the more success you have bringing birds to your backyard, the more you'll want. We bet you've seen yards in your neighborhood with whole arrays of different kinds of bird feeders, and wondered what was going on with those families. We'll tell you: They were having fun!

Now you can, too. In this chapter, we'll give you the basics of bird-attracting, so you can get results right away.

BACKYARD BIRDING ESSENTIALS

Backyard bird-watching is one of the easiest—and least expensive—hobbies around. Just keep your eyes and ears open and consider yourself a full-fledged bird-watcher. You can make the experience more enjoyable, however, by getting yourself a few basics. Check out a bird specialty store in your area like Wild Birds Unlimited or a birding destination with a great gift shop like Hawk Mountain in Kempton, Pennsylvania. Sporting-goods stores like Cabela's and country-living stores like Tractor Supply Co. might also be one-stop shopping destinations. So are online bird-supply sites like www.duncraft.com. Or get basic bird supplies in a pet, home, or hardware store; a field guide and birdsong CD from a bookstore like Barnes & Noble or Borders or online at Amazon.com or www.birds.cornell.edu; and a pair of binoculars at a sporting-goods or bird-specialty store.

To get started, try these suggestions.

- **A great tube feeder.** A well-made feeder can last practically forever. Look for one with a clear acrylic tube and metal top, bottom, feeder openings, and perches. (The metal perches can be covered with plastic, but here's another

5-MINUTE MAKEOVERS

Fast Ways to Attract Birds

Planting bird-friendly trees and shrubs or installing an in-ground water garden with features designed to bring in the birds can take time to produce the desired results. But there are plenty of quick—and inexpensive—things you can do to put out the welcome mat almost instantly. Jump in right now and see how you can boost the bird population in your yard or space with these five fast ways to attract birds.

1. **Hang a tube feeder.** Tube feeders are available at bird specialty stores, hardware and farm supply stores, and home centers, as well as at many pet stores and, at least seasonally, at discount retailers. Get one to start, along with a supply of sunflower seed to fill it. Black oil sunflower attracts the greatest variety of birds, but any sort of sunflower seed will draw birds to the tube. If your new tube feeder will hang in a place where cast-off sunflower hulls may pose a problem, avoid the mess by filling it up with shelled, or hulled, sunflower seeds. Look for more feeder and seed specifics in Chapter 2, "Seeds and Feeders," beginning on page 25.
2. **Set out water.** Water features for birds can be elaborate—see Chapter 6, "Water Features for Birds," beginning on page 177, for options—or they can be very simple. If you have a casserole or shallow bowl that you've never liked, you can donate it to the birds, and do a good deed while getting rid of something you've always hated at the same time. Set it out, fill it with water, add a few pebbles to help the birds find a perch, and voila!
3. **Grow a nectar plant.** Columbines, trumpet vine, cleome (spiderflower), impatiens, nasturtiums, annual red salvia, cardinal flower, rose-of-Sharon, snapdragons, coral honeysuckle, cannas, bee balm (monarda), zinnias, and many other nectar-rich plants are especially good hummingbird attractors. Add a few of these hummingbird flowers to your garden—or to a container or two on your deck or patio—and see how many hummingbirds you can bring in!
4. **Add a hummingbird feeder.** From the ruby-throated hummingbird on the East Coast to the many species in Texas, the Southwest, and the West Coast, it's easy to attract these flying jewels to your yard if you set up a nectar feeder. (You can buy ones ranging from standard plastic feeders to handcrafted glass and ceramic versions, or make your own from recycled soda bottles.) See Chapter 7, "Hosting Hummingbirds," on page 207 for everything you need to know to bring them into your yard.
5. **Set out some fruit.** Half an orange, apple slices, a piece of melon, an overripe peach, a handful of berries—birds love fruit as much as we do. Set some out on a plate (a plastic plate or even a piece of cardboard is fine) and watch the birds and butterflies come over for dessert! You can also attract orioles by hanging half an orange from an oriole or fruit feeder, readily available in bird specialty stores. (Some feeders even come with cups for jelly as well as hooks for fruit!) Or make your own: Pierce the rind of an orange half by running a skewer through the fruit parallel to the cut side. Then make a hanger from a length of twine, knotting it securely on each end of the skewer. Hang the skewered fruit from a branch or hook.

myth-buster—research has proved that birds' feet will *not* become stuck to bare metal perches, so plain metal is fine.) A top-quality feeder may seem outrageously expensive—hey, this is a bird feeder, for heaven's sake!—but look at it this way: By the time you've had to replace cheap all-plastic feeders two or three times, you might as well have bought the well-made model to begin with. Remember that you don't have to start with a gigantic feeder. Bigger feeders accommodate more birds and need to be refilled less often. But if you're willing to refill a smaller feeder a couple of times a day (and you won't have to do it that often except in peak winter feeder season), a well-built small model is great. The birds will make sure they get their turn!

- **A hook for the feeder.** Once you've chosen a tube feeder, you need a place to hang it. And here's the most important tip in this whole book: Make sure you hang the feeder where you can see it easily from the house. (This is, of course, true for *every* feeder you set up or hang.) It should be easily visible from a window, and not just any window, but a window you look out often. If you spend a lot of time in the kitchen, hang it near the kitchen windows. If your family gathers to eat and do homework and projects at the dining room table, hang it where you can see it from the dining room. Spend a lot of time on your enclosed porch? Hang it where it's easy to see from the porch. It may be satisfying to know that you're providing for birds even if you can't see a feeder, but you'll certainly have a lot more fun if you can watch the action at the feeder and be part of the experience.

  Once you've chosen the best location, you'll need some way to hang the feeder so it's off the ground and the birds can eat in safety. Fortunately, the manufacturers of bird feeders have also thought of this, and developed sturdy, weatherproof hanging double hooks in any number of lengths and sizes. If you have a convenient tree that's easy to see from your chosen window, select a hook that's big enough to fit over the best branch for the feeder. If it's a thick branch, choose a hook that's bigger on the end that goes over the branch and smaller on the end that holds the feeder. Eyeball your branch to see how long a hook or how many hooks you'll need to hold the feeder at a height where you can easily take it down for refilling. No tree nearby? You can also buy a feeder pole or shepherd's crook to hold your feeder. (Read about all the options in Chapter 2, "Seeds and Feeders," on page 25.)

- **Songbird seed mix.** We'll get into all the types of seed and seed mixes you can use to attract birds—including specific types of birds—in Chapter 2, "Seeds and Feeders." For now, let's concentrate on getting a seed mix that will attract the widest variety of birds. When you go to the store, you'll see mixes labeled "songbird mix," "songbird favorite," and so on. Buy the best songbird mix you can afford, and get ready to watch the birds fly in! Be aware that cheaper mixes often add seeds that birds aren't that fond of, like corn and safflower seed. (Cardinals will eat safflower seed, but they also enjoy other seeds.) Look for mixes with lots of sunflower seeds, millet, and other bird-friendly ingredients.

- **A tin for birdseed.** To keep bugs, mice, and other undesirables (including your dog!) out of your birdseed, you need a container to store it in. If you buy small bags—the size parrot or parakeet food comes in—a gallon container might be fine. But most of us buy bigger bags, since we quickly find that seed disappears faster than we might believe. To keep pests out, a tin cylinder is ideal. If your family enjoys those giant tins of chips, popcorn, and pretzels, you can use the empty tins to hold birdseed. You can find tins at bird specialty stores with gorgeous illustrations of birds on the outside, and they're also often available at pet stores, as well as hardware and home-improvement stores. They're inexpensive—maybe even free at pet stores with the purchase of pet food—lightweight, and pest-proof. Get a size that will hold the contents of the bag of birdseed you choose.
- **A scoop for the seed.** Okay, you've got the seed and something to put it in. But how do you get it out of the container and into the tube feeder? You'll need two things: a scoop and a feeder filler. Big plastic scoops are available at every pet store as well as bird specialty stores. If you buy one that's sized to the opening of your feeder filler, it makes life a lot easier, let us tell you. What's a feeder filler, you ask? Read on.
- **A feeder filler.** Trying to pour seed from a scoop into a narrow tube feeder is a pain. You'll probably spill as much seed from the sides as you get into the tube. To avoid the frustration and mess, and make filling tube feeders painless and fun, manufacturers have developed "seed dispensers"—wide-mouthed plastic bottles with long, narrow tubes in their lids. To fill your tube feeder, remove the lid from the dispenser, fill the bottle with seed, screw the lid back on, open the feeder top, invert the dispenser over the tube, and voila! The seed pours into the tube precisely and quickly. Buy a seed dispenser that's suited to the size of your feeder tube. (You can find all sizes, from jumbo to slender ketchup-dispenser size.)
- **A field guide.** Okay, you've got your feeder up and filled. Now, what's that bird at the feeder? To find out, you need a good basic field guide. The classic starter guide is *A Field Guide to the Birds* by Roger Tory Peterson, which has eastern and western editions. Other excellent field guides are the *National Geographic Field Guide to the Birds of North America, The Sibley Guide to Birds* (also available in eastern and western editions), *The Audubon Society Field Guide to North American Birds* (two volumes, eastern and western regions, with photographs), the *Stokes Field Guide to Birds* (also with eastern and western volumes, and also with photographs), and *The Backyard Bird Lover's Field Guide,* by Sally Roth. Check them out at your local bird store or bookstore, ask birding friends, or contact your local Audubon Society chapter (find one near you at www.audubon.org) or bird club and ask for recommendations.

  A field guide focused on your state or, even better, on the part of the state in which you live, will prove more useful for day-to-day bird-watching than a comprehensive guide to all the birds of North America or even all the birds of the eastern or western United States. When you've spotted a bird you don't recognize and want to look it up quickly, it's helpful to have the options pre-screened to take your location into account. Otherwise, you may find yourself flipping through pages and pages of unlikely candidates before you narrow down your choices to a possible match. Meanwhile, the bird in question has probably long since moved on, leaving you with just a memory to compare with the pictures in your guide.

Of course, this doesn't cover the possibility of an unusual or even rare bird showing up in your locale, and it won't help you identify the birds you see when your travels take you out of your usual haunts. Include a comprehensive bird guide in your collection, if at all possible, and use it when you encounter a bird that doesn't match any of the species covered in your local field guide. This book may also be helpful if you have time to "study up" on birds you might see while traveling. If bird-watching is on your agenda during a trip away from home, it's probably worth investing in a narrow-scope guide to the birds of the area you're visiting.

Match Sounds to Sights

Top-notch birder Rudy Keller of Boyertown, Pennsylvania, past president of the Baird Ornithological Club and contributor to *The Birds of Pennsylvania,* notes that it's easiest to learn to identify birdsongs if you get a CD that's keyed to your field guide. That way, as you page through the guide, you'll hear the songs in the same order.

In addition to bird song CDs, there are a growing number of more portable devices to help you match birds to their sounds. For the Birds, Inc., offers the IdentiFlyer, a handheld digital player that lets you choose the songs you want to hear from illustrated cards that slip into the player, and the iFlyer, a pen-style scanning wand that reads bar codes representing more than 200 birds and 10 frogs. At least two companies, birdJam and iFieldguides, have products that let you play bird sounds and view bird photos on an iPod, while National Geographic's Handheld Birds displays illustrations and range maps and plays songs and calls on a PDA.

- **Binoculars.** Why get binoculars for watching birds in your yard? Not only can you use them to identify feeder birds, they're also ideal when you see a bird in some tree near the edge of your property. Could that be a hawk? A quick look through your binoculars confirms that it is, and comparing the appearance of the hawk through your lenses to the identifying marks in your field guide will tell you which one. For hints on selecting and using binoculars to bring the birds in for a closer look, see Chapter 9, "Sharing Space with Birds," on page 269.
- **A birdbath.** Providing water is a great way to bring birds flocking to your yard. (See Chapter 6, "Water Features for Birds," on page 177 for lots of tips on how to do this.) It's true as we said earlier that a feeder alone will bring in birds, but water will bring in more (as well as butterflies) and keep them happier.

  A birdbath is great because it provides a shallow basin with perching all around the rim, so birds can drink without drowning, and it puts that basin on a pedestal to give birds an advantage over predators like cats—they can see them coming and fly off to safety in plenty of time. Birdbaths come in all sorts of designs, colors, and price ranges, so you're sure to find one that suits both your budget and style.

A TOUR OF YOUR YARD

The next step in bringing birds to your yard is to make the yard inviting to them. It's time to take a sheet of paper, a pen or pencil, a camera (if you have a camera phone, that's easiest), and this book, and take a walk around your yard. Usually, you see your yard from a human perspective. But this time, you're also going to get a bird's-eye view of your yard!

First, walk out to the street, and look "in" at your front yard from the outside. What do you see as you look across the yard to your house? Is there a fence or hedge around your property? How much of the yard is lawn? Is your lawn a single kind of grass, like Kentucky bluegrass or Bermuda grass, or is it a mix of grasses and other plants like clover and violets? Are there trees scattered across the lawn? If so, what's under the trees? Are there shrubs in the lawn? Do you have flower beds or mixed borders (small trees, shrubs, flowers, ornamental grasses, groundcovers)? What does your foundation planting (the strip of ground immedi-

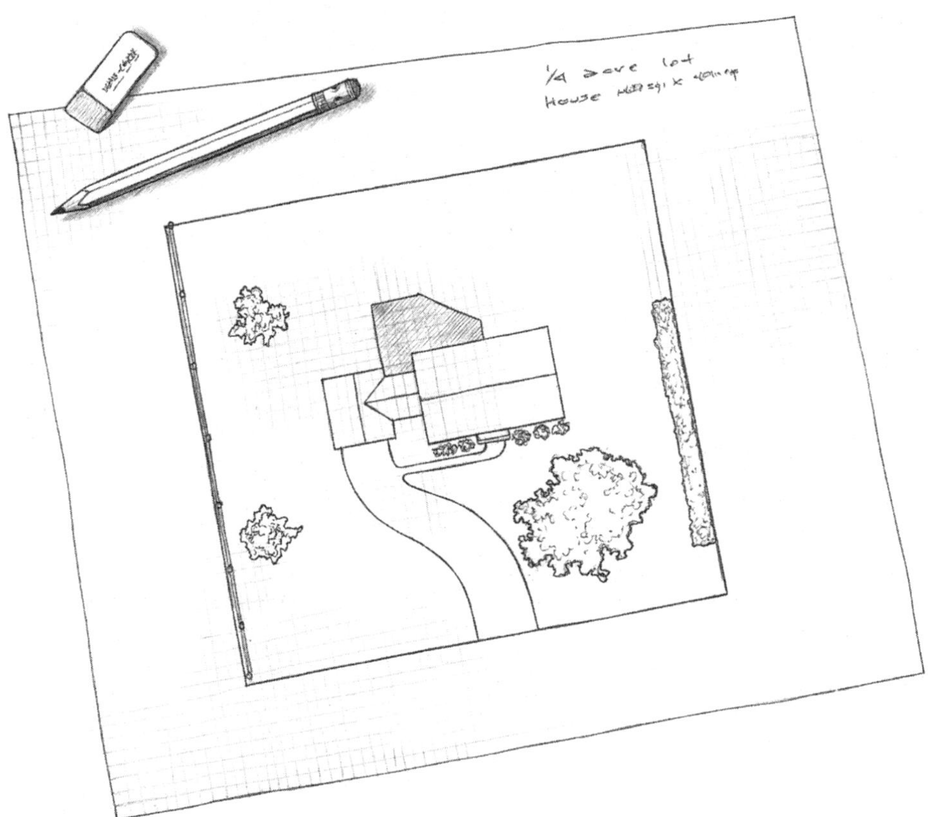

This is a typical suburban setup. *There's not much here to bring in birds, and the large expanses of thirsty grass will need to be mowed all summer long. Fortunately, there's plenty of room to create a veritable paradise for birds (and you, too).*

Watch That Spray!

Lots of us may be tempted to pour chemicals on our properties to control pests such as Japanese beetles, mosquitoes, fleas, ticks, ants, yellow jackets, and other creepy crawlers. But "bug spray" kills more than pests. It also kills butterflies and harms birds, which, after all, provide natural pest control by eating vast quantities of insects. Creating diversity instead of dumping on chemicals is the best way to bring balance to our yards. But it's not the only way.

Obviously, learning about organic pest controls and using them rather than harmful chemicals is one way to control pests without killing beneficial insects and other creatures like birds, toads, and tadpoles. (You'll find the latest in organic pest-control advice in books like *Rodale's All-New Encyclopedia of Organic Gardening* and *Rodale's Vegetable Garden Problem Solver.*) But learning a more tolerant attitude is an even better way. Try to think like Mother Nature: Things grow, things get eaten, things grow back.

If the Japanese beetles eat the leaves on your rose bushes, you're right, they look horrible. But if you've ever had it happen, you know that new leaves will grow. Rather than setting out hideous beetle traps or dumping on poisons, encourage a diversity of birds and other wildlife to visit your yard and get the beetles under control. The presence of moles means that nature is working to get the beetle grub population back to manageable levels. Patience and a holistic attitude can be the best pest control of all.

Two chapters in this book, Chapter 3, "Plants and Landscape Features for Birds," beginning on page 87, and Chapter 4, "Sharing Your Garden with Bug-Eating Birds," beginning on page 121, will give you lots of bird-friendly tactics for creating a beautiful yard and garden. Plant to attract birds and beneficial insects, avoid planting disease-prone varieties, and you're already well on your way!

ately surrounding your home) look like? Do you have any window boxes, containers, hanging baskets, or other accent plants? What about your neighbors' yards? Are there any trees, shrubs, or hedgerows in them that you could "borrow" for bird-attracting purposes? Take pictures of the front yard and any special features.

Let's proceed to the sides of the house. Do you have any plantings along the sides, or are you just waging a losing battle trying to grow grass in the shade? Are there fences or hedges along the sides of the property? Are there paths along the side, and if so, is there an opportunity to plant an inviting selection of groundcovers and perennials? If not, is there room to put in a path and some plants with "bird appeal?"

Now, let's head to the backyard. What's there now? A few trees, some thin grass, and a basketball hoop or volleyball net? Maybe a play gym and/or sandbox and slide? A swimming pool? A doghouse and yard? A fire pit and/or grill? Sketch or describe everything on your paper and take pictures.

What about the house itself? Do you have an open porch, deck, or patio off the front, back, or sides? If you do, do you currently spend a lot of time sitting out there? You can make an outdoor (or indoor/outdoor) seating area like this a centerpiece of your bird-attracting strategy, not only arranging feeders and plants so you can see them from your deck, patio, or porch, but also setting out feeders, hanging baskets, and container plantings to bring birds as close as you like!

Okay, you've looked at your yard from your perspective—a human perspective. What do you think? Are you pleased with what you see? If not, take a few minutes to envision your yard as you'd really love to see it. Let your imagination go. Do you see streams and ponds full of fabulous water

EVERYBODY WINS

Put a Little Life in Your Lawn

Americans are so obsessed with the idea of the perfect lawn that many neighborhoods have become little more than green deserts—huge expanses of a single type of grass that are regularly treated with so many chemical pesticides and herbicides that all other life forms have been destroyed. No wonder our honeybees are disappearing!

Lawns don't have to be barren and lifeless. They can be rich mixes of lush, low-growing plants, from beautiful white clover and bugleweed (ajuga) to beloved flowers like violets and scarlet pimpernels and herbs like thyme and prunella, with a mix of grasses forming the backdrop. Think of it this way: A diverse lawn is like a gorgeous Oriental carpet, a priceless treasure that seems new every time you see it because the pattern is ever-changing, while an all-grass lawn (especially a lawn with just one species of grass) is like wall-to-wall carpeting—boring.

A mixed lawn will attract all kinds of life to your yard, from insects like butterflies and bees feeding on the abundant nectar of flowering lawn plants to toads and ladybugs looking for an insect dinner. You'll get bonuses like fireflies (also known as lightning bugs), too, lighting up your summer nights. The life that's drawn to your lawn will bring birds flocking, looking for bugs, seeds, and nectar. A lawn like this is not only beautiful, it's exciting!

Many people think of a mixed lawn as an overgrown, weedy mess. But that is dead wrong: A lawn like this will thrive when it's kept mowed, just like an ordinary lawn. You may have heard that lawns do best when you set the mower higher than you may have learned to do, since even conventional lawn grass is healthier and grows best when its roots are shaded. The same is true of a mixed lawn: Raise the mower blade to 3 inches for the health of your lawn. And as with a conventional, all-grass lawn, you should always leave the clippings to fertilize your mixed lawn. We are always amazed at the people who bag and throw out their grass clippings, then dump chemical fertilizers on their lawns to replace the lost nutrients. What are they thinking?!

Finally, we'll leave you with a thought: If all the pesticides people dump on their lawns are killing "pests," what are they doing to your pets, kids, friends and relatives, and *you*—not to mention birds, butterflies, and other wildlife? If you encourage a mixed lawn of beautiful (and often useful) plants, nature will take care of any "pests" without additional help from you. Your lawn will look lush and inviting. You can watch your kids run barefoot across the lawn with the puppy without wondering, "How long has it been since the lawn service sprayed?" And you'll be rewarded with a wealth of birdlife.

Just think—you're actually gaining all these benefits from *not* doing extra work or going to extra expense. How great is that?

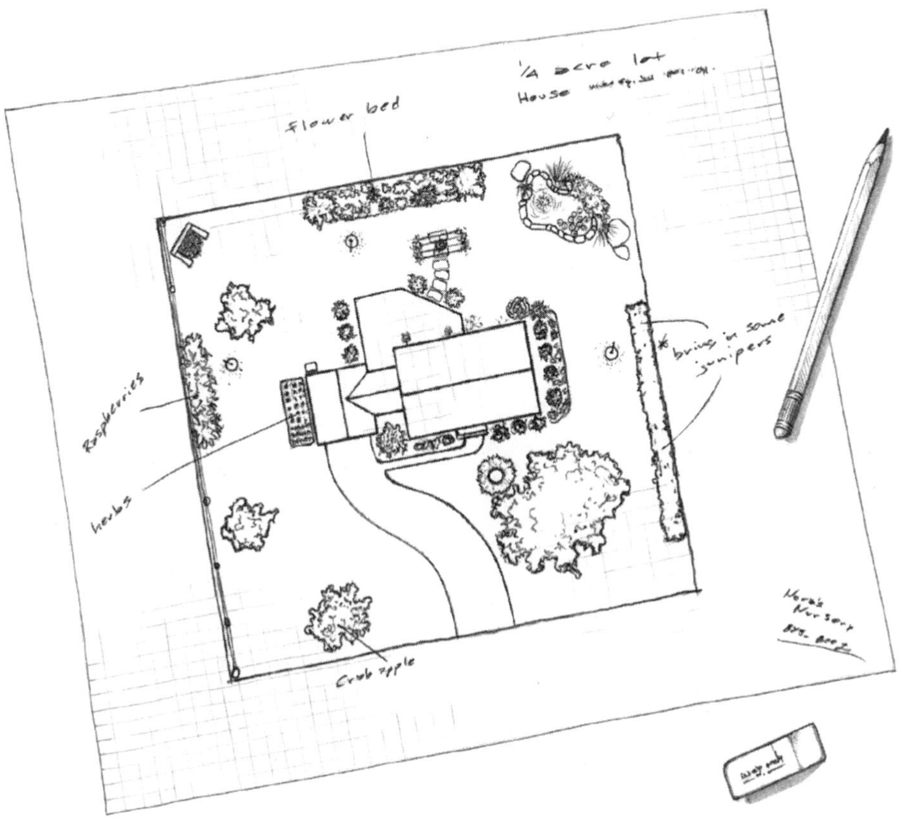

Bird's-Eye View: An Ideal Yard. *See how the typical ¼-acre suburban yard can be transformed from a sterile expanse of lawn to a bird-attracting paradise. It's easy, and you'll get more pleasure from your newly enhanced landscape, too!*

lilies; beds of flowers and succulent veggies; fruit trees, vines, and bushes; and beautiful shade trees, shrubs, hedges, and groundcovers?

As you read this book, add the bird-attracting features that appeal to you to your sketch (as we've done in "Bird's-Eye View: An Ideal Yard" above)—and to your landscape! Take more photos of the yard as you add each new feature, such as a birdbath, feeder, water garden, or hedgerow, and as your new gardens and plantings mature. Soon, you'll be taking photos and enjoying the company of visiting birds!

Think Like a Bird

Look at your yard from a bird's perspective. Here's where those four essentials (food, water, cover, and shelter) come in. That's because a bird will consider its basic needs: Is there an abundance of food? Is there water? Is it safe here—can I quickly escape from predators? And, in spring: Is there a place to nest and raise my young? Check out your current plantings from a bird's-eye view. Are there many sources of food and shelter? What about water? Are you giving the birds enough?

BRINGING IN THE BIRDS

How do you persuade birds to call your backyard home? Later chapters will give you all the details on choosing and setting up feeders, water features, nest boxes, and bird-friendly landscapes. We've already talked about setting up a basic tube feeder, a hummingbird feeder, nectar plants, and a water source. We've warned against poisoning your avian guests (and your family) with chemical pesticides. In this section, we'll give you an overview of quick ways to bring in birds, plus some simple things you can do now to attract a wide variety of birds in the near future.

10 TIPS FOR RAPID RESULTS

Planting a variety of bird-friendly trees and shrubs is probably the most effective way to attract the most birds to your yard over the long term. But what about now? Here are 10 hot tips to bring birds flocking.

Quick tip #1: Make a mess. No, we haven't lost our senses—we're still talking about attracting birds, we promise. Birds love the cover of a mixed hedgerow more than pretty much anything—we'll talk more about this on page 14—but it takes a while to grow a good hedge. In the meantime, give them some protection by setting up a brush pile in an out-of-the-way area of your backyard. Go around the yard picking up fallen limbs and branches, then pile them up where you won't have to look at them, with the biggest branches at the bottom to create some open spaces inside for the birds. (If your yard is twig-free, see if you can play "pick up sticks" at a friend's or a local park—with permission, of course! Wear gloves and watch out for poison ivy, oak, or sumac.) Pull some weeds and add them to the pile. Go on, make a mess! Your goal is to give songbirds a hiding place where they can quickly duck out of reach of cats, hawks, and other predators. The brush pile will help birds feel secure when they visit your yard.

Quick tip #2: Just add water. Experts say that water is more critical to birds' well-being than food, and this can be especially true in winter when accessible water is particularly hard to find. We've already recommended that you set up a birdbath, put a few pebbles in it for birds and butterflies to perch on (dragonflies like them, too), and keep it filled with fresh water. Help your feathered friends take a drink this winter by setting out a small water heater to keep the birdbath water from freezing over. These plug-in devices are readily available in bird specialty stores and catalogs. You just set one in your birdbath and plug it into an outlet on the exterior of your house—that's all there is to it!

Quick tip #3: Build a compost bin. As long as your compost bin is accessible—for example, pallets wired together to create a three-sided bin with an open front and top—and if you compost kitchen scraps, wild birds will be grateful. Tomato, pepper, and cantaloupe seeds; corncobs; white rice and stir-fry scraps; bread and pasta tidbits—all these things and many others will invite birds in to dine on your heap, as well as the earthworms and insects that will make their homes in a compost pile. Whatever your household provides will help nourish *all* life, including birdlife. (Remember not to compost meat scraps, bones, and fat, which can attract vermin.)

Pallets are a free and attractive way to set up a tidy compost bin that your birds will love. Wire three pallets together to form a three-sided box, with the top and front open, as shown. As you add materials from your kitchen and yard, you'll be providing nourishing seeds and scraps for birds. The birds will also enjoy any insects they find visiting the pile. If you find that you have more to compost than you can fit in one bin, wire two more pallets to the first set to form a second open-sided box, and so on until you have as many as you need.

Quick tip #4: Make a mud puddle. What's come over us? First we tell you to make a mess, and now it's a mud puddle. But we have a good reason for this one, too—like us, birds need their minerals to stay healthy, and one way they get them is by eating mud. (Yes, it sounds gross, but remember, we're talking about creatures that eat *worms*.) If you clear the grass off a shallow area and keep it watered, birds and butterflies will visit regularly to get their nutrients. You can set the freshly dug grass upside-down on the compost heap or brush pile, and watch the birds enjoy ripping through the soil and roots in search of nutrients and bugs.

Quick tip #5: Feather their nest. During breeding season, you can befriend birds by putting out nesting materials. Like seeing piles of bricks, concrete blocks, and 2-by-4s and sacks of concrete by the road with a big "FREE" sign in front, nesting materials are an invitation for birds to set up house in your yard. Popular choices include 4- to 8-inch (10- to 20-cm) pieces of yarn, string, or twine; hay or straw; pet hair; human hair (from your brush or comb); shredded paper; thread; feathers; thin ribbon (avoid plastic, Mylar, and other synthetic ribbons); even cotton balls (make sure they're real cotton) or pieces of Spanish moss. Drape them on a shrub you can see from a favorite window, or stuff them in a wire suet feeder, hang it up, and enjoy the show!

Quick tip #6: Create a container garden. If you enjoy the sight of a brilliantly blooming hanging basket, window box, or container, think how much more pleasure you'll have if the flowers are buzzing with hummingbirds! Think hot colors—red and orange, with hot pink and purple thrown in for good measure. A window box of annual scarlet sage *(Salvia splendens)* with gorgeous nasturtiums trailing down its sides; a sunny container filled with snapdragons or 'Purple Wave' petunias; a half-barrel with a massive red-flowered canna (like the purple-leaved 'Australia', green-leaved 'The President', or 'Valentine', with brilliant red-pink flowers); a shady pot of impatiens and a purple-flowered hosta with white- or cream-variegated leaves or a silver-leaved heuchera (coral bells); or a glorious red-and-purple or red-and-pink-flowered fuchsia in a hanging basket will spell heaven for your hummers. All these plants are readily available from garden centers and home improvement stores.

Quick tip #7: Butter them up. Here's a fast, fun way to give birds a nourishing treat, especially in cold weather: Collect some dried pinecones (you want cones with open scales) to garnish for a bird snack. If you'll want to hang them when you're finished, tie loops of twine around the stems now. Next, stuff peanut butter (plain or crunchy) in the openings among the scales. When you've packed the pinecones with peanut butter, roll them in wild birdseed mix so the seeds stick to the peanut butter. Then set them out on your tray feeder or hang them from hooks or branches where you can watch the birds enjoying their winter treat.

Quick tip #8: Help birds celebrate Christmas all winter. If you buy a real Christmas tree every year, resist the urge to drag it to the curb for trash collection when the holidays are over. Instead, take it to a discreet part of your backyard where it can provide shelter for birds all winter. (In fact, it could form the start of the brush pile we suggested in quick tip #1 on page 11.) One warning, though—don't set out a tinsel-covered tree. The synthetic tinsel can be harmful to birds just as it can be to your indoor pets. Skip the tinsel if you want to try this, so you don't have to take it off strand by strand before setting out the tree. If you'd rather not have a brush pile on your property, you can always haul your tree to the curb once the weather's warmed up in spring.

Quick tip #9: Up your color quotient. Try this great tip from birding enthusiast and author Sally Roth: Attract curious hummingbirds to your yard by adding some instant color in the form of red and/or purple gazing balls. You can set them on traditional birdbath-type bases or nestle them among your garden flowers—or both! Remember to put them where you can see them, so you can enjoy the hummingbirds' arrival. They won't mind your trickery if you have a nectar feeder or nectar-rich flowers like cleome (spiderflower), salvias

Birds, with their small bodies and high metabolisms, need plenty of calories to stay warm in winter. These peanut-butter-and-seed-coated pinecones are a fun homemade way to provide for their needs.

. . . Except for Slimy Pests

Are snails and slugs destroying your hostas and other prized ornamentals, or making mincemeat of your veggie garden? Get rid of them and give wild birds a treat with this simple control:

Next time your family has grapefruit for breakfast, instead of tossing the empty rinds, set them cut-side down around slug- and snail-infested plants. The next morning, turn the rinds over and you'll find that slugs and snails have crawled inside! Set these pest-filled citrus bowls, cut-side up, near trees and shrubs so the birds can feast on the escargot, then add the empty rinds to your compost pile.

(flowering sages), and red zinnias waiting for them when they arrive.

Quick tip #10: Set up a trellis. A lattice-type trellis provides lots of openings where birds can perch. If you don't have a lot of trees and shrubs on your property, this is an easy way to offer them instant shelter. Set it against a side wall, the back of the garage, or another relatively quiet place. You can, of course, plant a flowering and/or fruiting vine at its base to give birds food and even more shelter (see long-range tip #2 on the opposite page for some good choices). But for instant gratification, buy some of those half-baskets (hanging baskets with one flat side) to hang on your trellis. Three will make a good show. Plant them with colorful annual trailing plants like 'Empress of India' nasturtiums, trailing petunias, or cardinal climber (also called cypress vine morning glory, *Ipomoea quamoclit*). If your trellis is in the shade, choose impatiens instead, perhaps with golden creeping Jenny (*Lysimachia nummularia* 'Aurea') spilling over the side just for show.

10 TIPS FOR LONG-TERM RESULTS

Now it's time to take the long view. What can you do to make your yard a bird magnet year after year? You'll find plenty of ideas in the chapters that follow, but here are some simple, effective things you can do now for terrific results later.

Long-range tip #1: Plant a hedgerow. Nothing attracts birds like a hedgerow—not a hedge, but rather a mixed border of shrubs, small trees, vines, perennials, annuals and biennials, and grasses. The more diversity the better as far as birds are concerned! A well-planned hedgerow will provide abundant food, protection, and nest sites. Hedgerows can include small fruiting trees like crab apples, pawpaws, and mountain ash; plus fruit-bearing shrubs and bushes like elderberry, rugosa roses (see "Budget-Wise Birding" on page 8 for more on them), aronia, bush cherries, raspberries, and wineberries; nectar favorites like lilacs, weigela, and flowering quince; bird-attracting vines like passion vine, wild grape, Virginia creeper, honeysuckle, and American bittersweet; perennials like butterfly weed, asters, goldenrods, and coneflowers (including black-eyed Susans and purple coneflowers); and grasses like big and little bluestem, switchgrass, and sedges.

Basically, if you can plant a diverse hedgerow, then leave it to its own devices (removing, of course, invasive plants like European bittersweet and kudzu and misery-causing allergens like poison ivy and ragweed), your birds will be in clover—which, incidentally, is also a great plant for hedgerows! But a hedgerow can be much simpler, too. If you currently have a hedge of privet, forsythia, yew, boxwood, or euonymus that's been pruned to a box (rectangular) shape, if you let it grow out, you'll discover that these plants have a pleasing fountain shape, or—in the case of euonymus, boxwood, and yews—naturally form neat, rounded shapes. (Privet has an extra bonus—honey-scented flowers.) Just by letting it grow out, your hedge will be transformed into a hedgerow—with a beautiful, low-maintenance form, plus fruit and flowers for hungry birds. How easy is that?

Long-range tip #2: Plant a hummingbird vine. Trumpet vine *(Campsis radicans)* and vining honeysuckles (*Lonicera* spp.) provide a long summer season of bloom for hungry hummingbirds in search of nectar. There are many beautiful varieties, but the scarlet "trumpets" of the species form of trumpet vine and orange-red trumpet vine or coral honeysuckle *(L. sempervirens)* in the East—and Arizona

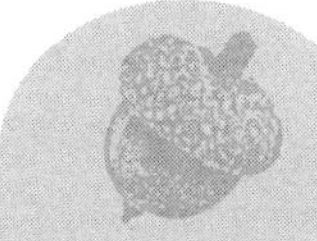

ACORN EFFORT, OAK TREE RESULT

Plant a Sunflower

Want to make a big difference with a small change? Plant a sunflower! Even one sunflower adds beauty to your property and delights children with its big, bold flower head. But best of all, it provides birds with one of their favorite foods—sunflower seeds! Tucking sunflowers into your flower bed or vegetable garden will brighten your yard, and once the seeds form and the head dries, you can shuck the seeds and add them to your bird feeders or simply hang up a dried head for the birds to enjoy.

In the past decade, sunflowers have become very popular with gardeners and many decorative varieties have come on the market. When you're planting with birds in mind, you'll want one of the big-headed types like 'Snack Seed' or 'Sunzilla' that forms lots of nutritious sunflower seeds, not a small, decorative type. The birds will thank you!

Another option is to take a tip from upscale garden catalogs and use one or more sunflower heads to make a bird wreath. You can make a beautiful, edible (from the birds' perspective, anyway) wreath with a sunflower head in the center and dried sprays of millet, wheat, grasses, ornamental mini-corn, and even foxtail framing it. (See Chapter 2, "Seeds and Feeders," beginning on page 25 for more on growing bird favorites.) Many farm stands now offer ornamental corn and grains during autumn harvest season, so even if you don't grow all the ingredients, you can still find a nice mixture to combine with your sunflowers in a wonderful bird-attracting wreath.

Whether you make an edible wreath from your sunflower seedhead or use it as is, hang it where you can watch the birds enjoying the bounty it provides. The easiest way to do this is to leave an inch of stem on the sunflower seedhead and pierce the stem through the center with an awl, then thread jute or other natural-fiber string through the hole and make a loop. You can hang the loop from a nail, a branch, or a hook such as the kind you use to hang your feeders.

honeysuckle *(L. arizonica)* in the West—will bring in the most birds. Both trumpet vine and honeysuckle are vigorous vines and require a sturdy trellis or arbor in full sun for best bloom.

Long-range tip #3: Set up a feeding station. A tube feeder or two will certainly bring birds flocking to your yard, but it probably won't be long until you're hooked and eager to provide food of all kinds to your winged visitors and residents. While you can certainly hang feeders all over the yard, the advantages of a feeding station are that it provides one-stop shopping for hungry birds and you can set it up where it's easy to see all the activity from your favorite window.

There are plenty of ready-made feeding stations available from stores, catalogs, and Web sites that cater to wild birds—stands with multiple hooks for feeders, platforms, and the like. (We'll review these in detail in Chapter 2, "Seeds and Feeders," beginning on page 25.) But it's also lots of fun to create your own—with tray feeders, suet feeders, hanging tube feeders, hummingbird nectar feeders, oriole fruit and jelly feeders, and even—if you're not squeamish—containers for mealworms, earthworms, and other squirmy treats.

Of course, each feeder you set up requires maintenance and restocking, so it's best to start slowly and add on as your knowledge and enthusiasm grow. Look over the options in Chapter 2, including specifics on how to attract your favorite birds. Go online to check out the offerings at wildbird sites like www.duncraft.com. Visit your local Wild Bird Center or other wild bird specialty store, and see what local pet stores, Agways, Tractor Supply Co. stores, and hardware and home-improvement stores are offering. Think about the best place or places in your yard to set up feeding stations. Sketch or describe some set-ups that appeal to you and suit your budget, providing options for later add-ons.

Long-range tip #4: Grow the "Three Sisters." Native Americans traditionally grew three crops together—corn, beans, and squash or pumpkins. The corn stalks formed poles for the bean vines to climb, and the squash or pumpkin vines trailed among the stalks, forming a shady, water-retentive mulch for the roots of the corn and beans. If you grow a "Three Sisters Patch" in your yard, you'll be able to benefit birds and enjoy some of the bounty yourself. Interplant one or more of the many varieties of colorful Indian corn or popcorn, scarlet runner beans, and pumpkins, winter squash, or gourds. These plants all prefer full sun, plenty of water, and average to rich garden soil. (See Chapter 3, "Plants and Landscape Features for Birds," beginning on page 87, for more gardening tips.)

Hummingbirds will be drawn to the brilliant scarlet blossoms of the runner beans, and you can harvest the beans green (to eat like snap beans) or allow the seeds inside to mature and eat them fresh or dry to eat later (birds will enjoy them, too). Once the corn matures, you can dry it on the cob and display it during harvest season. Then, after Thanksgiving, make wreaths for the birds (see Chapter 2, page 85, for more on this) with the smaller ears of popcorn. (Save a few ears for yourself!) Shell the big ears, crack the kernels, and add them to a homemade seed mix, or set whole cobs out for squirrels, deer, and other wildlife. Meanwhile, harvest mature winter squash and pumpkins. When you use them, scoop out the seeds and set them out for the birds. If you grow gourds, once you've cured them, you can cut a hole in the side, scoop out the seeds and feed them to the birds, and hang up the dried gourd—plain or decorated—as a birdhouse. (See Chapter 5, "Making a Birdhouse a Home," beginning on page 149, for more about making gourd houses.)

Long-range tip #5: Set out nest boxes. If you have lots of trees and shrubs on your property, chances are that you're already attracting lots of nesting birds. (One clue is to look for broken eggs on the ground in spring, and blown-down nests after storms with high winds.) But because birds tend to be cautious and site their nests where they're as inconspicuous as possible, if you want to enjoy watching parent birds flying to and from the nest and baby birds flexing their wings and taking that first tentative flight, it helps to set up nest boxes where you can watch them conveniently. Birds really do use nest boxes, and if you set them out, they're likely to have occupants—though not necessarily the ones you expect! (Mice, wasps, and undesirable birds like starlings are also fond of nest boxes.)

Nest boxes (also called birdhouses) are great alternatives if your property has few trees—or while your trees are growing. And they're especially important for cavity nesters like woodpeckers, since most people take down dead trees as soon as they see them, leaving no dead wood for the birds to drill into to make homes. Some of our best-loved birds make their nests in naturally formed holed in trees and posts, or in abandoned woodpecker nest holes. These birds include the eastern, western, and mountain bluebird, tufted titmouse, wood duck, white- and red-breasted nuthatch, purple martin, black-capped Carolina and chestnut-backed chickadee, American kestrel, barn owl, eastern and western screech owl, Carolina and house wren, tree swallow, great crested and ash-throated flycatcher, common goldeneye, hooded merganser, northern flicker, and a number of warblers, including the famous prothonotary warbler. It's up to us to make up the loss of natural habitat by providing nest boxes for these wonderful birds!

In Chapter 5, "Making a Birdhouse a Home," beginning on page 149, you'll find out all about choosing, establishing, and maintaining a wide variety of birdhouses, as well as making your own. Read it before you buy a bunch of birdhouses! But if you can't wait that long to get started, go online to the Cornell Lab of Ornithology's Birdhouse Network site (www.birds.cornell.edu/birdhouse) for its recommendations, then head to your nearest Wild Bird Center or other wild bird specialty store or online to a specialty supplier like Duncraft (www.duncraft.com) and select a basic birdhouse. Set it up where it will be shaded, secure, and out of reach of cats and dogs, but still easy to see from your windows, deck, or patio. Put out some nesting materials (see quick tip #6 on page 12) and you're in business!

Long-range tip #6: Add moving water. Birds love moving water—dripping water, sprays, mists, waterfalls. They enjoy flying through it and getting a bath on the fly. The sound of moving water also tells them that water is nearby and draws them to it. Hummingbirds are especially fun to watch as they fly through the mist or spray, but if you set up some form of moving water, you'll attract many other grateful birds.

BIRD MYTH-BUSTERS

Stop! Don't Pop!

Whether you grow your own popcorn or buy it at the grocery, don't spend time and energy popping it and stringing it into lovely white garlands for the birds' benefit. Strands of fluffy popcorn make fine decorations to our eyes, but birds won't feast on them. Offer dry popcorn on the cob to seed-eating birds and squirrels and watch it disappear.

Discover Rugosa Roses

If you have more patience than money, you can make a beautiful bird-friendly hedge from just a few plants. (You can start with just one plant if you're willing to wait, and three to five would provide enough to make a dense yard-long hedge in 5 years or less.) How? With rugosa roses. These dense, gorgeous plants are tough and handsome even when they're not blooming, unlike often-fragile hybrid teas.

Depending on the variety, their blooms can be single, semi-double, or double, and come in shades of red, white, pink, magenta, and purple. They bloom in late spring/early summer and often rebloom in late summer, and the fragrance of the rose blossoms is out of this world! As if this weren't enough, the handsome foliage turns a glowing gold in fall, and the plant is covered with huge, showy scarlet rose hips—nourishing for you as well as the birds, with their renowned vitamin C content. Plants quickly form dense, upright shrubs, providing plenty of thorny protection and shelter for birds.

Choose a variety that will reach the height you'd like your hedge to grow. That way, the only pruning you'll need to do is to remove dead branches, not cut back your plants or wonder why they're not getting as tall as they should be. *Rosa rugosa* 'Alba', with its large single white blooms and red hips, is an excellent choice, reaching 6 feet tall and wide, like its magenta-flowered sister, *Rosa rugosa* 'Rubra.' Other varieties can be as short as 1 foot tall or as tall as 12 feet. You can find rugosas at garden centers and also in nursery catalogs (and their Web sites), such as Heirloom Roses in Oregon (www.heirloomroses.com), Heirloom Roses in Canada (ships to United States; www.oldheirloomroses.com), and Direct Gardening (www.directgardening.com).

Rugosa roses make dense, low-maintenance hedges or handsome specimen plants. Covered in large, fragrant flowers during summer, their rich green foliage turns bright gold in fall and complements huge, showy scarlet rose hips. Rugosas send up suckers, or shoots, that you can dig and relocate as needed to form an attractive hedge in a relatively short time. Once you have as many plants as you need, mow along the sides of the hedge to control new suckers.

One obvious way to provide a spray of water is to turn on your lawn sprinkler. If you have a sprinkler and use it regularly, you already have a "bird shower" on your lawn. But because sprinklers waste so much water (most of it evaporates), it's better to localize the moving water where most of it will be recycled.

Wild bird specialty stores, catalogs, and Web sites now offer special drip and mist attachments for birdbaths, and you can buy birdbaths with fountain features already installed. You can also buy special nozzles that will turn an ordinary garden hose into a mister to attract birds. Read more about these options—and others, like circulating streams and waterfalls—in Chapter 6, "Water Features for Birds," beginning on page 177.

Long-range tip #7: Plant blueberries. Blueberries are fantastic landscape plants. These shrubs are almost entirely free of pests and diseases, so once you plant them, they're pretty much maintenance-free. Most grow 5 to 6 feet (1.5 m to 1.8 m) tall, but you can find low-growing varieties that reach only 3 feet and giants that grow to 10 feet (3 m) tall. They produce attractive foliage and white bell-shaped flowers in clusters in the spring, then ripen abundant (15 to 20 pounds, or 6.8 to 9 kg, of fruit from a mature bush), luscious blueberries in summer. And finally, the foliage turns a brilliant red in fall. If you live in that part of the West that has alkaline soil, acid-loving blueberries aren't for you. But the East Coast, South, Northeast, North Central States, Midwest, and West Coast are perfect for blueberries, and there are species and varieties that will thrive in all those areas. Because different varieties ripen at different times, you can plant several kinds that are suited to your area; with a careful selection, it's possible to harvest blueberries from May to November. You can find bushes for sale in nurseries, garden centers, even farm supply and home centers, usually in spring,

Plant a Birdy B&B

No tree offers more to birds in winter than the eastern red cedar (*Juniperus virginiana*). This commanding evergreen grows quickly, reaching an ultimate height of 70 feet (21.3 m) in a sunny, open site. Its dense, prickly branches afford plenty of nesting sites for birds, as well as protection from predators. And from summer through winter, it is covered with showy clusters of blue-green to blue-black berries (actually berrylike cones) with a whitish bloom. These berries are beloved by birds and by floral arrangers, who use them in Christmas wreaths and swags despite the branches' prickly scales. But even showier than the tall, berry-laden tree is the ever-changing assortment of birds flying in and out of its branches all winter, making it a living Christmas tree in the best possible sense.

Looking for an attractive, bird-friendly red cedar substitute for a yard in the West or the northernmost states? Balsam fir (*Abies balsamea*) stands up to extreme cold and partial shade, reaching 75 feet (23 m), while Colorado spruce (also known as Colorado blue spruce, *Picea pungens*) grows to 50 feet (15 m), can take full sun, and is drought-tolerant.

Birds will fly in to dine on juniper berries; the dense evergreens also offer plenty of prime real estate for nesting and roosting.

and can order a wide selection from mail-order and online nurseries specializing in fruit (see long-range tip #10 on this page for four of the best companies). Birds love the luscious fruit as much as we do, so be sure to save plenty for them!

Long-range tip #8: Grow a bird garden. What fun to grow a garden just for the birds! Ornamental sorghums and broom sedges have become available in recent years, supplementing the selection of ornamental grasses, colorful corn, millet, and sunflowers that are bird favorites. Don't overlook seed-producing flowers—black-eyed Susans (*Rudbeckia* spp., also called coneflowers), purple coneflowers (*Echinacea purpurea*), evening primroses (*Oenothera* spp.), and tickseed sunflower (*Bidens aristosa*) are great choices, and the daisy form of many of them attracts butterflies, too. Add some nectar favorites—wild bergamot (*Monarda fistulosa*) and bee balm (*M. didyma*), red clover, goldenrods, and butterfly weed (*Asclepias tuberosa*)—and you'll attract hummingbirds to your bird garden, too. (Not to mention even more butterflies.) We'll talk more about designing a garden specifically to produce birdseed in Chapter 2, "Seeds and Feeders," beginning on page 25. A garden that combines seed and nectar plants can be as ornamental as it is attractive: Visitors will think they're observing a beautiful ornamental flower bed with some unusual, sophisticated plants. Only the birds will know what you're really up to!

Long-range tip #9: Add a water garden. Birdbaths are great. And if you add moving water to your birdbath (see long-range tip #6 on page 17 for more on this), you'll enjoy the results as much as the birds will. But nothing beats the beauty and pleasure you (and birds and other visiting wildlife) can get from a water garden. We suggest that you start small—maybe a half-barrel garden with a little water fountain, a submersible pump, a few water plants, and a couple of goldfish. Once you've gotten the hang of water gardening and discovered how much you like it, your only limits are your time, budget, and property constraints! Water gardens with waterfalls, recirculating streams, a backyard pond—anything's possible. We'll give you all the how-to-do-its in Chapter 6, "Water Features for Birds," beginning on page 177. Luckily, in addition to specialty mail-order and online catalogs of water plants and accessories, most garden centers, pet stores, and home-improvement stores have water-garden sections, too. And there's probably at least one specialty water-garden store near you. Let us tempt you: Imagine looking out the back door and seeing a majestic great blue heron standing still as a statue in your water garden. It can—and often does—happen!

Long-range tip #10: Plant a sour cherry. If you've never grown a cherry tree on your own property, you may not realize what a bird magnet it is. Birds especially seem to love the sour cherries—the ones that are used for pies and jellies. If you just want to bring in birds, you might want to grow a full-size, standard cherry tree (maturing at 15 to 20 feet, or 4.6 to 6 m, tall), which will also provide shade and be decorative in bloom. But if you'd like to share some of the harvest yourself—or you don't have a lot of space—a semi-dwarf (10 to 12 feet, or 3 to 3.7 m, tall) or dwarf (6 to 8 feet, or 1.8 to 2.4 m, tall) cherry is your best bet (they're not only smaller, they're much easier to harvest—at least, if you're not a bird!).

If you choose self-pollinating varieties like 'Montmorency' and 'Dwarf North Star' (also sold as 'Northstar'), you'll only need a single cherry tree to produce loads of succulent fruit. You'll find them at nurseries like Edible Landscaping (www.ediblelandscaping.com, 800-524-4156), Miller Nurseries (www.millernurseries.com, 800-836-9630), Stark Bros. Nurseries & Orchards Co. (www.starkbros.com, 800-325-4180), and Raintree Nursery (www.raintreenursery.com, 360-496-6400).

THE 10 EASIEST BIRDS TO SEE

What are the easiest birds to bring to your yard? That depends on where you live and the time of year. You can go to the Cornell Lab of Ornithology's Web site (www.birds.cornell.edu) and search its Project FeederWatch site for the most frequently reported birds at feeders by state and region. Project FeederWatch is a winter count, as is another fun project sponsored by Cornell, the 4-day Great Backyard Bird Count (also state by state).

Another way to find out what birds are common in yards in your area is to check with your local Audubon Society chapter or ornithological club. (The Audubon Society sponsors the venerable Christmas Bird Count, now in its 108th year.) Read on to see what birds you might encounter in *your* yard. The page numbers after the bird names in the following lists means you'll find more detailed profiles of these species in the chapters ahead.

EASTERN BIRDS: SPRING-FALL

Here are the birds you're most likely to see once winter's gone and the warm-season residents have come back to their breeding grounds. Note that if you live in the country, you'll also see common field birds such as bluebirds, barn swallows, and red-winged blackbirds. If you keep a close eye out and provide conditions they like, you may see Baltimore orioles (page 101) and scarlet tanagers. Tufted titmice (page 76), house finches (page 330), blue jays (page 282), white-breasted nuthatches (page 125), and woodpeckers are year-round residents, although you might not see as much of them during the warm months unless you keep your feeders filled all year. You're bound to see lots of little birds, including gray catbirds (page 113) and many warblers, sparrows, and wrens. But this list is a start.

- American robin (page 278)
- Mourning dove (page 285)
- Northern cardinal (page 62)
- Ruby-throated hummingbird (page 216)
- European starling (page 320)
- American goldfinch (page 64)
- House (English) sparrow (page 324)
- Grackle, common and boat-tailed (page 288)
- Northern mockingbird (page 297)
- Chickadee, black-capped and Carolina (page 29)

EASTERN BIRDS: WINTER

In winter, different birds appear at eastern feeders. Some birds will stay through the winter, too, including the cardinal, mourning dove, and goldfinch (now in its brown winter plumage), as well as a wealth of sparrows. And you may be lucky enough to see showy birds like cedar waxwings, rose-breasted grosbeaks, common flickers, and pine siskins. If you want them, and you live in a rural area, you can attract wild turkeys to your yard. Here are other birds you're likely to see:

- Dark-eyed junco (page 42)
- Mourning dove (page 285)
- Blue jay (page 282)
- Downy woodpecker (page 126)
- Northern cardinal (page 62)
- White-breasted nuthatch (page 125)
- American goldfinch (page 64)
- Tufted titmouse (page 76)
- Black-capped chickadee (page 29)
- House finch (page 330)

Other common winter feeder birds in the East are the red-bellied woodpecker, hairy woodpecker, Carolina chickadee, purple finch, red-breasted nuthatch, American robin (page 278), Carolina wren, white-throated sparrow (page 36), song sparrow, house sparrow (page 324), northern mockingbird (page 297), European starling (page 320), brown-headed cowbird (page 327), American crow (page 309), and common grackle (page 288). In the Southeast, you'll also commonly see the eastern bluebird (page 156), eastern and spotted towhees (page 129), chipping sparrow, red-winged blackbird (page 196), and yellow-rumped warbler.

WESTERN BIRDS: SPRING-FALL

As you know if you live in the West, the most-seen lineup is quite different in your area. Make the Easterners jealous by attracting all these beautiful birds to your yard! (There are 12 of these!)

- Western scrub-jay
- Steller's jay
- Black phoebe
- Black-chinned hummingbird
- Mountain and Carolina chickadees (page 29)
- Western kingbird (page 139)
- Bewick's wren
- Red-breasted nuthatch
- Yellow-rumped warbler
- Western tanager
- Chipping sparrow
- Ruby-crowned kinglet

Of course, bird species vary depending on where you live. On the California coast, for example, Anna's and Allen's hummingbirds are very common. Check the lists for your area at the Cornell Lab site (www.birds.cornell.edu) or contact your local ornithological club or branch of the Audubon Society for the best local information.

Look It Up at the Lab

The Cornell Laboratory of Ornithology, that is. Cornell sponsors lots of what it calls "Citizen Science" projects, including the famous "Project FeederWatch," and collects and analyzes the data. Cornell presents the results of its country-wide research on its Web site, www.birds.cornell.edu, along with a smorgasbord of other benefits for backyard birders—everything from a shop with its picks of the best binoculars, guides, CDs, and much more, to its massive online subscription reference, *The Birds of North America*, with extensive, frequently updated information for more than 700 species, as well as a photo gallery and audio and video features for each species.

But for most of us, the best feature of all is the "All About Birds" section, where you can find a bird guide with descriptions, photos (adults, juveniles, nests, eggs, etc.), and an audio feature that lets you hear the songs, range, even "Cool Facts" for each bird! "All About Birds" also has features on how to identify birds, birding gear, attracting birds, landscaping for birds, and more. Check out the Web site and see for yourself. It's a wonderful online reference for all backyard birders!

11 Fly-By Birds

There are some birds that won't necessarily land in your yard or spend time there, but that you may be lucky enough to see flying over your yard fairly regularly or seasonally. Some, like the kestrel, may be perched on a telephone wire on a road near your yard where you can enjoy them without actually hosting them. Others, like the owls, may be heard rather than seen, or you may see them coasting silently over a road at dusk. You're bound to see flocks of pigeons (called "rock doves" by birders) in and around cities, and gulls are becoming common sights in shopping center parking lots and anywhere else they think there might be a handout at a dumpster. Here's a list of 11 common fly-bys you might see from your backyard. Get out that field guide, your birdcall CD, and those binoculars and see for yourself!

- Canada goose (page 333)
- Snow goose
- Mallard duck (page 204)
- Black vulture
- Turkey vulture
- Red-tailed hawk (page 245)
- American kestrel
- Great blue heron (page 200)
- Great horned owl (page 253)
- Eastern screech owl (page 163)
- Barn owl

WESTERN BIRDS: WINTER

In the winter, western feeders boast some of the same birds seen in top-10 lists in the East. But the lineup changes, too, both in terms of the relative number of each bird and the introduction of some different birds to the list. Enjoy these beautiful birds at your feeders and in the trees and shrubs in your backyard.

- House finch (page 330)
- Dark-eyed junco (page 42)
- House sparrow (page 324)
- Northern flicker (page 299)
- Mourning dove (page 285)
- American robin (page 278)
- White-crowned sparrow
- Pine siskin
- European starling (page 320)
- American goldfinch (page 64)

Other winter feeder favorites include the western scrub-jay; Steller's jay; lesser goldfinch; downy woodpecker (page 126); black-capped, mountain, and chestnut-backed chickadees (page 29); red-winged blackbird (page 196); curve-billed thrasher; Anna's hummingbird; song sparrow; eastern, spotted, and canyon towhees (page 129); white-winged dove; American crow (page 309); Cooper's and sharp-shinned hawks (page 249); and ruby-crowned kinglet.

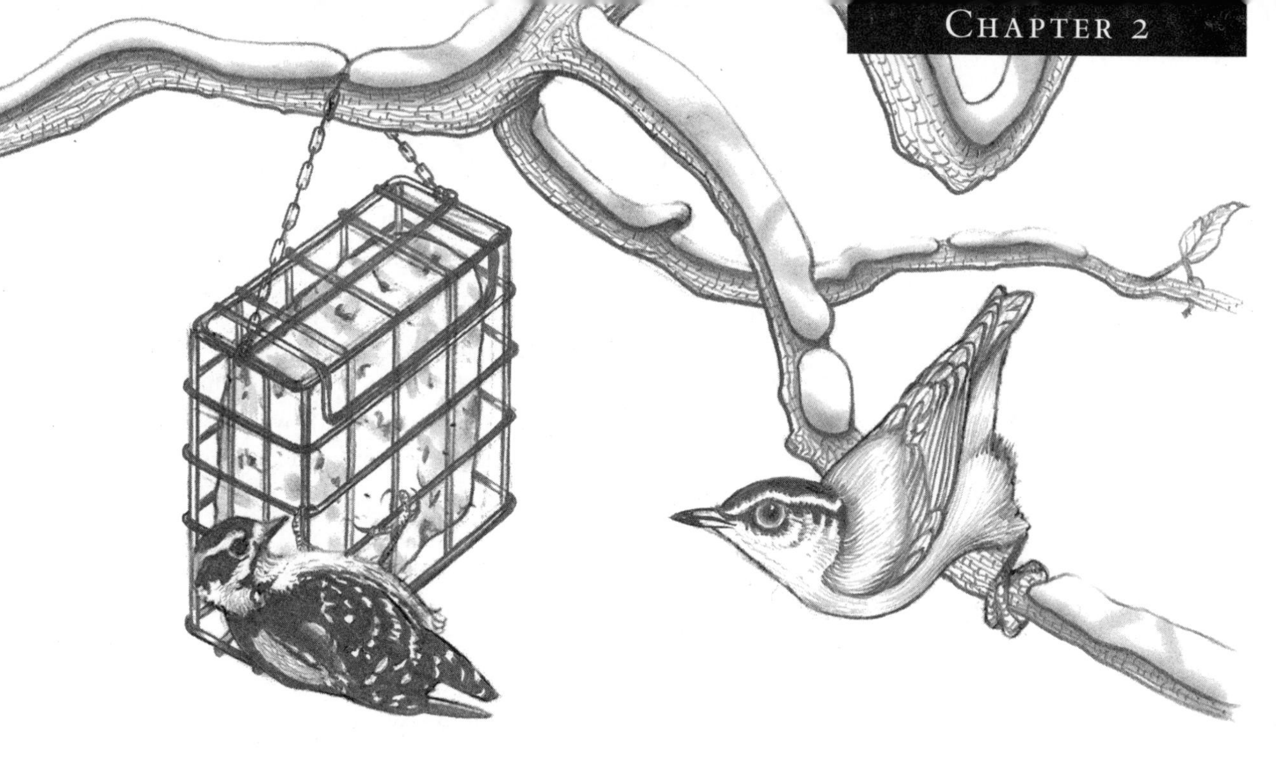

CHAPTER 2

SEEDS AND FEEDERS

Feeding backyard birds sounds so simple: Set out a feeder, fill it with seed, and sit back. And you'll certainly get some birds if that's all you do! But the world of backyard bird feeding is much broader and richer than that. This chapter will explore recent discoveries, as well as the basics, in detail. You'll find out what makes a good bird feeder; which seeds attract the birds you love; which seeds and mixes you should never buy; how to store seed safely; how to make your own mixes; how to create a backyard feeding station, both store-bought and from scratch; and how to attract birds that don't eat seed—the ones most homeowners never see.

In addition, in this chapter you'll find profiles of the most beloved feeder birds—cardinals, chickadees, finches, goldfinches, grosbeaks, juncos, sparrows, and titmice. You'll learn how to recognize them; which species you'll see, depending on where you live; whether you can expect to see them all year or just in winter; which foods and feeders they prefer; and how to provide extras they especially love. So read on, and get ready to bring in the birds!

FEEDING FRENZY

With so many feeder styles to choose from, how do you decide which one to buy? Consider your space, your budget, and the birds you want to attract. As you ponder your selection, consider this advice from Project FeederWatch: The best bird feeders should be easy to assemble and clean; they should be able to withstand the weather and keep seed dry; and they should be big enough so you're not constantly refilling them.

FEEDERS AT A GLANCE

If you're trying to decide what kind of feeders to put up in your yard, it's easy to get confused. Some feeders go by names that aren't familiar or don't seem to be appropriate (who'd think that a house-shaped feeder would be called a "hopper?"). Here's an at-a-glance guide to the most common feeder types.

- **Tube feeder.** These feeders are made from plastic tubes with caps on both ends. There are two tube types: The most popular is one designed with "ports," or round openings, with perches underneath, and is meant to hold sunflower seed or seed mixes; these attract finches, titmice, chickadees, cardinals, nuthatches, and woodpeckers. The other type has tiny openings for nyjer seed, which attracts finches, buntings, redpolls, and pine siskins.
- **Tray feeder.** Tray feeders are square, rectangular, or triangular platforms with screened bottoms and wooden or molded plastic sides. They're designed to be hung from a support, set on short legs on the ground, or pole-mounted. Birds that dislike using perches while feeding, such as cardinals and jays, prefer tray feeders to tubes, and ground-feeding birds like juncos, towhees, sparrows, and mourning doves will especially appreciate a tray set up at ground level.
- **Hopper feeder.** These house-or cabin-shaped feeders have a roof, one side of which lifts up so you can pour in seed. Many have solid ends but clear plastic sides so you can monitor the level of seed in the feeder. The base of the feeder extends out from the body to form a feeding platform; thanks to gravity, just enough seed comes out at the base to fill the platform lip. Some hopper-style feeders are made of wood; some have roofs and bases of recycled plastic; while others are designed to keep squirrels off and are made of metal with perches that drop down when a squirrel lands on them, sealing off the seed ports. Some hoppers have cages on one or both ends to hold suet cakes. Hefty hoppers usually are pole-mounted or hung from sturdy chains. They attract many species of birds, from nuthatches and titmice to cardinals and jays.
- **Platform feeder.** A platform feeder is basically a pole-mounted or hanging tray feeder with a solid surface instead of mesh. Some have a roof overhead with open sides, while others are open to the elements. In either case, it's important to put out only as much seed as birds will eat in a few hours, since seed on a platform is exposed to rain and snow, even with a roof. Birds that visit hoppers will also enjoy dining on platform feeders.
- **Steel "cage" (mesh) feeder.** Cage feeders are cylinders—tubes—of wire mesh with wood or recycled plastic bases and lids. The cylinders have smaller or larger mesh depending on

The Case for Four-Season Feeding

Probably the most-asked question in backyard birding is "Should I feed birds all year or just in winter?" We're firmly in the feed-all-year camp. Here's why:

In winter, you're providing much-needed calories for cold birds by setting out food. In return, you'll have the fun of watching dozens of birds cavorting around your feeders, adding color and life to the drab winter landscape and helping those seemingly endless months pass much more quickly.

Spring may actually be the most important time to feed birds. Many people put their feeders away when the weather gets warmer and the grass turns green, but the insects many birds rely on as a primary source of food in warm weather take a while to emerge, arrive, and/or build up sufficient numbers to sustain them. Meanwhile, the birds are establishing their territories, building nests, courting, and preparing to raise their young—all activities that require a lot of nutrition! Keeping your feeders active in the spring will ensure that you have a vibrant, diverse population of birds in your yard and that you're doing your part for the next generation.

Summer feeding may benefit you more than your backyard birds. With summer's dense foliage and plentiful insect populations, birds might feast in hiding where you can't see them. But if you keep setting out food, you'll bring birds—in their glorious summer plumage—up close where you can enjoy them. Summer's a great time to supplement your flowers with nectar, fruit, and jelly feeders to lure in orioles and hummingbirds. Fruits like apple halves and chunks of cantaloupe will also bring in jays, cardinals, tanagers, and a host of other wonderful visitors.

As flowers, fruit, insects, and even weed seeds begin to vanish with the onset of colder weather, it's important to supplement your backyard birds' diet with seeds, suet, and other feeder favorites. You'll find more birds arriving at your feeders as the fall migrations bring more species down from the North. Feeders that are already buzzing with birds will act like billboards to signal to these new arrivals that there's a diner in the area—and it's free!

What are the biggest benefits of feeding birds year-round? You'll always have plenty of birds nearby to enjoy, and you'll never have that agonizing wait every winter for the birds to "discover" your feeders. And you'll have the satisfaction of knowing that you're helping both bird populations and the environment. As the Droll Yankee Web site (www.drollyankees.com) explains, "When you feed birds, you help more baby birds survive. More birds will eat more insects, so you'll need fewer chemicals to control them. Using fewer chemicals will make the environment healthier for you, your children, your pets, our water supply . . . and wild birds."

whether they've been designed for nyjer or sunflower seeds, or shelled peanuts. Birds pull the seeds or nuts out through the mesh while clinging to the side of the cylinder. Birds that visit plastic tube feeders will come to wire mesh seed feeders; woodpeckers, nuthatches, and jays will patronize peanut feeders.

- **Suet feeder.** These square metal cages are designed to hold the prepared suet blocks that are readily available anyplace that sells wild bird supplies. People tend to think of woodpeckers and nuthatches when they think of suet, but many birds, including chickadees and cardinals, relish this calorie-dense food when temperatures drop.

- **Nectar feeder.** These glass, plastic, or ceramic bottles or tubes are designed to hold sugar water or commercially prepared nectar for hummingbirds or orioles. They have nectar ports on the sides or feeding tubes extending from their base.
- **Fruit feeder.** Fruit feeders tend to look like the planet Saturn, with an apple or orange half in the center and a circular perch surrounding it. Hang one from a branch and you might attract orioles, cardinals, mockingbirds, bluebirds, robins, and other fruit lovers.
- **Window feeder.** Window feeders are sturdy plastic squares or rectangles that attach to your window with suction cups. Because they attach to your window, they bring birds up close where they're easy to watch. Some window feeders are designed to fit *inside* your window, bringing wild birds almost into the house. Typically small, they'll attract the smaller feeder birds, including finches, chickadees, and titmice.

Serve Less in Summer

If you're on a budget, you may wonder where the money for a year-long stash of birdseed will come from. Our suggestion: Cut down the number of feeders you put out as the weather warms and insects and flowers become plentiful. Keep a tube feeder or two and one tray or platform feeder in operation where you're most likely to see and enjoy birds. Set out your fruit and nectar feeders for the season. Clean the others and store them until fall.

Project FeederWatch

We mentioned the Cornell Lab of Ornithology in Chapter 1 (see page 22), but it's worth bringing up again here because of its outstanding "Citizen Science" project, Project FeederWatch (cosponsored by Bird Studies Canada). Thousands of avid backyard birders across the United States and Canada note down what birds are visiting their feeders each month, and send the data to the Project FeederWatch site (www.birds.cornell.edu), where their data is analyzed, combined with other reports, and presented online.

Though Project FeederWatch itself is a subscription service—backyard birders pay a fee to be part of it—the site has a wealth of information that's available free to everyone. Check out the "About Birds and Bird Feeding" tab at the top of the FeederWatch page for its best advice on feeders, seed, setting up a feeder, troubleshooting, and more. If you click the "Explore Data" tab, you can find: listings of birds by state or province for each year since 1988; sightings of rare birds; top 25 feeder birds by state or province; maps of bird distribution; population studies; and locations of Project FeederWatch count sites.

As you become more enthusiastic about feeding birds, and more comfortable identifying your feeder visitors, consider participating in this wonderful project. The annual fee is just $15 ($12 if you're a Lab Member), and you'll get a kit, an electronic newsletter, and an end-of-year report, *Winter Bird Highlights*. It's a great way to get more from backyard birding—and to give more to your fellow backyard birders, too!

Take a Closer Look

Black-Capped Chickadee *(Poecile atricapillus)*

Black-capped chickadees are easy to identify by their black cap and "bib" and white cheeks. The back is gray, breast is white, and belly is a pale pumpkin-orange. Males, females, and juveniles look alike, and their plumage looks the same all year, though the colors become duller in summer. Adult birds are 5 to 6 inches (13 to 15 cm) long. Females nest in holes in trees and typically lay six to eight roundish white eggs with tiny brown speckles.

Feeder Favorites for Chickadees

- Sunflower seed, especially black oil and striped
- Peanut hearts and hulled peanuts
- Peanut butter mixed with hulled seed
- Suet
- Safflower seed

Regional Relations

Black-capped chickadees are common throughout the northern half of the country. In the Southeast and south-central states (through most of Texas), their smaller cousin, the Carolina chickadee (*Poecile carolinensis*), takes over. It's very hard to tell the two species apart, but the Carolina chickadee is 4¾ inches (12 cm) long and it has a more high-pitched call; it's also more likely to stay in the trees and shrubs than the adventurous black-capped chickadee is. If you live in the western part of the country, you have a chickadee of your own, the 5¼-inch (13.3 cm) mountain chickadee (*P. gambeli*). It looks like its cousins, too, but has a distinctive white eyebrow, which turns the black band over its eyes into a Zorro-like mask. Its underside is gray rather than pale buff-orange like that of the black-capped and Carolina chickadees.

Tempting Features and Treats for Chickadees

- Since chickadees are cavity nesters, they'll appreciate it if you set out nest boxes for them.
- Black-capped chickadees will visit feeders all year. They prefer feeders that are well off the ground, so choose these to replenish rather than low tray feeders.
- Chickadees appreciate a source of fresh water all year. A heated birdbath is ideal in winter.
- Offer special treats like pine nuts, mealworms, almond pieces, doughnuts, and raw hamburger.

Did You Know?

- Maine and Massachusetts claim the chickadee as their official state bird.
- Chickadees are considered to be a type of titmouse! (Both are in the Paridae family.)
- Chickadees typically mate for life, but occasionally a chickadee will get a "divorce" in order to pair up with a higher-ranking bird.
- Chickadees form flocks of six to ten (or more) birds for the winter. If your feeders are filled and ready when they migrate through your area, they may choose your yard to stay in for the winter.
- Chickadees stash their food, taking one piece at a time and hiding it by tucking it into crevices in bark and other secret places. A single chickadee can stash hundreds of pieces of food in a single day, and scientists have found that each bird can remember thousands of hiding places. They also remember which ones have the best treats, and which ones they've emptied. Because they usually cache food within 100 feet of its source, it's easy to watch this process if you use your binoculars to follow along as a chickadee leaves your feeder.
- It's not the song but the call of the chickadee—"chick-a-dee-dee-dee"—that gave the bird its name; the song is a high-pitched whistled "fee-bee-ee."
- Scientists have found that the chickadee's call is actually a complex language used to recognize other flocks and individual birds, warn of predators, and "speak" to each other.

THE TRUSTY TUBE FEEDER

Tube feeders seem like the quintessential bird feeders. When you say "bird feeder," a tube feeder is the one that pops into everybody's mind. So it's hard to believe that it was almost 1970 before the first tube feeder came on the market. And of course it took an engineer-inventor to think of it! (See "Feeder Files: Droll Yankees" on the opposite page for the story of Peter Kilham and the tube feeder.)

Most people start feeding birds by purchasing a tube feeder and a bag of seed, filling the feeder, and hanging it up. And that's a smart move. When we asked Pat Varner, co-owner with her husband Will of the Wild Birds Unlimited Store in Allentown, Pennsylvania, what feeder she'd suggest for someone just starting out in backyard birding, she replied without hesitation, "A tube feeder. If you

A tube feeder filled with sunflower seed will host a steady stream of chickadees and titmice, as well as finches, cardinals, and other seed lovers.

BIRD MYTH-BUSTER

Skip the Mix when Serving Seed in a Tube

Since different birds prefer different foods, offering a seed mix seems like the best way to attract the greatest variety of birds. Not necessarily, notes an experienced birder who explains that the type of feeder also determines which birds fly in for a meal. "The most important thing to tell people is not to put a seed mix in their tube feeder," says Rudy Keller of Boyertown, Pennsylvania, past president of the Baird Ornithological Club and contributor to *The Birds of Pennsylvania*. "Not all birds like to perch on tube feeders, and the ones that do prefer sunflower seed. They'll just throw the other seeds all over the place in an effort to get to the sunflower seeds in the mix." Rudy suggests just putting sunflower seed in tube feeders with feeding ports (the round openings like ship's windows) and nyjer seed in tube feeders designed exclusively for this finch favorite (see page 63 for more on nyjer).

But what about the mixes? They definitely have a place—it's just not in a tube feeder. "Put them on tray or platform feeders or on the ground where the birds who prefer those seeds can easily reach them," says Rudy. The editors of *Birdwatcher's Digest* agree. We'll talk about those options on page 67. Have we used seed mixes in tube feeders ourselves? Sure, plenty of times—we didn't know better. And it didn't keep the birds from coming. But it's true that a lot of the seed ended up on the ground (and on every other surface near the feeders)—a boon for ground-feeding birds like juncos and mourning doves, but a mess as well.

FEEDER FILES: Droll Yankees

Peter Kilham, an artist, engineer, and inventor, founded Droll Yankees, located in Foster, Rhode Island, and invented the first tubular bird feeder, the Droll Yankees A6 feeder, in 1969. Over 35 years later, almost 2 million Droll Yankees A6 feeders (which have six feeder "ports," or holes where birds can access seed, and six perches) have been sold worldwide.

There is now an extensive line of Droll Yankees tube feeders, with weather-proof, squirrel-beating zinc lids and bases (many in their "New Generation" series are powder-coated in attractive copper or rich burgundy or green), stainless hangers, durable crack-resistant polycarbonate tubes that won't yellow, squirrel-proof zinc feeding ports and perches, and a selection of lengths. Feeders are designed for sunflower or seed mixes, nyjer seed, or peanuts.

Droll Yankees also makes a series of Bird Lovers tube feeders, which have heavy plastic rather than metal lids, bases, and perches, range from 8 to 23 inches (20 to 58 cm) long, and are extremely affordable. Bird Lovers feeders are designed for sunflower seeds or general seed mixes, with the standard rod perch or a special U-shape perch. There's also a special Bird Lovers feeder for nyjer seed to attract finches. Like Droll Yankees' classic tube feeders, Bird Lovers feeders are made from UV-stabilized polycarbonate plastic, which won't degrade or yellow in sunlight.

In addition, Droll Yankees makes a seed, suet, mealworm, and fruit feeder, the Seed Saver, with a domed top and circular deep-dish bottom. It has drainage holes to help keep seed dry and an easy adjustment system so you can position the dome at the height you desire above the base, allowing only the smaller birds to feed or moving it higher to permit birds of all sizes to enjoy the feast. The domed top also protects the seed from rain and snow.

Droll Yankees also produces poles, seed-catching trays, and squirrel baffles. And it offers a line of special squirrel-repelling feeders, the Yankee Flipper, Tipper, Dipper, and Whipper (the last three have different types of collapsible perches that flip down under a squirrel's weight, while the Flipper has a battery-powered motor that actually flips squirrels off the feeder when they land on the perch).

Droll Yankees' reputation for quality is outstanding. It offers lifetime warranties on its bird feeders, and has repair specialists in stores that carry its feeder line so if anything goes wrong with your feeder, you can conveniently have it repaired. One of North America's most famous birding hot spots, Hawk Mountain Sanctuary, carries exclusively Droll Yankees feeders in its gift shop because, as a Hawk Mountain store clerk said, "We know that they hold up well against the elements." Some of our own Droll Yankees feeders are still going strong after 15 years of continuous use.

Visit Droll Yankees' Web site at www.drollyankees.com and check out its feeders for yourself. (You can't order feeders on the Web site, but you can buy them in wild bird specialty stores as well as pet stores, Agway, and other local venues. The Web site will give you a list of nearby sources.) Highly recommended!

have one feeder in your yard, you want one that you can see from all sides, and you want to be able to see the level of seed from the house easily."

But all seeds are not equal when it comes to filling that feeder—and for that matter, all tube feeders aren't equal, either. Here's the scoop.

Choosing a Tube Feeder

So now you have your sunflower seed. How do you select a good tube feeder from the dozens of models available? First, think about where you plan to hang it. If you're planning to hang it from a slender branch or a shepherd's crook, one of the smaller feeders would work better than a large tube that will be quite heavy when it's full of seed. If, on the other hand, you're planning to mount your feeder on top of a pole or post, hang it from a sturdy branch, or use a multi-hanging pole system specially developed to support feeders, a larger feeder will not only mean less frequent filling, it will also usually have more feeder ports, and that translates into more birds at your feeder.

BIRD MYTH-BUSTERS

Metal Perches Don't Freeze Feet

Here's an enduring misconception about tube feeders: Birds' feet will freeze onto metal perches when temperatures drop below 32°F (0°C). Let us say once and for all: It just isn't so. Think about it: Have you ever seen a bird stuck to a feeder perch? No, you haven't, and neither has anyone else. Feeder manufacturers would certainly not keep making feeders with metal perches if they endangered wild birds—it would put them out of business! So let go of this baseless bird myth and buy the most durable feeder you can afford. You—and your hungry visitors—will be glad you did!

The number of feeder ports—those circular holes, usually with a perch under each, that give birds access to seed—is another consideration when choosing a feeder. While a tube with just two ports at the bottom will work fine and attract plenty of birds, you'll have a better show with more ports, since more birds can feed at a time. (The drawback is that the more ports in your feeder, the more often you'll need to refill. But we think it's worth it.)

Next, think about durability. The best plastic tube feeders have tough polycarbonate tubes that won't yellow or become brittle over time, and will withstand everything nature can throw at them with nary a chip or crack. The tops, bases, and perches are made of squirrel-resistant metal, and the port holes are also surrounded by metal to keep sharp squirrel teeth from enlarging the openings. Hangers are sturdy stainless steel or cable. The perches are securely attached to the feeder.

Now consider ease of use, from the human rather than the bird perspective. Lift up the lid to see how easy it will be to lift it off and refill the feeder. Consider how it will feel when it's half-full of seed and swinging from its hook. Will you still be able to lift it down easily, then lift the lid and refill it, replace the lid, and hang it back up? Is the model you're looking at easy to clean? Some tube feeders have sections—either "ribbons" or cubes—to hold different kinds of seed. They certainly look snazzy in photos, but we think they're a cleaning and filling nightmare. If you can only put up one feeder and you want to go this route, we'd suggest choosing a model with three separate tubes attached to the same base and top to reduce and simplify filling chores.

BUDGET-WISE BIRDING

B.Y.O. (Build Your Own) Soda Bottle Seed Feeder

If your family drinks soda, you can make a big, attractive tube feeder for less than $3. Remove the label from a 2-liter soda bottle, rinse it out, dry it thoroughly, and discard the cap. Buy a soda bottle feeder packet (ours cost $2.99 at the local Agway), which contains a plastic feeder base and a hanging attachment. Using an awl or other sharp implement, punch two holes on opposite sides of the base of the soda bottle, about an inch from the bottom, and push the hanger into place. Turn the bottle upside down and fill with seed, then screw on the feeder base (a circular tray with perches) in place of the cap. Hang the bottle outside and you're good to go! It's easy to refill by turning the plug in the bottom of the feeder base, pulling it out, and pouring seed in. A 2-liter feeder holds plenty of seed—one of the "good feeder" requirements of the Cornell Lab of Ornithology. And you're not only recycling the soda bottle—the plastic feeder attachments are also made from recycled plastic! What a deal.

Have any questions? We thought so.

Q: *Will birds really come to a soda bottle feeder?*

A: You bet.

Q: *Won't a soda bottle feeder look unsightly in my yard?*

A: We were surprised and delighted to see that our soda bottle feeder was at least as attractive as any of our tube feeders, even the most expensive models, at less than a tenth of the cost. Frankly, we thought it was more attractive than the other feeders.

Q: *Okay, what's the catch?*

A: You're right, there is one. If squirrels are tearing your other feeders apart, they'll find this one as well, and while a soda bottle is great at surviving the elements, it's no challenge for a hungry squirrel. If your yard is plagued by destructive squirrels, the best way to save money on feeders and seed is to buy the best squirrel-proof feeder you can afford. (See Chapter 11, "Less-Wanted Guests," beginning on page 315, for more on dealing with squirrels.)

Wire "Cage" Tube Feeders

A different style of tube feeder is made from durable steel mesh or hardware cloth formed into a cylinder. The ends are blocked with wood or sturdy (often recycled) plastic. The lid lifts up on its wire or cable hanger. Tubes (and their wire mesh or hardware cloth) are sized to contain sunflower seed, nyjer, or peanuts.

Look for well-made wire tube feeders that are securely welded or otherwise sealed where the two edges of the wire connect, and that all edges are smooth, including the opening at the top. You don't want to be stabbed by a protruding wire while filling, hanging, or cleaning the feeder. Because the wire mesh is exposed to the weather, choose a tube made from stainless steel mesh—it's worth it! These feeders—especially the ones made for sunflower seed and peanuts—can be heavy when they're full, so check the handle carefully to make sure it's securely attached to the feeder. Lift the top up and down on the handle several times to make sure that it's easy to lift and replace on the tube after cleaning or refilling.

These feeders have their own advantages and disadvantages.

PROS

- Unlike plastic tubes, which restrict access to feeder ports and/or bottom trays, birds have access to the entire length of a wire tube feeder. More access means more birds can use the feeder at the same time.
- Since they have no perches, these feeders attract birds that can feed while clinging, such as nuthatches, chickadees, titmice, and goldfinches, rather than the heavier birds.
- A well-made wire feeder, such as the ones made with thick recycled plastic tops and bottoms and stainless steel mesh, will last for decades.
- If you're handy, you can make your own from ½-inch (1.3 cm) stainless steel mesh or hardware cloth for a peanut feeder, ¼-inch (0.6 cm) stainless steel mesh or hardware cloth for black oil sunflower seed, or window-screen-size mesh for nyjer seed. Use pieces of untreated wood cut to fit for the top and bottom (for example, 6-inch, or 15 cm, squares or circles for the sunflower tube) and a wire or thin steel cable for hanging.

CONS

- All those openings make these feeders messy to fill. You can fill them over a newspaper and collect the spilled seed (a good choice for nyjer), or fill them over a tray or platform feeder or where you typically ground-feed and leave the spilled seed where it falls.
- The infinite openings also make the seed more vulnerable to rain and snow. If birds empty your wire tube feeders quickly—and we've noticed that they tend to, once they've discovered them—you can simply refrain from refilling them when a snow or thunderstorm is predicted, bring the feeders indoors or into your garage or toolshed so they'll stay dry, and then refill and rehang them after the storm. Or add a protective dome (such as a plastic squirrel baffle) over the feeder to try to keep out the worst of the weather.
- A cheap wire feeder will rust eventually when left unprotected and exposed to the elements.
- The very speed with which hungry birds can empty these feeders could be considered a drawback by some, but we think the spectacle is worth it!

A Tube Feeder Just for Goldfinches

Well, it's not really "just" for goldfinches; buntings, redpolls, pine siskins, house finches, and purple finches all love the tiny nyjer seed, too. But nobody loves nyjer like goldfinches! Nyjer feeders don't have ports like ordinary tube feeders—they have tiny openings that let the birds remove just one of the minute seeds at a time.

If you don't want other birds depleting your nyjer feeders, you can buy a model with openings *below* the perches. Goldfinches can eat upside down, but other nyjer lovers like house finches can't. However, studies have shown that goldfinches would much rather eat right side up! We suggest that you share the wealth.

On the plus side, squirrels and starlings ignore nyjer. That means that instead of investing in a feeder with metal portals and other protective parts, you can buy a cheap all-plastic model instead. A nyjer feeder with a yellow plastic lid and base will echo the cheerful color of breeding male goldfinches in all their glory. And you don't have to worry about vandals chewing up the feeder. Which means . . . well, it means that if you love goldfinches, jewel-bright buntings, and other nyjer-eaters, you should check out "Nyjer: Sock It to Me" on page 63 for a pleasant surprise.

Extra! Extra!

What about extras—the domed squirrel baffles that attach above hanging feeders and both above and below pole-mounted feeders; the seed trays that attach to the bottom of the tube feeders to catch spilled seed; and the silica crystals to keep seed dry? We propose that you let spilled seed fall to the ground to allow ground-feeding birds like juncos and towhees to enjoy the bounty. A seed tray attached to the bottom of a tube feeder will simply fill up with rain or snow and create a perfect repository for wet, moldy, solidified seed, unless you pair it with a domed squirrel baffle, and even that will offer scant protection from slanting rains.

The exceptions here are if you're trying to attract cardinals and other big birds to a tube feeder (see "Take a Closer Look: Northern Cardinal" on page 62 for more on this), or you're an apartment dweller trying to keep seed-related debris from getting all over the sidewalk, the landscape, or a downstairs neighbor's balcony. In this case, choose the biggest tray you can, pair it with a domed baffle of the same size, and make sure you clean it out whenever you fill the feeder and after every rain. (Make sure feeders are permitted in your complex before you spend the big bucks!)

If squirrels are likely to attack and damage your tube feeders, by all means get a domed baffle. If you're pole-mounting your tube feeder, use one baffle above the feeder and one below. Squirrel-resistant feeders are available with metal tubes. The drawback of these is that you can't see the seed level to tell at a glance when to refill, but we suspect that beats tubes that have been gnawed open. Other designs, like tube feeders inside coated wire cylinders, keep out both squirrels and larger birds—a great solution if squirrels have been destroying your feeders or simply eating large quantities of seed. (Duncraft even sells a cage that lets you retrofit your own tube feeder.)

Or try the latest and greatest in squirrel-deflecting tube feeders—they're built with circular perches at the bottom that either drop down under the weight of a squirrel (or starling or pigeon) or use batteries, again weight-activated, to spin the perch and toss off the squirrel or heavy bird. Both these and the caged tube feeders let you see the

Take a Closer Look

White-Throated Sparrow *(Zonotrichia albicollis)*

White-throated sparrows are easy to distinguish from other sparrows and little brown birds because of their prominent white throat. They also have a bold black stripe on the crown of their heads and another at their eyes, and yellow "eyebrows" in front of their eyes that either turn white farther back in the white-striped (or white-crowned) form of sparrow and tan in the tan-striped (tan-crowned) form. Both males and females are rusty brown above and gray below, and they look the same all year, though their colors are brightest in spring. Juveniles' sides and breast are heavily streaked, and their throats and eyebrows are grayish. Adult birds are 6 to 7 inches (15 to 18 cm) long; the males are slightly larger than the females. Females lay a clutch of one to six pale blue eggs with dark markings in nests built on or near the ground.

Feeder Favorites for Sparrows

- Sunflower seed, especially black oil sunflower
- Millet, red and white
- Cracked corn
- Peanut hearts

Regional Relations

White-throated sparrows are hardly the only ones you're likely to see at your winter feeders. Look for song sparrows (*Melospiza melodia*) across the country, and fox sparrows (*Passerella iliaca*) in the Southeast, Texas, the southern half of New Mexico and Arizona, and along the West Coast. Unlike other sparrows that visit feeders, most of which breed in Canada, the chipping sparrow (*Spizella passerina*) breeds through most of the United States (as well as in Canada), so you may find it visiting your feeders from spring until fall, but not in winter, unless you live in the Deep South. Golden-crowned sparrows (*Zonotrichia atricapilla*) visit West Coast feeders in winter. White-crowned sparrows (*Z. leucophrys*) visit winter feeders across most of the United States, and American tree sparrows (*S. arborea*) can be found at winter feeders in all but the southernmost states. Distinctive markings help identify the various species, but there are more than 32 species in the United States alone, so it takes practice to determine which is which. To sort out the ones visiting your yard, you'll want a good field guide and a pair of binoculars.

Tempting Features and Treats for Sparrows

- Put platform or tray feeders near dense shrubs, hedges, or evergreens; sparrows prefer to feed near cover.
- Plant some flowers for your sparrows! They love the seeds of annuals like cosmos and marigolds, as well as perennials like asters and goldenrod.
- Make sure your sparrows have a source of fresh water all year. A heated birdbath is ideal in winter.
- Sparrows also appreciate salt; put a handful in a saucer and place it on the ground at your feeding station.

Did You Know?

- White-throated sparrows are one of the most abundant winter feeder birds, along with dark-eyed juncos and song sparrows, according to Project FeederWatch.
- White-throated sparrows are more likely than other sparrows to visit feeders in urban areas.
- Although adapted to tray and platform feeders, white-throated sparrows are ground feeders that forage by kicking through leaf litter in search of seeds.
- According to the Cornell Lab of Ornithology, white-throated sparrows occasionally mate with dark-eyed juncos and produce hybrids that look like grayish sparrows with white outer tail feathers.
- White-throated sparrows seek mates based on color form: All the females prefer tan-striped males, while all the males prefer white-striped females. Because the white-striped birds are more aggressive than the tan-striped, they tend to get what they want!
- The song of the white-throated sparrow has been described as "Oh sweet Canada, Canada, Canada" or "Old Sam Peabody, Peabody, Peabody."

seed levels, too. (See page 54 for other options.) If squirrels aren't a problem, however, we suggest that you simply hang a good-quality tube feeder and leave it at that.

Now . . . about those silica crystals. If you've ever tried dried-flower crafts, you've probably used silica gel (which, despite its name, is also crystalline) as a desiccant to dry fresh flowers quickly while maintaining their color and shape. Or you may have seen those little packs of silica gel in shoe boxes, added to keep shoe leather from molding in damp conditions. One of the latest innovations in birding products is the use of loose silica crystals—this time water-absorbing silicon dioxide. These crystals, sold as Feeder Fresh, absorb moisture to keep seed drier and are nontoxic if consumed by birds. The idea is that you put the crystals in the bottom of your tube or other feeder to keep seed from molding and/or clumping, then simply discard them when you clean your feeder and replace with fresh crystals before refilling with seed.

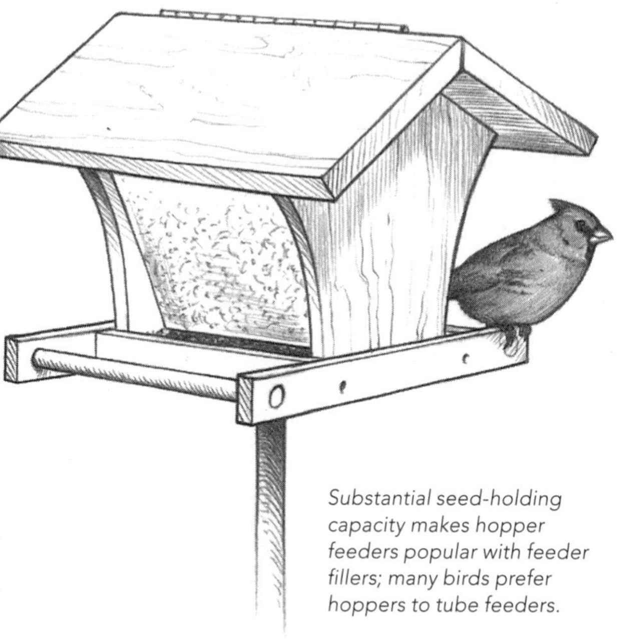

Substantial seed-holding capacity makes hopper feeders popular with feeder fillers; many birds prefer hoppers to tube feeders.

If it takes birds a while to eat the seed in your feeder during warm to hot, humid weather when mold is most likely, by all means give this a try. But as long as birds are emptying your feeders quickly—within a day or two of filling them—you don't need to worry. We were concerned that hulled seed, like hulled sunflower, might be more vulnerable to dampness and mold. This was a special concern since it's so expensive. But when we asked birding pro Rudy Keller, he just laughed. "Birds love hulled sunflower so much, it will never stay in a feeder long enough to mold!"

THE WHOPPER HOPPER FEEDER

Hopper feeders combine the convenience of a tube feeder with the platform feature of platform and tray feeders. This means that they attract more birds than tube feeders, since birds that dislike tube feeders—such as sparrows, woodpeckers, and jays—will visit them, as will favorites like cardinals, titmice, chickadees, nuthatches, and finches. But we call them "whopper" because they hold a lot of seed—up to 10 pounds!—making refilling a weekly (okay, twice weekly) rather than a daily chore. This comes in especially handy when you're leaving for a week's vacation and don't want to make the pet sitter refill the feeders as well as feed the animals, water the plants, and collect the mail.

Hoppers actually look like small cabins, a resemblance that is reinforced by the fact that many of them are made of wood for a rustic look. One side of the roof lifts up to allow you to fill the hopper, which then dispenses seed from openings along the bottom onto a ledge or narrow tray. As birds eat the seed, more is automatically dispensed until the feeder is empty. (But of course you wouldn't let *that* happen!)

Cabin Fever

Wooden hoppers usually have plastic sides that let you monitor seed levels. These feeders blend attractively into the landscape, especially after a year or two as the wood begins to weather. And they can usually be either pole-mounted or hung by a stout chain from a large tree branch. (Remember, these things are *heavy,* especially when filled! If you're putting the chain around a tree trunk for stability and ease of viewing, add a bracket—wooden for looks, metal for durability—beneath the hopper to keep it upright.) Many come with dividers so you can offer two or three types of seed—say, black oil sunflower or sunflower and safflower in one half and a mix of small seeds in the other—at a time. Some also let you adjust the height of the plastic sides to regulate the seed flow. And many models come with a suet cage attached at one or both ends.

If you opt for a wooden hopper, choose the most durable model you can afford, with sturdy wood construction and tough acrylic plastic panels in the sides. The bigger the feeding tray, the more easily birds can feed, and the broader the roof, the drier seeds (and birds) will stay. A broad roof also offers the diners some protection from hawks. Make sure it's easy for you to lift up the movable part of the roof to pour in seed. If you're buying a model with suet cages attached, make sure they're sturdy, protected by the roof overhang, and easy to fill.

Heavy Metal

If squirrels are a problem in your area, or you're spending too much on seed because the big birds (starlings, grackles, doves, and the like) are eating you out of house and home, a metal hopper feeder can provide many of the advantages of wooden hoppers with the additional benefit of being squirrel-proof.

Metal hoppers are also cabin-shaped, but the walls, roof, and other parts are solid metal, often enameled an attractive dark green. They typically have ports at the bottom that offer access for birds that land on a perch to feed. The perches are specially constructed to bear the weight of songbirds, but if a squirrel or heavy bird lands instead, the perches drop down, closing off the feeder ports behind a metal barricade and often causing the unwanted squirrel or bird to lose its balance and topple or fly off.

Like wooden hoppers, metal models can be hung or pole-mounted. Unless your property is invaded by hungry bears, they'll last practically forever. But because the sides are solid, you can't visually monitor seed levels.

Plastic Fantastic

If you're mounting a hopper feeder on a sturdy post, pipe, or stout pole, or hanging it from a large branch or tree trunk, its weight is no issue. But if you're using one of the popular adjustable pole-mounted feeder setups designed to hold several feeders, weight is a consideration. A good choice in this case is a plastic hopper feeder.

We recommend that you opt for one made from recycled plastic and help the environment along with your birds. (See "Everybody Wins" on the opposite page for more on wild birds and recycled plastic. For more on pole systems, see page 54.) Like the wooden hoppers, they have clear plastic sides so you can easily monitor seed levels, and they also often come with suet cages attached at one or both ends. Even if you're choosing a plastic hopper feeder, we suggest that you mount it on top of your pole system rather than hanging it from a pole arm. It will be much more stable, which you'll appreciate as much as the birds when it's time for a refill!

EVERYBODY WINS

New Life for Old Plastic

One trend we heartily applaud is the wild bird business community's embrace of recycled plastic in its feeders, houses, and other products. For years we've all read about the horrors of birds being trapped in plastic six-pack packaging and the like. Now, for once, the birds are benefiting from our plastic waste—and so is the environment.

Small specialty companies like Garden Gate Enterprises of Bethlehem, Pennsylvania, make their entire line of feeders from recycled plastic. (Check out the wonderful tube, hopper, suet, and tray feeders at www.gardengatebirdhouses.com.) And franchises like Wild Birds Unlimited proudly feature durable feeders and birdhouses made from recycled plastic milk jugs. In fact, we were thrilled during a visit to a Wild Birds Unlimited store to see that it was even selling birdseed in recycled plastic water jugs—with the original labels still visible under the new seed labels!

Sure, recycled plastic is good for the environment, but what does it look like? If you've seen the thick, tough plastic "wood" that's used to edge beds and make lawn furniture, you know what we're talking about. Naturally, the recycled plastic "wood" used in the feeders is thinner than a board! But it's still plenty thick and strong. (As Garden Gate Enterprises notes, plastic lumber won't fade, peel, rot, chip, crack, or warp.) You might think plastic feeders would look ugly, but they don't. The greens, browns, tans, and grays of the plastic look great in the landscape—you have to go up and examine or even touch them to tell they're not wood.

Opting for a Hopper?

A hopper feeder is a great component of a feeding system. But before you rush out to shop, there *are* a few drawbacks to keep in mind.

1. First, as noted, hoppers tend to be big and durable, which means they also tend to be expensive. If you're birding on a budget, you might want to put a hopper feeder on your Christmas list. And bear in mind that while you might want several tube feeders, a single hopper feeder is enough for most yards.
2. Hoppers allow birds to feed from both sides, but because you'll almost certainly set up yours so one long side faces you, you'll miss the show going on around back. Fortunately, we've found that the birds switch sides constantly as they feed, so you may not see every bird all the time, but you can be sure you'll see every bird.
3. A metal hopper won't let you visually monitor seed levels, so you'll have to manually check it to make sure it's not running low.
4. Wooden hoppers will eventually deteriorate, they're not squirrel-proof, and they're harder to clean than metal or plastic.
5. The feeding area on hopper feeders is usually a narrow strip on each side (or a perch, in the case of metal hoppers), limiting the number of birds that can feed at any given time. However, though hoppers can feed fewer birds than platform or tray feeders, they can still host more birds at once than most tube feeders.
6. Rain and snow can make the dispensed seed at a hopper feeder soggy and prone to mold. Make sure you clean and dry off the feeding area on both sides of your hopper after every rain or snow to allow the birds access to fresh, dry seed.

KEEP IT CLEAN

A dirty feeder can spread disease to the birds you're trying to nurture. If you set out feeders for wild birds, it's up to you to maintain them. If you don't, seed can mold and/or harden in clumps that block birds' access to your feeders. Regular maintenance and some good old common sense can prevent seed hygiene problems. Here's how to keep your feeders clean.

- **Choose good seed.** Old, dusty, bug-infested seed is no more attractive to birds than it is to you. Buy fresh seed, and buy seed that birds will actually eat (see "Seed Savvy" on page 55 to find out more about this), so the seed mix doesn't just sit and molder in your feeder.

- **Monitor seed consumption.** Set out no more seed than your birds will eat, so you don't have seed sitting around exposed to rain and snow, which can cause clumping and mold. It's better to set out smaller quantities more often than to leave seed uneaten.

- **Choose a feeder that's easy to clean.** The best feeders are designed with cleaning in mind. They're made of easy-to-clean materials and they open up (or come apart and fit back together) quickly and easily. Companies are constantly updating their designs to make feeder maintenance simpler: Droll Yankees, for example, redesigned the base of its New Generation tube feeders to bring the seed up closer to the lowest ports, so birds could easily reach *all* the seed rather than leaving unreachable seed in the bottom to clump and/or mold. That's the kind of innovation you want to look for.

- **Clean your feeders.** Use a bottle brush or brushes designed specifically to clean tube feeders (available from all stores and Web sites that sell wild bird supplies), removing all hulls and seed residue before refilling. Once a month, wash the feeders in a cleaning solution. Droll Yankees recommends a 50/50 solution of hot water and white vinegar, while the editors of *Birdwatcher's Digest* suggest a solution of ¼ cup bleach in 2 gallons of warm water. Whichever solution you choose, scrub thoroughly, rinse, and dry. When feeders are thoroughly dry, refill them and replace them on their hook or pole. By rotating your cleaning schedule, you'll always have some feeders in operation while you're cleaning others. Use a spatula to scrape damp or encrusted seed off a tray feeder, and a long-handled brush (like a hearth sweeper) to remove hulls and debris.

- **Clean under feeders.** Many birds, including juncos, sparrows, cardinals, and mourning doves, prefer feeding on the ground, so spilled seed from your feeders is like manna from heaven to them. But after a while, seed hulls can build up, inviting mold and disease. And sunflower seed hulls contain a substance that can prevent other plants from sprouting, which can affect your lawn and garden if you grow plants from seed. Allow ground-feeding birds to enjoy the spilled bounty, but prevent problems by removing hulls under your feeders when they start to build up.

- **Don't forget the finches.** Nyjer seed is so small you might think it couldn't gum up or mold, but wet nyjer can make an ugly mess of your feeder. Monitor your finches' seed consumption, and don't put out more than they'll eat in a few days. (For more on nyjer, see page 63.)

- **Watch the nectar feeders.** It's even more important to make sure nectar feeders are clean, since uneaten nectar ferments quickly and can mold. Make sure you change the nectar regularly and don't put out more than your orioles and hummingbirds will consume. (See Chapter 7, "Hosting Hummingbirds," beginning on page 207, for more on keeping your nectar feeders shipshape, and "Jelly Junkies, Fruit Fiends, and Nectar Nuts" on page 80 for more on attracting orioles.)

- **Make suet seasonal.** Talk about gross! If you've ever seen—or smelled—rancid fat, you'll know why it's a bad plan to put suet out in hot weather. The suet-based cakes that are made to fit neatly in commercial suet cages will hold up better, but even they aren't impervious to summer heat. We suggest that you feed suet from fall through spring, and keep birds coming to your suet feeders with bakery and peanut-butter-based treats once the weather warms up. (For more on suet, see page 74; for bakery treats, see page 84; and for tips on feeding peanut butter, see page 85.)

Birds aren't the only ones who can pick up diseases from feeders and the area surrounding them—some diseases (including histoplasmosis, a serious lung fungus) can be transmitted to humans from bird droppings, which tend to collect where feeders are located. If you'd like to attach a feeder pole to your deck railing so you can enjoy wild birds almost within arm's reach as you relax outside, make sure you position its feeder arm so that it hangs over the lawn or border planting rather than over the deck itself. Some longtime backyard birders, including Bill Adler Jr. in his book *Impeccable Birdfeeding,* suggest wearing protective rubber or latex gloves while cleaning feeders or sweeping up seed hulls and debris from under feeders. At the very least, wash your hands after you refill, clean, or sweep up around your feeders.

Where Are the Birds?!

If you're just setting up a new feeder, or if you set out feeders in the fall rather than feeding birds year-round, it may take a while for birds to discover your feeder(s). Give them a week or two. Remember that, active and colorful as they are, birds are prey animals, and are naturally cautious—they don't want to end up as someone else's dinner because they've come to a feeder for a meal of their own! Help them feel confident by putting your feeder near shrubs and/or trees where they can reach cover fast if danger threatens.

If you're adding a new feeder to your yard and already have some established feeders, take a tip from the feeder pros at Droll Yankees: Place the new feeder near your older feeders until the birds have become used to it and are eating from it regularly. At that point, you can move it to its real destination in your yard.

The folks at Havahart, who make an extensive line of feeders as well as their famous live traps, have an idea that strikes us as ingenious. They suggest that if you're setting up the first feeder in your yard, put some seeds in a shiny pie plate under it as well as in the feeder. Birds will come to investigate the plate and will discover the feeder as well. If you already have feeders in the yard, Havahart recommends emptying your old feeders and placing the full new feeder near the old ones until the birds start using it. Then refill all the feeders and move the new one where you want it.

Take a Closer Look

Dark-Eyed Junco *(Junco hyemalis)*

Male dark-eyed juncos (slate-colored form) have a dramatic dark gray-black head and back and snowy-white underparts. Their dark tails have white outer feathers that flash as they fly. Females are a brownish gray rather than gray-black. Colors are the same all year. Juveniles display thin streaks on the head, breast, and back, but otherwise look like adults. Adult birds are 6 to 6¼ inches (15 to 16 cm) long. Females lay three to five bluish white eggs covered with tiny brownish speckles in nests built in small cavities on the ground—on slopes, among tree roots, in rock faces, even on the verges of roads.

Feeder Favorites for Juncos

- Sunflower seed, especially hulled and black oil
- Mixed seed
- Millet seed
- Cracked corn
- Peanut hearts

Regional Relations

The dark-eyed junco is a composite of seven forms that were once considered to be separate species: the slate-colored junco of Canada and Alaska that winters in the eastern United States, the Oregon junco of the West, the pink-sided junco of the central Rockies, the gray-headed junco of the southern Rockies, the white-winged junco of the Black Hills, the red-backed junco that lives in mountainous areas near the Mexican border, and the Guadalupe junco of Baja California. The backs of the Oregon and gray-headed juncos are reddish-brown, but the head of the Oregon junco is black (male) or brown (female), while as its name suggests, the gray-headed junco sports a gray head. Sometimes the Oregon form will appear at eastern feeders in winter. Some juncos live year-round in the higher elevations of the Appalachians and the mountains of the West.

Tempting Features and Treats for Juncos

- Juncos are ground feeders, so put their seed directly on the ground or on a tray feeder, preferably near dense shrubs or other cover so they can escape from predators.
- Treat your juncos to some bread or cracker crumbs.
- Smear peanut butter or a suet mix on top of a small log and set it on the ground where you're feeding juncos.
- Juncos will also relish finely chopped suet set out in a saucer or on a tray feeder.

Did You Know?

- The dark-eyed junco is the No. 1 feeder bird in the United States.
- Juncos are actually a type of sparrow.
- Juncos are called "snowbirds" because their arrival means that winter is coming, and also because, as dark-backed ground feeders, they're easiest to see against a snowy backdrop.
- Juncos form winter flocks of up to 30 birds, though the typical size is six to nine.
- Juncos feed by scratching among leaves and grass with both feet as they look for seed.
- In addition to the many forms of dark-eyed junco, there is a second recognized species, the yellow-eyed junco (*Junco phaeonotus*), but it lives in the forests of the Southwest and is not a feeder bird.
- Though juncos are ground feeders by preference, they will venture onto platform feeders as well as decks and deck railings (if they're under a tube feeder) in search of seed.
- The junco's song is a musical trill, but its call is a sharp "tick" or "smack."

TRIED-AND-TRUE: TRAY AND PLATFORM FEEDERS

Tray and platform feeders were probably the first bird feeders wild bird lovers came up with—at their simplest, they're just flat pieces of wood set on the ground or mounted on a pole, just a step or two above tossing seed on the ground. (Which isn't a bad idea at all, as long as you toss it around or under dense shrubs, hedges, a woodpile, or other protective cover.) As a rule of thumb, the trays are the ones that sit directly on the ground or on short legs, or are hung from branches or metal crooks. Platforms are elevated and mounted, usually on poles.

Well-Grounded: Tray Feeders

A tray feeder usually has short legs to hold it up off the ground or a sturdy wire or thin piece of steel cable for hanging (they tend to be heavy, even without seed or birds). Most tray feeders are square or rectangular, but we've seen one ingenious model (from Garden Gate Enterprises, www.gardengatebirdhouses.com) that's triangular. It has both a hanger and fold-down legs, so you can use it either way.

Tray feeders aren't complicated; you can easily make your own, even if you don't know one end of a hammer from the other. (See "5-Minute Makeover" on page 44 for directions.) A good tray is big enough to host lots of hungry birds. It should be sturdily built so it won't be blown around by the wind or toppled by squabbling birds. It should feature a rigid stainless screen or plastic mesh feeding surface for good drainage and wood or recycled plastic sides (and feet, if it's not a hanging model). The sides should be high enough to keep most of the seed in the tray, but no more than a couple of inches, since you want to be able to see the birds as

Ground-feeding birds such as juncos and sparrows will fly up to feed at hanging tubes and pole-mounted hopper or platform feeders, but they prefer to dine at a tray feeder that's raised just a few inches above the ground.

they come in to eat. Of course, some seed will inevitably be kicked, tossed, or blown out.

Some tray feeders have roofs, usually set on four posts attached to the corners of the tray. A roof offers birds some protection from the elements and from flying predators like hawks, and it also helps keep seed dry. But it's much harder to see the birds if the tray feeder is on the ground, since you're looking down on it from above.

Site your tray feeder where the ground-feeding birds that visit it can quickly fly to shelter if a predator (like a hawk or the neighborhood cat) appears. In front of a dense shrub, hedge, or evergreen tree is ideal. Place it where you can enjoy the spectacle from the house, deck, or patio—wherever you typically sit to watch birds.

Ground feeders generally prefer a mix of small seeds—millet, canary seed, even a little flaxseed. They also enjoy some sunflower seed and cracked corn. And of course they appreciate treats like pieces of bread, crushed crackers, Cheerios, and raisins. Don't overdo it, though. Start small, with just a handful or two of seed, and introduce more when you see that the birds are eating it quickly. Uneaten seed and other food will attract squirrels, mice, and other seed robbers—even deer!—and the unprotected surface of an unroofed tray feeder lets seed and other food spoil quickly once it's wet.

Clean your tray feeder regularly: Knock, sweep, or brush off seed hulls, clumped seed, and other debris, and compost or trash it, then hose off the feeder and let it dry before refilling.

5-MINUTE MAKEOVER

A Speedy Tray Feeder

If you have an old window screen and a few bricks lying around, you can make your own tray feeder in a flash. Put the bricks on the ground where you want your feeder, and position them under the four sides of the screen. Use a screen with metal mesh rather than plastic if you have one—the metal will hold up better under the weight of birds and seed. Your new tray feeder will be unobtrusive, capacious, and best of all, free!

Party Time: Platform Feeders

There is no doubt about it: Platform feeders are the most fun of all. These pole-mounted feeders are easy to make at home, even with minimal skills. And they provide everything a backyard birder (not to mention feeder birds) could want: lots of room for lots of birds, easy viewing, and the perfect surface to set out a wide variety of foods.

The simplest homemade platform feeder is a piece of plywood or lumber nailed or screwed to a stout pole (often made from a straight, sturdy branch) or tree trunk (after the tree has been cut down). Backyard birders often hammer long nails sharp-end-up through the platform (before attaching it to the pole) so that they can "spear" orange, pear, and apple halves onto the feeder for orioles, cardinals, jays, and other fruit-loving birds. (The spikes are also good for keeping doughnuts, bagels, and other baked goods in place—at least for a while.) Bird feeder builders may also attach plastic cap "cups" (this time nailing them down) to hold treats like jelly, mealworms, chopped suet, grit, and salt.

Most DIY birders leave it at that—no seed-containing sides, no drainage holes (though you

A simple plywood square atop a post is all you need to serve tasty tidbits to all manner of feathered guests. Secure an old jar lid to the platform to hold jelly or other treats; drive a nail or two up through the platform to create "spikes" for skewering pieces of fruit, doughnuts, or other goodies.

can certainly drill them in if you want). That's because platform feeders are so popular with birds that there's seldom any seed left to be ruined by bad weather. Of course, if it rains or snows, an unprotected platform feeder will get soaked. Use good sense and don't put out more seed than birds can consume quickly if bad weather is predicted; save the bread and other treats for after the storm. Sweep or brush off seed debris regularly, and follow that up with a blast from the hose when rains haven't cleaned the surface for you. (Let the feeder dry before restocking.)

If you buy a platform feeder, you can easily find models with screen bottoms for drainage or drilled drainage holes, sides to provide convenient perching and help contain seed, even roofs to ward off the elements (not to mention hawks). Commercial platform feeders are designed to fit securely on the poles sold by their manufacturers. (For more on poles, see page 54.) Because your platform feeder will get a lot of use, buy the sturdiest, most durably constructed model you can afford.

Site your platform feeder where you'll get the best view of the avian action. You can pole-mount the feeder from waist to chest high. The higher pole will help bring the birds into view if your yard slopes down to where you've sited your feeding station. Just make sure you don't (or your much taller spouse doesn't) mount the pole too high—you should be able to fill and clean it easily, without straining.

Like tray feeders, platform feeders are open season for squirrels, wasps, yellow jackets (if you set out fruit), and other marauders. If squirrels are Public Enemy No. 1 in your book, another type of feeder will be a better option. (See "Those @#!*%!! Squirrels" on page 46 and Chapter 11, "Less-Wanted Guests: 'Pest' Birds and Other Wildlife at Your Feeders," beginning on page 315, for suggestions and pest-beating tips galore.)

Catering Your Platform Party

Go to town! The platform's the place to try out anything you think your birds might like. Besides sunflower and safflower seed and small seed mixes, you can set out fruit (both fresh and dried) and vegetables, nuts, cereal, chips, crackers, and baked goods of all kinds (see "Bird Bread and Baked Goods" on page 84 for ideas). Get in the habit of saving a few fresh peas, strawberries, cherries, or other bits of fruits and veggies as you prepare your family's meals, then setting them on the platform feeder. Don't forget the summer fruits, either. Birds love chunks of luscious fruits like cantaloupe, pineapple, peach, banana, and watermelon as much as we do. Save a few for them!

Share your table scraps—bits of scrambled, fried, and hard-boiled egg (not to mention the toast and bacon!), the corners of sandwiches, a little salad, a teaspoon or tablespoon of a side dish, a fragment of pizza or piecrust, a little cheese. Don't overdo it, and remove any leftover scraps at the end of the day to avoid attracting vermin, or more often in hot weather to prevent spoilage. Keep track of what the birds like and what they won't eat so you'll know what to set out. And remember,

Those @#!*%!! Squirrels

No doubt about it, squirrels are the critters backyard birders love to hate. Whole books have been written about foiling their attempts to destroy feeders and consume mass quantities of expensive seed, including the best-selling *Outwitting Squirrels*. You'll find more tips for keeping squirrels under control in Chapter 11, "Less-Wanted Guests: "Pest" Birds and Wildlife at Your Feeders," beginning on page 315. But we wanted to say a few things here about feeders that foil squirrels.

Droll Yankees proclaims its squirrel-foiling Yankee Flipper feeder the "Hottest Selling Bird Feeder in the Industry," and store owners from Agway to Wild Birds Unlimited say that the feeders customers buy most often are the ones that are sold as "squirrel-proof." In fact, most wild bird specialty stores and Web sites feature continuous-play videos of squirrels being foiled at their feeders and stores boast special displays of them.

Pat Varner, co-owner with her husband, Will, of the Wild Birds Unlimited store in Allentown, Pennsylvania, says the most popular product in her store is a feeder called the Eliminator. She points out that you should look for certain features in a squirrel-proof feeder to avoid trouble. "Many manufacturers sell feeders that they say are 'squirrel-proof' when in fact they are only squirrel-resistant," Pat says. "Squirrels can't get to the seed, so they destroy the feeders trying. Wild Birds Unlimited's Eliminator and Fundamental both close with the squirrel's weight, not allowing squirrels access to the seed or making the feeder vulnerable to destruction. And the Eliminator carries an in-store lifetime guarantee." The Eliminator is Pat's personal favorite product of the gazillions offered in her Wild Birds Unlimited store.

Birding pro Rudy Keller also endorses the feeder styles with perches that drop down their preferences may change in fall and winter when it's cold and new birds are arriving.

If you're a gardener, you have even more options for your platform buffet. When you're weeding, set out weeds that have gone to seed—birds love the seeds of lamb's-quarters, pigweed, dandelion, and many other gardening nightmares. If your roses form hips, cut a few and put them on the platform feeder so you can watch what happens; try other seeds and berries from around the garden, too.

Mealworms have become a popular feeder item, since insect-eating birds appreciate the high fat content of these wormlike grubs. (See "Mad about Mealworms" on page 82 for more on mealworms.) But birds will be equally grateful for any grubs, caterpillars, and other creepy-crawlies you discover while gardening and set out on the feeder. (Make sure you can identify the caterpillars of beautiful butterflies like monarchs and swallowtails, and those of luna moths, though, before you start harvesting bugs.) There's a certain satisfaction in dumping some Japanese beetle grubs or Mexican bean beetle larvae on the feeder—payback time!—not to mention cutworms, tomato hornworms, and other garden pests.

under a squirrel's weight, pulling a metal barrier down over the seed ports. "Squirrels are persistent," he says, "and they'll keep trying for a few days. But once they realize that they really can't get any seed, they give up and don't come back."

You can also exclude squirrels by creating your own low-cost baffle system. "Baffles are good if the feeders are far enough away from the trees," says backyard birding enthusiast Joan Silagy of Leesport, Pennsylvania. At nearby Blue Marsh Lake, a simple feeding station setup has been foiling squirrels for years. Blue Marsh staffers chose a half-inch thick metal cable to hang their feeders, then slipped two 3-foot-long pieces of PVC pipe along the cable before attaching it to sturdy metal posts at each end. Then they hung the feeders on the cable between the two pieces of pipe. "When a squirrel tries to cross the cable to reach the feeders, he can't," Joan says. "The pipes spin. Bye-bye squirrel!"

You can also try the hot pepper plan. Because they know that birds don't feel the burning sensation hot peppers cause in mammals, including squirrels, many people buy bags of seed with dried peppers included or mix their own dried hot peppers into their seed. But since, like us, squirrels can eat the seed and avoid the peppers, a more effective trick is to buy seed that's been treated with hot pepper extract. Birds eat it; squirrels don't.

Another approach is the "live and let live" tactic: to feed squirrels preferred foods away from your feeding station. Most stores and Web sites that sell bird supplies also sell squirrel feeders, usually to hold dried corn on the cob or a mix of corn and peanuts. "After all," as Rudy says, "squirrels are entertaining to watch, too."

WOODPECKER WONDERLAND: SUET FEEDERS

Back in the day, if you wanted to set out suet for woodpeckers, hawks, and other feathered lovers of fat, you went to your butcher and requested a bag of hard, white chunks of beef fat (suet is technically fat that surrounds the kidneys of cattle). And you can still do that. (See "Suet and Other High-Fat Fixations" on page 74 for more on that and on all types of suet, peanut butter, high-fat mixes, and meat treats in general.) If you wanted to prevent the suet from going rancid as it sat outside, or to add seeds and other goodies to it, you had to melt (render) it twice in a laborious, greasy process, then reform it into a solid block.

Times have changed, as you know if you've been in a store that carries wild bird supplies anytime lately—including pet stores, supermarkets, and home centers, at least during the winter months. Nowadays, backyard birders are more likely to set out preformed suet cakes in suet cages that are (conveniently) just the right size for them. These cakes come in an astounding variety, including ingredients from nuts and raisins to papaya and bugs, allowing you to select the "flavor" you feel your suet samplers would prefer, or to try a different kind every week. And the cakes won't melt or get rancid, even when the temperature hits 90°F (32°C).

Suet feeders attract woodpeckers of all kinds—downy, hairy, red-bellied, red-headed, pileated, flickers, and more. (Sorry, we haven't seen an ivory-billed woodpecker at our suet feeders yet, but we're still hoping.) But that's just the cream of the crop. Beloved birds like nuthatches, chickadees, titmice, bluebirds, and jays love suet, too. Unfortunately, so do squirrels, raccoons, starlings, crows, and even cats.

Choosing a Suet Feeder

If you're like most backyard birders, you'll want to hang or set up a suet "cage" that will hold those convenient cakes of suet from the store. You can choose a simple square suet cage that you can hang like a tube feeder; a hopper (cabin-style) feeder with a suet cage on one or both ends; a tray for suet cakes that attaches to a feeder station pole; a "varmint-proof" suet cage enclosed in a wire cylinder that you also hang like a tube feeder; a cage-style suet feeder with a "roof" to protect the contents from the elements; a tube feeder designed to hold suet balls; or a suet feeder with a solid top and sides that only allows feeding from the bottom, intended to discourage starlings and other suet hogs that can't hang upside down to eat.

Because woodpeckers brace themselves against tree trunks as they feed, using their tails for support, you can also buy hanging suet feeders that are designed with a wooden or recycled plastic brace and suet cages attached on one or both sides. The woodpeckers cling to the mesh and brace their tails against the support, which extends downward from the wire cage(s), while they feed in comfort.

Of course, you can also choose two or more of these options instead of limiting yourself to one. Whichever style or styles you choose, look for a sturdy suet cage that's easy to open to fill or clean. A latch or metal clip to secure the feeder's opening will deter squirrels and raccoons from helping themselves to the entire block of suet. Most suet cages are made of heavy wire that is coated with vinyl or enamel, often in forest green, to withstand the elements (it looks good, too).

SETTING UP A FEEDING STATION

Ready to get started? As with the famous potato chip, it's hard for backyard birders to stop at just one feeder. And why should you? (A survey of Project FeederWatch participants revealed that they averaged seven feeders in their yards, including hanging feeders, suet feeders, and platform feeders.) We recommend that you go to stores that sell lots of wild bird supplies and/or check out specialty Web sites for ideas for just what kind of setup you'd like in your own yard. (See the "Feeder Files" features in this chapter for leads on where to start.) And before you get out your checkbook or pull out the plastic, review "Before You Start" on page 51.

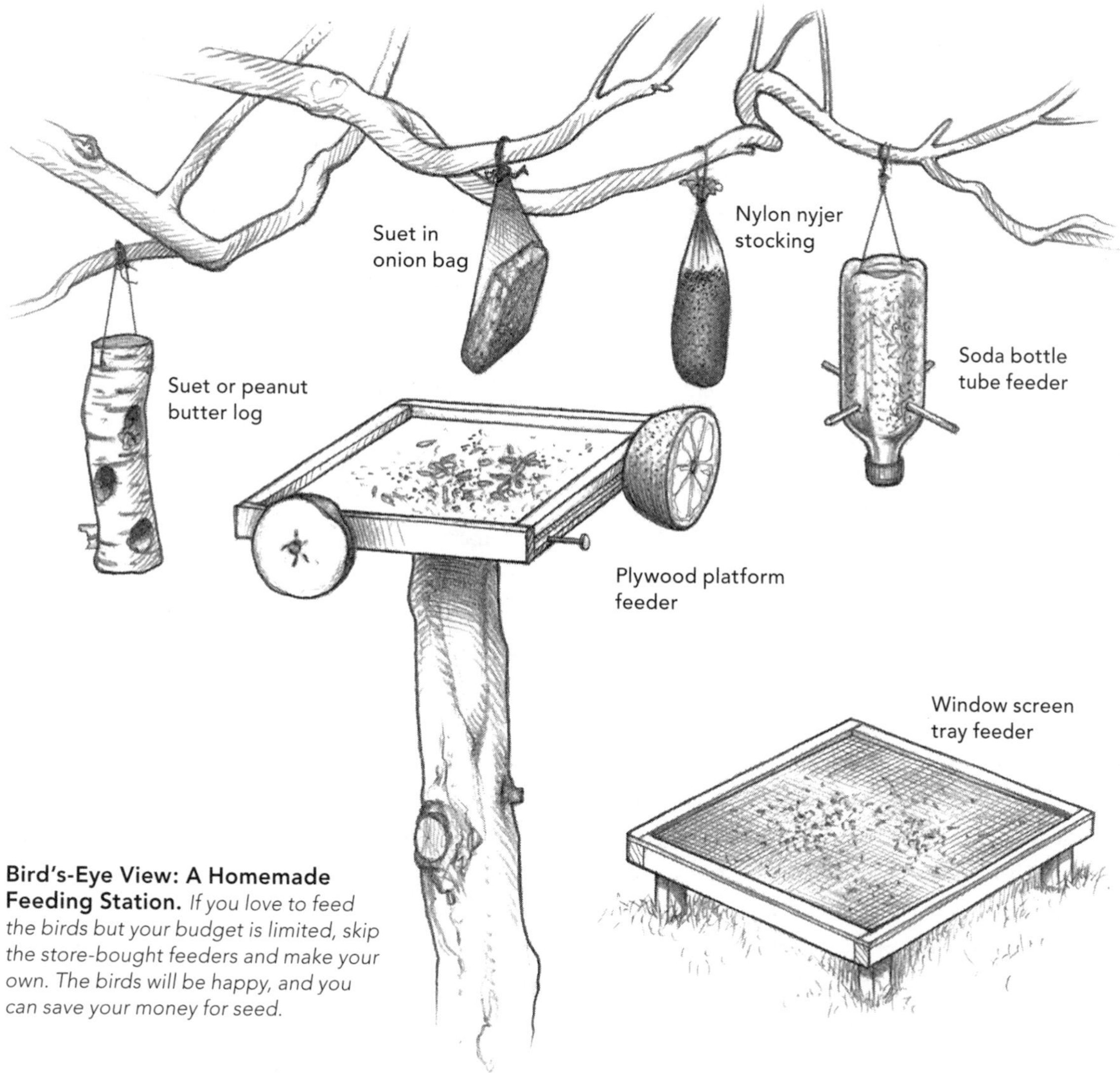

Bird's-Eye View: A Homemade Feeding Station. *If you love to feed the birds but your budget is limited, skip the store-bought feeders and make your own. The birds will be happy, and you can save your money for seed.*

SITING YOUR FEEDING STATION

The first and most important consideration is where to put your feeding station. You want to site it where you can see it easily from the kitchen window, the sliding glass door, the deck or patio, the family room, or wherever you and your family like to relax and look at birds. You want it to be convenient to the house, so it's not too much of a trial to head out every day or two with fresh seed, water, and treats.

But your preferences aren't the only ones that matter. Many birds won't venture out into the open to feed, preferring to stay near protective cover like trees, shrubs, and hedges so they can quickly escape from predators, loud noises, and other perceived threats. For their sake, site your feeding station where you can see them *and* they can quickly head for cover.

"Do *not* place a feeder out in the middle of the lawn. The birds become hawk bait if you do that!" warns Joan Silagy, who with her husband, Bob, set up the ultimate feeding station in their yard in Leesport, Pennsylvania. "If you need to place a feeder out in the open, plant bushes close by or tie a discarded Christmas tree at the base of the feeder to offer protection. Always try to keep the immediate area around the feeding station clear, at least for a few feet, so birds can see predators such as feral or free-roaming cats approaching and make their escape."

No cover where you want to put your feeding station? Create instant cover with a brush pile. Pile branches, twigs, pulled weeds, leaves, and other plant debris near your feeding site, keeping the pile structure open enough so that birds can move in and out quickly but predators can't.

Even backyard birding pros with plenty of trees and shrubs around their feeding stations often build brush piles simply because birds love them. Joan has a brush pile by her feeders even though they're placed in what most of us would consider a woodland setting at the edge of her lawn. "In winter, I move the brush pile closer to the feeders, since without their leaves the trees provide less protective cover," she says. "Then I move it a little further back in spring after the trees and shrubs leaf out."

You don't have any shrubs or trees nearby, but brush piles aren't part of your landscape plan? We suggest a compromise. Put a modest brush pile beside your feeders this fall, but plant a dense, twiggy shrub like privet (*Ligustrum* spp.)—you have to promise not to shear it!—or a shrubby, red-hipped rugosa rose (*Rosa rugosa*), or an evergreen tree or shrub to provide permanent cover in future years. You can remove the brush pile once the trees and shrubs have leafed out in the spring.

Siting feeders in a sheltered location helps you as well as the birds if you live in a windy area. If you've ever tried to capture a tube feeder for a refill as it swayed in a strong breeze, you'll know what we mean! And watching seed blow off a platform feeder isn't much fun, either.

Finally, because windows and glass doors reflect the trees and sky, making them a hazard for birds, how far you locate your feeding station from the house can be critical. Joan Silagy has this to say about siting: "Either have the feeders up very close to the window to prevent window kills from birds hitting the window when they're flushed, or have the feeders at least 15 feet or more from the windows." See "No More Knockouts" in Chapter 9, "Sharing Space with Birds," on page 279 for the scoop on making windows safe for birds.

EVERYBODY WINS

Get a Closer Look

You can really bring birds up close and personal by attaching feeders directly to your windows. Small clear plastic feeders suction onto the glass. The feeders are usually square (one suction cup) or rectangular (often with two feeding compartments and two or three suction cups), with hoods over the feeding compartment to keep out rain, snow, and debris. You can also find house-shaped window feeders with pitched roofs (three suction cups), tray feeders for windows, and even hummingbird feeders designed for window use! Even the suction cups are clear so they don't obstruct the view. This is a great backyard birding project for kids, and it has an unexpected benefit, too: The feeder will keep birds from flying into the window and injuring or killing themselves.

BEFORE YOU START

Siting your feeding station for your viewing comfort and your birds' safety is the first step. But deciding what to put there is the second. Before you head to the store or hit the button for a hefty online order, consider these points. They can save you money and aggravation, both now and later.

- **Start small.** The costs of feeders and seed can quickly add up, especially once you start discovering all the feeders, pole attachments, birdbaths, seed and suet mixes, and accessories available. And birds go through seed fast, so your startup costs are literally only the beginning. But cost is only part of the picture. There's also your responsibility for keeping your feeders and water features clean and filled. By starting small, you can see if, like so many backyard birders, you become "hooked" and find this the most enjoyable hobby ever. If so, you can start to add feeders and accessories to your heart's content. But add them one at a time. That way, you can keep track of maintenance and costs and make sure you're enjoying your newfound passion every step of the way. The last thing you want is for this wonderful hobby to become a source of guilt and remorse!
- **Face some bird facts.** To enjoy having a feeding station, you need to seriously consider how you and everyone else in your family feel about three things: cleanliness versus mess, noise and chaos, and bird mortality. Will you freak out if you see spilled seed on the lawn or bird droppings around the birdbath and on the platform feeder? The more feeders you set out, the more mess you'll have. And birds aren't the only issue. Feeders may attract bugs, rodents, and other unwanted visitors. Know your tolerance level before you start. That's true of noise and chaos as well. Birds at feeders often squawk and fight, sing and call. The never-ending show is part of the pleasure of backyard birding for most of us, but if you're sound-sensitive, fewer feeders will mean lower volume. Finally, the reality is that birds are fragile creatures and they die. Every year, you'll probably lose at least one to cold or disease, a hawk or cat, or a sky-reflecting window. If finding a dead bird is going to destroy your pleasure in hosting birds, recognize that the fewer feeders you put up, the less your chances of losing one.

- **Plan for storage.** You'll need a place to store birdseed, as well as a place to keep any feeders that you don't plan to fill year-round. Big bags of seed can take up serious space. Ideally, you should store them where they'll be convenient for you but out of the weather, where they're out of reach of seed vandals like raccoons, and where they'll stay cool and dry. A garage, toolshed, or mudroom is a great choice. So is a *dry* basement with a door to the outside. We'll talk more about seed storage containers on page 71.
- **Keep track.** Who's coming to your feeders and when? What are they eating and what are they avoiding? When do you need to get more seed? Are you attracting unwanted visitors? How are the feeders holding up? Are you spending too much or staying within budget? There are plenty of pertinent questions that will help you keep track of what's working and what's not, which will let you fine-tune your feeding station protocol and avoid repeating mistakes. If you have a great memory, simple observation might be enough, but you may want to keep a backyard birder notebook or diary to remind yourself. It's also great for noting who's arriving at your feeder, when they come and go, and what they like to eat.

3 Feeders Every Backyard Birder Should Have

Ready to take the plunge? Start to build your feeding station with these three feeders, which we consider backyard essentials: a good sunflower-type tube feeder, a platform feeder, and a suet feeder. That's all you really need for a lifetime of enjoyment.

Want to add on? Once you have the "Big Three," consider expanding to a nectar feeder for hummingbirds. But remember, this is a big commitment! Nectar feeders need regular cleaning and refilling with homemade or store-bought nectar. If you're a gardener, you might consider planting "hummingbird flowers" like columbines, salvias, trumpet vine, rose-of-Sharon, jewelweed or impatiens, bee balm, and butterfly bush. By choosing plants that bloom from spring through fall (and winter, in mild-winter areas), you'll be able to host hummingbirds year-round without a nectar feeder. And you can enjoy the flowers, too!

Another good option for adding-on is a nyjer feeder for goldfinches, house and purple finches, buntings, and redpolls. A hopper feeder will provide your feathered friends with a hefty seed supply, while protecting the seed from bad weather and reducing refill chores. (Choose a model with suet cages on the ends to expand your suet-lovers' options.) A tray feeder will give ground feeders a comfortable place to eat. Orioles and other fruit-loving birds will thank you if you add a fruit feeder to your array—or better yet, a fruit-feeding station that serves up jelly as well as fruit. Or you might try a mealworm feeder for bluebirds and other insect eaters.

Instead of (or in addition to) adding different kinds of feeders, you can always add more of what you find works for you and your birds—more tube feeders, a second platform feeder, another hopper, suet feeder, or nectar feeder. You'll know you've joined the elite corps of backyard birders when you find yourself setting up feeders you'll seldom even see, simply because you know the birds will appreciate them.

When you're just starting out, though, stick to the "Big Three": tube, platform, suet. Simple—but so much fun!

FEEDER FILES: Stores Just for Birds

When you walk into a store that sells supplies just for wild birds, you may feel like the proverbial kid in a candy store. Everywhere you look, you'll find a mind-boggling assortment of marvelous feeders, houses, birdbaths, seed, suet cakes, and other foods, and gizmos to attract birds of all kinds. You'll also find quite an array of ingenious devices to foil squirrels, ants, and other undesirables (though you'll find some fun squirrel feeders as well). Most stores carry an assortment of field guides and other books and magazines on wild birds and birding, plus binoculars and other useful supplies.

The oldest and largest of the franchise stores is Wild Birds Unlimited, founded in 1983 in Indianapolis. It now has over 300 Wild Birds Unlimited Nature Shops across the United States and Canada, featuring literally hundreds of bird-friendly products, many of which are Wild Birds Unlimited exclusives. It also has a wonderfully helpful and informative Web site (www.wbu.com), which offers backyard birders a wealth of how-to information and displays its products as well. Wild Birds Unlimited recognizes the importance of education and is a sponsor of Project FeederWatch as well as many other programs.

Second in age and size is Wild Bird Centers of America, founded in Maryland in 1985 and now offering 85 stores from coast to coast. Like Wild Birds Unlimited, Wild Bird Centers offer an incredibly diverse array of products in well-designed, inviting stores. They also sponsor Project FeederWatch and many other programs and have educational features on their Web site (www.wildbirdcenter.com). Both Wild Birds Unlimited and Wild Bird Centers offer free e-newsletters on their Web sites.

Nature centers and popular birding spots may also feature shops that cater to backyard birders as well as to folks venturing farther afield to look at birds. These stores can be great places to get expert advice on choosing binoculars and field guides. Purchases made at such sites often will help to support wildlife conservation or other worthy causes.

You might also be lucky enough to have a local, family-owned wild bird business near you, such as the All Seasons Wild Bird Stores in Minneapolis and St. Paul (www.wildbirdstore.com), the Wood Thrush Shop in Nashville, or the Bird House in Bethlehem, Pennsylvania (www.thebirdhouse-bethlehem.com). Check your telephone directory's yellow pages under "Birds—Feeders and Houses" to see if there's a private or franchise store in your area. Whether the store is one of a kind or part of a chain, we promise you'll be in for a treat!

As you walk through entire rooms devoted just to birdhouses, feed and feeders, hummingbirds, and birdbaths, you can begin to feel overwhelmed by the wealth of sheer ingenuity that's passing before your eyes. How can you tell the difference between all those models? Which ones are best for your needs? We suggest that you begin your search by checking out the companies' Web sites, exploring the products from the safety of home before plunging in for a hands-on experience. Make a note of any that look intriguing and check out pricing, too. Once you arrive at the store, look at the products in person to make sure they're what you expected and compare them to the other choices the store offers. Finally, ask the store personnel for their advice. The staff at a dedicated wild bird business tends to consist of people who love birds and backyard birding. They also know their products and will be happy to share their expertise with you.

Hang 'Em High or Set 'Em Straight

You've bought some feeders. Now it's time to set them up. You have two basic choices: Hang them from a branch, bracket, line, or tree trunk, or pole-mount them. Both are good options, and stores, Web sites, and catalogs that specialize in wild bird supplies have lots of options to help you.

Feeder hangers. Branches come in all sizes, and if you want to hang your feeder from one, you need to be able to do two things: Fit the hanger over the branch and reach the feeder easily to fill and clean it. Fortunately, some bright souls realized that the easiest way to do this would be by using hooks. Pretty much every source of bird supplies (beyond grocery stores) sells a variety of hooks for bird feeders. Choose hooks that are weatherproofed metal for strength and durability; hand-forged iron hooks may look gorgeous, but they'll rust.

Once you've decided which branch you'll hang your feeder on, choose a hook with one end that's wide enough to fit over the branch. The other end should be narrow enough to hold the feeder securely. If the branch you choose is too far off the ground to let you reach the feeder with just one hook, you may need to buy two or more to bring the feeder within reach. Only the one that fits over the branch will need a wide end; the rest can all be narrow. Some hooks are very short, like open S-hooks, to allow you to attach a feeder to a lower branch, clothesline, or wire. (The last two are often recommended for squirrel-proofing.)

Poles. You can make your own feeder pole from a straight, stout branch or trunk; buy a wooden pole or length of 4 × 4; or use a sturdy length of pipe. The key is to choose something that will support the weight of one or more filled feeders and the birds (and squirrels) that will be jumping all over them. (Don't forget to buy one that's tall enough to fit in its support hole and still extend as high as you want it to be.) Dig a hole deep enough to provide solid support—at least a foot, and better yet 18 inches—and secure the post in the hole with concrete or hard-packed earth.

Not into hole digging? Go for convenience and buy one of the many poles available at wild bird supply stores. Stability is the key—if you opt for a store-bought version, look for a pole that has a stable anchoring system. Some twist or screw into the ground with corkscrewlike augers. Others have three or four "feet" that extend from the feeder's base and anchor it to the ground. And still others have wide circular bases that sit on top of the ground.

Most store-bought poles are either adjustable (from 41 to 73 inches, or 104 to 185 cm, high) or come in 18-inch (45.7 cm) sections so you can adjust the height. You'll want a taller pole if you put shepherd's-hook-type hangers or other hanging arms on top and hang all your feeders from the arms, and a shorter height if you plan to mount a tube, platform, or hopper feeder on top, with or without others hanging from an arm system beneath the top feeder. You can also buy a steel or wrought-iron shepherd's crook for a single hanging feeder, but in our experience these aren't sufficiently stable to take all the swaying that goes on when birds visit the feeder.

There are also plenty of poles designed to fit on deck railings and bring your feeders almost within arm's length as you sit on your deck. While this is a delightful idea, let us remind you again that spilled seed, hulls, feathers, and bird droppings are an inescapable part of the bird-feeding experience, and the deck is not the best place for this mess. Instead, we suggest hanging a tube feeder or two from a tree near (but not over!) the deck. But if you just can't resist, at least position the pole so it holds the feeders away from and not over the deck.

SEED SAVVY

Now that you have your dream feeding station—or at least a feeder—in mind, it's time to turn our attention to the nitty-gritty—the stuff you put in it. And mostly that will be seeds. We'll talk about suet, nectar, fruit, and even mealworms later in this chapter. But let's start with a look at our most frequent visitors' favorite seeds. Then we'll review the kinds of seeds and seed mixes that are available. Some are stars, some are duds, and some are misrepresented (see "Bird Myth-Busters: Misleading Seed Stories" on page 56). And of course, we'll tell you how to spot seed that's not fresh, how to save money on seed, how to store it safely, and lots more.

FAVORITE BIRDS, FAVORITE SEEDS

As backyard birding has become more sophisticated, manufacturers and backyard birders alike have focused their attention on trying to attract their favorite birds, often while trying to exclude "undesirable" species. (What are undesirable species, you ask? Usually they're unattractive birds that make nuisances of themselves in one way or another—by being feeder bullies, preventing favorite birds from eating, or by traveling in huge flocks, emptying feeders, making a racket, and/or depositing droppings and other detritus everywhere. Starlings and house sparrows are classic examples.) We say, if you want to spend your time waging feeder wars, good luck to you! We'd rather focus our energy on attracting as many of our favorites as possible. And the first step is knowing which seeds they prefer.

We've provided lists of favorite foods for every bird profiled in this book, so you can find your own favorites and read all about them. But we'll give you at-a-glance lists of the "best of the best" here for easy reference, by bird and by seed. Note that when we say "sunflower," you can't go wrong with black oil sunflower seed. And we discuss peanuts in the "Suet and Other High-Fat Fixations" section on page 74, but we list peanut hearts here since they're included in some seed mixes (peanuts *are* seeds, after all!).

When you're ready to buy seed, you might want to photocopy this page and take it with you to the store. It will help you stay focused when you're surrounded by dozens of choices!

Birds and the Seeds They Love

- **Cardinals:** Sunflower, safflower, peanut hearts
- **Chickadees:** Sunflower, peanut hearts
- **Titmice:** Sunflower, safflower, peanut hearts
- **Nuthatches:** Sunflower, safflower, peanut hearts
- **Juncos:** Sunflower, millet, peanut hearts
- **Goldfinches:** Nyjer, sunflower
- **Grosbeaks:** Sunflower, safflower, peanut hearts
- **Finches:** Sunflower, nyjer, safflower, peanut hearts, millet
- **Woodpeckers** (including flickers): Sunflower, peanut hearts, cracked corn
- **Jays:** Sunflower, cracked corn, milo, peanut hearts
- **Buntings:** Nyjer, millet
- **Pine siskins:** Nyjer, hulled sunflower

- **Sparrows:** Sunflower, cracked corn, millet, peanut hearts
- **Towhees:** Cracked corn, sunflower
- **Doves:** Cracked corn, millet, milo, sunflower

Seeds and the Birds That Love Them

- **Sunflower, black oil:** Cardinals, chickadees, titmice, nuthatches, juncos, goldfinches, grosbeaks, finches, woodpeckers, jays, sparrows, towhees, doves, and so on
- **Sunflower, gray striped:** Cardinals, grosbeaks
- **Sunflower, hulled:** Cardinals, chickadees, titmice, nuthatches, juncos, goldfinches, grosbeaks, finches, woodpeckers, jays, pine siskins, sparrows, towhees, and so on
- **Safflower:** Cardinals, titmice, nuthatches, grosbeaks, finches
- **Nyjer:** Goldfinches, finches, buntings, pine siskins
- **Millet:** Juncos, finches, buntings, sparrows, doves
- **Mixed seed:** Cardinals, chickadees, titmice, juncos, goldfinches, finches, jays, buntings, sparrows, towhees, doves, and so on
- **Cracked corn:** Woodpeckers, jays, sparrows, towhees, doves, and so on
- **Peanut hearts:** Cardinals, chickadees, titmice, nuthatches, juncos, grosbeaks, finches, woodpeckers, jays, sparrows, and so on

Now it's time to take a closer look at the seeds birds love best. We'll start with the most popular choice (you know what that is by now, right?) and move on through the others that have more specific fans.

BIRD MYTH-BUSTERS

Misleading Seed Stories

Here are three common misconceptions about birdseed that we'll bet you've heard.

1. **Cardinals love safflower seed.** Wrong! Cardinals love *sunflower* seed, like most feeder birds. But unlike most feeder birds, cardinals will eat safflower seed. (So will grosbeaks and woodpeckers.) The real benefit of putting out safflower seed for your cardinals is that it doesn't attract squirrels, starlings, and other undesirables to your feeder.
2. **Nyjer (niger) is a kind of thistle.** Wrong again! This finch favorite is not related to thistles. The plant that produces this tiny black seed is a yellow daisy that's native to Africa. See "Nyjer: Sock It to Me" on page 63 for more about this popular and pricey seed.
3. **Wild birds won't eat milo.** Milo, a round, reddish seed that resembles a small pearl, is used as filler in less-expensive bird mixes. (It's actually the seed of sorghum, as in sorghum molasses.) Most reputable sources will tell you to avoid mixes with milo, since wild birds won't eat it. Not so, says Project FeederWatch—at least in the West. It's found that western jays are fond of milo. Pheasants, wild turkeys, pigeons, and doves eat it, too, all over the country. So if you're an eastern backyard birder, go with the received wisdom and skip mixes with milo unless you want to attract game birds; in the western half of the country, especially if you love the big, bad jays, go for it.

Clean It Up

You'll probably want to clean up under your bird feeders no matter what you're offering, just to get the mess swept up and keep your landscape looking good. Or you may be conscientious about seed cleanup because you're concerned that a buildup of debris under your feeders might promote mold or spread disease. But in the case of sunflower seed, there's a special reason to clean it up.

A chemical compound in the hulls of sunflower seeds causes what's known as an allelopathic reaction: It prevents seeds from germinating. This means that you may find bare patches under your feeders (although this could also be caused by birds scratching the ground in search of seeds). Of course, you could avoid potential problems by feeding shelled sunflower seed exclusively, but we suggest that you be kind to your wallet and simply sweep up the hulls on a regular basis. Dispose of them rather than composting them, since you don't want to compromise your garden seeds' germination!

SUNFLOWER SEEDS: FEEDER FAVORITES

Sunflower seeds are the stars of the birdseed universe. They are the favorite feeder fare of all feeder birds whose beaks can handle the shells. But be aware that not all sunflower seeds are alike. There are several kinds of sunflower seed sold, individually and in mixes, for bird feeders, not to mention the choicest treat of all: hulled sunflower seeds (sometimes sold as sunflower meats or hearts). Virtually all feeder birds love the expensive hulled seed, but if you're buying it in the shell, focus on black oil and gray striped.

Black oil sunflower seed, with smaller, all-black seeds, was originally developed (as its name implies) as a source of sunflower oil. But it proved to be a bonanza for backyard birds. The oil-rich seeds are their very favorite fare. If you put out only one kind of seed for backyard birds, this should be it. When you shop for black oil seed, look for clean, plump, glossy seeds without any sign of insect holes.

Gray striped (also called black striped) sunflower seeds are the largest sunflower seeds—they're the ones with cream-colored shells with dark gray stripes. Cardinals and grosbeaks enjoy the big seeds—their stout bills are up to the challenge of hulling them. So do bobwhites. In tests conducted by Dr. Aelred D. Geis of the U.S. Fish and Wildlife Service, tufted titmice, jays, and grackles also ate striped sunflower seeds with as much enthusiasm as black oil seeds. So don't shy away from mixes with these big sunflower seeds—as long as they also contain black oil seed!

If you're pricing straight sunflower seed, for once you'll be in for a pleasant surprise: black oil sunflower seed costs significantly (almost a fourth) less than gray striped seed! That's because the gray striped seed is also a popular human snack. Fortunately for us, the birds aren't such fans! Your luck will run out, though, when you turn to the hulled seed, which costs well over twice as much as black oil seed.

We suggest that you treat your birds to the occasional small bag of hulled seed and make black oil seed your staple. Use it alone in tube feeders, and alone or in combination with other seed (such as millet) in tray, platform, hopper, and other feeders, or tossed directly on the ground for ground-feeding birds.

Fun with Sunflower Heads

Have you seen those edible "wreaths" made of a dried sunflower head, usually with a raffia ribbon and some wheat, milo, and berries tied decoratively at the top? We think they're adorable—and so do sunflower-loving birds! Fortunately, it's easy to grow your own for pennies.

Sunflowers have become the darlings of the garden world in the last decade, and if you look in a garden catalog or search online for sunflowers, you'll find dozens of varieties to choose from. Many of these are small and decorative, with red, orange, or multicolored petals, multiple blooms, and smaller flowers than the old-fashioned sunflowers. But while these new varieties may be more colorful and ornamental, and are better suited for cut flowers, we recommend that you grow the dinner-plate size if you're aiming to provide seed for birds.

Choose varieties like 'Snack Seed', 'Sunzilla', 'Kong Hybrid', 'American Giants Hybrid', 'Mammoth Russian', or 'Super Snack Hybrid' that have been bred to provide a huge head packed with edible seeds in a home garden setting. (Note that many of them grow really tall—up to 14 feet!!!—so check the plant description before you buy and choose a variety that's suited to the area where you plan to grow it.) Packets of sunflower seed for gardening are widely available. Check your favorite catalogs or stores or go online to sites like Renee's Garden (www.reneesgarden.com) or Burpee (www.burpee.com).

Remember that most of these big varieties produce only one sunflower head per plant, so it will take a lot of room to harvest more than a few heads. Support tall sunflower plants by growing them against a fence, wall, or trellis, or the heavy heads may cause them to topple over. Of course, you can just let the mature heads dry on the plant and leave them there until the birds have eaten all the seeds—the birds won't mind! But you can also cut off the heads when the petals have shriveled and the seeds have started to dry, then use them to make your own sunflower "wreaths," or just set one out on your platform feeder every now and then and watch the fun!

Use your imagination to come up with wonderful ways to display your sunflower heads. One of our all-time favorites was in a rural backyard where the homeowners had tied sunflower heads, spaced at regular intervals, along the top of the wire fence that surrounded their yard. They attached the sunflower heads between the topmost and second wires, with the heads facing into the yard so they could enjoy the sight of the birds feasting on their treat.

To learn more about growing your own seed for the birds, see "Growing Your Own Birdseed Garden" on page 72.

A dried sunflower head serves as a self-contained feeder for finches and other small birds. If you grow your own sunflowers, you may want to cut the seedheads in late summer and hang them in a sheltered spot to finish drying. Otherwise, the birds will gather your harvest for you, perhaps sooner than you intended to offer it!

SAFFLOWER: BOLD AND BEAUTIFUL

Safflower didn't come by its name by accident. Its beautiful saffron-orange flowers, borne abundantly in thistlelike heads on sturdy annual plants, make it a natural for the flower garden (or the birdseed garden—see "Growing Your Own Birdseed Garden" on page 72 for more on this). Its flowers dry easily, retaining their brilliant color, so they're perfect to brighten up dried arrangements and wreaths, too; just hang the flowers upside down by their stems in a warm, dry place or lay them on a screen to dry.

Safflower seed is hard, white, angular, and plump, smaller (but fatter) than black oil sunflower seed. Cardinals are the most famous safflower eaters, but other birds will eat it, too, including nuthatches, finches, titmice, and grosbeaks.

Since safflower seed is apparently something of an acquired taste, it's best to accustom your birds to it by mixing a little in with your black oil sunflower seed, then gradually increasing the amount of safflower seed as the birds discover it. You can set out special safflower feeders, but we're fans of continuing to offer a black oil sunflower/safflower mix, which all safflower eaters prefer to straight safflower. If you buy seed in bulk, it's easy and cost-effective to blend your own; otherwise, look for a "cardinal's favorite"-type mix in which the two seeds are already blended.

You can offer safflower or a safflower-and-sunflower mix in a regular tube feeder and/or tray and platform feeders. Or toss some directly on the ground beneath a dense shrub or hedge.

FEEDER FILES: Duncraft

If you started feeding birds before the advent of the Internet, there's a good chance that you spent many happy hours with a Duncraft catalog in your hands. Duncraft has been selling backyard bird feeding products since 1952, when its founder, Gil Dunn, invented a tray feeder that clipped onto windowsills in his workshop in Penacook, New Hampshire. (Like Droll Yankees, another tale of Yankee ingenuity!) They still offer a windowsill tray feeder today.

Today, Duncraft still operates from Penacook, run by Gil's children, Mike and Sharon Dunn. They have produced their famous catalogs since the 1960s that are still as enjoyable today as they were back then. You can request one from their wonderful Web site, www.duncraft.com, or order an amazing assortment of products directly from the site, which features free e-newsletters, bird ID and feeding tips, and a blog. You can also find Duncraft products offered in retail stores that specialize in wild bird supplies. Or, if you're lucky enough to be vacationing in beautiful New Hampshire, you can visit their store in Concord. Like Droll Yankees, they offer a guarantee for their feeders and other products, whether you buy them online, through their catalog, or in a store.

Duncraft also pioneered the Duncraft Food Club, offering automatic deliveries of its many seed mixes, suet cakes and balls, mealworms, seed blocks, and other products that you personally select, as well as their Seed-by-Month service, which offers 5- or 10-pound bags of different seeds and seed blends that Duncraft has found most appropriate for each month of the year.

BUDGET-WISE BIRDING

Arithmetic for Bird Feeders

A bag of seed or a suet cake may not seem to cost much, but over a season or a year, those costs can add up—especially when you're filling several feeders. In a survey of backyard birders participating in Project FeederWatch, the average amount of seed set out per household each winter was more than 300 pounds (136 kg)! And that's not taking the rest of the year into account, much less the additional 20 pounds (9 kg) of suet and suet-based products purchased per household.

Let's try a little math. Crisscrossing between stores and the Internet and checking different types of seed and seed mixes, we decided to make it easy on ourselves and assign $15 to an "average" 10-pound (4.5 kg) bag of seed (actual costs ranged from $7.95 for an inexpensive blend to $24.95 for a high-end blend). We chose the lower end of the price spectrum and put suet cakes at $1.10 per 11-ounce cake (we found them from 99 cents to over $3). Okay, let's go: $15 for 10 pounds of seed is $150 for 100 pounds and $450 for 300 pounds; 16 ounces per pound puts the suet cakes at $1.60 per pound or $16 for 10 pounds and $32 for 20 pounds, for a grand total of $482—plus tax and/or shipping—and we're still just talking about winter!

Mind you, not everyone is as enthusiastic about backyard bird feeding as Project FeederWatch participants. And even if you are, it would take you a number of years to acquire the number of feeders (and the number of birds) to use that much seed and suet. But you can see why serious backyard birders are serious about saving money on seed! At the same time, they're not about to serve their beloved birds bad seed just because it's cheap. Read on for some of their time-tested seed-smart tips. (For suet, see "Suet and Other High-Fat Fixations" on page 74.)

- **Buy in bulk.** Almost always, the bigger the bag of seed, the lower the cost. (For example, $10.95 for 5 pounds, or 2.2 kg, but $76.95 for 50 pounds, or 22.7 kg—a savings of 65 cents a pound or $32.50 for the 50-pound bag!) Bulk seed that's not sold pre-bagged will save you even more. "I don't know any serious birder who doesn't buy seed in bulk at a feed store," says birder Rudy Keller. And some birders won't buy at just any feed store. Lillian Karch of Kutztown, Pennsylvania, is so serious about backyard birding that she and her husband planted more than 1,000 trees on their property after seeing how many birds came to the feeders at Hawk Mountain Sanctuary's wooded feeder display. Like Rudy, she buys her seed in bulk from a feed store—but she has to drive more than an hour to get there. "I checked out all the closer stores before I settled on this one," she says. "I was really impressed by how fresh their seed was and I've been going there ever since."
- **Buy clean seed.** You're not saving money if you buy old, moldy, insect-infested, or debris-rich seed. Birds can't derive the nourishment they need from bad seed, and you're doing them no favors by putting it out—as you'll find out when they fly off in search of better fare.

  Before you buy, check the bags for signs of insect infestation—small beige moths flying around the area, tiny holes in the bag, perhaps even a minute caterpillar crawling along a seam. Lift a bag—is it as heavy as you'd expect from the stated weight? Old, dried-up seed will weigh less than fresh seed. If you're buying a bigger bag, it will probably be paper, so you can't actually see the seed inside. But the store will often have small plastic bags of the same seeds and mixes for sale. Look at them and see how the seed looks to you. Can you see little pieces of twigs, lots of empty hulls, and other detritus? If so, pass it up. If not, and everything seems fine, keep those seeds in plastic bags in mind when you get your big paper sack home. Open it. Does the seed look the same as the seed in the plastic bags? A reputable company will put the exact same quality of seed or mix in both its clear plastic and its paper bags.

- **Join the club.** Many stores, catalogs, and Web sites offer incentives to keep buyers coming back, often in the form of buyer's clubs. You register with them and each time you buy seed, they record your purchase. When you've bought a certain amount of seed or number of bags, you get a free bag of seed, a discount on your next bag, or some other reward. If you always buy your seed at the same place, make sure you ask if they offer this service, and if so, sign up to collect your savings.

- **Split the difference.** Save even more by going in on a bulk order with some of your birding friends. A group of you can order a much bigger quantity than you could by yourself, and those savings will add up. And there's another bonus—the only thing more fun than shopping for backyard bird supplies by yourself is shopping for them with friends!

- **Watch the bottom line.** If you order seed from a catalog or Web site, make sure it charges shipping based on price, not weight, or those heavy bags of seed can cost a lot more than you think. Based on the cost of the seed, compare the shipping and handling charges to your state sales tax (and local, if you have one)—which you'd pay instead of shipping costs if you went to a store. Of course, some companies, including eBirdseed.com, offer free shipping. As a rule of thumb, we suggest comparing total costs from several sources before "shelling" out cash for seed. Don't forget to account for your own time and transportation costs if you have to drive very far to buy seed and suet.

- **Protect your investment.** Once you've hauled your seed home, keep it cool, dry, and safe from pests of all kinds. See "Careful Storage Saves Seed, Contains Costs," starting on page 71, for tips on how to store seed safely.

Keeping costs in mind certainly makes good sense. But we also want to remind you to keep a sense of perspective. You can buy a 20-pound bag of birdseed for less than $25—often considerably less—and it might last a couple of weeks. For that $25, you'll be getting hours of delight and just plain *fun* watching the birds cavort at your feeders. It's a lot less than it would cost to take your family to a movie and buy them popcorn and soda, or to take them out to dinner just once, and it's a pleasure the whole family can enjoy. That's a great value any way you figure it!

Take a Closer Look

Northern Cardinal *(Cardinalis cardinalis)*

Male cardinals are bright red with black facial markings around their sturdy, cone-shaped orange beaks. Females are a duller red-brown color with splashes of bright red; both males and females wear a characteristic red crest. Colors are the same year-round. Juveniles resemble females, but lack any red and have dark beaks. Adult birds are 7½ to 9 inches (19 to 22.5 cm) long. Females nest in small trees or shrubs and usually lay a clutch of three eggs that are buff white; the nests typically are no higher than 10 feet (3 m) above ground level.

Feeder Favorites for Cardinals

- Sunflower seed, especially black oil
- Safflower seed
- Cracked corn
- Shelled peanuts
- Apple pieces
- Ground or chopped suet

Regional Relations

In southern Arizona, New Mexico, and Texas, you might see a bird that resembles the cardinal in size, shape, and song but wears gray feathers marked with bright red on the face, breast, wing tips, and tail. The pyrrhuloxia (*Cardinalis sinuatus*) looks a lot like its cardinal cousin and the two species may be seen together along the southwestern border between the United States and Mexico.

Tempting Features and Treats for Cardinals

- Dense vines (sweet autumn clematis or grapes) or hedges (especially shrub or climbing roses) provide desired nesting sites.
- Offer low-level bathing with a spray or mister attachment.
- Toss a handful of rock salt in a saucer and place it on the ground at your feeding station.
- Provide coarse sand to supply the grit cardinals need to digest seeds from your feeder.

Did You Know?

- Seven states have the cardinal as their official state bird—Illinois, Indiana, Kentucky, North Carolina, Ohio, Virginia, and West Virginia—making the red bird the most popular choice, with the western meadowlark second with six states and the mockingbird coming in third with five states.
- If you want to attract cardinals to your tube feeder, add a bottom tray. Wild Birds Unlimited store owner Pat Varner in Allentown, Pennsylvania, points out that while the perches on tube feeders can be too small for cardinals to land on, they can easily land instead on a bottom tray to feed. And as Pat says, "Everyone wants cardinals!"
- Cardinals mate for life; during courtship and nesting, male cardinals may be seen feeding their mates.
- Bright-red males can not only flash a warning to potential predators ("Don't eat me!"); they're also more successful at getting the best territories and the most food. And apparently the females find the most colorful males more attractive than males with duller plumage, based on the brighter males' better reproductive rate. (Then again, perhaps the females are practical and are also after that food and choice territory.)
- Male cardinals are very territorial and may become nuisances when they take to attacking their reflections in your windows.
- Cardinals are year-round residents of their range across the eastern United States to the Rocky Mountains and along the Mexican border in the Southwest.
- The cardinal's distinctive song is said to sound like "cheer, cheer, cheer, what, what, what, what," and its call sounds like "chip."

NYJER: SOCK IT TO ME

Nyjer, niger, niger thistle, thistle. What *is* this little black seed? Well, first of all, it's not a thistle. It's actually a yellow daisy in the composite family, more closely related to sunflowers than thistles. (Its botanical name is *Guizotica abyssinia.*) So why on earth did someone call it a thistle, a misconception that lingers to this day? Well, maybe the tiny seed reminded somebody of thistle seed. Or maybe the fact that finches, who love thistle seed, also love nyjer seed and thus prompted somebody to call it niger thistle. Or maybe they were struck by how invasive the plants were, just like thistles. Sheesh!

Whatever the case, the name stuck, and to this day, many people are afraid to put nyjer in their feeders because they don't want any thistles in their yards. So let us say it one more time: Nyjer is *not* a thistle. Yes, the plants can be invasive, but they won't invade *your* yard, because the seed is sterilized before it's sold so it can't germinate and spread.

But what about the nyjer/niger part? Initially, the seed was called niger after Nigeria, since the plants are native to Africa. (Almost all nyjer seed sold in the United States is still imported from Ethiopia and India.) But backyard birders didn't pick up on the connection, so the spelling was changed to nyjer to make the pronunciation more obvious.

Whatever you call it, goldfinches and other beautiful birds (like jewel-toned blue buntings and purple finches) love it. It's more expensive than many seeds, but a little goes a long way, and you don't have to worry about any big birds or squirrels gobbling it up—they don't like it. Besides, you can recoup the money you spend on it by saving on feeders, since birds who love nyjer will eat it from . . . a sock!

BUDGET-WISE BIRDING

Serve Nyjer in a Sock

Nyjer seed is notoriously expensive (perhaps because it's so small it takes bazillion seeds to make a pound)—it costs almost twice as much per pound as the black oil sunflower seed that ranks at the top of almost every bird's menu selections. But, since squirrels and other feeder raiders couldn't care less about nyjer, you can recoup the cost with an inexpensive plastic tube feeder, or even a sock feeder. Sock (or sack) feeders look like white fishnet stockings with tiny holes that allow goldfinches and other nyjer enthusiasts access to the seed.

You can buy a sock full of nyjer seed, ready to hang, for less than $4 wherever wild bird supplies are sold. Or, if you'd rather buy nyjer in bulk and save even more, you can buy unfilled socks or sacks for just $1.99 and fill them yourself. In either case, once they're full, simply hang them out, enjoy the show, and refill them as they empty.

To make a free nyjer feeder, cut the foot and lower leg from an old pair of pantyhose, filling it with nyjer, and securing it to a hanger with an ornament hook or paper clip that you use to pierce the nylon sides. The finches will figure out how to extract their beloved nyjer seed, never fear!

No matter what type of container you choose for serving nyjer seed, you'll want to fill it with care to avoid losing the pricey seed as it slithers through the multiple holes of the feeder. Fill your nyjer feeder over a sheet of newspaper so you can easily recapture any seed that escapes.

Take a Closer Look

American Goldfinch *(Carduelis tristis)*

Male goldfinches, with their sunny yellow bodies and dramatic black head patch and black-and-white wings and tail, rank with cardinals and blue jays among the most-recognizable feeder birds—at least in spring and summer. In fall, they shed their gorgeous plumage and assume more drab yellowish olive tones, looking much like the nondescript female (that's olive-brown and lacks the black-and-white wings) until breeding season rolls 'round again. The females become still plainer in winter, turning grayer and losing some of their olive color. Juveniles resemble males in winter plumage. Adult birds are 4 to 5 inches (10 to 13 cm) long. Females lay two to seven bluish white eggs in nests in shrubbery.

Feeder Favorites for Goldfinches

- Nyjer seed
- Sunflower seed, especially black oil and hulled

Regional Relations

The Southwest is home to the lesser goldfinch (*Carduelis psaltria*), and California also hosts Lawrence's goldfinch (*C. lawrencei*). Like their more famous cousin, the males of both species have predominantly yellow bodies in spring and summer, though their other markings differ. Other close relatives include the pine siskin (*C. pinus*), with its yellow-, black-, and white-striped wings, which winters throughout the United States and often joins goldfinch flocks, and in Canada, the common and hoary redpolls (*C. flammea* and *C. hornemanni*), which lack yellow coloring and substitute jaunty red caps for the black cap of the American goldfinch.

Tempting Features and Treats for Goldfinches

- Tempt goldfinches by planting some of their favorite seed-producing flowers—perennials like asters and purple coneflower, and annuals like cosmos, zinnias, and sunflowers.
- Because goldfinches consume a plant-based diet year-round, they need more water than most species, and they love to bathe. Keep that birdbath full and the water fresh!
- Goldfinches enjoy salt, too. Toss a handful of rock salt in a saucer and place it on the ground at your feeding station, or set out a salt block.

Did You Know?

- The goldfinch is the official state bird of New Jersey, Washington State (where it's called the willow goldfinch), and Iowa.
- Goldfinches are sociable and feed in flocks small and large. (According to Project FeederWatch, the average for January is 10 goldfinches per feeder.) They can also form mixed flocks with sparrows and chickadees.
- Unlike many birds, goldfinches molt (shed old feathers and grow new ones) twice a year, in spring and fall (most birds molt only in fall). Because the goldfinch lays its eggs so late—in summer, when the seeds it eats are abundant—it can afford to molt in spring as well as fall. Species that lay their eggs in spring must save their energy for producing and rearing young.
- Goldfinches are one of the few songbirds that are almost completely vegetarian, eating very few insects. Even their young are fed prechewed plant matter rather than "bug stew."
- Goldfinches can satisfy their need for water by eating snow; they sometimes roost under snow as well for its insulating warmth.
- Some manufacturers make nyjer tube feeders designed so goldfinches must hang upside down to feed. The design discourages house sparrows, which also enjoy nyjer and can quickly deplete a standard nyjer feeder. But in tests, goldfinches preferred to feed upright.
- The goldfinch's song, a long series of varied warbles and twitters, is so beautiful that the goldfinch has been called the wild canary.

MILLET AND CANARY SEED: THE LITTLE GUYS

After sunflower, the staple seed of backyard birds is millet, sometimes called proso millet. Millet is beloved by juncos, finches, buntings, sparrows, towhees, thrushes, Carolina wrens, doves, and many other backyard birds. They'll eat both white and red millet. White millet is ideal for tray, platform, and hopper feeders, and is a good choice for seed mixes. Try sprinkling red millet directly on the ground, where it's enjoyed by sparrows, juncos, buntings, cardinals, pyrrhuloxias, thrashers, towhees, and other ground-feeding birds.

Millet seed is tiny and round—you'll know it well if you grew up with parakeets, since it's a staple of commercial parakeet seed, too. Speaking of which, you can offer tray and platform feeders a treat by purchasing sprays of millet next time you're in the pet store. You'll find them with the caged-bird supplies.

Canary seed, which is also pale but is long and slender rather than round, is also a staple seed of the caged-bird trade, as you might suspect from its name. It's also relished by backyard birds, including house and purple finches, goldfinches, buntings, sparrows, and redpolls. You're most likely to find it with black oil sunflower, nyjer, and millet in blends designed just for finches.

There are plenty of other small seeds, too, including oil-rich red-brown flaxseeds that are as good for the birds as they are for us. We suggest feeding these seeds in store-bought or homemade mixes (see "Mixing It Up: Seed Blends" on page 67). If you want to make your own mix or offer a seed like red or white millet by itself, ask for it in wild bird specialty stores or go online to birdseed specialty sites like eBirdseed.com. You'll enjoy a wealth of bird favorites like cardinals, chickadees, titmice, juncos, goldfinches, finches, jays, buntings, sparrows, towhees, and doves.

What about grass seed? If you suspect that birds who love little seeds would go for grass seed, you're right. And if you happen to have a bag with some leftover grass seed still in it, feel free to set it out or add it to your tray- and ground-feeding mix—*if* it's organic. Lots of grass seed is treated with pesticides, fungicides, and other substances that are bad for birds. Make sure yours is safe before you put it out.

If you raise chickens, you'll have noted that house sparrows, doves, starlings, and blackbirds can't resist scratch grain, a mix of cracked corn, wheat, and sometimes oats and other grains used to supplement hens' pellet rations. Available at feed stores and farm stores like Agway and Tractor Supply, scratch grain is an inexpensive choice for ground feeding. Serve it away from your other feeders to distract these greedy diners. Needless to say, game birds like wild turkeys, pheasants, and bobwhites will enjoy it, too.

Take a Closer Look

Purple Finch *(Carpodacus purpureus)*

The male purple finch (*Carpodacus purpureus*) wears a raspberry-hued purple-red color over most of its body with brown wing and tail tips and a whitish belly. The female is a brown bird with a distinct white eyebrow and cheek patch and a white-streaked breast; adult birds are 6 inches (15 cm) long. Young birds resemble the females. Purple finches spend their winters in the eastern half of the United States where they are frequent feeder visitors. Summer finds them in the northern reaches of the Great Lakes and New England and across Canada, nesting in conifers at woodland edges. Females build tidy cup-shaped nests 5 to 60 feet (1.5 to 18 m) above the ground and lay three to six dark-speckled blue-green eggs. Purple finches were once abundant at northern feeders in winter, but now are more common in the South. This was at first thought to be caused by the expanding house finch population, since house finches are dominant, but is now believed to be due to habitat disruption by humans. There is also a race of purple finches that's native to the West Coast and is a bit less highly colored than the eastern race.

Feeder Favorites for Purple Finches

- Sunflower seed, especially black oil
- Millet
- Cracked corn
- Peanut hearts
- Nyjer seed

Regional Relations

It's easy to mistake the similar-size male house finch (*C. mexicanus*) for a male purple finch—until you see the two species side by side. The male purple finch's wine red color covers almost his entire body, while the male house finch's cherry red is primarily found on his head, breast, and back. Female house finches are duller and less distinctively marked with white than female purple finches, but still much harder to tell apart than their mates. House finches range across the United States year-round. Cassin's finch (*C. cassinii*) is yet another purple-red-tinted bird, slightly larger than the purple and house finches. The male Cassin's finch is less colorful than the purple finch and more pink-hued with a bright red crown; female Cassin's finches look similar to female purple finches. Cassin's finch is a western bird, ranging from Mexico to Canada's Pacific coastline.

Tempting Features and Treats for Finches

- Purple finches relish pumpkin seeds and also enjoy safflower seeds.
- Finches prefer a platform feeder on a tall pole, but will visit other feeders as well.
- Offer finches grit in the form of builder's (coarse) sand.
- A winter water source is a big attraction for all finches.

Did You Know?

- The purple finch is the official state bird of New Hampshire.
- Both purple and house finches were once sold as caged birds for their color and beautiful warbling songs.
- The male purple finch may lift the feathers atop its head slightly, creating the appearance of a crest.
- The tail of the purple finch has a more pronounced notch than the house finch's tail.
- In flight, the purple finch's call is a metallic yet musical "pick."

MIXING IT UP: SEED BLENDS

Seed mixes or blends offer all-in-one convenience, attracting lots of different birds with a single bag. But there are so many mixes on the market that it's easy to be overwhelmed. How do you choose a mix?

Pat Varner, co-owner with her husband, Will, of Wild Birds Unlimited in Allentown, Pennsylvania, helped us out when we asked her what sort of seed mix she'd recommend if someone only wanted to buy one mix. "I'd probably recommend our Deluxe Blend," she said. "It has black oil sunflower, a favorite of most birds; striped sunflower, popular with blue jays and cardinals; safflower, a seed also popular with cardinals and chickadees; and millet, for birds like doves, sparrows, and other ground feeders. It's a good all-around mix and a favorite with our customers."

But even Pat couldn't choose just one. "Another bestseller is our No-Mess Blend—black oil sunflower, safflower, peanuts, and millet, but all without shells. No mess!" These hull-less blends are an especially good choice if you don't want to spend time cleaning up hulls, or if you're an apartment or condo dweller who can't afford to make a mess. And there are plenty of "no waste" mixes to choose from. But bear in mind that the extra work involved in producing them is passed along to you in terms of higher costs, and that birds eat them super-fast, since they don't have to work to get at the seeds, so you'll be refilling feeders more often.

Whatever mix you buy, check the ingredients list to make sure you—and your birds—are getting your money's worth. As with any food, ingredients are listed by proportion, with the most abundant ingredient first. Make sure the mix you buy has bird favorites like sunflower, millet, peanut hearts, and/or safflower listed first, not cheap fillers like cracked corn and less-preferred seeds such as milo, wheat, oats, or rice—or you may be paying too much.

Make Your Own Mix

You can save money—and have fun—by buying seed in bulk, then mixing it up yourself. If you've used a store-bought mix that worked well for you in the past, it's easy to read the list of ingredients, eyeball the proportions, and try to reproduce it at home. As long as you use quality seed as your base, the birds will come flocking, and you can tweak the proportions as you see what gets eaten.

Don't have a favorite mix? Here are some make-at-home mixes to try:

- **Basic blend.** Three-fourths black oil sunflower to one-fourth white proso millet. This simple mix will attract a wealth of backyard birds, including cardinals, chickadees, titmice, nuthatches, juncos, goldfinches, finches, woodpeckers, jays, buntings, sparrows, towhees, doves, and many more.
- **Cardinal classic.** Half black oil sunflower, half safflower. This mix will attract lots of other birds, too, including titmice, nuthatches, grosbeaks, chickadees, and finches. For an added thrill, you can always mix in a scoop or two of hulled sunflower hearts or chips.
- **Finch favorite.** Bring goldfinches, buntings, redpolls, house and purple finches, and pine siskins flocking with a mix of equal parts millet (white or red, or half of each, depending on what's available), nyjer, and black oil sunflower. You can increase the appeal by adding a scoop or two of canary seed and/or flaxseed.

Take a Closer Look

Indigo Bunting *(Passerina cyanea)*

Similar to sparrows in size and shape, indigo buntings (in the East) and lazuli buntings (in the West) stand out among small seed-eating birds by virtue of the males' showy plumage. From late spring to early fall, indigo buntings mate and raise their young in pasture lands, orchards, and woodland edges across the eastern United States. During the breeding season, males are solid bright blue with slightly darker blue-to-purple head feathers. When it's time to return to their winter quarters in Mexico and Central America, their blue feathers give way to a subdued mix of brown and blue. Rarely seen females are dull brown with touches of blue on their wings and tail. Adults are 4½ to 5½ inches (11 to 13 cm) long.

Feeder Favorites for Indigo Buntings

- Millet
- Chopped peanuts
- Canary seed, as sold for pet birds
- Chopped nuts
- Grass seed (untreated)

Regional Relations

But for the bars of white on its wings and its sturdier conical bill, you might mistake a male lazuli bunting (*P. amoena*) for a western bluebird—both birds have a blue back, head, and tail, a rusty red breast, and a white belly, and they share similar range and habitat. Lazuli buntings cover the western United States from the coast to the plains and from southern Canada to southern California, spending the winters in southern Arizona and Mexico. Where their ranges overlap, lazuli and indigo buntings will flock together and sometimes interbreed.

In Texas and the Southeast, the painted bunting (*P. ciris*) gives birders a thrill with its colorful plumage. Males have purple-blue heads, red breasts and bellies, and green backs; female painted buntings are bright green with yellow-green bellies.

Tempting Features and Treats for Indigo Buntings

- Blackberries and raspberries tempt indigo buntings with fruits and shelter amid the thorny canes.
- Serve chunky rock salt or a salt block in a waterproof container on the ground or on a low platform.
- Hedges, brushy areas, and shrubs provide preferred shelter and nesting sites for buntings.
- Plant a birdseed garden of fast-growing annual flowers such as cosmos, zinnia, coreopsis, and marigolds; include white proso millet, lettuce, and mustard for additional appeal.
- Offer water in low, shallow containers; add a dripper to attract birds' attention.

Did You Know?

- Warm-weather-loving indigo buntings travel northward later in spring than many other migratory birds, and they are quick to head south at the first sign of cooler weather in fall.
- Human activity in the eastern United States has increased the brushy open spaces and woodland edges where indigo buntings prefer to hunt for weed seeds and insects, making them one of the few songbirds that have become more populous as a result of development.
- Male indigo buntings migrate northward to establish their territories a week or two before the females arrive. Males court prospective mates with song until they find a partner and begin nest building.
- A bunting nest may include pieces of snakeskin woven in among the usual building materials of grass, twigs, and weeds.
- The pretty voices and colorful feathers that give birders so much pleasure have historically spelled trouble for buntings: In their winter range, these beautiful songbirds sometimes are trapped and sold as caged birds in Europe.

FEEDER FILES: Don and Lillian Stokes

For 25 years, Don and Lillian Stokes have been the public faces of backyard birding, appearing in their own TV series on PBS (*Stokes Birds at Home*) and the DIY cable and satellite network (*DIY Bird Watching Workshop*). The Stokeses have written 32 books, including their own series of *Stokes Field Guides* and the *Stokes Bird Feeder Book*, as well as innumerable newspaper and magazine articles. In addition, they have their own line of binoculars, as well as their Stokes Select bird feeders, accessories, and seed blends, available through bird product Web sites like BestNest.com and eBirdseed.com as well as in stores nationwide.

The Stokeses own Web site (www.stokesbirdsathome.com) is a great resource for the beginning backyard birder. With a free e-newsletter, bird blog, tips log ("Webnotes"), and Q&A log (you can also submit your own questions), as well as an educational section on birding, it will help you start out right with bird identification, feeding, housing, and much more.

The Stokeses clearly practice what they preach. Besides being avid avian educators, they donate a portion of the proceeds from their product sales to bird habitat and conservation projects. And they've made their own New Hampshire home, Bobolink Farm, into a nature preserve that has attracted 165 species of birds. (Now, *there's* a goal to aspire to!)

- **Woodpeckers' choice.** Flickers, chickadees, jays, and titmice will also love this blend of equal parts black oil sunflower, striped sunflower, and peanut hearts. Add a scoop or two of mixed nuts, pumpkin seeds (pepitas), golden raisins, and/or whole peanuts for a truly deluxe mix.

Serving Seed Mixes

Birds will get the most from seed mixes if you feed them in tray or platform feeders, directly on the ground, or in hopper feeders. (As we've noted, you can put mixes in tube feeders, too, but a lot of the mix will end up all over the ground, since tube feeders tend to prefer sunflower seed.) It's such a delight to watch a Carolina wren eating breakfast at a hopper feeder with titmice, chickadees, sparrows, and nuthatches, or a family of cardinals sharing the wealth with jays and woodpeckers at a platform feeder. Part of the fun is that you never know what you'll see!

Solidified Seed Mixes: Seed Blocks

Seed blocks are big cubes (usually 6 inches, or 15 cm, or slightly larger) of solidified seed, the ultimate in convenience food for birds. You just take a block out of its package, set it on a tray or platform feeder, and voila! You can find blocks made of black oil sunflower seeds or a mix, such as black oil and striped sunflower seeds, safflower, millet, and cracked corn.

Seed blocks are also sold for critters like squirrels and game birds. These usually have a mix of corn, peanuts, sunflower seeds, and wheat, or are simply mixed from corn and black oil sunflower seed. You can place these blocks directly on the ground. Put them some distance from your bird feeders if you want to divert squirrels and flocks of ground feeders.

Take a Closer Look

Evening Grosbeak *(Coccothraustes vespertinus)*

Male evening grosbeaks look like bulked-up goldfinches, with big, bright yellow bodies and prominent yellow eyebrows, dramatic black-and-white wings, dark heads, and the large bills that give grosbeaks their name. Females are grayish tan with black-and-white wings and tails. Colors are the same all year. Juvenile females resemble adult females, while juvenile males fall between the adult male and female in appearance, with a golden brown body. Adult birds are 6 to 8 inches (15 to 20 cm) long. Females usually lay three or four light blue to blue-green eggs with a faint brown scrawling pattern; the nests are saucer-shaped and are built in trees or large shrubs.

Feeder Favorites for Grosbeaks

- Sunflower seed, especially black oil
- Safflower seed
- Cracked corn
- Peanut hearts or pieces

Regional Relations

The handsome male rose-breasted grosbeak (*Pheucticus ludovicianus*), with its black-and-white body and rose-red breast, is one of the most striking of all feeder birds. (The female resembles an oversize sparrow.) Its summer breeding range is from the Yukon east to Newfoundland and south to North Dakota, Nebraska, and New Jersey, as well as down the Appalachians to north Georgia. In winter, it migrates to southern Mexico, northern South America, and the Caribbean.

The male black-headed grosbeak (*P. melanocephalus*) looks like an oriole, with its orange body, black head and tail, and black-and-white wings; the female has a buff-orange body and brown where her mate has black. Blue grosbeaks (*Guiraca caerulea*) look a lot like overgrown indigo buntings, and their ranges overlap. Look for the heavy grosbeak bill surrounded by black, a slightly grayer blue body, and chestnut wing bars to tell the two apart (females are brown).

Tempting Features and Treats for Grosbeaks

- Every time you eat cherries, instead of tossing the pits, rinse, dry, and store them in a labeled plastic bag in your freezer. When evening grosbeaks arrive at your feeders, give them a real treat—cherry pits are their favorite food!
- Grosbeaks appreciate plenty of water as they make their winter rounds. A heated birdbath is ideal. Clean it often and refill with fresh water.
- Toss a handful of rock salt in a saucer and place it on the ground at your feeding station or set out a salt block.

Did You Know?

- Evening grosbeaks and pine grosbeaks are members of the finch family (Fringillidae).
- Unlike most songbirds, evening grosbeaks don't have a migration path and don't seem to follow any routine in their decisions to travel. Instead, there are what birders call "irruptions," years when large numbers of grosbeaks pour down from their breeding grounds in Canada and move around the United States, seemingly at random.
- Evening grosbeaks' appetite for sunflower seeds is legendary. A single grosbeak is capable of eating almost 100 sunflower seeds in 5 minutes! Once grosbeaks find a sunflower feeder, they'll aggressively keep other birds away, and males will also prevent females from eating if supplies aren't plentiful. You can attempt to outsmart your raucous visitors once you know the inside scoop: Evening grosbeaks prefer breakfast served on a high platform feeder. Some birders put out a moderate amount of sunflower seeds in the morning, then wait a few hours before setting out more. Others provide tube sunflower feeders well away from their platform feeder to give the other birds a chance.
- Evening grosbeaks typically travel in flocks of 15, though in irruption years, flocks of over 100 have been reported.

CORN: CRACKED BUT NOT CRAZY

Cracked corn has gotten a bad rep among some birders, most likely because it's often used as a cheap filler in lower-end birdseed mixes. But plenty of birds love cracked corn—just not necessarily the birds you want to see at your tube feeders. Woodpeckers, jays, sparrows, towhees, cardinals, red-winged blackbirds, doves, and many other birds consider cracked corn a treat, and it's a high-protein as well as a cost-conscious choice.

Set cracked corn out on tray or platform feeders or directly on the ground. Adding sunflower seed and millet—both red and white on trays and platforms, red alone if ground feeding—will attract virtually all feeder birds. As with every type of bird food, cracked corn is vulnerable to spoilage, especially on damp ground, so use a "less is more" approach and don't set out more than the birds will eat in a day.

As you might expect, corn attracts a lot more than songbirds. Game birds like wild turkeys, quail, and pheasants relish it. So do chipmunks and squirrels, which is why you see squirrel feeders that offer whole ears of dried corn on the cob. Woodpeckers can also eat dried corn off the cob, and woodpeckers, cardinals, and jays will take whole kernels.

CAREFUL STORAGE SAVES SEED, CONTAINS COSTS

Even though most birds dine on insects during at least some part of their lives, insect-infested birdseed is a big turnoff for those birds that also show up at your feeders for a meal. Birds will turn up their beaks at seed that harbors weevils or grain moths, just as they'll bypass a feeder full of moldy or rancid seeds. That's because the seed has been consumed so there's nothing left but hulls, it no longer tastes good, and it's been robbed of any nutritional value. When you stock your bird-feeding pantry, take smart steps to keep those foods fresh until you serve them to your avian guests.

- Keep your birdseed in a cool, dry place. An unheated garage, basement, or mudroom is ideal. To keep out pests, transfer it from paper or plastic bags into tightly sealed metal or plastic containers. Clean trash cans with tight-fitting lids work well for this purpose. Choose metal containers if you know mice are about—mice will chew through a plastic pail to get at an all-they-can-eat birdseed buffet.
- If you go through large quantities of seed quickly, you might find it convenient to store it outside. But if you do, you must use metal containers (again, like trash cans) with tight-fitting lids that clamp firmly to the containers. Putting a weight (such as a concrete block) on the lid will also help keep critters like raccoons from pulling it off.
- Store suet in a refrigerator year-round (or in the freezer during the summer months) to prevent spoilage and protect it from mice and other critters.
- When you buy new shoes or electronics, keep the little bags of silica gel that manufacturers use to protect their products from moisture. Drop one or two into your stored birdseed to protect it from moisture; replace with new bags after your next shoe-shopping excursion.
- Tuck a few bay leaves into your stored birdseed to repel insect pests, just as they do in your own pantry.

Growing Your Own Birdseed Garden

Growing a birdseed garden is a lot of fun, and it's educational, too—you'll find out what all those seeds look like on the plants that produce them. But be realistic—you'll add to your birdseed stash, sure, but you won't replace it. You'd need a farm field to grow enough seed for a season! Instead, grow a small birdseed plot and enjoy the adventure.

Prepare the bed just as you would for a vegetable garden, turning the soil when the growing season ends in fall or when it can be worked in spring, breaking up clods, removing weeds and debris, and smoothing the surface. Cover the bed with black plastic or straw mulch to keep it weed-free until you're ready to plant. For a first-time birdseed garden, we suggest that you start small—prepare a bed 6 feet (1.8 m) wide by 8 feet (2.4 m) long, with the long sides running north and south.

When the soil has warmed in spring and all danger of frost is past, it's time to get going. Mark off a 2-foot (0.6 m)-wide section running the length of the bed on the northern side. Then divide the remaining bed into four short strips, 4 feet (1.2 m) long by 2 feet (0.6 m) wide. Plant sunflowers down the length of the 2-by-8-foot strip (see page 58 for suggested varieties). Plant blocks of seed in the 2-by-4-foot strips: safflower, peanuts, white millet, and corn, or safflower, white millet, and two blocks of corn. Or plant safflower in the blocks on each end and a block each of red and white millet. Use the spacings recommended on the seed packets.

Or just take a chance, as backyard birding author and naturalist Sally Roth does, and sow handfuls of seed right from the birdseed bag! Whatever you choose, if you sow birdseed—whether it's a mix or a single type—instead of buying your seed from

- Keep a broom and dustpan handy to sweep up spilled seed before it leads pests to your supply.

Stop That Moth!

Try these tactics to keep grain moths—the kind that infest birdseed—at bay: Buy clean, fresh seed, store it securely in bug-proof metal or food-grade plastic tins or bins, and use it up quickly. If you suspect your seed is infested, moth traps are excellent monitors: Set one out and you'll know for sure by the following day.

You can buy sticky traps for grain moths under brand names like Pantry Pest and Flour & Pantry Moth Trap, available online. These traps work because they contain grain moth pheromones—sex attractants that drive the moths wild. But in our experience, the pheromones cause all the grain moths to go wild, including those that don't come into the traps, resulting in a lot more mating and egg laying.

If your traps confirm your suspicions, dispose of the infested seed, clean all containers and the room they're in thoroughly, and buy better seed-storage containers if necessary. Temporarily store containers and seed in another room, outdoors, or in your freezer, and set out another trap in the original room a week or two later to see if the problem has been resolved.

a nursery or garden center, make sure it hasn't been sterilized before you plant it. If it has, it won't germinate. That's why we don't recommend that you try planting nyjer; because the plants are invasive, all nyjer seed is sterilized before it's sold.

Once you've planted your seeds, water them in, then watch for them to germinate. Continue to water your bed when the soil dries out, and thin plants if they start to crowd each other. (If you dig the thinnings carefully with some soil around their roots, you can transfer them to fill in gaps where seeds didn't come up.)

Anytime after your sunflower seeds have germinated, you can set up a trellis for them along the northern side of the bed. Use bamboo poles, stakes and twine, wire fencing, or the trellising material of your choice. Just remember that sunflower plants grow tall and their seedheads can be large and heavy. Anchor the trellis firmly, and tie the plants securely to your trellis as they grow taller.

Continue to water and weed as your plants grow, just as you would any garden bed. Enjoy the sight of the beautiful safflower and sunflower blooms! It's a bonus you'll enjoy as much as your birds will enjoy the seeds.

Once the seedheads have matured and the plants have yellowed and dried (yellowed plants indicate mature peanuts as well), it's time to harvest the seedheads and compost the stalks. (Sunflowers are harvest-ready when the petals dry and the heavy heads hang down.) Hang the cut heads in a warm, dry place (like the attic or garage) to finish drying, then set them out whole, one at a time, when you want to give the birds a treat. Or shell and store the seeds in pest-proof containers until you're ready to serve them up.

Smart Dispensers Save Spills

Getting seeds into bird feeders can be messy, but you can lessen the mess with the right equipment—a sizable dispenser with a wide mouth for fast, easy filling and a spout for precision pouring. (If the container has a narrow mouth, it will take forever to fill, and you'll spill as much as you put in.)

Our favorite seed dispenser is a big plastic bottle with a spout in its screw-on lid, looking for all the world like a giant mayonnaise jar with a ketchup or mustard spout. Its capacious size ensures that you won't have to keep running back and forth from the seed storage tin to the feeder, even when filling a roomy hopper feeder, and the spout pours seed easily into even a narrow tube feeder without spilling. And it's translucent, so you can see how much seed you have left to distribute among your feeders. Wild Bird Center stores sell these dispensers.

Another useful tool for safely transferring seeds into a feeder is a wide-mouthed scoop with a narrower tubular handle that doubles as a funnel. You can use the scoop to fill feeders with ample openings, or fill the scoop and upend it with the narrower handle in the opening of a tube feeder. Duncraft is one source of such scoops.

Even a rinsed and dried recycled gallon milk jug can be used to save seeds from spilling. Cut away the bottom of the jug, keeping the handle and lid intact, then use it as a combination scoop and funnel.

SUET AND OTHER HIGH-FAT FIXATIONS

Woodpeckers, nuthatches, titmice, chickadees, and lots of other birds—including, believe it or not, orioles—are crazy about suet. But isn't suet beef fat, and aren't birds seed eaters? Well, no, birds aren't strictly vegetarian: These are the same birds that are ridding our gardens of insect pests during the growing season. Like us, they're omnivores (with a few exceptions, like carnivorous hawks and vegetarian goldfinches) and opportunists, that will eat whatever they find that tastes good. That's why you should think about branching out in your meat offerings, not just to mealworms (see "Mad about Mealworms" on page 82 for more about them) but to all kinds of meaty treats (see "Think Outside the Cake" on page 77 for ideas).

The simplest—and cheapest—way to set out suet is to buy some at the grocery, put it in a mesh onion bag, and hang it up in a tree in your yard. It won't look as appealing as a cute suet cage or suet log feeder, but it does the job. And you can't beat the price! When we checked with our local grocery, the butcher told us that he'd cut any amount upon request throughout the year, and sets packages of suet out in the meat case every winter—at 79 cents a pound!

Mind you, suet that's fresh from the grocery or butcher shop will spoil rather quickly if temperatures rise above freezing. Wait until consistently cold weather arrives before you serve fresh suet chunks. In warmer weather, you need to prepare the suet by melting it twice—a process called rendering—and letting it harden between meltings, to make it more resistant to spoilage. (See text on this page for the how-to details.) Otherwise, stick with store-bought suet cakes, balls, or plugs, or the lard-based mixture described on the opposite page.

Did we mention how birds gobble the stuff up? Birds love suet, and some of them are big birds—like woodpeckers and jays—that can demolish a suet cake in no time. If you want your suet cakes (or your bird-feeding budget) to last longer, try this savvy birders' trick: Just remove the front of the suet-cake packaging and set it in the suet cage package and all. (Make sure the open side faces the house, so you can see the birds at the feeder.) It will take the birds longer to eat the suet when they can only reach the suet cake from one side. Cakes will last longer in the house-style feeders that birds can only access from below for the same reason.

HOMEMADE SUET CAKES AND CONCOCTIONS

If you don't mind messing around with grease, you can save money and have fun making your own high-fat blends for birds. Here are two options you can try, with lots of fun variations. Use the basic techniques and then customize to create your own special bird food blends!

Starting from Scratch

Carolyn Reider in Pennsylvania makes her suet treats the old-fashioned way—she renders chunks of suet on her stove. "I go to the butcher and get slabs of nice white fat," she says. "Then I cut it into chunks and render it on the stove. Don't let it get too hot, or the fat will scorch and turn brown. I occasionally stir it around and smoosh the fat globs to squeeze out more. It takes a while and the house stinks of rendered fat.

"Eventually, you will have a pot of fat with chitlins," Carolyn continues. "You can scoop out the chitlins with a slotted spoon and discard them, or set them outside for the birds and other animals to eat. The fat is dangerously hot, so be very careful with it. I usually let it cool off a little, then pour it into empty coffee cans. If I want to, before pouring it into the cans, I'll add some cornmeal and/or peanut butter and mix it in.

"Do not put the plastic lids on the cans until they're cool!" Carolyn warns. "I store mine in the refrigerator or freezer. Then I have to let it warm to room temperature before I can smush it into the holes in my log feeder."

Lard-Based Luxuries

Want to try an easy-to-make mix that wild birds can't resist? Try this tried-and-true recipe from backyard birder extraordinaire Joan Silagy of Leesport, Pennsylvania. Joan, a longtime member of the Baird Ornithological Club who travels to the Southwest regularly in search of great birding sites, has one of the best backyard feeding stations we've ever seen—and it's mostly homemade, thanks to the talents of her husband, Bob. Here's how to make the mix she swears by.

"I use about a cup of lard, or sometimes Crisco, and ½ to ¾ of a cup of peanut butter. It can be smooth or chunky," Joan says. "Then I microwave it just long enough to soften it up, just a minute or two, until it's almost melted. Once it's soft, I mix it with flour as if I were making dough for a piecrust. Then I add a little water, cornmeal, oatmeal, crumbled day-old bread—whatever I have available. I keep it refrigerated and smear some on my log feeder as the birds eat it."

Joan's friend and longtime backyard birder Anna Kendall has her own secret source for stale bread—her local farmers' market. "I can buy a whole loaf for pennies," she says. If you have a farmers' market in your area, it's worth asking at the bakery stands shortly before the market closes on its last day. You can score a loaf or two, too! (Remember, you can always freeze what you don't use right away.)

Do birds like Joan's lard-based concoction? "They love it!" she says. "Not only the woodpeckers but the blue jays, cardinals, catbirds, orioles, juncos, and even the crows." Joan sets out her mix in spring as well as fall and winter. "It's especially welcomed when the migrants return to the area in spring," she says. "They burn a lot of body fat during their journey, and it's a welcome addition to their diet and gives you an opportunity for up-close observation of many species."

You can find lard in the grocery case along with butter and margarine. Like suet, it's easy on the wallet—just $1.19 for a 1-pound tub.

A "Grate" Treat

Pennsylvanian Anna Kendall has her own favorite recipe for suet-loving birds. She waits until the stale bread she buys at deep discount from the farmers' market gets hard. Then she takes a loaf and grates it, mixes the crumbs into bacon grease or other drippings, and sets out the mix for her woodpeckers, chickadees, titmice, and nuthatches. Anna uses a handheld grater, but you could also break off chunks of stale bread and whiz them in your blender or food processor to make crumbs. Depending on how much fat you mix in with the crumbs, you can make a thick suet pudding or work it with your hands to form suet crumbles and set them out on your platform feeder. As always, refrigerate what you can't use right away.

Take a Closer Look

Tufted Titmouse *(Baeolophus bicolor)*

With their triangular crests, tufted titmice resemble little gray cardinals, but they're actually chickadee relatives. Males and females are gray above and whitish below with rusty sides and a black forehead. Because their bright black eyes are surrounded by grayish-white, they seem more prominent than many birds'. Juveniles lack the forehead coloration and the rust color is much fainter. Adult birds are 6 to 6½ inches (15 to 16 cm) long. Females lay three to nine white eggs with tiny reddish dots in a nest built in a tree hole.

Feeder Favorites for Titmice

- Sunflower seed, especially striped, black oil, and hulled
- Safflower seed
- Shelled peanuts and peanut hearts
- Apple pieces
- Suet

Regional Relations

Native to Texas and Mexico, the black-crested titmouse (*Baeolophus atricristatus*) has been considered both a separate species and a form of the tufted titmouse; thanks to DNA testing, currently the separate species classification seems to be winning out. The black-crested titmouse looks like a tufted titmouse with a white forehead and black crest. What was formerly thought to be the plain titmouse has also been split into two species, the juniper titmouse (*B. ridgwayi*) and the oak titmouse (*B. inornatus*). Both are gray birds with short crests, but the juniper is slightly larger and grayer, while the oak has a gray-brown back. Though both are woodland birds, the oak titmouse is a year-round resident of California, while the juniper titmouse makes its home in the Southwest. The bridled titmouse (*B. wollweberi*) extends its year-round range up from Mexico into the wooded mountains of southern New Mexico and Arizona. This handsome little gray bird has a black throat, a black-edged crest, and a black "C" on each cheek.

Tempting Features and Treats for Titmice

- Give titmice a thrill by providing peanut butter with (hulled) seeds pressed into it.
- Titmice are nut lovers that especially enjoy acorns. If you pass an oak tree on your walks or know of another good acorn source, collect some and set them out on a platform feeder as a treat.
- Treat your titmice to a doughnut, bread, crushed crackers, or cereal.
- Fruit-loving titmice will appreciate it if you share a few cherries with them when your family is having some.

Did You Know?

- Titmice forage for insects and insect cocoons in trees, sometimes hanging upside down while they search.
- Tufted titmice may forage in mixed flocks during the breeding season, but in winter they stay in family groups. That's why you won't see large flocks of titmice at your feeders, but the two or more you do see will be faithful visitors.
- Like chickadees, titmice cache their food. They'll take one seed at a time from your feeder and dash off, returning immediately for another seed.
- Tufted titmice are year-round residents of their range across the eastern United States to Minnesota and along the Mexican border south of Texas.
- Titmouse beaks may be small, but they're strong. Tufted titmice thrive on acorns and beechnuts, while their western relatives enjoy acorns and pine nuts.
- The titmouse gets its name not because it reminded someone of a mouse, but from a combination of the Old Icelandic word *titr*, "small," and the Anglo-Saxon *mase*, "small bird."
- The song of the tufted titmouse has been described as a whistled "peter-peter-peter" or "here-here-here." Its call sounds like "tsee-day-day-day."

THINK OUTSIDE THE CAKE

Suet cakes are the ultimate fast food for birds: Unwrap the cake, drop it in the suet cage, hang it up, and enjoy the show. But they're not the only show in town. Fat-loving birds will devour any number of high-fat meat treats, without gaining weight (thanks to their stellar metabolisms) or getting clogged arteries. Aren't you jealous?

Indulge your birds' fat cravings with some of these tempting morsels.

- **Pepperoni.** Yes, you read that right. Share a piece or two with the birds next time you make (or buy) a pizza. They enjoy it as much as we do.
- **Pizza.** Speaking of pizza, those greasy pizza crusts will bring fat-lovers flying. And just like your dog, they'll love it if you leave on some toppings for them!
- **Fat, skin, and other good stuff.** If you leave fat on steaks, skin on chicken, and so on while you cook them for that fabulous flavor that only fat can give—but then remove it before serving so as not to threaten your family's and friends' waistlines and heart health—don't throw it out! Give that yummy fat and skin to the birds. They'll love it!
- **Bacon and sausage grease and other drippings.** Fat left in the pan after you cook bacon, sausage, and other meats is a bird delight. Mix it with bread crumbs, cornmeal, and other carbs (see page 75 for more on this), heat it up, and stir in some peanut butter for a super treat, or just serve it straight—smeared on a log, filling holes in a log feeder, or in a cup on a platform feeder.
- **Meat scraps.** Don't forget the birds when you're scraping the dinner plates! Bits of beef, chicken, turkey, pork, and other meat scraps will "beef up" your backyard birds' diets. That goes for tidbits of bacon, sausage, ham, soup bones, and lunch meats, too.
- **Deep-fried food.** We're not the only ones who think fried foods are finger-lickin' (or maybe feather-lickin') good! We've mentioned doughnuts already, but red-headed woodpeckers and other fat-loving birds will also relish fritters, hush puppies, corn dodgers, and other deep-fried favorites.
- **Eggs.** We cholesterol-conscious humans may not want to eat too many eggs, but birds love them! Bits of scrambled, fried, and hard-boiled eggs, pieces of omelet, corners of quiche, a little morsel of eggs Benedict—the richer, the better.

Stud Suet with Shell-Free Seed

Store-bought suet cakes often are studded with seeds, fruit, and all kinds of tempting tidbits. So when you're making your own suet-, lard-, or Crisco-based concoction, it seems like a good idea to toss a few handfuls of seed into the mix. But in this case, all is not as it seems. "Don't embed seeds in fat unless they're hulled," warns birding pro Rudy Keller. "Birds hull their seed—even little seeds like millet—before they eat them, and fat-coated seeds are too slippery to hull. If you want to add seed, try hulled sunflower seed. Or toss in some cheap nut meats."

GOING NUTS

Backyard birds and peanuts—like peanut butter and jelly—are a natural combination. Peanut butter (like us, many birds prefer crunchy, but they'll also go for smooth), peanut hearts, split and whole shelled peanuts, unshelled peanuts: Every kind has its feathered fans. Rich in fat, protein, and fiber—not to mention calories!—peanuts have what it takes to help birds through a cold winter.

Peanut hearts and pieces are popular bird treats alone or in seed mixes. They'll attract cardinals, chickadees, titmice, nuthatches, juncos, grosbeaks, finches, woodpeckers, jays, and sparrows. You can offer them on tray and platform feeders as well as in hopper feeders. Because there are no shells, there's no waste. No fuss, no muss!

BUDGET-WISE BIRDING

Make Your Own Suet Log

You can buy a suet feeder that's made from a log, but if you know how to use a drill, it's easy to make your own. Here's how backyard birder Carolyn Reider of District Township, Pennsylvania, does it:

"Get a hunk of firewood or a section of log that's 12 to 16 inches (30.5 to 40.6 cm) long and about 3 to 6 inches (7.6 to 15.2 cm) thick," says Carolyn. "It can have the bark still on, but eventually the bark will fall off. Nail a heavy fence staple most of the way into the middle of the top or use a heavy-duty screw eye for hanging. The weight of the log will depend on the wood, but you need something sturdy to hang it by.

"Use a drill to make holes at whatever spacing you like," Carolyn adds. "I drill mine about 2 inches (5 cm) apart. Use a drill that will make holes about 1 inch (2.5 cm) wide. If you're using hand tools, use a brace and an augur bit. Clamp the log into a vise. For power tools, the way to go is to use a Forstner bit and an electric drill or—best of all—a drill press. The Forstner bit makes a nice, clean, hollowed-out hole. I usually make the holes 1 to 1¼ inches deep.

"If you're using a log with the bark still on, the holes should be deeper, not only as deep as the bark," Carolyn warns, "or when the bark comes off, the holes will disappear! Make sure you drill into the wood itself. That's all there is to it—just fill the holes with suet or a mix of suet and peanut butter and hang the log up."

Do you already have a log feeder and plenty of woodpeckers, flickers, nuthatches, titmice, jays, and chickadees clamoring around it? Maybe it's time to step up to the ultimate log feeder. At Hawk Mountain Sanctuary in Kempton, Pennsylvania, the backyard bird feeding station has a cafeteria-line log feeder: A 6-foot (1.8 m)-long section of log, about 6 inches (15 cm) in diameter, rests atop sturdy log poles at about knee height, like the top of a gate or fence. The sides of the log are drilled down its whole length with inch-wide holes, spaced about 2 inches (5 cm) apart, and stuffed with suet. Suet-loving birds can perch comfortably on top of the log while reaching down for the suet treats, while you enjoy the show!

Some manufacturers offer suet "plugs" especially for log feeders. You buy them in rolls, then cut off pieces to fit your feeder holes. Duncraft offers them in four "flavors:" sunflower, peanut, hot pepper, and suet-free pecan. Of course, you can also make your own fillings (see page 75 for recipes and techniques).

Whole or split shelled peanuts are favorites, too, especially with titmice, chickadees, nuthatches, jays, and woodpeckers. You can set some out on your tray or platform feeder, or pour them into a special tube feeder made from ½-inch (1.3 cm) wire mesh—just the right size for shelled peanuts. There are also plastic peanut feeders that look like they came from outer space—brilliantly colored tubes riddled with irregular circles. But we say if the birds like them, and you like them, then go for it!

You can even use peanuts in the shell—woodpeckers and jays can shell their own. Set a handful on your platform feeder or use a specially designed wire tube feeder just for unshelled peanuts. With both shelled and unshelled peanuts, you can buy bags just for birds or share your own stash.

What about peanut butter? Buy a big jar of the cheap generic brand and stuff it into the holes in a log feeder (See "Budget-Wise Birding" on the opposite page for more on log feeders) or smear some directly onto its bark. Or mix it up with lard, Crisco, or suet and cornmeal for a high-fat bird favorite (see "Lard-Based Luxuries" on page 75). Slather some on a slice of bread and cut it into bird-size bites. Birds love to pull the peanut chunks out of chunky peanut butter, but smooth is fine, too. And if you like to snack on peanut butter and crackers, don't forget your feathered friends. Make an extra cracker "sandwich" with peanut butter filling, then crush it in a plastic bag and set out the pieces.

True Nuts: All Mixed Up

It's not a big secret that peanuts aren't really nuts at all—they're legumes, like beans. But birds also love real nuts—the pecans, walnuts, almonds, hazelnuts, cashews, Brazil nuts, macadamias, and pistachios that we all crave.

As with other "people food," set aside a few nuts for the birds while you're adding them to a recipe. Putting almond slivers on a salad? Adding pecan or walnut pieces to brownies or banana bread? Tossing pine nuts into your pesto? Set some out on your platform feeder and enjoy the antics of woodpeckers, jays, chickadees, titmice, nuthatches, and others.

This is also a great solution if you love mixed nuts but have never liked certain ones, like Brazil nuts or macadamias, which are part of the mix. Finally, you can refuse to eat them and not feel guilty! Tell critics that birds are especially grateful for these high-fat treats. (And see if the mention of "high fat" causes your fellow guests to suddenly decide to donate their former favorites to the birds as well.) Don't worry if the nuts are roasted and/or salted—birds love salt, and though raw nuts are great, roasting won't hurt them.

Of course, you'll attract more birds if you reduce the nuts to bird-size bits in a blender, coffee grinder, or food processor. "Bits" is the operative word here—don't make nut meal!

Acorns and Other Wild Nuts

Backyard birds aren't snobs like us, who only enjoy rich, sweet-tasting nuts like cashews, almonds, and pecans. Birds also love acorns, which are so bitter that it takes an indescribable effort to make them fit for human consumption. And shade-tree nuts like black walnuts, hickory nuts, chestnuts, and buckeyes will be gratefully accepted—especially if a squirrel or human cracks them open.

Nut-producing shade trees may be a headache for homeowners, but they spell survival for birds and other wildlife. And how hard is it really to rake up the acorns or nuts when they fall and stash them in an out-of-the-way place, such as underneath a tree or hedge?

ACORN EFFORT, OAK TREE RESULT

Give 'Em Grit (and a Side of Salt)

When winter restricts birds' diets to a narrower range of foods, nutrient deficiencies can result, leading to weak-shelled eggs when spring rolls around. Adding a source of calcium to your feeding station gives birds a welcome boost and helps promote the survival of struggling songbird species.

Birds also seek grit to help them break down the hard seeds in their diet. In a bird's gizzard, small stones and grit grind its food into a digestible state. Flocks of birds often can be seen along roads pecking at sand and fine gravel for this purpose. This is especially true in winter, when ice-fighting applications of sand and salt make road surfaces safer for vehicles and more attractive to birds seeking grit and minerals. Offering grit and other minerals at your feeding station helps keep birds off the streets—literally!

You can sprinkle grit and other crunchy treats on the ground near your feeders or offer them in tray feeders. Serve salt in a solid-bottomed tray or saucer to keep it from washing through in rain or snow and killing plants below.

GOOD GRIT AND MINERAL SOURCES

Builder's sand (sharp or coarse sand)

Natural aquarium gravel, rinsed

Crushed eggshells

Crushed oyster or clam shells

Cuttlefish bone (as for pet birds)

Salt block (mineral or plain)

Rock salt

Wood ashes

JELLY JUNKIES, FRUIT FIENDS, AND NECTAR NUTS

We aren't the only ones who love our PB&J, or a little jelly on our morning toast. Orioles love the sweet stuff too. Manufacturers of bird feeders have picked up on this, and you can now find quite an assortment of fruit and platform feeders that include little jelly cups. There are even jelly feeders that you can attach over an open jar of jelly, making frequent refills unnecessary. (We don't want to think about all those sticky-headed birds, though!)

No need to break the bank on exotic jellies: Cheap grape jelly suits orioles just fine. Get a store brand and go for it! No diet jellies, though—unlike us, birds don't need the calorie savings. Quite the opposite!

A FONDNESS FOR FRUIT

Because orioles have become more common at feeders over the past decade, bird supply stores have begun to cater to them, and now many of us know that orioles love orange halves. (Maybe it's just the association of orange fruit, orange bird that makes this easy to remember.) But orioles aren't the only orange lovers at your feeding station: cardinals, bluebirds, mockingbirds, robins, and woodpeckers are also orange aficionados.

But oranges are only the beginning. Orioles also enjoy peaches and pears, apples and figs, and berries of all kinds—including blueberries, elderberries, blackberries, and mulberries. So do plenty of other birds, including robins, cardinals, tanagers, waxwings, vireos, titmice, chickadees, sapsuckers, finches, jays, mockingbirds, grosbeaks, thrashers, thrushes, flickers, woodpeckers, wrens, catbirds, and phoebes. Cherries are favorites, and so are plums, grapes, and chunks of cantaloupe and other melons.

Different birds have different favorites—just as orioles adore oranges while robins love apples. When you're preparing fruit for your family, set out a few pieces on your platform feeder and see what comes to eat them. The same goes for dried fruit: Save those raisins that stick to the bottom of the box or the last few "Craisins" or apricot pieces for your platform feeder. Birds can't resist dried fruit! Make sure you chop large pieces, such as dried apple slices or whole dried apricots, into bird-size bites before offering them.

Don't forget wild fruits. If you have rugosa, sweetbriar, or other roses in your garden that produce fat rose hips, birds will appreciate them on the bush, or cut some for your tray and platform feeders. That goes for other fruits like ornamental quinces, serviceberries, dogwood berries, some crab apples, and many more. You can even design part or all of your landscape with birds in mind. Find out how to create a bird-friendly landscape in Chapter 3, "Plants and Landscape Features for Birds," beginning on page 87.

An Easy Orange Add-On

Rather than buying separate orange and nectar feeders for orioles, try this tip from owners Dan and Gordon of eBirdseed.com: Double up! Punch a hole through an orange half with an awl, large nail, or screwdriver, then push it over the hook on your nectar feeder and down the hanger to rest over the feeder. Orioles get two treats for the price of one! Duncraft even produces a dual-purpose nectar feeder designed just for this purpose.

NECTAR FOR ORIOLES

Like hummingbirds, orioles also enjoy our substitute "nectar"—a sugar-water mix served up in special nectar feeders. For orioles, which are famous for loving oranges, store-bought nectar often includes orange flavoring and sometimes even orange coloring. (See Chapter 7, "Hosting Hummingbirds," beginning on page 207, for recipes for making your own nectar.) Because orioles are bigger than hummingbirds, bird specialty stores offer special oriole nectar feeders that are larger, with larger nectar ports, and are usually orange rather than red.

Many models come with bee and wasp guards at the nectar ports, since bees and wasps enjoy nectar, too. (So do ants, but you can buy some pretty flower- or umbrella-shaped ant excluders to hang over your nectar feeder.) Are these guards necessary? Not according to Leesport, Pennsylvania, backyard birder Joan Silagy. The sight of a bee or wasp at the feeder may disturb us, but as Joan reminds us, "These birds eat insects!"

If you can't get orioles to come to your nectar feeders, try this tip from the backyard birding pros: Hang the feeders closer to your trees. Once the orioles start visiting the feeders, you can gradually move them closer to the house.

MAD ABOUT MEALWORMS

Love bluebirds? If you can attract these meadow-loving birds to bluebird houses on the perimeters of your yard, you can lure them in for a closer look—and more in-yard time—with mealworms. These inch-long tan "worms" are actually the larvae of grain-loving darkling beetles. They're readily available in bird specialty shops like Wild Birds Unlimited as well as pet and bait stores, or you can order them online from sites like eBirdseed.com (www.ebirdseed.com) and Duncraft (www.duncraft.com). Because online quantities tend to be large (1,000 mealworms and up), if you go that route you might want to split an order with your bird-feeding friends.

Another option is to buy canned, roasted, or freeze-dried mealworms, also available from bird specialty stores, catalogs, and Web sites. The canned mealworms are processed to retain their plumpness, increasing their appeal to birds—though of course nothing beats the movement of live mealworms to attract them.

Once you've started offering live mealworms, you can keep canned, roasted, or freeze-dried worms on hand as a backup to use if you run out of live ones. Refrigerate canned mealworms after opening the container, and discard any uneaten mealworms after 48 hours. (No need to discard living mealworms, of course!) Freeze-dried and roasted mealworms require no refrigeration.

Mealworms aren't the only "worm" you can offer your birds. You can always set out grubs,

Even if bluebirds are active in your neighborhood, they may not make an appearance at your feeders. These cheery birds feed on insects and small fruits, so you won't see them lining the perches of tubes filled with sunflower seed. To bring bluebirds to the table, serve up a tray or dish filled with mealworms. These light brown grubs are a particular favorite of bluebirds and are particularly welcome in early spring when other insects are hard to find.

Stockpile Seeds and Other Bird-Worthy Leftovers

When cleaning fresh produce for your own meals, it's hardly any extra effort to set aside seeds you don't plan to eat. Save seeds of apples, pears, peppers, pumpkins, squash, melons, and other fruits. When you have a small supply, set them out on a tray or platform feeder or broadcast them over your lawn for the birds to enjoy.

Other leftovers from your kitchen may also meet with favor when offered at the backyard feeding station, but it's wise to serve "people food" in small quantities until you know how well it is received—and by whom. Bread crumbs, stale bread, pizza crusts, cooked vegetables, cooked pasta, bits of cooked eggs, and scraps of ham or bacon are some of the many foods that may find an appreciative audience among the birds. But such foods may also be attractive to other wild animals—raccoons especially—and to loud, bossy birds such as crows, starlings, and blue jays.

To avoid these potential pest problems, put out small amounts of any new food and wait to see what happens before proceeding further. If your supply of bird treats from the kitchen is larger than the current demand, don't despair that the excess will go to waste. Label a large, resealable freezer bag "For the Birds" and toss any likely candidates for the feeding station into the bag, making sure to cut up large items into bird-bite sizes before you stow the bag in your freezer. Pull it out when your supplies of normal bird foods run low and you don't have time to get to the store or in winter when hungry birds are less choosy about their meals. You can dole out the treats so that they're eaten quickly—less risk of attracting nocturnal animals—and have the satisfaction that your leftovers aren't going to waste.

caterpillars, and other larvae you discover while gardening or doing lawn chores. Keep a small container handy when you're turning the soil in your lawn or gardens. If you encounter grubs, cutworms, wireworms, or other subterranean pests, toss them into your "holding cell," then add them to a tray feeder for hungry birds to find. The same practice works if you find caterpillars dining on your crops—pick them into a container and serve them to the birds. And some wild bird stores and catalogs, like Duncraft, offer roasted wax worms—actually the larvae of bee moths. These "WaxSnax" look like shorter, fatter mealworms and attract the same insect-eating birds that love mealworms. They require no refrigeration. If you have a bait store nearby, check their coolers for tasty tidbits to serve to birds. In addition to earthworms and mealworms, many bait shops also sell containers of live wax worms. You can use these insect larvae to bring in the birds just as reliably as anglers use them to reel in the fish.

Note: See "Take a Closer Look" at bluebirds on page 156.

GROW YOUR OWN MEALWORMS

Save money and aggravation by growing your own mealworms. It's sort of like sourdough starter: You'll only have to buy them once, and then you'll have a supply on hand indefinitely. Mealworms are very easy to raise, and can be an interesting home "livestock" project for the whole family. All it takes is a carton of oatmeal, a raw potato, and a refrigerator. To find out how to do this, see "Growing Mealworms, Step by Step" on page 142.

BIRD BREAD AND BAKED GOODS

Like us, birds love bread and baked goods. Their super-fast metabolisms make them carboholics with no fear of packing on the pounds—or even ounces. But what kind of bread do birds love best?

Think back for a minute to your childhood, when your parents took you to the local park to feed the ducks. We'll bet they brought along a bag of Saltine-type crackers and stale white bread—the kind of bread that modern nutritionists say is as bad for you as eating sugar straight from the bag, the kind of bread that's used as the starting point for the Glycemic Index, which is to say, "empty" calories. And we'll bet the ducks gobbled it all up. So will backyard birds. The sad truth is that birds prefer the "white stuff," the spongy "balloon bread," to the most nutrient-dense multigrain bread we can make or buy. Maybe it's because the white color helps them see it better than brown bread. Maybe it's because they need those "empty" calories, especially in cold weather, without having to work to get them. Nobody seems to be sure.

Do we advocate feeding birds white bread and crackers? If that's what you feed your family, absolutely—break some up and set it on your platform feeder. The same is true of doughnuts, a calorie-dense treat that birds love as much as Homer Simpson does, not to mention muffins, pancakes, biscuits, and other treats. But if you give your family, and you'd rather give your birds, more nutrient-dense goodies, here are some tips to help you.

- **Use common sense.** You've heard that chocolate is bad for animals; don't give it to your birds, either. Save those chocolate doughnuts for the family! The same goes for ooey-gooey frostings and fillings: If birds get them on their feathers, they might not be able to get them off.
- **Give them the leftovers.** Several whole books have been devoted to the topic of recipes for birdy baked goods, including two we especially enjoy, *My Recipes Are for the Birds* and *Bird Food Recipes*. But frankly, it makes more sense to save part of the baked goods you're already making for your family and feed them to the birds rather than making separate recipes. Birds will love your breads, muffins, biscuits, pancakes, cornbread, and rolls; just reserve a few slices or pieces when you pull them from the oven, and set them out once they've cooled. Birds also enjoy piecrust; roll the unbaked leftover bits into a rope and bake it along with the crust, then break the rope into pieces (once it's cooled) and set them on your platform or tray feeder.
- **Use white whole wheat.** If you typically use whole-wheat flour and find that the birds aren't flocking to your wholesome fare, try switching to white whole wheat. It has the same nourishing whole-wheat goodness, but is made from white rather than red wheat so it bakes up paler. The lighter-colored goods will bring in the birds! Look for white whole wheat in your supermarket (King Arthur Flour is one brand) or health food store.
- **Use white cornmeal.** Substituting white cornmeal for yellow will not only create whiter baked goods, which will attract more birds, but it's sweeter, too, not bitter like yellow

BUDGET-WISE BIRDING

Deck the Yard with Edible Ornaments

Do you covet the boxes of beautiful seed-coated "bird ornaments" that are featured in gift catalogs around Christmas? We'd love to buy a few boxes and hang the decorative treats in trees all over our yards, but they're pricey, and the holidays are a time when many of us are watching our budgets.

Instead, make your own edible ornaments for the birds! Take slices of stale bread and punch out festive shapes with cookie cutters. (You can set the leftover scraps out on your platform or tray feeder.) Coat one side of each shape with a thin layer of peanut butter; use the crunchy kind for a special treat. Then press *hulled* sunflower and/or millet seeds into the peanut butter. Punch a hole in the center of each "ornament" and hang them outside with twine or colorful yarn.

For sturdier ornaments, use crackers as your base. Buy (or make) crackers in fun shapes—Pepperidge Farm makes butterfly-shaped crackers, and we've seen flowers and stars, too, as well as diamonds and circles. Coat one side of each cracker with peanut butter, and press in hulled seeds (or press the crackers peanut-butter-side down into a plate of hulled seeds). Use a nail and carefully push it through each cracker, then hang them with ornament hooks.

Or use slices of bagel to make peanut butter and birdseed "wreaths." Of course, you can always make sugar-cookie ornaments as you do for your own tree, "ice" them with peanut butter, press in the seeds, and hang. Or set out some of all of these and see which ones your birds prefer.

---

cornmeal. Try it and see if your family doesn't prefer it, too!

- **Up the appeal.** Adding apple or apricot pieces, raisins and/or "Craisins," sunflower seeds (hulled, of course), and similar goodies to your muffins, breads, and pancakes will make them more delicious for your family as well as for your feathered friends.
- **Think wholesome but high-calorie.** With their high metabolisms, birds need a lot more calories for their size than we do. Help them out with oil-rich treats like zucchini and pumpkin bread; fruit- and nut-laden fruitcake; bread pudding; cornbread; and the occasional croissant (oops, did we say "wholesome?!").
- **Get a "bottom of the box" (or bag) mind-set.** Instead of eating or tossing those broken crackers, chips, popcorn fragments, and the like that seem to inevitably lurk at the bottom of boxes and bags, get in the habit of taking them out to the platform or tray feeder and letting the birds share your crunchy snacks. Just be sure to break them into bird-size bites before setting them out—using a rolling pin or the bottom of a mug will quickly crush them down to size.
- **Save some cereal.** Speaking of boxes, birds eat cereal, too. Set out a handful of Cheerios or Rice Krispies or some crushed cornflakes on the platform or tray feeder and watch the action.

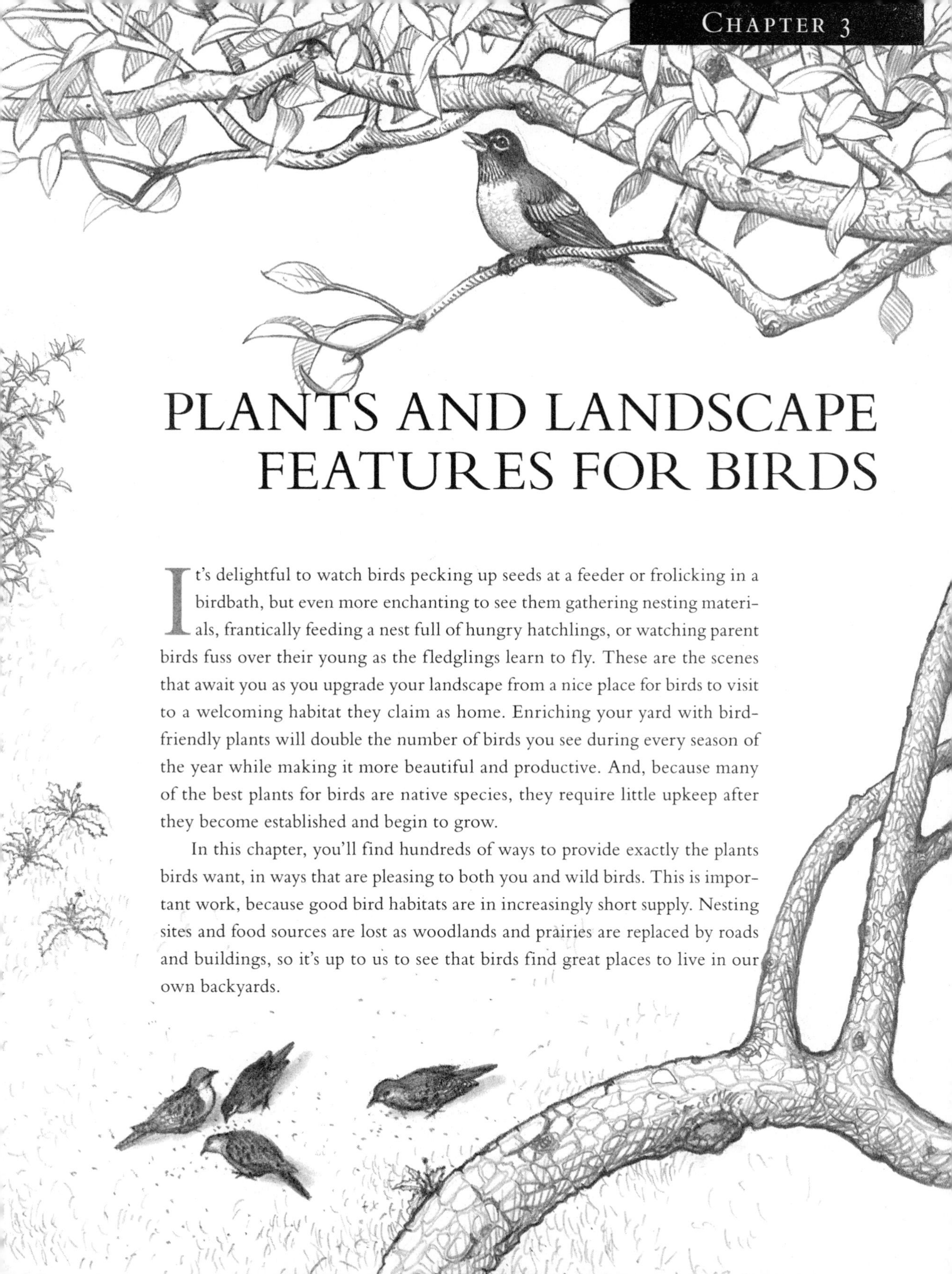

CHAPTER 3

PLANTS AND LANDSCAPE FEATURES FOR BIRDS

It's delightful to watch birds pecking up seeds at a feeder or frolicking in a birdbath, but even more enchanting to see them gathering nesting materials, frantically feeding a nest full of hungry hatchlings, or watching parent birds fuss over their young as the fledglings learn to fly. These are the scenes that await you as you upgrade your landscape from a nice place for birds to visit to a welcoming habitat they claim as home. Enriching your yard with bird-friendly plants will double the number of birds you see during every season of the year while making it more beautiful and productive. And, because many of the best plants for birds are native species, they require little upkeep after they become established and begin to grow.

In this chapter, you'll find hundreds of ways to provide exactly the plants birds want, in ways that are pleasing to both you and wild birds. This is important work, because good bird habitats are in increasingly short supply. Nesting sites and food sources are lost as woodlands and prairies are replaced by roads and buildings, so it's up to us to see that birds find great places to live in our own backyards.

TAKING YOUR PLACE IN ECOLOGICAL HISTORY

For tens of thousands of years, dozens of different species of birds inhabited the place where you now live. Perhaps it was once a dense hardwood forest, or maybe tall pines, spruces, and other conifers ruled. If you live in the Central Plains, your backyard may have been a hip-high field of grasses and wildflowers. As civilization came, the ecological history of your home changed, and your neighborhood may have spent several decades as a farm field before it was developed with roads and houses. Now it's your turn to create changes that will bring new integrity to the land that is yours, to enhance or restore it on behalf of birds. Your most powerful tools are plants.

Birds depend on plants for food, cover, nesting sites, and places to court and rest. In this chapter, you'll learn about more than 100 plants that attract different types of birds, including many plants that are easy to fit into smallish yards. Many of these are North American native plants—the same species that supported healthy bird populations long before Homo sapiens appeared on the scene. Times have changed, but birds haven't changed their minds about what they need from the landscape.

To many people, a landscape intended to serve as a bird sanctuary must be a wild place where plants are allowed to ramble as they will, but birds easily accept landscapes that follow more orderly styles. While it's true that many of the bird species that are threatened or endangered require the rarest of modern landscapes—dense forests where the highest treetops reach 100 feet into the sky—there's much you can do to support an amazing diversity of birds even if you live in the suburbs or a large city.

DEVELOPING A "BIRDBRAINED" LANDSCAPING STYLE

If birds were in charge of designing your landscape, they would probably chatter on endlessly about the plants described later in this chapter, and then make these simple suggestions you may not have considered.

Success in the City

Roads and buildings make poor habitats for most birds, but a few species have adapted to urban life quite well. Pigeons had already taken to nesting on roofs and window ledges in Europe before they were brought to North America in the 1600s, and our native mourning doves sometimes move close to people by building their nests in hanging baskets. Two other imported species, house sparrows and starlings, have adapted to city life a little too well. Colonies of house sparrows take over store signs and the eaves of buildings, while starlings can turn any crevice into a secure home. Learn more about these opportunistic birds that often make the most of human habitation, sometimes to the point of being considered pests, in Chapter 9, starting on page 269, and Chapter 11, starting on page 315.

- Limit concrete and asphalt. Hard surfaces are unbeatable for driveways and main entryways, but substitute mulch-covered paths in shady areas, or a porous patchwork of crushed rock and flagstone in sunnier spots. Impermeable hard surfaces have nothing to offer wild birds, but birds can peck up insects and grit from mulch or gravel.
- Skirt raised decks with dense shrubs to create excellent shelter for birds during every season of the year.
- Start from the highest treetops in your yard and work your way down. Tall trees are what birds see first, and once they've perched on a branch they inspect what lies beneath the canopy. They know they've found a promising place when they see that the puddles of sun along the edges of the tree canopy are lush with berry-bearing shrubs and vines, or flowers that produce nectar and seeds.
- Locate feeding stations, nesting boxes, perches, and other bird activity areas near evergreens or twiggy shrubs, without blocking the birds' flight paths or providing predators with secret stalking space. Birds prefer not to be watched as they come and go from their nests, and ground feeders need to hop to cover close by when they sense danger.

Follow That Wasp

If you see a wasp or hornet's nest in a tree, don't be surprised to find a bird's nest nearby. Wrens, orioles, and finches often nest near stinging insects, which may help defend their nests from some types of predators.

Seed-Planting Machines

Most birds swallow small seeds whole, which get scratched up a bit as they pass through the birds' gizzards. The seeds then exit the birds coated with nitrogen-rich droppings, sometimes miles from the plant that produced them. Numerous native plants from dogwoods to wild grapes depend on birds to disperse their seeds, but birds serve equally well as seed-planting machines for exotic invasive plants. This is all the more reason to eradicate invasive species such as Oriental bittersweet or Japanese honeysuckle. Once these plants produce seeds, where they end up is far beyond your control.

MAKING A BALANCED PLAN

You don't need to let your yard grow into a jungle to enjoy the company of a wide variety of birds. If you enjoy gardening, many birds will follow your lead, appearing when certain insects become numerous or edible fruits begin to ripen, or you may see a large increase in seed eaters if you grow bachelor buttons, cosmos, and other annual flowers. But before you launch into an ambitious planting plan, take stock of what you already have, and see what you can do to correct existing conditions that have a negative impact on birds.

After you've worked your way through the "Birdscaping Balance Sheet" on page 90 and fixed serious problems, you'll be ready to begin adding plants and features that will make your yard irresistible to birds.

YOUR BIRDSCAPING BALANCE SHEET

As a first step toward making your yard a better place for birds, inventory its good and bad points, just as you might compare assets and liabilities on a financial balance sheet. Once you have this information, you can increase your assets while modifying features that don't work well for birds. The result will be a yard that includes a wealth of winged wildlife.

KEEP AND GROW THESE ASSETS

- *Tall seed-bearing trees* like maples, oaks, and birches provide food and habitat at heights that other plants can't match. Many small birds specialize in gleaning small insects from the bark of tall trees. See plant lists on pages 116 and 117.
- *Evergreen trees* such as pines, junipers, and hemlocks provide food and shelter during every season of the year and are invaluable in winter. See plant lists on page 116.
- *Small fruit-bearing trees* including cherries, hawthorns, and dogwoods always get noticed by birds, and they're easy to fit into small yards. See plant lists on page 117.
- *Dead trees* are gold mines for birds, whether bluebirds are nesting in cavities or woodpeckers are chowing down on wood-boring insects. With its highest and longest branches trimmed off in the interest of safety, a dead tree (often called a snag) can stand as a landscape treasure for many years.
- *Hedges, thickets, or mixed shrub borders* make ideal habitats for many birds, especially if they include berry-bearing native shrubs. Keep reading for dozens of ways to arrange native shrubs so they look as good as they work.
- *Nectar- and seed-bearing flowers* are present in most flower gardens, but you can increase visits from birds by growing more of their favorites. See plant lists on page 119.
- *Water* is a basic necessity for all birds, and they won't be able to resist a birdbath or water feature located where they can come and go safely. Water also may attract birds seldom seen at feeders, for example warblers and vireos. See Chapter 6, starting on page 177, for dozens of ways to provide birds with a dependable source of water.

EVERYBODY WINS

Berry Nice Neighborhoods

In many neighborhoods, residents with green thumbs work together to enhance entrances and medians with attractive plants. Many berry-bearing shrubs and seed-producing perennials make good choices as long as they are *not* located where birds must fly across a busy street to get to them. Fruit-eating birds including robins, brown thrashers, and cedar waxwings become obsessed when holly or dogwood berries are ready to harvest, and goldfinches never stop and look both ways before crossing a street to get to bachelor's buttons or sunflowers that are holding ready-to-eat seeds. To avoid casualties, locate plants that attract birds where moving cars will not pose a hazard to flying diners.

SHRINK OR ELIMINATE THESE LIABILITIES

- *Invasive plants* crowd out native species, but hungry birds are often quite willing to accept an exotic substitute if their preferred wild food is not available. Birds are credited with spreading many of the most aggressive invasive plants that have come to North America from other continents (see "Seed-Planting Machines" on page 89). When you allow an invasive plant to continue to produce fruits or seeds on your property, you are participating in this process. To set things right, identify invasive plants in your yard and make a plan to bring them under control. Persistence is often needed, but several seasons of digging out and chopping back will tame even the worst offenders.
- *Domestic (and not so domestic) cats* kill more than 10 million birds a year, and gawky fledglings that are learning to fly make easy prey. For cats, bringing down birds is pure instinct, and many cat owners have received dead bird presents from their feline companions. Keeping your cat indoors—especially during the summer nesting season—is the best way to keep Kitty from hunting songbirds for sport.
- *Big windows and sliding glass doors* are invisible to birds. Many birds die tragic deaths when they crash into large glass barriers. Unable to see the glass, they fly toward things they see inside your house (like large houseplants or colorful shiny things) and you hear that awful thud. Many birds that are knocked out by window collisions regain consciousness after a while, but others die. See "No More Knockouts" in Chapter 9 on page 279, for easy ways to avoid such casualties.

Great Trees for Birds

More than 20 trees that birds especially like are listed on pages 116 and 117, but the following species often top the lists of birdscaping trees:

- **Red maple (*Acer rubrum*)** has it all—moderate to fast growth, excellent fall color, and plenty of nutlike fruits, called samaras, for birds to gather in winter when other foods are scarce. Small trees transplant easily. Native to the East, red maples grow well in moderately moist soil in the West, too. Hardy in Zones 3 to 9, red maples grow 40 to 60 feet (12 to 18.5 m) tall.
- **The branches of hawthorns (*Crataegus* spp.)** are usually armed with thorns, which makes it a great place for birds to feed with few worries about predators. Fragrant spring flowers give way to tiny applelike fruits. A western species, the Washington hawthorn (*C. phaenopyrum*) also grows well in the East. Hardy in Zones 3 to 8, hawthorns grow to about 30 feet (9 m) tall.
- **Conifers that shed their needles are rare, but two trees—bald cypress (*Taxodium distichum*) in the East and larch (*Larix* spp.)** in the West—provide dense cover in summer yet don't block warming winter sun. Bald cypress grows 50 to 100 feet (15 to 30 m) tall in Zones 4 to 9; larches can grow to 150 feet tall (45 m) in moist western sites.

Take a Closer Look

Cedar Waxwing *(Bombycilla cedrorum)*

Both male and female waxwings will catch your eye with their sleek bodies and finely etched markings—a yellow band on the tip of the tail, a black eye mask outlined in white, and a dashing brown crest. Red waxy appendages on waxwings' secondary wing feathers give this bird its common name. Females lay two to six pale gray eggs lightly speckled with brownish gray. Adults are 6 to 7 inches (14 to 17 cm) long.

Feeder Favorites for Waxwings

- Dried tart cherries
- Boughs of juniper berries
- Raisins

Regional Relations

The robin-size Bohemian waxwing (*Bombycilla garrulus*) is about an inch longer and generally stockier of body than its cedar cousin, but otherwise the two species appear quite similar. While cedar waxwings range across most of North America, from southern Canada to southern Mexico, Bohemians spend most of their time in the North, nesting in northernmost Canada and Alaska during the breeding season. Occasionally, however, the species will flock together where their ranges overlap, and Bohemians will be sighted well beyond their usual haunts.

Tempting Features and Treats for Waxwings

- Wild cherries are among waxwings' favorite foods, and they find berry-bearing junipers irresistible.
- Waxwings passing through your area in search of food are likely to stop for a bath if they hear the trickle of running water.
- If nesting pairs have settled in or near your yard, they may be attracted to a platform feeder stocked with chopped apples and dried fruits.
- Plants with bright red berries—honeysuckles, dogwoods, and sour cherries—are almost guaranteed to attract waxwings when the fruit is ripe.

Did You Know?

- Waxwings are fruit nomads, moving in flocks as new food sources are found. They also eat insects caught on the wing, often feeding them to newborn chicks.
- Mated pairs work together to build nests high in trees. While the female incubates the eggs, her mate brings her food.
- When food is abundant but space is tight, waxwings sometimes share food by passing berries to one another. Food sharing is also a common courtship ritual.
- Well-known as fruit lovers, waxwings are actually flycatchers that dine on insects during the summer months.
- The cedar waxwing's song is a high-pitched repetition of "sreee" sounds.
- Flowers, the buds of deciduous trees, and sap are other items that sometimes are included in waxwings' diet.

A Waxwing Comeback

For 200 years, cedar waxwings and their close relatives, Bohemian waxwings, were captured and sold as caged birds. Taking captives became illegal in North America in the early 20th century, and then Mexico banned the export of captive waxwings in the early 1980s. Meanwhile, reforestation programs and the planting of berry-bearing shrubs in home landscapes helped cedar waxwings make a comeback. In the past 40 years, waxwing populations in North America have doubled.

KEEPSAKE TREES

Birdscaping from the top down means starting with trees. From a bird's-eye point of view, treetops are your yard's front door. Located as they are up in bird space, trees attract birds like beacons. Bigger is generally better when it comes to good trees for birds, so the best trees for birds may be the ones you already have. But even fast-growing trees grow slowly, so replacing existing trees (unless they're invasive species) is seldom practical in a single lifetime. Slow-growing oaks and other nut-producing trees are true treasures in a bird-friendly landscape, as are dense evergreens like pines, cedars, and spruces.

Except for meadowlarks, quail, and other birds that make their homes in grasslands and prairies, birds seldom stay long in landscapes that do not include trees. Migratory birds may spend a few days gathering fruits from a specimen shrub in your lawn—or weed seeds in your vegetable garden—but you'll see few nesting pairs or year-round residents if your landscape lacks trees. Trees give birds the vantage points they need to keep an eye on their territories, provide nesting sites, and often serve as a major source of food. In addition to producing flower nectar and seeds, trees support large numbers of insects that are eaten by birds. From leaf-eating caterpillars to weevils feeding beneath the bark, trees are year-round cafeterias for titmice, woodpeckers, and other bark gleaners. See "*Tree Gleaners at Your Service*" on page 124 in Chapter 4 for more information about these and other insect-eating birds.

Let in the Light

If you have so many trees that little sun gets through their branches, open portals of light for nearby plants by pruning off the lowest branches. Removing branches within 12 feet (3.6 m) of the ground also improves the view for year-round bird-watching and may help protect nesting birds from some types of predators.

Just inside the shade canopy of large, established trees, you can often slip in small shade-tolerant species such as dogwoods, redbuds, or tree-form serviceberries. Look for puddles of light where bunchberries (*Cornus canadensis*) or another shade-tolerant groundcover might grow; otherwise let fallen leaves form their own mulch beneath established trees.

EVERYBODY WINS

Let Dead Trees Support Life

When a tree in your yard gets seriously injured or killed, don't rush to have it taken out. Instead, remove (or have someone else remove) any branches that might break off and fall as they become brittle, but leave 20 feet (6 m) or so of the main trunk intact. As the years pass, woodpeckers will chip out holes as they gather insects; cavity-nesting birds will later use these holes as homes. Dress the base of your snag with bird-friendly vines or small shrubs to ensure plenty of return visits from birds that eat both insects and fruits.

KEEPING A BIRD-FRIENDLY LAWN

There is usually a place in a bird-friendly landscape for a small swath of open lawn, which often will be visited by robins, mockingbirds, and other earthworm eaters. Crows, ravens, jays, and magpies like to include a patch of lawn in their territory, and many ground-feeding birds peck into turf in search of seeds.

There is but one ironclad rule you must follow if you want to support birds *and* have a good lawn, which is that the turf must be managed organically. This is easier than ever thanks to the improved availability of organic fertilizers. In another happy coincidence, organic pre-emergent herbicides made from corn gluten prevent crabgrass seeds from germinating and then serve as fertilizer as they break down and join the soil food web.

Your lawn will also be of more interest to birds if you mow it high, which tends to keep the surface shady, moist, and peckable. Allowing the clippings to decompose right where they fall will encourage earthworms, or you can bag your clippings and use them as mulch in other parts of your yard.

Who's Eating the Dandelions?

As fluffy dandelion seeds blow about on summer breezes, many of them are collected by seed-eating birds including goldfinches, buntings, chipping sparrows, and finches.

What Ground Feeders Want

Ground feeders can become the most familiar of birds, but until they accept new things (like you) as safe, they are understandably nervous. And, although you may think doves and pigeons are dangerously slow to take off when chased by a child or dog, birds that feed on the ground have well-developed talents for finding shelter fast. When given exactly what they want in terms of feeding space, juncos and sparrows will become a constant presence in your yard. Here are three key features.

An open swath of lawn that is separate from your main bird feeding station. Most ground feeders prefer to feed away from the noise and chatter of aboveground feeders, and it's healthier for them to

Doves and other ground-feeding birds will clean up spilled seeds beneath hanging and pole-mounted feeders, but they'd rather have their own space where they can dine undisturbed by noisy feeder birds. Add a low basin where they can drink and bathe to create the perfect spot for these down-to-earth guests.

The Incredible Shrinking Lawn

It is tempting to use the lawn as a feeding station, but most lawn grasses hold up poorly to the constant trampling, pecking, and showering of seeds that goes on beneath a feeder. This situation provides the perfect excuse to convert the best site for your main feeder from lawn into a bed filled with bird-pleasing plants. Here are four more smart strategies for converting lawn space to bird space.

1. Frame it up.
Framing the lawn with berry-bearing shrubs and seed-producing flowers will turn it into a stage where a wide variety of birds will come and go, including many that like scratching into the moist soil beneath plants in search of soil-dwelling insects. A lawn's frame, or border, need not be limited to a few types of plants. Part of the frame might include low-growing evergreen groundcovers like cotoneaster or creeping juniper, with other sections filled with colorful flowers such as black-eyed Susans and zinnias.

2. Add a backdrop.
Remote areas of a lawn often suffer from neglect, so they are the ideal place to create a thicket, or simply a well-chosen group of shrubs birds are guaranteed to love. The dark contrast provided by backgrounds that include tall evergreens improve backyard bird-watching, too.

3. Connect island beds.
The root-ridden area beneath trees is often difficult to mow, and most plants—including grass—struggle to grow in dry shade. Cover the ground under trees with biodegradable mulch, and see if there are ways you can connect trees with curved beds. To keep maintenance to a minimum, fill the beds with bird-friendly native shrubs or trees listed on pages 117 and 118.

4. Use select specimen shrubs.
If you only want to shave a little space from an already smallish lawn, you can do it with a neatly mulched specimen shrub. Native viburnums are excellent for this job, or you could use a sculpture-like group of dwarf conifers.

5. Put in pathways.
Although paths aren't strictly for the birds, they will make it easier for you to tend landscape features that are. Create walkways that give you access to feeding stations and bird baths so you can refresh food and water with ease. Paths also reduce the amount of turf you have to care for, and they look nicer than grass that's been trampled by frequent trips over the same route.

dine on a site that's not littered with a layer of cast-off shells and droppings from a feeder overhead.

Shelter from strong winds, especially in winter and during nesting season. If winter winds often blow from the North, look for a spot close to the south side of your house—or on the sheltered side of evergreen trees or shrubs.

Twiggy shrubs, evergreens, or other shelter plants within 10 feet (3 m) of at least one side of the feeding space. Leave at least one broad side open as a ground-feeder flyway.

A place to bathe and drink is important to all birds, no matter what or where they eat. Place just the basin from a standard bird bath on the ground—or sunk slightly into the ground—in an open area where ground feeders dine. See Chapter 6, "Water Features for Birds," for tips on safely siting a low-level water supply.

STOCKING YOUR LANDSCAPE'S PANTRY

The seeds and suet you use to fill your feeders are certainly appreciated by birds, but your feeders are small cafés compared to the banquets provided by plants. As trees, shrubs, grasses, and flowers provide natural food season after season, their menus change from month to month, and sometimes from day to day. Birds often show tremendous patience (or perhaps pickiness) as they wait for huckleberries or sunflower seeds to ripen and then they swoop in and can't seem to get enough. If you think of your landscape as your biggest and best bird feeder of all, capable of providing the very foods birds have sought out for thousands of years, you're on the right track toward tripling the number of bird species that pass through your yard.

Putting the food supply first is also a smart strategy because plants that produce berries, nuts, seeds, and other foods birds like to eat also provide safe places to nest, roost, or hide from predators. Food plants create habitats for insects, too, so insect-eating birds derive benefits from plants they never directly consume.

If you want your avian restaurant to get five-feather ratings from birds, you'll need to keep it open year-round, and you'll need to serve fresh, local food in season along with standard feeder fare. To help you develop a landscape that can accomplish this feat, the pages ahead will look at outstanding food plants, sorted by the season in which they are in highest demand by birds.

WHAT DO YOU WANT?

One of the reasons you're making your yard more bird-friendly is so it will be more enjoyable for you, too. If you have wonderful visions of what you want, great! But if you need more focus as you imagine enhancing your yard with bird-friendly plants and features, here are six guidelines to keep in mind.

1. Clear viewing scapes between bird activity areas and indoor windows are a top priority. As a practical matter, you may need to shield large windows or take other precautions to keep birds from crashing into them (see "No More Knockouts" in Chapter 9, on page 279,

ACORN EFFORT, OAK TREE RESULT

Be a Restrained Snipper

As long as a shrub is holding berries, stay away from it with your pruning shears. Birds wait until late winter to eat many berries such as those from some sumacs, pyracanthas, choke berries, and hollies, which become more palatable as they begin to ferment.

BUDGET-WISE BIRDING

Spreading Shrubs

No matter where you live, there are spreading shrubs that will help fill empty pockets in your landscape without emptying your pockets in the process. In addition to multiplying themselves at a rapid pace (usually beginning the second year after planting), spreading shrubs including stately staghorn sumac (*Rhus typhina*) in the East, gray dogwood (*Cornus racemosa*) in the Midwest, blueberry elder (*Sambucus caerulea*) in the West, and rugosa roses (*Rosa rugosa* and hybrids) and viburnums (*Viburnum* spp. and hybrids) in most regions all provide food for dozens of species of birds.

for a variety of ways to keep birds from colliding with windows).

2. Make no compromises when it comes to easy access to feeders, birdbaths, or perhaps a secret bird-watching blind. Flat stepping-stones are easy to place in grass, gravel, or in soft, biodegradable mulch. The easier it is for you to reach feeders and baths, the more likely you are to keep them clean and filled.
3. Open up closed, choked-off views that are caused by invasive plants. Substitute native species after the invasives have been brought under control.
4. Enhance stark views of a bare landscape with evergreen and deciduous shrubs and trees. Until these plants have time to grow, use cosmos, sunflowers, zinnias, and other seed-bearing annuals to lure in birds.
5. Choose planting sites with care. Location is everything when it comes to certain bird-beloved plants, such as mulberries and oaks. If these big trees are too close to your house (or where you park your car), the constant rain of fruit or acorns becomes a seasonal nuisance. When deciding where to grow food-bearing plants, make sure that fallen fruits or nuts won't stain your house, dent your car, or create sidewalk messes that stick to people's shoes.
6. Save the best seat for yourself. Be sure to include places in the landscape where you can sit outside and enjoy the company of your feathered guests. Put a comfortable bench in a spot with a view of a basin where birds come to drink and splash, or set up a feeding station where you can see it from a seat on your deck or patio.

Birds That Eat Summer Fruits

Brown thrashers	Robins
Cardinals	Thrushes
Catbirds	Towhees
Grosbeaks	Waxwings
Orioles	Woodpeckers

FRUITING PLANTS FOR SUMMER

There are plenty of birds that depend on summer's fruit to help them suddenly take on the task of filling a nest full of hungry mouths. This drill gets repeated up to 100 times a day. As anyone knows who has watched a family of wrens, doves, or pigeons go through its intense 4- to 6-week nesting cycle, mother and father birds don't get a lot of rest when food is scarce. A more plentiful fresh fruit supply makes things much easier for parents and fledglings of fruit-eating birds. Brown thrashers, robins, and catbirds often volunteer to "help" gardeners harvest their blueberries or cherries, although they would really prefer wilder fruit like spring serviceberries, summer huckleberries, or wild plums. Showy cedar waxwings follow the harvest of wild fruits in small flocks, moving to a new place when a promising fruit approaches perfect ripeness.

Reducing Fruit Theft

Birds have special talents for watching blueberries, huckleberries, and other fruits until they begin to ripen. Then they swoop in and eat their fill, which is not what many gardeners want to happen. We want our berries first, and the best way to beat the birds is to cover ripening berries with bird netting or wedding net, often called tulle. The fine mesh of tulle keeps birds from plucking fruits through the net—something they'll do quite readily with the 1-inch (2.5 cm) mesh typical of most garden netting.

If you opt for netting to help save at least some of your berry crop for yourself, be sure to secure the net at ground level to prevent birds from sneaking under the barrier and feasting on your fruit. Robins, in particular, are well known for outsmarting an unsecured net to get at ripening berries. Covering cherries and other tree fruits is difficult or impossible, but many gardeners have luck with other deterrents like shiny CDs or pie pans hung from branches. A newer defense strategy that works surprisingly well is to tie plastic grocery bags to tree limbs or to a string or wire suspended over berries. As the bags flap in the wind, they spook birds that are after your fruit. Whatever defense you choose to protect your fruit, keep in mind that moving "scare" devices are more effective than stationary ones. A flapping bag is more likely to deter berry-nabbing birds than a scarier-looking but motionless rubber snake.

Summer Fruit Plants for Birds

Blackberry	Honeysuckle
Blueberry	Mulberry
Chokecherry	Plum
Grape	Raspberry
Hawthorn	Serviceberry

Little Berries Are Best

You may like nickel-size blueberries, but few birds can handle berries this large. Even robins and thrushes must spear big berries and then tear them into smaller pieces. Smaller berries like those produced by junipers and elderberries are enjoyed by a much longer list of bird species compared to persimmons or plums.

Serviceberries at Your Service

No matter where you live, there is a native serviceberry to add to your bird garden. Often called amelanchiers (ah-meh-LAN-chers), serviceberries cover their bare branches with lightly fragrant white blossoms in spring, followed by blueberry-like fruits in midsummer. Fall color of all serviceberries is yellow to red. If the birds seem to have plenty of berries to spare, pick a few for a batch of hot serviceberry muffins!

Check native plant nurseries for these species and set out dormant plants in late winter.

Shrubby Serviceberries

Shrub-size serviceberries make great specimen shrubs in partially shaded lawns, or you can mix them into shrub groupings.

- **Often called juneberry, Saskatoon, or western serviceberry, *Amelanchier alnifolia*** is native to the West but adapts to life in most regions where winters are cold (Zones 3 to 7). Plants grow 6 to 12 feet (1.8 to 3.6 m) tall.
- **In the East, adopt a smooth serviceberry (*A. laevis*)** and watch it develop multiple trunks as it grows to 15 to 20 feet (4.5 to 6 m) tall. Also called Allegheny serviceberry, this species is adapted in Zones 4 to 9.

Tree-Form Serviceberries

Tall serviceberries make fine little trees for small yards, and require little or no maintenance after they're established.

- **Downy serviceberry (*A. arborea*)** is hardy to Zone 3 and grows 20 to 40 feet (6 to 12 m) tall, depending on growing conditions.
- **Often called Pacific serviceberry, *A. florida*** stays small in dry locations or can grow to 20 feet (6 m) with ample moisture and fertile soil. It's hardy to Zone 2.

Groundcover Serviceberries

Use these low-growing types as groundcovers in open woods or on rocky hillsides.

- **Bartram or mountain serviceberry (*A. bartramiana*)** grows 1 to 3 feet (0.3 to 0.9 m) tall and is hardy to Zone 5.
- **Running serviceberry (*A. stolonifera*)** forms 2- to 3-foot-tall (0.6 to 0.9 m) thickets and often colonizes rocky spots to Zone 5.

NECTAR-BEARING SUMMER FLOWERS

Hummingbirds need plenty of sugary flower nectar to keep their little wings beating 55 times a second, and you'll find dozens of ways to catch their eye with favored flowers in Chapter 7, "Hosting Hummingbirds." Orioles sip flower nectar, too. Many of the same plants that attract hummingbirds do double duty as butterfly magnets.

Nectar-rich flowers also attract other insects in droves, the majority of which are beneficials that help rather than harm plants. Should destructive insects become numerous, birds are an important natural control, and many bird species that normally eat seeds or fruit become bug-nabbers during nesting season when they need extra protein. See Chapter 4, "Sharing Your Garden with Bug-Eating Birds," for tips to help you explore the bug-bird connection.

Give Them Sun

From petunias to salvias, nectar-producing flowers will bloom longer and stronger if they get plenty of sun. Bright-colored bloomers are more eye-catching in full sun than pale pastel flowers, too. To get the biggest impact—and guarantee that birds will appreciate your efforts—try to plant flowers in broad masses or drifts.

The Missing Sense

Birds have fantastic eyesight (hawks and other birds of prey can see eight times better than we can!), but except for vultures and a few other birds, they can hardly smell a thing. The allure of fragrant flowers is therefore wasted on birds, although they benefit from flower perfume indirectly, when the scent attracts moths and other insects that birds like to eat.

Fine Vines for Fences

When trained to grow over a fence or wall, flowering vines form a vertical curtain of foliage and blossoms that provides excellent cover for birds that feed on the ground. Beware of invasive species of Asian origin, which won't be a problem if you stick with native species like those listed here.

Bittersweet (*Celastrus scandens*) bears bright red berries on vigorous, rambling vines that can grow 25 feet (7.6 m) long. Adapted in Zones 3 to 8, it's a fantastic fencerow plant.

Coral honeysuckle (*Lonicera sempervirens*) produces clusters of red and yellow blossoms in early summer, followed by scarlet berries. Adapted in Zones 4 to 9, this native deciduous vine will quickly turn a chain-link fence into a bird-friendly thicket.

Trumpet vine (*Campsis radicans*) is easier to manage in tight spaces if you start with a well-behaved cultivar like 'Yellow Trumpet' or 'Madame Galen'. Adapted in Zones 3 to 9, trumpet creeper blooms intermittently from summer to fall.

Take a Closer Look

Baltimore Oriole *(Icterus galbula)*

Male orioles are hard to miss because of their bright orange breasts, dark black hoods, and flashy white wing bars. The female is less colorful, with a dull orange breast and gray wings and head. Adults are similar in size to robins, from 7 to 8 inches (18 to 20 cm) long. Intricately woven oriole nests are elongated, 5-inch (12 cm)-long pouches lined with soft plant fibers and hair; into these remarkable nests, the female lays three to six pale blue-gray eggs with irregular streaks and spots of brown and black.

Feeder Favorites for Orioles

- Suet crumbled on tray feeder
- Orange slices or halves
- Cups of grape jelly
- Sugar water in a nectar feeder
- Nut meats

Regional Relations

The orchard oriole (*Icterus spurius*) may nest in small colonies with others of its species; orchard oriole males are dark chestnut orange and black with white wing markings more subtle than those of the Baltimore oriole. Females are olive colored with yellowish undersides. Smaller than Baltimore orioles, orchard orioles share the same range across the eastern United States as their better-known cousins and may join Baltimores to migrate in late spring and early fall.

West of the Great Plains, the striking yellow breast of Bullock's oriole (*I. bullockii*) is often seen flashing through treetops. Where the ranges of Baltimore and Bullock's orioles overlap, interbreeding between the two species is common, creating confusion for birders attempting to identify the resulting hybrids. For a time, Bullock's and Baltimore orioles were grouped into a single species and dubbed "northern orioles," but their status as distinct species has since been restored. In the Southwest, bright yellow covers the head of the hooded oriole (*I. cucullatus*), which appears to be wearing a black mask over its eyes and beak.

Tempting Features and Treats for Orioles

- Place 4- to 8-inch-long (10 to 20 cm) pieces of white string on shrubs near where you think orioles may be building a nest. As she weaves her nest, a female oriole may gather 200 pieces of grass, string, and hair.
- Orioles often visit black locust trees, trumpet vines, and other plants that offer abundant nectar.
- Water is a priority for orioles, so they are more likely to nest in yards that include water features.
- Insects, including caterpillars and grasshoppers, make up approximately half of an oriole's diet.

Did You Know?

- The Baltimore oriole is the state bird of Maryland. Wherever they live, orioles scour trees for caterpillars, weevils, beetles, moths, and other insects.
- Orioles typically return to their northern breeding grounds at about the time apple trees bloom in spring.
- Should a cowbird sneak an egg into an oriole nest, the parent orioles are smart enough and strong enough to toss out the alien egg.
- Orioles often "ant" themselves by jabbing ants into their tail and wing feathers. Ornithologists believe the birds use the ants to help control mites and other parasites in hard-to-reach places.
- Orioles are perhaps the most colorful members of the Icterid family of birds. Among their cousins are blackbirds, grackles, meadowlarks, and cowbirds.
- Although they have similar plumage colors and markings, the orioles of the Americas are not closely related to the Old World orioles (family Oriolidae). These brightly colored birds are mostly tropical and subtropical species, found in South Asia, Africa, Indonesia, and Australia.

SUMMER WILDFLOWERS AND GRASSES

A wildflower meadow composed of a tapestry of perennial and reseeding wildflowers laced together with a sprinkling of native grasses is a dream home for smart territorial birds, such as meadowlarks and quail, which nest on the ground. The continuous rain of seeds from wildflowers attracts seed eaters, and a meadow is also a rich hunting ground for bluebirds, grasshopper sparrows, and other bug-nabbers.

A meadow can be large or small, and it's important to include pathways that can be kept open with a lawn mower so you can walk through the meadow and enjoy the buzz of life there. It often takes a few years of adding new plants (and taking out others) to create a meadow that is both beautiful and beckoning to birds, but once established a meadow can perpetuate itself with well-timed mowing. Most meadows benefit from mowing once a year to control woody plants and weeds, but you'll need to observe a no-mow policy from spring to fall to keep from disturbing the peace of your summer residents. Wildlife specialists in the Great Lakes region recommend keeping fencerows and ditches unmowed at least until August 1st to allow fledglings to leave the nest. If you want to provide winter food and habitat for quail, turkeys, and other big year-rounders, delay mowing until early spring. When in doubt, mow only the pathways and perimeter and use loppers and pruning shears to nip out unwanted plants within the meadow itself.

Plants for a Birder's Meadow

Bachelor's button	Purple coneflower
Black-eyed Susan	Sea oats
Goldenrods	Sunflowers
Little bluestem	Tickseed coreopsis
Prairie dropseed	Touch-me-nots

Who's Down in the Ditch?

Attacking overgrown plants in a ditch is a dirty job, and many birds prefer that you neglect a ditch anyway. Ground nesters including quail, bobolinks, and even pheasants sometimes raise their young in ditches, and insect-eating birds always find plenty of choices in a damp ditch. In Great Britain, leaving ditches uncut for 2 years was found to increase the number of bird species present by 30 percent. Even more exciting was finding that the uncut ditches served as homes to four times more nesting pairs of frequently-seen birds.

If looking at an overgrown ditch bothers you, screen it from view with a hedge of well-mannered shrubs or a wall of ornamental grasses. The birds that live in the ditch will appreciate the enhanced privacy, and you'll get plenty of glimpses of them as they venture out in search of food and nesting materials.

A messy ditch looks like home to bobolinks and other birds that nest on the ground.

Birds of Grassy Meadows

- Bluebird
- Bobolink
- Goldfinch
- Grasshopper sparrow
- Indigo bunting
- Junco
- Meadowlark
- Mourning dove
- Nighthawk
- Ovenbird
- Pheasant
- Red-eyed vireo
- Towhee

Go for a Walk

If you're stumped for ideas about the best bird plants for unusual sites, like a damp meadow or a dry prairie, visit a nearby natural area with hiking trails that traverse a variety of terrains. Look at how grasses, shrubs, vines, and wildflowers grow when left on their own, and mimic the groupings in similar sites in your yard.

EVERYBODY WINS

Rescuing Native Plants

In many areas, members of native plant societies and other gardening groups volunteer to dig and relocate native plants destined to be killed when land is developed for roads, houses, and other buildings. Whenever possible, these plants are relocated to plant preserves, but frequently there are extras to take home. Participating in plant rescues is a great way to learn about native plants and help preserve them while stocking your town and your yard with the plants birds want most.

Plant a Mini Meadow

The word "meadow" often conjures a vision of wide open spaces, but even a small plot packed with seed-producing plants will keep birds busy and look beautiful at the same time. For example, you might:

- **Give a clump of black-eyed Susans a backdrop of 'Purple Majesty' or 'Jester' ornamental millet.** Long after you enjoy the show of bright yellow flowers contrasted with purple spikes of millet seeds, sparrows, juncos, buntings, and other seed eaters will gather the seeds from the faded blossoms or from the ground.
- **Combine purple coneflowers with dwarf native asters and a clump of tall native grass such as big bluestem.** Finches will gather some of the coneflower seeds in early fall, while other seeds will stay safely beneath snow until eaten in early spring.
- **Fill a sunny space with sunflowers, mixing varieties of different sizes and colors.** Invite hummingbirds to the party by allowing cypress vine morning glory (*Ipomoea quamoclit*) to run up some of the sunflowers. Goldfinches and nuthatches will start harvesting sunflower seeds as soon as they ripen, and the show will last for weeks.
- **Edge a partially shady pathway with sea oats or another handsome native grass.** After freezing weather turns the grass into a dry mass of foliage and seeds, it becomes a well-stocked storm shelter for juncos and other small ground feeders.

THE AUTUMN HARVEST

From a bird's point of view, some of the most important plants in your landscape produce fruits in the fall. When days become short in early autumn, migratory species look for high-calorie berries to help them build up the fat reserves they'll need for their long southbound journey. Year-round birds know that several lean months lie ahead, so they often compete with temporary summer residents for fall's bounty of berries.

Don't assume that birds don't like a certain berry because they show no interest in eating it in fall. The berries of some plants (see "Food Plants for Winter" on page 106) become more palatable to birds after they've been subjected to several bouts of freezing weather.

A Dogwood for Every Niche

Dogwoods (*Cornus* spp.) are among the most useful, beautiful, and versatile of bird-friendly plants. All produce fleshy drupes (a type of berry) in fall, which are eagerly gathered by birds. Here are eight great native species that are easy to grow when given an appropriate site.

- **Pagoda dogwood (*C. alternifolia*):** Moist partial shade, Zones 2 to 8, large spreading shrub or small tree
- **Silky dogwood (*C. amomum*):** Moist soil in sun, Zones 4 to 8, medium-size shrub, white berries in early fall
- **Bunchberry (*C. canadensis*):** Moist shade in acid soil, Zones 2 to 7, spreading groundcover, useful in shady rock gardens
- **Flowering dogwood (*C. florida*):** Moist partial shade, Zones 5 to 8, slow-growing small tree, beautiful in all seasons, bears big red berries in fall
- **Brown dogwood (*C. glabrata*):** Moist stream banks in warm, arid climates, Zones 8 to 10, thicket-forming shrub bears fruits in fall
- **Red-osier dogwood (*C. stolonifera*):** Moist soil in sun to partial shade, Zones 2 to 8, clusters of white berries in fall, bare branches color up in late winter
- **Pacific Coast dogwood (*C. nuttallii*):** Fertile soil in sun to partial shade, Zone 9, small tree (20 to 30 feet, or 6 to 9 m), features great fall color and big crops of berries
- **Gray dogwood (*C. racemosa*):** Fertile soil in sun to shade, Zones 5 to 8, thicket-forming shrub turns bright red in fall, produces abundant white berries

Flocks of robins may arrive to feast upon ripening dogwood berries in fall.

Fall-Bearing Fruit Plants for Birds

- Bayberries
- Buffaloberry
- Cotoneasters
- Dogwoods
- Elderberry
- Hollies
- Mountain ash
- Oregon grape holly
- Persimmon
- Sassafras

High-Contrast Berries

Plants that depend on birds to disperse their seeds often produce bright red berries guaranteed to catch a bird's eye. On plants that shed their leaves in winter, it's often the contrast between ripe berries and colorful foliage that calls birds in for a taste. For example, birds can't miss juicy clusters of black elderberries on red stems, displayed against a background of buttery yellow fall foliage. The white berries of red-osier dogwood are irresistible as the plants' leaves turn red and gold in early fall.

3-Day Company

It's been said that company is like fish—after 3 days it starts to smell bad. Migratory birds often provide 3 days of company when they visit your yard during their trip, but it's not because they fear overstaying their welcome nor do they become malodorous. Rather, many birds spend the first day of a stopover feeding lightly as their bodies become accustomed to a new food supply. On the second day they gorge themselves and on the third day they rest up and prepare to be on their way.

Birds That Eat Fall Fruits

- Catbird
- Cedar waxwing
- Chickadees
- Eastern bluebird
- Grosbeaks
- Northern flicker
- Pheasant
- Purple finch
- Quail
- Robins
- Tree swallows
- Warblers
- Wood thrush
- Woodpeckers

Don't Feed the Ducks

If migratory ducks, geese, gulls, or swans stop in at your place, resist the urge to feed them. Doing so may delay their progress or lead to more birds hanging around than you can handle. Besides, traditional "duck food" like old bread and crackers are low in nutrition compared to these big birds' main diet of insects, grasses, and aquatic plants. Worse yet, waterfowl that are frequently fed bread are more likely to swallow dangerous items that look like bread, such as pieces of litter or Styrofoam. In 2003, the state of Rhode Island banned feeding waterfowl.

Food for the Road

Migratory birds burn up plenty of calories as they fly south in fall, so a high-fat diet suits their autumnal needs. Because of their high fat content, dogwood and sassafras berries make especially great flying food.

Collect Dry Berries

The fruits of many winter food plants are dry and leathery, which makes them easy to keep indoors. Gather a few berry-bearing sumac or cedar branches in fall, enjoy them in dry indoor arrangements for several weeks, and put them out for the birds in late winter.

FOOD PLANTS FOR WINTER

You may think sumac or snowberry fruits look ripe by late fall, but birds know better. Freezing and thawing breaks down indigestible compounds in these bitter berries, turning them into late-winter feasts for dozens of species of birds. In addition to those that fly in, often in small flocks, to gather these goodies, ground-feeding birds will get their share by cleaning up fruits that fall to the ground. Any berries left on these plants by winter's end may be harvested overnight when migratory species arrive in early spring.

For many birds of the deep forest that eat insects in summer, winter survival depends upon finding plenty of broken nuts and acorns left behind by other animals, and sometimes bashing nuts open themselves. Following a good nut year, nut-eating birds find plenty of food to scavenge, which often leads to bigger families in spring. By planting native species that produce winter nuts and fruits, you provide crucial winter food and year-round habitat for many flocks and families of birds.

Conserve Conifers

The elegant, long-lived trees known as conifers often qualify as miniature bird sanctuaries all by themselves. Densely needled conifer branches provide great cover when a predator appears, they make wind-resistant nesting sites, and the seeds of conifers are a major food source for crossbills and several other small birds. Conifers come in a huge range of shapes and sizes. Where space is limited, you can substitute dwarf forms of native species of pines, junipers, cedars, and others.

Winter Nut and Fruit Plants for Birds

- American highbush cranberry
- Arborvitae
- Ash
- Bittersweet
- Butternuts
- Cedars
- Crab apples
- Firs
- Junipers
- Maples
- Oaks
- Pines
- Pyracantha
- Snowberry
- Spruces
- Virginia creeper

Birds That Eat Winter Nuts and Berries

- Blue jay
- Brown thrasher
- Catbird
- Cedar waxwing
- Crossbills
- Grosbeaks
- Northern flicker
- Northern mockingbird
- Pheasant
- Turkey
- Woodpeckers

Take a Closer Look

Red Crossbill *(Loxia curvirostra)*

The strong beaks of crossbills cross at the tip, making them easy to distinguish on sight from other finches. Male red crossbills have ruddy red breasts and heads, with blackish wings and a short, notched tail. Usually brick red, males may also wear shades of orange or yellow. Females are olive green to yellowish, with gray wings. The white-winged crossbill has bold white wing bars. Adult birds are 6 to 8 inches (14 to 20 cm) long. Red crossbills are numerous wherever conifer forests are found—in the mountains in California and the western United States, throughout western Canada, and across Canada to the Great Lakes and New England. Crossbills nest near the ground in their preferred habitat, tending three to five greenish-white brown-spotted eggs.

Feeder Favorites for Crossbills

- Pine nuts
- Sunflower seeds
- Conifer cones

Jaws of Life

Instead of using their odd bills to peck, crossbills use them to pry into prickly conifer cones and then flick out the seeds with their tongues. They are such specialists at harvesting conifer seeds that they even feed them to their young. Nomads that wander year-round, crossbills don't run from winter as long as their habitats include plenty of seed-bearing pines, spruces, firs, and hemlocks.

Regional Relations

Similar in size, habit, and range to their red crossbill relatives, white-winged crossbills (*Loxia leucoptera*) are most readily distinguished by the pair of bold white bars on their wings. The white-winged crossbill's beak is smaller than that of the red crossbill, and as a result, it prefers to feed on the smaller cones of conifers such as hemlock and larch.

Tempting Features for Crossbills

- Large seed-bearing conifers are the perfect crossbill version of a bed-and-breakfast.
- Sunflower seeds offered at a tray-type feeder will often catch the attention of crossbills as they travel about in search of seed-bearing trees. At feeders, crossbills are often here today and gone tomorrow.
- Crossbills prefer to spend their time in the deep forest, so they're most likely to visit remote areas of home landscapes.
- Crossbills often take grit and salt from the edges of walkways, driveways, and roads.

Did You Know?

- As long as there's plenty of food available, crossbills will breed and rear young at any time of year, even in winter.
- Crossbills often live together in informal groups, moving in a flock when they need to find a new supply of oil-rich conifer seeds.
- In winter, skiers may be more likely than backyard birders to see crossbills. Snow-covered conifer forests are great places to find crossbills.
- Members of the finch family (Fringillidae), crossbills are related to purple and rosy finches, goldfinches, and evening grosbeaks.

CREATING LANDSCAPE FEATURES FOR BIRDS

For many people, choosing plants they want to grow is easy; it's deciding where to put them that keeps them up at night. But weaving a bird-friendly tapestry of plants that also makes your landscape more appealing to people is simple, because nature has already provided several tried-and-true planting plans. From enriched woodland edges to food-bearing green fences and berry thickets, there are unlimited options for grouping plants so that birds can't help but make use of them, and people can't help but admire them.

In the following pages, you'll discover dozens of ways to arrange plants so that they meet birds' needs, but it's up to you to decide where to begin. If you have a large yard, you may want to work from the outside inward, by planting trees and shrubs along the outer edges of your yard, and leaving open space for bird feeding closer to your house. In a smaller yard, concentrate first on the areas you see most often from your windows, or from your deck or patio.

Incredible Edges

If your yard already includes several trees or large shrubs along one or more of its edges, you're in luck! A woodland edge that borders a sunny, open area is an ideal setup for birdscaping, because you usually can add a layer of bird-friendly shrubs in the partial shade near the trees. Wildflowers and seed-bearing grasses can take over in spots where plenty of sunshine gets through the treetops.

WORKING YOUR PROPERTY LINE

To make good use of all the space you have, you may plan to fill your yard with plants from one end to the other. This approach will be fine by the birds, but might not go over so well with your town, neighborhood, or your neighbors.

- **Stay low under power lines.** Trees that grow too close to power lines may be cut back without your permission. Stick with mound-forming shrubs instead.
- **Plant inside shared property lines.** Avoid conflicts with neighbors by planting trees and shrubs far enough inside your property lines so that they won't encroach on your neighbor's land when they reach mature size.

Sizing Up Green Fences

If you live in a town or city where the height of fences is restricted by local ordinances, it's likely that laws address the size and location of hedges, too. For example, hedges within 10 feet (3 m) of a street or road often must be kept to 30 inches (76 cm) or less so as not to interfere with drivers' ability to see around corners or curves. In your backyard or along the sides of your property, hedges may be subject to the same height restrictions as fences. Take the time to check local ordinances before planting a new hedge, and talk with your neighbors, too. Bigger is better where birds and hedges are concerned, so a wildlife-friendly hedge that spans more than one yard will attract more birds than a short hedge meant to hide your garbage cans from view.

Two Viburnums Are Better Than One

Woodland edges are prime real estate for elegant viburnums, but most of the beautiful viburnums planted in North American yards are descended from Asian ancestors. Yet North America is rich with native species that bear flowers in spring, colorful green foliage that turns bright red or gold in autumn, and berries in fall and winter. When planting native viburnums, include at least two plants of a given species to make sure they pollinate well enough to set heavy clusters of fruit. Viburnums do not come in male and female forms, but having multiple plants can greatly increase berry production.

- **In the East, try arrowwood viburnum (*Viburnum dentatum*) or possumhaw viburnum (*V. nudum*),** both of which are available as named varieties selected for superior color, fruiting, and growth habit.
- **In the West, both western cranberry bush (*V. ellipticum*) and squashberry (*V. edule*)** readily make themselves at home in moist partial shade.

- **Respect setbacks and easements.** In many communities, local laws define front yard "setbacks"—open margins between the street and where you can plant trees or erect buildings. Limit plantings in utility easements to small plants that can easily be replaced if they must be dug up to make repairs to buried cables or pipes.

HEDGES, THICKETS, AND OTHER GREEN FENCES

You can turn your property line into a haven for birds (and the insects they eat) by creating a hedge or thicket of bird-friendly plants. By definition, a hedge is a linear planting made up of a limited number of different types of plants, which is used to define boundaries, exclude intruders, or divide different areas of the landscape. A thicket is a wilder form of green fence that is best suited to larger yards where growing space is not in extremely high demand.

To many people, the word "hedge" brings to mind pruned evergreen hedges that have been used since the Middle Ages and still give structure to spaces in large formal gardens. The gardens of many old European castles include elaborate hedge mazes of boxwood or yew, but a hedge planted for wildlife is much less formal—and needs only a few hours' maintenance each year. In addition to serving as wildlife habitats, hedges and thickets can be situated so that they tame persistent winds and blowing snow, muffle traffic noise, and filter dust from nearby roads. They also can deter unwanted intruders, while providing a pleasing visual backdrop for the rest of the landscape.

Make a Brush Pile for Birds

To a wren or brown thrasher, a loose pile of brush is almost as desirable as a bramble thicket (see page 11). These birds and others will seek temporary shelter from hawks and similar threats in a brush pile.

ANATOMY OF A WILDLIFE HEDGE

At its best, a hedge created to serve birds should be broad at the base and include tall plants whenever possible. If you include a number of different plants, the hedge will have an informal look, whereas limiting yourself to three kinds of plants, set in a repeating pattern, will make the hedge appear more orderly.

For the most appealing results, choose two or three species of native plants that are the right size for your yard, even if this means the hedge itself may be somewhat small. For example, you might combine dwarf junipers with viburnums to create an all-shrub hedge, or opt for a simple tapestry of compact hollies underplanted with strawberries. The three-way combination of mound-forming shrubs, evergreen shrubs, and small trees is hard to beat from a bird's point of view, and you usually can maintain such a grouping simply by pruning out dead or poorly placed branches once each winter.

WORKING WITH BRAMBLES

Thorny raspberries, blackberries, and other brambles grow so well in many climates that they're considered pest plants, but as bramble fruits grow into a thicket, their tangled canes create ideal habitat for many types of birds. Fruit-eating birds like brown thrashers and catbirds often nest in bramble thickets, and many other species eat the juicy, seedy fruit.

Taming Wild Brambles

You won't face aggravation from chiggers and snakes if you bring order to your wild bramble patch in winter, when critters are inactive. Here's how to bring enough order to a wild bramble thicket to create good picking conditions for you, healthy growing conditions for the plants, and great nesting and feeding space for birds.

- **Choose a patch that's easily accessible and not near a busy road.** Roadside picking is dangerous, and roadside berries may carry a heavy dose of pollutants and dust.
- **Dress for the job by wearing thick pants,** a jacket that's unlikely to be snagged or ripped by sharp thorns, and heavy gloves.
- **Use pruning loppers to prune back the tips of young, fruit-bearing canes to 6 to 8 feet (1.8 to 2.4 m).** Young canes of bearing age may be green, pink, or reddish brown, while older canes are dark brown to black. Prune out the old canes at ground level.
- **Sprinkle a balanced organic fertilizer over the plants' root zones,** and then blanket the ground with a 6-inch (15 cm)-deep mulch of leaves, straw, or other organic material. Also mow and mulch the perimeter path you'll use when picking your crop.
- **In spring, control the plants' spread by lopping off the sprouts that appear out of bounds.** A swing blade will slice down unwanted canes and accompanying weeds in one swipe.
- **Pick the berries you can reach** and leave those in remote sections of the thicket for birds.
- **After the berries finish ripening, prune out dead canes and pinch back the tips of the longest new canes of erect varieties.** Fertilize and mulch the patch again. Do a bit more cleaning up in winter to remove dead canes you missed and you'll have a self-perpetuating berry patch.

Berry-Bearing Brambles

Black raspberries (*Rubus occidentalis*) are native to North America, and the birds know it! "Blackcaps" are birds' favorites, in part because birds have no trouble pulling the berries from the plants. You'll need to use bird netting or wedding net to cover branches you want to harvest yourself.

Red raspberries (*R. idaeus* and other species) are easy to grow and less attractive to birds than black raspberries, so there's less competition for the harvest. Summer-bearing varieties produce in early summer, while 'Heritage' and other primocane (first-year growth) varieties that are pruned back in winter will bear their berries in fall.

Yellow raspberries (*Rubus* hybrids) are grown like red raspberries. Many gardeners find that birds leave yellow-fruited raspberries alone, which increases their value in the garden but limits their usefulness as wildlife plants.

Blackberries (*Rubus* spp.) include dozens of native and introduced species, and blackberry or dewberry patches usually produce enough berries for birds and people to share. Thornless varieties such as 'Navaho' and 'Triple Crown' are more gardener-friendly than thorny strains and can easily be grown tethered to a pillar in a small yard.

You don't have to turn your yard into a prickly obstacle course to avail yourself and birds of the benefits of these plants. Instead, use brambles to cover fences or grow them on a fixed trellis or pillar. See "Taming Wild Brambles" on the opposite page, for tips on sharing your landscape with a wild patch of bramble fruits.

Birds in the Bramble Patch

These birds use bramble thickets for food, cover, or nesting sites.

Bluebirds	Jays
Cardinals	Pheasant
Catbirds	Tanagers
Flickers	Thrushes
Grosbeaks	Towhees
Grouse	Woodpeckers

Bird-Friendly Mulches

If the base of a hedge is not planted with bunchberries, strawberries, or some other groundcover plant, keep it mulched year-round with shredded leaves, grass clippings, or another organic mulch generated in your yard. The mulch will deter weeds and help retain soil moisture, and give ground-feeding birds fertile space for scratching for insects and seeds.

EVERYBODY WINS

Be a Messy Picker

As you gather blackberries for cobbler or jelly, don't worry about dropping a few fruits. Small birds that are not able to snap up whole berries will peck up those that shatter as they fall, and ground-feeding birds will find their dinner underfoot—right where they want it.

FENCEROWS AND HEDGEROWS

North America is crisscrossed with fences, particularly barbed wire and livestock fencing intended to keep large animals in their pastures. When wild plants grow to cover such a fence, the result is called a fencerow or hedgerow, and a managed fencerow can be an amazing habitat for birds. The biggest challenge for a fencerow's keeper is to monitor the site for invasive plants, which are a constant threat in fencerows along roads (cars and trucks are not as efficient at dispersing seeds as are birds, but they often do spread seeds from one place to another). If allowed to grow, invasive plants such as Japanese honeysuckle, multiflora rose, privet, kudzu, and bindweed have no trouble overtaking slower-growing native species. As soon as you spot an invasive plant in a fencerow, use pruning loppers to cut it off at the soil line.

The Coppice Option

For thousands of years, English gardeners have used slender stems gathered from willows and hazels to weave wattle fences. To ensure a steady supply, these plants were grown in special plots that were cut back to the ground, or coppiced, every 2 or 3 years. Wildlife hedges that become unruly can be handled the same way. When cut back to the ground in winter, most hedge plants waste no time staging a strong comeback first thing in spring. The first year after they're cut back, young stems of red-osier dogwood and purple willow show beautiful late-winter color, and you can even harvest some of the stems for use in craft projects.

GIVE CHAIN-LINK FENCING A MAKEOVER

Chain-link fencing is affordable and hard to beat for retaining pets and kids, but it falls short in the looks department and is of little use to birds. You can help chain-link blend in with its surroundings by painting it dark green (in sun) or black (in shade). Then put the fence to work as a trellis for annual vines or plant zinnias at its base. Over time, you can hide the fence from view completely by planting its base with bird-friendly vines, shrubs, and groundcover plants.

Historical Hedgebanks

As sheep farming came to the English countryside in the late 1500s, parliament passed a series of Enclosure Acts that authorized landowners to plant dense hedges to fence off their land. Many of these were "hedgebanks"—hedges planted on the banks of streams, often by mixing seeds of oak, hawthorn, and ash in a straw rope that was buried in the ground. As the hedge plants grew, the enclosed space became enforceable as private property, which was quite unpopular among the common folks because it placed new limits on where they could keep their gardens and livestock. Yet these hedges became quite popular with songbirds, particularly hedges that included berry-bearing hawthorn trees. Today, many of these 500-year-old hedgebanks are being restored because they have been found to make such excellent habitat for birds.

Take a Closer Look

Catbird *(Dumetella carolinensis)*

Male and female catbirds are slate gray with black caps and have a chestnut patch beneath their tails. These vocal birds often imitate the sounds made by other birds and animals, with their unique addition of drawn-out "meow" sounds. Thicket dwellers by nature, catbirds are often heard long before they're seen. Adult birds are 8 to 9 inches (20 to 22 cm) long. Female birds incubate four to six blue-green eggs; both parents share the task of bringing food to their hatchlings.

Feeder Favorites for Catbirds

- Dried or fresh fruit, especially raisins and soft berries
- Suet
- Peanut pieces, scattered on the ground

Regional Relations

The catbird shares much of its range with another famous imitator, the northern mockingbird (see "Take a Closer Look" on page 297). The catbird is smaller, lacks white wing bars, and always wears its distinctive dark cap. Catbirds are far less territorial than mockingbirds. They typically fly southward in September and return to their northern breeding grounds across most of the United States in May.

Tempting Features for Catbirds

- Berry-bearing native trees including serviceberry, hawthorns, persimmons, and black cherry are catbird favorites.
- Berry-bearing native shrubs including wax myrtle, blackberry, and blueberry provide both food and nesting sites for catbirds.
- A blanket of mulch beneath shrubs and trees makes an ideal feeding ground for catbirds in search of ground-dwelling insects.
- Catbirds build cup-shaped nests in dense bushes. As she works, the female may change her mind and abandon a partially-finished nest in favor of a better location.
- Catbirds love water. Put a birdbath near a patch of brambles or a dense hedge and these somewhat secretive birds will emerge to drink and bathe.

Did You Know?

- In summer, catbirds eat thousands of insects, including caterpillars, ants, cicadas, dragonflies, and even termites.
- As catbirds migrate back and forth from Florida, the Gulf Coast, and Central America, they usually fly at night.
- Catbirds are quite shy and are most likely to feed on the ground late in the day, when few other birds are active.
- Should a catbird discover a cowbird egg in its nest, it may add a second story to its home, laying a new clutch of eggs in the new nest atop the old one (killing the first clutch along with the alien egg).
- Catbirds have been known to nurture orphaned broods of northern cardinals.

Watching Catbirds

If you watch a pair of catbirds coming and going as they build their nest deep in a shrub or thicket, your best view of their family life may be on the ground. Quietly spread a dark-colored towel or blanket on the ground and lie on it so you can look up into the bush. Catbirds become unusually quiet when the female is incubating a clutch of eggs, but become more vocal as they raise their young. If you come near to a bush where fledglings are hopping about testing their wings, the parents may hop close and warn you to stay away with their mewling calls.

LIFE IN THE GREEN LANE

In the language of wildlife-friendly landscaping, a green lane is comprised of two parallel hedges or hedgerows with an open lane between them. The lane might be a gravel driveway, a seldom-used dirt road, or a wide path that meanders through your backyard. When both sides are flanked by bird-friendly hedges, thickets, or a mixed shrub border and the interior surface is unpaved, a green lane is second only to a woodland edge when it comes to providing great habitat for birds. Birds have little talent for filling out questionnaires, but it's believed that the combination of open feeding space and dense cover is what makes green lanes so irresistible to birds.

You may not have room for a green lane inside your yard, but how about sharing one with your neighbor? Instead of sharing a fence or hedge, agree to leave a 5-foot (1.5 m)-wide walking space down the property line and flank it on both sides with boundary plantings of native shrubs and trees.

Greenbrier Can Be Good

The bane of gardeners who seek to enrich a woodland edge, thorny greenbrier (*Smilax* spp.) sneaks into shrubs and perennial plantings—and *stays*. The vines quickly regrow from root buds after stems are cut back to the ground, so you might just as easily train the vine to grow up a small tree or shrub, where you won't be injured by its thorny stems. Over 40 species of songbirds and woodpeckers eat black greenbrier berries. If you live in the Southeast, you can grow the thornless species commonly called Jackson vine (*S. smallii*) that graces many old porches. In other regions, forgive greenbrier its thorns long enough to make a mature vine available to your feathered friends.

WANT A WILDLIFE MAZE?

Many gardeners dream of creating a path flanked by a tapestry of fragrant flowers, handsome shrubs, and winsome ornamental grasses that leads to a private hideaway beneath the branches of a muscular tree. It's possible that birds dream the same dream, because songbirds reach maximum occupancy rates in exactly such a landscape. Your maze might be as simple as a curved path to a bench in the shade, or maybe you have room for something more dramatic—perhaps a small platform lawn (or moss lawn) surrounded on three sides by flowers, shrubs, and trees. As birds move about in the open area they'll be easy to watch, especially if you stay still in a quiet corner. You'll also get to know the feeling that you're the one being watched, because birds rule in enhanced habitats like wildlife mazes and green lanes. Expect to be fussed at when nearby nests are holding hatchlings. Curious hummers will check you out if you stand still long enough on a summer day.

TRIUMPHANT TRANSPLANTING

To keep your birdscape evolving at a steady pace, you'll need to add (and sometimes subtract) plants as the seasons pass. Successful transplanting involves good timing, sound techniques, and a generous attitude toward first-year watering.

Timing

As a general rule, spring is the best time to set out deciduous shrubs and trees, as well as hardy perennial flowers and grasses. As these plants emerge from their winter rest and grow new leaves and stems above the ground, a similar growth spurt takes place in their roots. When in doubt, set out new plants just as they're entering their most active phase of growth.

Many container-grown plants also can be set out in late spring and summer, provided the roots are not disturbed and are kept moist before and after transplanting.

Evergreens make most of their new growth from spring to early summer, but because they conduct photosynthesis year-round, they also can be transplanted in fall.

Techniques

Plants are built to stay in one place as opposed to moving around, so do everything you can to prevent transplanting trauma. Rather than pulling and twisting plants from their containers, place the watered pots on their sides and strike them several times to loosen the roots from the pot. Jiggle the plant out and promptly set it in its planting hole. Plant it slightly higher than it grew in its pot to allow room for a blanket of mulch.

Native plants do not require extensive soil preparation. Remove rocks and roots as you dig a planting hole slightly deeper than and twice as wide as the pot. You can add compost or organic matter to the soil as you backfill around the rootball, but do not use fertilizer.

After the plant shows new growth, you can applaud its efforts by sprinkling a light application of a balanced organic fertilizer over its root zone.

Water

Even drought-tolerant native plants usually need supplemental water during their first year. For the first 2 to 3 months after planting, water as needed to keep the soil from drying out completely. In the second year, provide water during serious droughts.

Only newly planted evergreens should need water in winter.

A mulch of pine needles, shredded leaves, or other organic material will go a long way toward conserving water.

Biomass Plants for Birds

Among the most renewable energy sources are biomass plants, which are grown for the purpose of burning in coal-fired power plants. When combined with coal, biomass plants such as baled switchgrass and dried, chipped willow stems give a cleaner burn resulting in reduced airborne emissions.

In New York and Oregon, willows grown for biomass have proven particularly attractive to birds. The willows are allowed to grow for 3 years and then cut back to the ground, after which they quickly regrow. Dozens of bird species use the willow branches as nesting sites, so growers are careful to harvest alternate rows in any given year, insuring thick, hospitable stands for songbirds.

80 FINE PLANTS FOR BIRDS

The plants listed here will get you started making your yard more beautiful—and irresistible to birds. Most of them are native to North America and may be easier to find at native plant nurseries than at garden centers. As you shop for plants, carefully read the plant tags, which offer important information on the plant's mature size and planting techniques needed to get it off to a good start.

The zone numbers refer to the USDA Plant Hardiness Zone Map as shown on page 356. The letters after the zone numbers stand for North (N), South (S), East (E), and West (W). Many of the plants listed here will grow in a wide geographical area, but those that are native to the high-rainfall areas of the East will struggle to grow in the dry climates of the West and viceversa. Whenever you can, stick with species that are native to your area.

Evergreen Trees

Cedar, eastern red (*Juniperus virginiana*): Zones 2-9; N, E, S

Firs (*Abies* spp.): Zones 3-9; all regions

Hemlock, eastern (*Tsuga canadensis*): Zones 3-7; all regions

Pines (*Pinus* spp.): Zones 3-8; all regions

Spruce, Colorado (*Picea pungens*): Zones 2-7; N, E, W

Deciduous Trees

Ashes (*Fraxinus* spp.): Zones 3-9; all regions

Ash, mountain (*Sorbus americana*): Zones 2-5; N, E

Bald cypress (*Taxodium distichum*): Zones 4-9; S, E, N

Host an "Official" Habitat

Once you begin to transform your yard into a paradise for birds, butterflies, and other wildlife, you should think about making the change official. The National Wildlife Federation's Backyard Wildlife Habitat Certification Program lets you register your yard as one of their certified habitats. You can even order a plaque to put out in your yard!

Check out their program online at www.nwf.org/backyard, which walks you through all the steps you need to make your yard wildlife (and environmentally) friendly. More than 70,000 yards across America have already been certified. Registration costs $15 and includes membership in the National Wildlife Federation (including a year's subscription to *National Wildlife* magazine), a certificate recognizing your yard as a certified Backyard Wildlife Habitat, and a subscription to their online quarterly newsletter, *Habitats*, which provides tips on how to make your yard more attractive to wildlife.

Chokecherry (*Prunus virginiana*): Zones 2-7; N, S, E

Crab apples (*Malus* spp.): Zones 4-8; all regions

Dogwood, flowering (*Cornus florida*): Zones 5-8; all regions

Dogwood, mountain (*C. nuttallii*): Zones 8-9; W

Hawthorns (*Crataegus* spp.): Zones 3-8; all regions

Larches (*Larix* spp.): Zones 4-9; W, N

Maples (*Acer* spp.): Zones 3-9; all regions

Mesquite (*Prosopis velutina*): Zones 8-10; W

Mulberry (*Morus rubra*): Zones 5-9; all regions

Oaks (*Quercus* spp.): Zones 3-9; all regions

Persimmons (*Diospyros* spp.): Zones 4-9; all regions

Plum (*Prunus americana*): Zones 4-8; all regions

Sassafras (*Sassafras albidum*): Zones 4-8; all regions

Serviceberry, downy (*Amelanchier arborea*): Zones 3-7; N, E

Serviceberry, Pacific (*A. florida*): Zones 4-9; N, E, W

Willow, desert (*Chilopsis linearis*): Zones 8-10; W

Evergreen Shrubs

Arborvitae (*Thuja occidentalis*): Zones 2-7; all regions

Bayberry (*Myrica pensylvanica*): Zones 3-7; N, S, E

Cotoneasters (*Cotoneaster* spp.): Zones 5-8; all regions

Grape holly, Oregon (*Mahonia aquifolium*): Zones 4-8; all regions

Hollies (*Ilex* spp.): Zones 4-9; all regions

Junipers (*Juniperus* spp.): Zones 2-9; all regions

Myrtle, Pacific wax (*Myrica californica*): Zones 7-9; W

Deciduous Shrubs

Blueberries (*Vaccinium* spp.): Zones 2-9; all regions

Buffaloberry (*Shepherdia argentea*): Zones 2-6; N, E, W

Bunchberry (*Cornus canadensis*): Zones 2-7; N, S, E

Cranberry, American highbush (*Viburnum trilobum*): Zones 2-7; N, E, W

Cranberry, western (*Viburnum ellipticum*): Zones 6-8; W

Chicago's Magic Hedge

Many bird-watchers in the Great Lakes region have heard of the Magic Hedge—a 150-yard-long tangle of shrubs and trees that stretches out into Lake Michigan where up to 300 species of birds have been identified. Initially planted with honeysuckle, the Magic Hedge now includes viburnums, serviceberries, sumacs, and other plants that provide food and shelter for migratory birds that follow Lake Michigan's long shoreline as they fly north in spring and south in fall.

Currant, clove (*Ribes odoratum*): Zones 4-7; N, E

Currant, flowering (*R. sanguineum*): Zones 4-7; N, E, W

Currant, golden (*R. aureum*): Zones 3-7; N, E, W

Dogwood, brown (*Cornus glabrata*): Zones 8-10; W

Dogwood, gray (*C. racemosa*): Zones 5-8; all regions

Dogwood, pagoda (*C. alternifolia*): Zones 2-8; all regions

Dogwood, red-osier (*C. stolonifera*): Zones 2-8; all regions

Dogwood, silky (*C. amomum*): Zones 4-8; all regions

Elderberries (*Sambucus* spp.): Zones 3-9; N, S, E

Elderberry, blue (*S. caerulea*): Zones 6-9; N, W

Holly, California (*Heteromeles arbutifolia*): Zones 7-9; W

Holly, winterberry (*Ilex verticillata*): Zones 3-9; N, W, E

Try Thimbleberries

Migratory birds in particular are attracted to raspberry-like thimbleberry fruits. The 2- to 4-foot-tall (0.4 to 0.9 m) shrubs thrive in beds that get partial shade. In the West, white-flowered western thimbleberry (*Rubus parviflorus*) is easy to find in native plant nurseries. In the East, look for purple-flowered thimbleberry (*R. odoratus*) when selecting bird-friendly plants.

Juneberry (*Amelanchier alnifolia*): Zones 3-7; W, N, S

Pyracantha (*Pyracantha coccinea*): Zones 5-8; all regions

Quailbush (*Atriplex lentiformis*): Zones 6-8; W

Serviceberry, Pacific (*Amelanchier florida*): Zones 2-7; W, N

Serviceberry, running (*A. stolonifera*): Zones 5-8; W, E, S

Serviceberry, smooth (*A. laevis*): Zones 4-9; E, S

Snowberry (*Symphoricarpos* spp.): Zones 3-7; N, E, W

Spicebush (*Lindera benzoin*): Zones 4-9; all regions

Squashberry (*Viburnum edule*): Zones 2-6; N, W, E

Sumac, smooth (*Rhus glabra*): Zones 2-9; all regions

Sumac, staghorn (*R. typhina*): Zones 3-8; all regions

Thimbleberry, purple-flowered (*Rubus odoratus*): Zones 5-8; all regions

Thimbleberry, western (*R. parviflorus*): Zones 7-9; W

Viburnum, arrowwood (*Viburnum dendatum*): Zones 2-8; all regions

Viburnum, possumhaw (*V. nudum*): Zones 6-9; E, S

BUDGET-WISE BIRDING

Straggly Spring Potpourri

As birds end their northward migrations in spring, they often feed on withered flowers left on the ground since the previous fall. Why not give them more of what they want? As you clean up your flower garden after winter's first freeze, bundle up dry bud-bearing stems and pack them away in a cardboard box kept in a cold place. In spring, scatter the stems on tray feeders, or simply place them on the ground and watch the birds glean them for seeds and insects.

Deciduous Vines and Brambles

Bittersweet (*Celastrus scandens*)**:** Zones 3-8; all regions

Blackberries (*Rubus* spp.)**:** Zones 5-9; all regions

Grapes (*Vitis* spp.)**:** Zones 4-9; all regions

Honeysuckle, coral (*Lonicera sempervirens*)**:** Zones 4-9; all regions

Honeysuckle, desert (*Anisacanthus therberi*)**:** Zones 8-10; W

Raspberries, black (*Rubus occidentalis*)**:** Zones 5-7; N, E

Raspberries, red or yellow (*R. idaeus*)**:** Zones 4-8; all regions

Trumpet vine (*Campsis radicans*)**:** Zones 3-9; N, S, E

Virginia creeper (*Parthenocissus quinquefolia*)**:** Zones 6-9; all regions

Flowers and Grasses

Bachelor's button (*Centaurea cyanus*)**:** annual; all zones and regions

Black-eyed Susans (*Rudbeckia* spp.)**:** Zones 3-9; all regions

Coreopsis (*Coreopsis* spp.)**:** annual and perennial; all zones and regions

Goldenrods (*Solidago* spp.)**:** Zones 3-8; all regions

Jewelweed (*Impatiens capensis*)**:** annual; all zones; N, S, E

Little bluestem (*Schizachyrium scoparium*)**:** Zones 5-9; all regions

Prairie dropseed (*Sporobolus heterolepsis*)**:** Zones 3-9; all regions

Purple coneflower (*Echinacea purpurea*)**:** Zones 3-9; all regions

Sea oats (*Chasmanthium latifolium*)**:** Zones 4-9; all regions

Sunflowers (*Helianthus* spp.)**:** annual and perennial; all zones and regions

CHAPTER 4

SHARING YOUR GARDEN WITH BUG-EATING BIRDS

A feeder stocked with seeds will give you a front-row seat for watching finches and other seed eaters, but when you share your garden with bug-eating birds, the best bird-watching seat in the house is far from the chaos of the feeding station. As a general rule, birds that eat insects have little interest in feeders during summer, when there are plenty of bugs to catch. Before the food supply dwindles at summer's end, many bug eaters take to the air to migrate thousands of miles southward. Only those equipped to peck or pry out insects hiding in bark crevices stick around through the cold winter months.

In this chapter, you'll meet more than a dozen birds whose summer diets consist of insects and other live prey like slugs, spiders, and salamanders. From nighthawks that nest on gravel rooftops in the city to flycatchers of the deep forest, insect-eating birds can be found in a huge range of habitats. Your yard is one such habitat, and having plenty of insect-eating birds around means there will be fewer creepy critters eating your plants. Best of all, bug-eating birds eat ants, flies, gnats, mosquitoes, and other insects that bug people, so your birds help make the garden more comfortable for you.

THE IMPORTANCE OF BUG-EATING BIRDS

Of nearly 9,000 species of birds, about 60 percent include insects in their diets. This makes perfect sense when you consider the fact that both birds and insects are able to fly, so they form an airborne community of hunter and hunted that's all their own. In most healthy ecosystems, birds consume about 40 percent of the insects present in an average season. When the ecosystem in question is your yard, a healthy bird population can make the difference between plants that have few pest problems and a garden that seems to go from one pest crisis to another.

Birds specialize in the kinds of insects they prefer and often have body parts built for harvesting them. Woodpeckers and nuthatches have strong talons that help them cling to tree trunks as they forage for food, while brown thrashers' feet are better suited to riffling through moist mulch. Nighthawks can gather loads of insects in their huge mouths during their evening hunts, and various flycatchers use cat-and-mouse hunting techniques to glean spiders, caterpillars, or ants from shrubs and low tree branches. Taken together, insect-eating birds are a remarkably efficient cleanup crew. Without them, naturally balanced ecosystems can't exist.

EVERYBODY WINS

Stay or Go?

Insect-eating birds can be sorted into those that stay in their territories year-round, those that commute a few hundred miles between the North and South, and neotropical migrants—species that spend winter thousands of miles from their summer breeding grounds.

Year-Round Resident Insect Eaters

Chickadees	Titmice
Nuthatches	Woodpeckers

Short-Distance Migrant Insect Eaters

Brown thrasher	Northern mockingbird
Eastern bluebird	Robin
Eastern phoebe	Towhee

Neotropical Migrant Insect Eaters

Flycatchers	Tanagers
Hummingbirds	Vireos
Kingbirds	Warblers
Nighthawks	Wood thrush
Swallows	

THE CHALLENGES OF GETTING CLOSE

Except for woodpeckers, nuthatches, and other insect eaters that also like nuts, bug-eating birds aren't seen at feeders often enough to get to know them. Serious nature photographers use live mealworms (a beetle larvae cultivated as fish bait) to entice insect-eating birds into camera range, which often takes place in the bird's habitat rather than the photographer's. Mealworms are always worth a try, and you can grow them yourself (see "Grow Your Own Mealworms" on page 142). In addition, try these three tried-and-true strategies.

A Double Dose of Diversity

Many insects undergo metamorphosis, changing from eggs to larvae to pupae to adults. This diversity of form increases the diversity of bug-eating birds' food supply—and enhances birds' value as pest controllers. For example, a vireo might not find a flying moth particularly attractive, yet it will gobble up the same insect in its larval caterpillar form. The same species of moth might meet its end as a pupa, scratched up by a foraging wood thrush. Or if it were found fluttering around a light at nightfall, it might become a nighthawk's evening appetizer.

1. **Watch for nesting pairs.** Most insect eaters are quite territorial during breeding season, so don't expect to see more than one nesting pair of kingbirds, flycatchers, or brown thrashers. Keep field glasses handy to watch for these birds feeding in nearby trees and shrubs.
2. **Learn familiar songs.** Several bug eaters are among the most melodious of singers. The wood thrush has the voice of a four-note flute, the flycatcher's song comes through as a piercing whistled tune, and the red-eyed vireo sounds like it's asking and then answering the same three-word question over and over. Check your local library for recordings—the fastest way to expand your repertoire of bird songs is to listen to them.
3. **Track migration patterns.** After their first year, birds follow similar migration patterns for the rest of their lives. Most species stop to feed along the way, so if you do see visiting migrants in your yard one year, you're likely to see them again in future seasons. Coastal, mountain, and wetland areas are the most heavily used stopover sites. Like high-end hotels, these preferred rest stops come with plenty of gourmet food, fresh water, and dense vegetation for a peaceful period of rest.

Don't be alarmed by a rustle in your hedgerow: Secretive brown thrashers forage for insects by picking through moist mulch and leaf litter. Hidden by sheltering branches while they hunt, these large birds are often heard rather than seen.

Support Land Preservation

In your own area, get behind efforts to create large, connected tracts of conservation land. Many bug-eating birds are seriously challenged by the parasitic egg-laying practice of brown-headed cowbirds (see page 327) when the bug eaters nest along the edges of forests. Deeper inside a large tract of wild land, cowbirds rarely sabotage the same species' nests.

YEAR-ROUND RESIDENT BUG EATERS

Along with year-round birds that eat seeds, several bug eaters stick around in cold winter weather. To survive, they switch to a mixed diet of fruits, nuts, and whatever insects they can find. Shrubs and trees serve up all three courses, although in winter insects tend to be in short supply. Short-distance migrants (see page 122) simply move far enough south to be sure they'll find a few insects during mild breaks in the weather, while better-equipped nuthatches, titmice, and chickadees settle in to spend the cold months gleaning overwintering insects from the bark of trees. Most woodpeckers stick around in winter, too, pecking out hidden caches of borers, beetles, and other insects that inhabit dead wood.

Handyman Nuthatches

When bugs are hard to find, nuthatches have been observed using pieces of bark as tools in their search. Holding a piece in its beak, a nuthatch inserts it into a bark crevice to pry away loose bark to get at the insects hiding underneath. Nuthatches also use their beaks as brooms, sweeping their nest area with the bodies of beetles and other pungent insects, perhaps to deter squirrels or other predators.

Adept at climbing, nuthatches scour tree trunks and branches for insects tucked into nooks and crannies in the bark.

TREE GLEANERS AT YOUR SERVICE

Numbers of important tree pests such as spruce budworms and gypsy moths vary from year to year, and so do populations of bug-eating birds. When a food supply becomes available, bird populations increase rapidly and then decline after most of the insects have been eaten. Neotropical migrant species (see page 122) do extensive gleaning of insects from leaves and stems in summer, but from fall to spring the gleaning of codling moth larvae, pine beetles, and other tree pests is done by year-round residents. Although small trees may have more insects for bark gleaners to find, birds generally prefer to feed on larger trees.

COMING DOWN THE MOUNTAIN

Most migratory birds travel north in summer and south in winter, but a few year-round birds migrate vertically, by moving from high elevations to valleys. Chickadees, juncos, and grosbeaks often migrate vertically, as do mountain quail and grouse, which make most of their journey on foot rather than on the wing.

Take a Closer Look

White-Breasted Nuthatch *(Sitta carolinensis)*

Small, elegant-looking slate gray birds with white underparts and black crowns, white-breasted nuthatches are easily identified by their ability to climb *down* a tree trunk, head toward the ground. Males and females look alike. Stocky adult nuthatches are less than 6 inches (15 cm) long. The female nuthatch incubates a clutch of four to ten creamy white eggs with red-brown spots, sitting on a nest of bark, grass, twigs, feathers, and hair built within a cavity or nest box. The male brings her food.

Feeder Favorites for Nuthatches

- Sunflower seed
- Suet
- Raw peanuts
- Peanut butter

Regional Relations

Three other nuthatches are native to North America, though they seldom make appearances at feeders. The red-breasted nuthatch (*Sitta canadensis*) lives and feeds in cold-climate conifer forests, while the brown-headed nuthatch (*S. pusilla*) lives in dry pine forests of the South. In the West, the tiny pygmy nuthatch (*S. pygmaea*) can be found in forests dominated by ponderosa pine.

Tempting Features and Treats for Nuthatches

- Nuthatches nest in tree cavities and may inhabit the same nest site for several seasons. If a dead tree is not available, they will accept nesting boxes built for wrens or bluebirds.
- Suet feeders that hang from tree limbs are more likely to be visited by nuthatches than feeders placed in an open site.
- Pinecones rolled in peanut butter mixtures (see page 13) and hung from tree branches are sure to get the attention of hungry nuthatches.

Did You Know?

- Nuthatches feed exclusively on insects in summer, but in winter switch to a seed-based diet.
- Going headfirst down a tree trunk may help nuthatches spot hidden insects that other birds have missed.
- Bowser beware! In gathering nest-lining materials, a nuthatch may help itself to some hair of the dog—literally—and may do so by grabbing a beak-full directly from a slumbering pet.
- Curved claws and strong hind toes help nuthatches cling to tree trunks. They use their sharp beaks to gather insects from bark crevices, gather caterpillars from leaves, and sometimes pluck up weevils and other small insects found on the ground.
- If hand feeding birds is your goal, you'll soon get to know the nuthatch. These relatively tame birds quickly adjust to human activity around the feeder and can be tempted to alight on your palm in exchange for pieces of peanuts or other nuts.
- Nuthatches have large families, often laying eight or more eggs. In early fall, small flocks seen feeding together may be family groups.
- Thinking ahead, nuthatches sometime stash acorns in bark crevices, then return to get them when food is scarce.
- When dining on nuts or seeds, a nuthatch wedges its food into a crack and uses its sharp beak to hammer the food into bite-size bits.

Take a Closer Look

Woodpeckers *(Picoides* spp. and *Melanerpes* spp.*)*

Downy woodpecker

Red-headed woodpecker

Of the 25 woodpecker species native to North America, most are year-round residents of forests and wooded neighborhoods. A few, such as the sparrow-size downy woodpecker, do migrate southward in winter, but larger woodpeckers stick around to defend their territory season after season.

Woodpecker size and markings vary with species, but all are basically black-and-white birds with some type of red marking. From smallest to largest, five of the most commonly seen species include:

Downy woodpeckers (*Picoides pubescens*) are small black-and-white woodpeckers found from Alaska to Florida. Males have a small red patch on the back of their heads. Growing 6 to 7 inches (14 to 17 cm) long, downy woodpeckers gather insects from weeds when they're not feeding in trees.

Hairy woodpeckers (*P. villosus*) look like larger versions of the downies and occupy much of the same range. Black-and-white with only a small red patch on the back of the males' heads, hairy woodpeckers grow 7 to 10 inches (18 to 26 cm) long.

Red-headed woodpeckers (*Melanerpes erythrocephalus*) live year-round in the South and East, and some birds move to the Great Lakes region to breed. Males and females have bright red heads, white chests, and black wings barred with white. This species grows to 9 inches (24 cm) long and must have dead trees in which to nest. In addition to insects, the red-headed woodpecker eats many types of nuts, seeds, and berries.

Red-bellied woodpeckers (*M. carolinus*) actually have but a faint rose blush on their bellies, but they're easily identified by their zebralike black-and-white wing bars and orange-red head stripes. Seen east of the Rocky Mountains, red-bellied woodpeckers grow to be about 9 inches (24 cm) long.

Pileated woodpeckers (*Dryocopus pileatus*) are the largest of North American species, growing 16 to 19 inches (40 to 49 cm) long. Their showy red crests atop crow-size black bodies with a few white markings make them easy to identify.

Feeder Favorites for Woodpeckers

- Suet
- Peanut butter mixtures (see page 75)
- Sunflower seeds
- Shelled peanuts
- Apple pieces

Tempting Features and Treats for Woodpeckers

- A large dead tree, at least 20 feet (6 m) tall and 18 inches (46 cm) in diameter, is a rare treasure that woodpeckers will use for roosting, nesting, and gathering food.
- Berry-bearing shrub groups that include viburnums, elderberries, or sumac may be visited by woodpeckers in late fall.
- Woodpeckers love to drum on resonant objects during nesting season, from spring through early summer. To a drumming woodpecker, a hollow section of metal downspout attached to a wood post and painted dark brown may sound like the best "tree" in the neighborhood.
- Wire suet feeders provide good places for woodpeckers to hang onto with their strong claws.

Did You Know?

- Mated pairs often call to one another as they feed, or they may let their mate know where they are by drumming on a hard tree.
- Woodpeckers often have large territories, which they keep secure by checking their roosting holes for intruders several times a day.
- Hatchling woodpeckers are fed a diet of regurgitated insects by their attentive parents.
- In fall, woodpeckers often stash away acorns and other nuts in small holes in trees. The birds return to get them when food becomes scarce.

SHORT-DISTANCE MIGRANTS

Several familiar birds that eat insects in summer switch to a fruit and seed diet in winter, making it easy for them to remain in North America through the winter months. But unlike species that maintain year-round territories, many other birds abandon summer homes in the North in favor of winter homes in the South. This short-distance migration makes for great bird-watching where winters are mild, yet puts pressure on resident birds that suddenly find their territories occupied by winter visitors. The availability of winter habitat and food is therefore crucial for these birds, especially species such as towhees and brown thrashers that prefer the cover of dense thickets.

THE EARLY-BIRD ADVANTAGE

The early bird may catch the worm, and another advantage of short-distance migration is getting a good choice of nesting sites come spring. Most short-distance migrants begin moving back north in late winter, often appearing unexpectedly during the first mild spells of spring. As the soil thaws, they're able to begin gathering insects, seeds, and fallen fruits. Most pair up and begin building a nest by the end of April, when neotropical species are just getting in from their longer flights.

THE BIRD-SPIDER CONNECTION

Insect-eating birds that feed on the ground harvest thousands of beetles and other small bugs, and they seldom pass up spiders, as well. But spiders mean more than food to many birds. Vireos, hummingbirds, wrens, and woodpeckers have been seen taking a feeding shortcut by plucking old insects from abandoned spiderwebs, and some naturalists think that the patterns within large webs spun by orb spiders and writing spiders are intended to keep birds from flying through them. In spring, numerous birds use spiderwebs to help weave their nests together. Hummingbird nests often include a large amount of webbing, whereas larger birds like turkey vultures use only enough spiderwebs to bind their nest materials together.

Real-Life Snowbirds

These birds move south in winter, but most remain on American soil. Migration distances vary from no movement (in the South) to less than 600 miles.

- American robin, page 278
- Brown thrasher, page 128
- Eastern bluebird, page 156
- Eastern phoebe
- Eastern towhees, page 129
- Northern mockingbird, page 297

Take a Closer Look

Brown Thrasher *(Toxostoma rufum)*

Larger than thrushes or even robins, both male and female brown thrashers have yellow eyes, cinnamon-brown backs and wings, two white wing bars, and white breasts streaked and spotted with brown. Their long legs make them look tall. Adult birds are 11½ inches (29 cm) long. Brown thrashers range across eastern North America to the Rocky Mountains and from Florida and Texas to southern Canada, but are most often seen in the Plains. Thrashers lay two to six blue- or green-tinted whitish eggs with red-brown spots in low-lying nests made of grass, twigs, and dry leaves. Both parents sit on the nest, although the female typically spends more time incubating the eggs.

Feeder Favorites for Brown Thrashers

- Suet
- Shelled peanuts
- Cornbread
- Raisins
- Dried berries

Regional Relations

Several western thrasher species require specific native plant habitats, so they seldom move outside small geographic areas. The California thrasher (*Toxostoma redivivum*) resides in chaparral hillsides near the coast, while the Crissal thrasher (*T. crissale*) lives among mesquite and willow in the desert Southwest. Curve-billed thrashers (*T. curvirostre*) ensure the safety of their nestlings by building their nests among spiny cholla cacti.

Tempting Features and Treats for Brown Thrashers

- Dense bramble thickets or vine-covered fences flanked by shrubs are required for nesting. Brown thrashers nest in thickets within a few feet of the ground.
- Mulches beneath shrubs and trees make rich hunting grounds for thrashers seeking beetles, grasshoppers, caterpillars, snails, and other favored foods.
- The edges of a shady compost pile make a fine foraging spot for brown thrashers.
- Thrashers enjoy bathing—in water or dust. A birdbath or other water feature will make them feel welcome in your landscape.
- Melodic and active singers, the brown thrasher has an extensive song repertoire, mostly consisting of paired or tripled phrases.

Did You Know?

- The brown thrasher is the state bird of Georgia, where many pairs maintain year-round homes. Many brown thrashers that spend summers in northern areas return to the Southeast for winter.
- Chicks are ready to leave the nest after 9 days or so. Many adult pairs produce two broods by the end of summer.
- Cowbirds often manage to sneak an egg into a brown thrasher nest and the thrasher parents wind up raising the cowbird chick as their own.
- Like mockingbirds, brown thrashers often imitate the calls of other types of birds, usually by calling out the notes twice.
- A mixed diet of juicy berries and insects satisfies brown thrashers in summer. In winter, they gather seeds shed by berry-bearing shrubs.
- Brown thrashers use their beaks to riffle through mulch in search of beetles and other insects.

Take a Closer Look

Eastern Towhee *(Pipilo erythrophthalmus)*

The largest of the sparrows, towhees are showy orange and black birds with white chest markings. Males and females differ only in head color, with the males sporting jet black heads compared to females' muted brown ones. Most towhees have red eyes, but yellow-eyed towhees are common in coastal climates. Adult birds are 7 to 8 inches (17 to 21 cm) long.

Feeder Favorites for Towhees

- Sunflower seed
- Cracked corn
- Shelled peanuts
- Cracked acorns

Regional Relations

The spotted towhee (*Pipilo maculatus*) sometimes migrates from Montana to Mexico, but lives year-round in much of the West. White wing bars make the spotted towhee even showier than the eastern towhee. The ranges of these two species overlap in parts of the Midwest, where they have hybridized.

Tempting Features and Treats for Towhees

- A brush pile or thicket is just what towhees want to find when looking for a place to nest. Towhee populations are declining due to lack of shrubby habitat.
- Thickly mulched shrubs and trees provide towhees with a steady supply of insects, snails, and millipedes they can scratch up with their feet.
- In hot weather, towhees love to settle into a birdbath for a thorough drench.
- Vine-covered fences near open areas are often used as lookout towers by towhees in search of food. Rather than visiting raised feeders, towhees prefer to peck up grain that has fallen to the ground.

Did You Know?

- Towhees and field sparrows have been known to work cooperatively in feeding one another's young. Young towhees closely resemble sparrows.
- Towhees escape harsh winter weather by flying a few hundred miles south, but they stay year-round in mild winter climates.
- Insects, spiders, and other creepy crawlies make up much of towhees' summer diet, but in winter they eat wild berries and seeds found on the ground.

Help Out with Habitat

Populations of towhees, brown thrashers, and other short-distance migrants often drop when farmland is developed into roads and houses, because these birds thrive in the thickets that grow up along fencerows or small streams. Bramble thickets are especially attractive as nesting sites, and many native berry-bearing brambles bear enough delicious fruits for you and the birds, too. Black raspberries are towhee favorites, as well as dewberries and blackberries. Consider planting a thicket of these brambles along the outskirts of your yard (see page 110).

NEOTROPICAL MIGRANTS

Neotropical migratory birds live south of the Tropic of Cancer (23 degrees north of the equator) in winter and breed in the United States and Canada in summer. About 200 species are neotropical migrants, including songbirds like thrushes and vireos, as well as many shorebirds and some hawks.

WHY DO THEY DO IT?

In their tropical winter homes, some migratory birds establish territories and most find plenty of fruits and insects to eat. So why should they bother to spend a month or more flying north in spring? Scientists think these three motives are neotropical migrants' best reasons to keep on the move.

- In North American breeding grounds, there's little competition for summer's plentiful supply of insects and more time to eat them because of longer daylight hours.
- Fewer predators are likely to bother nests and young hatchlings in temperate climates compared with tropical ones, where snakes, small parasites, and other problems could cause many nests to fail.
- Migration gives birds a fair shot at sufficient territorial space for successful family life. Compared with the dense chaos of tropical rain forests, northern breeding areas are luxuriously spacious and quiet.

Birds' motivations for migrating southward in fall might seem more obvious, especially to human "snowbirds" who likewise flee winter's cold in favor of warmer weather. Even though migration takes a substantial physical toll on birds, the advantages of spending the winter months in a warm climate where food is abundant outweigh the rigors of the trip itself.

THE NEOTROPICAL FLIGHT PLAN

If a swallow, nighthawk, or other neotropical migrant were to work up a flight plan, it would include the following important bits of information:

Departure and Arrival Times

In North America, as days become noticeably shorter in August, birds know that it's almost time to fly. Changes in day length are much less dra-

Refuges for Migrating Birds

As birds move along their routes, many stop to rest and feed in refuges that are part of the National Wildlife Refuge System. Comprised of 548 refuges in all 50 states, these sanctuaries often encompass coastlines and wetlands and follow heavily used migratory routes. In addition to the nearly 100 million acres in the United States' system, Environment Canada manages nearly 30 million acres in its Protected Areas Network. Many of those acres are included in 92 designated Migratory Bird Sanctuaries, which naturally cluster along the coastlines and are also scattered across the provinces.

matic closer to the equator, so birds probably use other cues when deciding when to fly north in spring. Perhaps they start thinking about the juicy caterpillars and beetles awaiting them in Ohio, or maybe they're motivated by a need to breed. Whatever the triggers, most neotropical migrants begin appearing in North America in late March, and the incoming stream continues until early May.

Best Times to Fly

Many birds commute between continents at night, when temperatures are cooler and they're less likely to be nabbed by predators. However, birds that eat insects as they travel usually fly by day. Swallows, nighthawks, and other bug-eating migrants check into roosting trees at night and fly low during daylight hours, where they share air space with insects. Many nighttime fliers use the stars as navigational aids, especially the North Star and the nearby constellation we know as the Big Dipper. In addition to navigating by the stars, birds also use the Earth's magnetic field to guide their long-distance travels.

Cruising Speed and Altitude

Large birds may fly as fast as 45 miles (70 km) per hour, while smaller birds do well to make 15 miles (25 km) per hour. Birds may take advantage of strong tailwinds by flying much farther in good weather than when the wind is blowing against them.

Most migratory birds fly less than a mile high, but a mallard duck that struck an airplane at 21,000 feet (almost 4 miles, or 6,400 m) is the highest-flying North American bird on record. Night-flying birds often fly higher than those that fly during the day. High-altitude flight is also more common when birds are following a long flight path over water.

Stopovers for Refueling

As birds run out of fat reserves or simply need to rest from flying, they often stop for 1 to 5 days to feed. The stopover will be short if there's little to eat, or longer should they luck into a fine supply of caterpillars or other foods. But even an open buffet of squirmy delicacies will not distract migrants for long. If birds linger too long at stopovers, they won't get first choice at the best breeding or overwintering sites ahead.

One of the biggest threats facing many neotropical migrant species is the loss of these essential stopover sites. When human development disrupts natural areas where birds routinely stop during their migration, it jeopardizes their chances of survival almost as significantly as does habitat loss at either end of the route.

If you live along one of the major migration routes (see maps on pages 136 and 137), having a bird-friendly landscape can make an important difference to birds on the move. A diverse, healthy landscape will welcome migrating birds in search of a stopover and you'll find yourself enjoying a greater variety of birds just outside your windows.

A Hazardous Journey

Scientists estimate that nearly half of all birds that migrate south in fall will not return to northern breeding grounds the following spring. Some are killed by predators or unfavorable weather during migration, while others are unable to recover from the physiological costs of the trip itself. Habitat loss further amplifies the stresses of migration by reducing the availability of food, water, and nesting sites.

Take a Closer Look

Tree Swallow *(Tachycineta bicolor)*

Only three clues are needed to identify a tree swallow: iridescent greenish-blue back and wings, white underparts, and a notched tail. Males and females look alike, although the female's color tends to be duller. Adult birds are 5 to 6 inches (12 to 15 cm) long. Tree swallows are cavity nesters that often move into holes previously occupied by woodpeckers; where no natural cavities are available, they will move into bluebird-style houses. They tend four to seven white eggs in a nest made of grass and lined with feathers.

Regional Relations

With summer breeding grounds stretching from Arizona to Alaska, the violet-green swallow (*Tachycineta thalassina*) often shares space with tree swallows in the West. This species gets its name from the color of its back and wings, which always have a greenish hue, but are sometimes more bronze than violet. Like tree swallows, violet-green swallows nest in natural or artificial cavities and will move into nest boxes intended for bluebirds.

Tempting Features and Treats for Tree Swallows

- Save old feather(down) pillows. Scatter their contents near nesting sites in early spring; swallows will use them to line their nests.
- Dead trees that are at least 14 feet (4.3 m) high and 27 inches (70.4 cm) in diameter are ideal nesting sites for tree swallows. Or you can provide nesting boxes.
- Include a wax myrtle (bayberry) in your landscape. Tree swallows love them!

Did You Know?

- Tree swallows migrate northward early, often arriving in Montana before the end of March. They begin flying south in late summer, soon after their nesting duties are finished.
- Large flocks of tree swallows form to migrate.
- On their southward journey, tree swallows may stop to check out potential nesting sites or to fill up on bayberries, a favorite in-flight food.
- Perhaps because they have a taste for mosquitoes, tree swallows often make their homes near water. Small colonies may form around desirable locations.
- Cold, wet summers are rough on hatchling tree swallows. In a lean year, only about 20 percent make it to adulthood.

Nesting Box Know-How

Tree swallows eat mostly flying insects, so they seldom are seen at bird feeders. Yet they happily accept the same type of nesting box used for bluebirds (see page 156). The entry hole should be no larger than 1½ inches (5 cm), and the box should be mounted 5 to 6 feet (1.1 to 1.4 m) off the ground. Make sure that the front door faces an open area such as a grassy space or a wildflower meadow—great places for tree swallows to find flies, beetles, ants, and other food. If tree swallows beat bluebirds to the nest box, putting up a second box 15 to 25 feet (4.5 to 7.6 m) away may accommodate both species.

Take a Closer Look

Barn Swallow *(Hirundo rustica)*

As barn swallows fly from nests beneath bridges or in barns or other buildings, look for their blue-black heads, backs, and wings, with pale reddish brown chests and darker ruddy throats. Barn swallows grow 6 to 7 inches (15 to 19 cm) long and have long, deeply forked tails. Their buff chests and bellies help to distinguish them from the similar looking but slightly smaller tree swallow (on the opposite page), which is creamy white underneath, and the slightly larger but all dark purple martin on page 160. But it's the barn swallow's tail that confirms its identity—long and deeply forked, it clearly differs from the notched tails of martins and tree swallows. The female barn swallow builds a characteristic mud and straw nest and lays four to six brown-spotted white eggs.

Regional Relations

Closely related cliff swallows (*Petrochelidon pyrrhonota*) share the same range as barn swallows, but have shorter tails and brighter ruddy colors. These are the famous swallows of the San Juan Capistrano Mission in Orange County, California, which generally arrive each year on March 19 and depart on October 23. During their nesting season, they occupy the oldest building still in use in California.

Tempting Features and Treats for Barn Swallows

- Like tree swallows, barn swallows tend to feather their nests with waterfowl feathers, such as those found in down pillows and comforters. White feathers are preferred.
- Barn swallows need mud to make their nests, so a gloppy puddle may get plenty of visits from nest-building females in late spring.
- A sprinkler may invite barn swallows to your yard for a fly-through shower.

Did You Know?

- Among barn swallows, males with very long tails are true Casanovas, often winning temporary sexual favors from mated females.
- A single barn swallow nest may require as many as 1,000 trips from the mud supply to the building site.
- A lining of fresh mud may turn last year's nest into this year's model, and barn swallows often return to the same nest year after year.
- When barn swallows re-use nests built in previous seasons, they tend to have more problems with mites and other parasites. Destroy their old nests in winter to force them to build new ones.
- When chasing after flying insects, barn swallows may beat their wings 15 times a second.
- As barn swallows migrate in fall, they often cover 500 to 600 miles in a single day.
- Barn swallows drink in flight, swooping down over water to take a sip.
- As North American forests have been transformed into farms, barn swallows have given up nesting in caves in favor of barns, bridges, boat docks, and even the eaves of houses. Open areas to feed make working farms particularly attractive, and farmers welcome barn swallows because of their insatiable appetites for insects.
- The ability to adapt their nesting habits to make use of manmade structures has been a benefit to barn swallows and their populations have increased accordingly. No other swallow species is as widely distributed or populous as the barn swallow.

URBAN BUG-EATING BIRDS

Nighthawks and swallows have adapted to urban and suburban life better than most other bug-eating birds, and it takes only one or two pairs of bug-eating birds to put a big dent in your garden's supply of leaf-eating caterpillars and other insects. In addition to the birds described in this chapter, the following six birds often are important allies that help urban gardeners keep pests under control.

Bluebird	Eats small insects and spiders
Chipping sparrow	Eats small crawling insects
House wren	Eats small insects and spiders
Phoebe	Eats small insects and spiders
Purple martin	Eats flying insects
Yellow warbler	Eats caterpillars and small crawling insects

Keep Your Help Happy

The simplest way to enlist the help of these and other bug-eating birds is to install numerous perches around your garden from which birds can watch for signs of their favorite foods. A tomato stake with a narrow horizontal crosspiece will serve just fine, as will tomato cages, wire garden fencing, trellises, and other common garden structures.

Peckable Beds

In spring, let bug-eating birds peck through prepared beds to rid them of cutworms, overwintering bean beetles and potato beetles, and other common vegetable garden pests. Short-distance migrants are specialists at this task.

First thing in spring, rake back the mulch over beds prepared the previous fall for peas, potatoes, onions, and other cool-season spring veggies.

Turn up patches of lawn you want to convert to garden space as early as the ground can be worked. Cutworms often are numerous where grass or weeds grew the year before, so these are prime spaces to encourage spring gleaning by bug-eating birds.

Pull weeds growing beneath fruit trees, and let birds gather insects from the disturbed soil for a week or two before spreading a fresh blanket of biodegradable mulch.

Before you plant in spring, give birds a chance to scour your gardens to reduce the numbers of hungry pests waiting to munch on your crops.

Take a Closer Look

Common Nighthawk *(Chordeiles minor)*

With mottled black and gray head and back, a nighthawk can pass for a patch of withered weeds or coarse gravel as it sits quietly in a field, a grassy spot, or on the roof of a building. Not related to hawks, nighthawks are most often seen in the evening or early in the morning, when they take to the air to hunt for food. Males and females sport similar camouflage colors, but the male has a white patch on its throat, whereas the female's patch is yellow. The birds' whitish underparts have numerous dark brown bars. In flight, you can see white bars on nighthawks' long outstretched wings. Adult birds are 8 to 9½ inches (22 to 24 cm) long.

Regional Relations

The lesser nighthawk (*Chordeiles acutipennis*) is common in the Southwest and looks almost exactly like a common nighthawk. However, the lesser nighthawk is more territorial and will chase away common nighthawks that try to nest nearby. The lesser nighthawk also has a shorter commute to its winter digs in Mexico, Central America, and the northern part of South America.

Tempting Features and Treats for Nighthawks

- Open grassy fields are nighthawk territory. A log or boulder that creates a protected spot where the ground is bare or covered with gravel is a preferred nighthawk nesting site.
- Gravel-covered roofs often serve as nest sites in urban areas, but not if the gravel has been covered with a rubber coating.
- In towns and cities, nighthawks often hunt for insects that gather around streetlights.

Did You Know?

- A nighthawk's bill may be small, but the bird has a large mouth—useful for nabbing large insects or for collecting a number of smaller ones.
- On a hot day, a female nighthawk may sit beside her clutch of eggs rather than on top of it and use her outstretched wings to shade the eggs from midday sun.
- Nighthawks hardly sing at all, yet often make nasal "spee-yah" calls as they hunt for flying food. When defending her eggs from intruders, a female nighthawk makes almost catlike spitting and hissing sounds.
- Commuting between Ontario and Argentina, some nighthawks migrate more than 6,000 miles. Nighthawks often live to be 5 years old, so they log tens of thousands of migratory miles.
- If you were to gain the same proportion of body fat needed by a migratory bird during the last few weeks before takeoff, you would need to pack on more than 10 pounds a day! While you might have to eat sticks of butter to gain that much weight, long-distance migrants like nighthawks bulk up on high-fat seeds, bugs, and berries.

Nose-Diving Nighthawks

When a male nighthawk wants to impress a female, frighten a rival, or deter an intruder, he may fly upward and then fold his wings and zoom straight back down, stopping a short distance from the ground with a loud rush from his outstretched wings. He then returns to the female, strutting and displaying his tail in classic show-off style.

SHARING YOUR GARDEN WITH BUG-EATING BIRDS

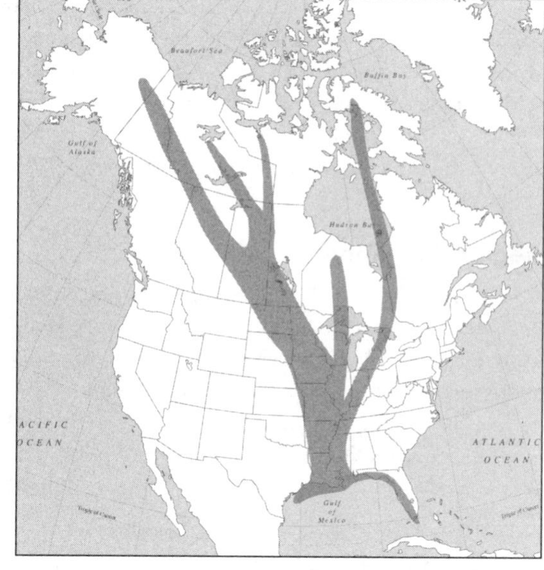

A feeder stocked with seeds will give you a front-row seat for watching finches and other seed eaters, but when you share your garden with bug-eating birds, the best bird-watching seat in the house is far from the chaos of the feeding station. As a general rule, birds that eat insects have little interest in feeders during summer, when there are plenty of bugs to catch. Before the food supply dwindles at summer's end, many bug eaters take to the air to migrate thousands of miles southward. Only those equipped to peck or pry out insects hiding in bark crevices stick around through the cold winter months.

In this chapter, you'll meet more than a dozen birds whose summer diets consist of insects and other live prey like slugs, spiders, and salamanders. From nighthawks that nest on gravel rooftops in the city to flycatchers of the deep forest, insect-eating birds can be found in a huge range of habitats. Your yard is one such habitat, and having plenty of insect-eating birds around means there will be fewer creepy critters eating your plants. Best of all, bug-eating birds eat ants, flies, gnats, mosquitoes, and other insects that bug people, so your birds help make the garden more comfortable for you.

Marathon Fliers

One of the most amazing of all migratory flights is that of the little blackpoll warbler (*Dendroica striata*), which takes an ocean route from Canada to South America. Individual birds may stay in the air for 80 hours or more between stops for food and water.

THE IMPORTANCE OF BUG-EATING BIRDS

Of nearly 9,000 species of birds, about 60 percent include insects in their diets. This makes perfect sense when you consider the fact that both birds and insects are able to fly, so they form an airborne community of hunter and hunted that's all their own. In most healthy ecosystems, birds consume about 40 percent of the insects present in an average season. When the ecosystem in question is your yard, a healthy bird population can make the difference between plants that have few pest problems and a garden that seems to go from one pest crisis to another.

Birds specialize in the kinds of insects they prefer and often have body parts built for harvesting them. Woodpeckers and nuthatches have strong talons that help them cling to tree trunks as they forage for food, while brown thrashers' feet are

ESTABLISHING AND DEFENDING TERRITORIES

Among most neotropical migrants, male birds appear at summer breeding grounds about a week before the females arrive. Perhaps they like to feel well-oriented before settling in to court, or maybe they need to spend some time exploring food and nesting resources in preparation for taking a new mate—or reuniting with an old one.

The size of a pair's territory varies with species. Swallows often nest in colonies, whereas a huge pileated woodpecker pair may maintain a 20-acre territory. Birds that do not directly compete for the same food sources and nesting sites are allowed, but rivals of the same species are quickly chased away.

Males that helped rear a successful nest the year before often return to the same place the following spring. Those that are songbirds by nature promptly begin singing to proclaim their presence. Early on in the scramble for real estate, male birds often sing for more than half the day—their general way of deterring new settlers. But until birds form pairs and begin nesting (see page 300), males bow out of direct conflict with rivals unless the site is so fine that it's worth the risk of serious injury.

You may not catch a glimpse of a male red-eyed vireo as he hunts for insects high in the treetops. But you might hear him singing up there as he claims his territory and advertises for a mate to share it.

The Coffee Connection

If you think there's nothing you can do to help ease the habitat pressures migratory birds face in their tropical winter homes, think again. When you buy organic shade-grown coffee, you're helping to provide winter habitat for vireos, warblers, and many other neotropical migrants.

Seeing "shade-grown" labels on coffee is a recent phenomenon, but it was the traditional way coffee was grown for hundreds of years. Only within the past 20 years have higher-yielding sun-tolerant coffee varieties displaced those that grow best in partial shade. This change has resulted in 95 percent fewer birds in those areas. When coffee shrubs are grown in the company of trees, both the number of birds and the diversity of species present increase dramatically in response to the greater availability of food and shelter.

Take a Closer Look

Eastern Kingbird *(Tyrannus tyrannus)*

Stately eastern kingbirds have charcoal-black heads, backs, and wings, and white breasts. Look closely for a thin white band on the tips of the tail feathers. Male and female kingbirds look alike, although the male has a small, concealed crown of red to orange feathers that's visible only during displays meant to impress a prospective mate. Kingbird colors are brightest early in the spring season, becoming faded in fall. Adult birds are 8 to 9 inches (20 to 23 cm) long.

Regional Relations

The western kingbird (*Tyrannus verticalis*) has been known to build nests on utility poles, which offer a great vantage point for watching for predators and flying food at the same time. Slate-gray feathers cover this bird's head and shoulders, and its yellow underside contrasts with blackish wing feathers, edged with white. The territories of eastern and western kingbirds overlap in the Great Plains. Compared to eastern kingbirds, the slightly larger westerners make a shorter migratory flight, spending winter in central Mexico and Costa Rica.

Tempting Features and Treats for Kingbirds

- Insects are often abundant near water, so kingbirds are attracted by water features.
- High perches make ideal spots for kingbirds to watch for prey.
- The highest branch crotches of dead trees are prime real estate for nesting kingbird pairs.

Did You Know?

- In fall, kingbird pairs merge into small flocks of 10 or more birds that fly during daytime hours to Central and South America. They stay in flocks through winter.
- Kingbirds occasionally eat honeybees and were once believed to be such significant honeybee predators that they were called beebirds. Until this myth was disproved, many kingbirds were shot by orchardists and beekeepers.
- Strong, agile fliers, kingbirds are able to catch wasps, moths, and other flying insects in midair.
- A kingbird seen doing crazy somersaults and false falls is probably a male trying to impress a female with his excellent flying skills.

Tyrants of the Sky

Kingbirds sometimes show passing interest in fruit offered at feeders, but their taste for fruit is mostly reserved for winter, when they eat fruits in South America's Amazon basin and other tropical feeding grounds. Higher up in the treetops, kingbirds are sometimes called tyrant birds because of their aggressive attacks on other species that come too close to their nests—including crows, hawks, and other large birds of prey. Flying insects make up most of kingbirds' summer diets, but these birds sometimes capture small lizards and frogs, too. With a scientific name that echoes their nature, tyrannical kingbirds regard your entire yard as a feeder. If a pair is nesting nearby, use binoculars to watch a bird catch a large insect, fly back to its hunting perch, and immobilize the bug before eating it or taking it back to its nest.

Take a Closer Look

Red-Eyed Vireo *(Vireo olivaceus)*

The most common of the vireos is a small olive green bird with a puffy white breast. Both males and females have a white eyebrow over a deep-red eye. Vireos are watchful, thoughtful little birds, seldom seen at feeders but often heard singing high in the trees where they glean insects from leaves and branches. Red-eyed vireos range across the eastern United States, the Great Plains, and much of Canada during the summer breeding season, migrating to South America for the winter months. Adult birds are 5 to 6 inches (12 to 15 cm) long. Males and females look alike, but male birds are slightly larger. Female vireos sit on their two to five eggs, which are white with small dark spots; while the female handles incubation, her mate gathers insects and brings them back for her. After the eggs hatch, both parents collect insects to feed their young.

Regional Relations

The Philadelphia vireo (*Vireo philadelphicus*) is slightly smaller than its better-known red-eyed cousin but otherwise similar in appearance, range, and feeding habits. Philadelphia vireos breed farther north than other vireo species, spending the summer across Canada and in the very northernmost United States. Several western species of vireo commute between South America and the American Southwest, including the thick-beaked plumbeous vireo (*V. plumbeus*) and the warbling vireo (*V. gilvus*). Varying in color from greenish to gray, these black-eyed vireos wear the same white eyeliner as other vireos and are often seen in woods near streams.

Tempting Features and Treats for Vireos

- Tall, leafy trees are required for vireos to stick around, because 85 percent of their summer diet consists of small insects gleaned from trees.
- Old spiderwebs and spider egg cases attached to upturned boards, bricks, or flowerpots are a gold mine of preferred nest-building materials for vireos.
- Vireos eat fruit when they migrate southward in early fall and may pause en route to snap up a few elderberry or jimsonweed berries.

Did You Know?

- Vireo females build elegant cup-shaped nests suspended between tree branches, often using spiderwebs, lichen, bark, and bits of spider egg cases.
- When they catch an insect that's too large to eat in one bite, vireos may hold it in their feet to chomp it into pieces.
- Vireo nests are frequent targets of brown-headed cowbirds, at least in part because vireo eggs and cowbird eggs are similar in size and color.
- In western and central South America there are year-round and summer (breeding) populations of red-eyed vireos. Some scientists believe that the resident vireos are a separate species.
- The insect-eating vireo's winter diet may consist almost entirely of fruit.

Virtuoso Vireos

Stationed high in the treetops, male vireos never run out of songs to sing. In a 24-hour period, a vireo may sing more than 20,000 times. The vireo's song varies, often sounding like a three-word question followed by a three-word answer. Vireos sometimes incorporate notes learned from other birds. If you hear a bird singing from high overhead in a tree, and he sings the same song over and over again, chances are good that you're hearing a virtuoso vireo. Female vireos rarely sing, leaving the vocalizing to the males.

THE NEED TO SING

All birds call, screech, or make some type of sound, but only about half of all bird species sing. These are collectively called passerines (they're classified within the order Passeriformes), which translates as perching birds. The estimated 4,000 species of passerine songbirds are able to perch on branches using their three forward and single rear toes.

Scientists think these birds are born knowing the basics of their song, but learning also plays an important role. Young birds must practice hundreds of times to get their species song close to right and then may need to add extra touches to make it work. With the help of recording equipment, several previously unknown secrets have been revealed about birds' songs.

Many birds have regional accents, or dialects, that are reflected in their song. Unless a bird can sing like a native, its song may not attract a mate or deter rivals.

Singing requires strength and energy, so well-fed, healthy birds sing louder than weaker birds. Loud, clear song makes a male bird a top choice as a mate.

Adding an extra note or flourish often dazzles the ladies. Males with beautiful plumage and strong songs are often granted sexual privileges by mated females.

THE DAWN CHORUS

At 5 a.m. on a spring Saturday, when you'd hoped to sleep in, it sounds as if every bird from miles around is perched outside your window, singing its heart out. Birdsong is beautiful, but must they sing all at once, and can't they wait until the sun comes up? The dawn chorus is so loud and rowdy because early morning is such a great time to sing. The still air helps sound carry well, nocturnal predators have returned to their daytime haunts, and daytime troublemakers are not yet active. Insects are sluggish until temperatures rise, so bug-eating birds are in no hurry to start feeding. So just in case an interloper needs to be scared away or a potential mate needs to be impressed, songbirds belt out their best at dawn.

Look, Listen, and Learn

Learning to identify birds by their songs and calls is similar to learning a new human language. In the case of birds, however, you're actually learning dozens of languages—a unique set of sounds for almost every bird species that you encounter. It takes time and practice to begin to associate particular notes and phrases with the species that makes them, but it's a tremendous thrill to make the connection between a familiar song and a familiar bird. In some cases, learning to recognize a bird's song is the best way to verify that bird's presence. Warblers, vireos, and other insect-eating birds that nest and feed in the treetops are among the most vocal avian singers, but they rarely linger closer to the ground where you might make a positive visual ID.

Many excellent recordings are available to help you train your ears to the songs and calls of your favorite birds. The best of these are accompanied by visuals—DVDs that offer both sights and sounds, or field guides coded to match CDs or digital audio files—to let you see the bird and hear it at the same time.

GETTING INTO MEALWORMS

Bug-eating birds may visit seed feeders in winter, but in summer mealworms are the best way to lure these birds to a feeder—or to attract nuthatches or swallows into an area that includes a likely nesting box. The same mealworms often fed to eastern bluebirds (see page 156) will get the attention of most birds that eat summer insects. In addition to the bug-eating birds in this chapter, robins, wrens, warblers, and many other species love mealworms. Mealworms can easily squirm off the edges of a tray type feeder, but making a mealworm feeder takes only a few minutes (see page 44).

You can buy mealworms in pet shops (they're sold as food for lizards, snakes, and other exotic pets) or through mail-order sources. Shop carefully, because prices vary quite a bit. Offer only 20 or so mealworms at a time and keep those you won't use right away in the refrigerator. Be sure to label the container holding the mealworms and to let other refrigerator users know about them—happening on a surprise cache of mealworms may be pleasing to birds, but unsuspecting humans often react less positively!

What Are Mealworms?

Mealworms are not worms at all, but rather the larvae of the darkling beetle (*Tenebrio molitor*). They're called mealworms because of their ability to flourish in nearly dry stored grains and flours. The dark brown adult beetles are about half an inch (1.25 cm) long. Females can lay more than 100 eggs, which hatch and feed as squirmy larvae for about 6 months. At any size, the larvae can be harvested and fed to birds. Most people who raise their own mealworms harvest them in batches and keep the extras in small containers in the refrigerator. Mealworms are dry to the touch rather than slimy and don't bite.

GROWING MEALWORMS, STEP BY STEP

Once you've watched birds go for a container of mealworms, you'll definitely want more! Growing your own mealworms is easy, interesting, and can save you a tidy sum over buying them. And every few months when you change the mealworms' bedding, you'll gain a fantastic fertilizer for outdoor-container or garden plants. Here's what to do.

1. Obtain a 1-gallon plastic bucket with a snap-on lid, such as a clean paint pail. Use a hammer and nail or an ice pick to make 15 to 20 holes in the lid.
2. Place a cup each of whole wheat flour, oatmeal, and plain cornmeal in the container (the mix need not be perfectly balanced). Gently mix in several dozen live mealworms purchased at a pet shop or a few adults captured from stored flour.
3. Slice a small potato in half lengthwise and gently press it cut side down into the surface of the flour. Lightly mist the flour's surface with water and snap on the bucket's lid. Except for the potato and the lightly misted surface, the flour mixture should be dry. Keep the container in a warm, dry place. Mealworms grow fastest at around 80°F (27°C), but will also make good progress in the 70°F (21°C) range.

4. Once a week, remove the old piece of potato and replace it with a similarly moist piece of vegetable, for example lettuce cores or thick cabbage leaves.
5. To collect a few mealworms, place two sheets of damp paper (such as from a grocery bag) over the surface of the flour mixture. Within a few hours, mealworms will congregate between the sheets of paper or may cluster beneath them. Collect them by jiggling or scooping them into another container.
6. To collect adults to start a new colony, cut an apple into quarters and press the pieces into the bedding. Overnight, any adults present will feed on the apple pieces in a swarm. Scoop up the apple pieces and quickly drop them into a new container filled with a flour mix.

Whether you grow your own mealworms or buy them from a wild-bird supply store, these beetle larvae are almost guaranteed to attract bluebirds to your yard. You can serve them in a specially designed mealworm feeder, as shown, that includes a sheltering roof, or put them out on a tray or platform feeder.

7. Every 5 to 6 months, prepare a fresh new container. Harvest most of the worms from the first colony and save some of the crumbly bedding for fertilizing outdoor plants. In addition to a starter handful of worms, adding a small amount of the old bedding will insure that the new colony also includes a nice supply of eggs.

SERVING MEALWORMS

Once you have the mealworms, put some out on a platform feeder or in a hanging plastic domed feeder and watch as insect-loving birds like robins, purple martins, Carolina wrens, tanagers, warblers, catbirds, thrushes, and woodpeckers—as well as bluebirds—discover them. Or place them in a special mealworm feeder designed for bluebirds that resembles a bluebird house (most bird specialty stores and Web sites carry them). Don't put them out more than one layer deep to avoid suffocating them. You can keep the mealworms you don't put out right away by storing them in the fridge in a container with 1 inch to 1½ inches (2 to 4 cm) of oatmeal and/or cornmeal.

Worms Welcome, Warm or Cold

You can offer mealworms year-round. Because they're alive, mealworms will freeze in very cold weather, so if you're putting them out in winter where temperatures drop below freezing, set out fewer at a time. As with suet, though, even an ice-cold mealworm will be appreciated by a hungry woodpecker!

TAKE A CLOSER LOOK

Flycatchers *(Empidonax* spp.*)*

Nearly a dozen species of flycatchers within the genus *Empidonax* nest in different regions of North America. While each species has characteristics that allow ornithologists to separate it from its flycatcher cousins, as a group these birds are rather similar in their appearance. It can be difficult for casual birders to distinguish one from another in areas where species overlap.

These small gray-green birds blend in beautifully with their leafy habitats. A greenish tinge darkens flycatchers' gray heads and backs, and their wings are charcoal black with two thin white bars. Flycatchers have large black eyes and short sharp beaks. Adult birds are about 5½ inches (14 cm) long.

Regional Relations

North America's most familiar flycatchers vary by region.

The least flycatcher (*Empidonax minimus*) breeds in the North from Nova Scotia to Alaska, as well as in the Upper Midwest. Its summer diet consists mainly of ants and beetles. As its name suggests, the least flycatcher is one of the smallest in this group of birds; it is also grayer than other flycatchers. By contrast, the Acadian flycatcher (*E. virescens*) is the largest in this genus, and its feathers are greener than those of its closest relatives.

The Acadian flycatcher spends summers along the rivers and streams of the Mississippi River basin. It eats mostly spiders and caterpillars in its range from Louisiana to Pennsylvania.

The dusky flycatcher (*E. oberholseri*) is the most common flycatcher in the West, breeding throughout the Rockies and most of California. It eats whatever it catches, from caterpillars to damselflies.

The willow flycatcher (*E. trailii*) nests in wet, brushy sites across the United States and southern Canada, spending the winter months in Central America and northernmost South America. This small, olive-brown bird may capture insects by pouncing on them in a hawk-like manner or by hovering as it gleans them from tree branches and foliage.

Understory Bug Hunters

You're most likely to see flycatchers in your yard if there are trees and large shrubs nearby, because flycatchers feed in just such places. Flycatchers catch all sorts of flies and other insects "on the wing" and sometimes use dragonfly wings to line their nests. But the hunting method you're most likely to see goes like this: The bird perches on a small branch and when it sees an insect it wants, it quickly sallies out to grab it. Most of these are short trips, less than 5 feet (1.5 m) from the perching branch.

Did You Know?

- Flycatchers are long-distance migrants that spend winter in Central America and Mexico. Their one-way flight time ranges from 25 to 32 days.
- Flycatchers that live deep in the forest seldom have their nests sabotaged by cowbirds, but the situation is different along forest edges, where cowbirds are much more likely to sneak an egg into a flycatcher's nest.
- Flycatchers vigorously defend their territories, often chasing off larger species that attempt to nest there.
- Like most other birds that migrate long distances, a flycatcher's chest muscles are specially built to hold its wings outstretched through many migratory miles in spring and fall. To minimize air resistance, many other migratory species, including swallows, have long, pointed wings in addition to powerful pecs.

THE WONDER OF WETLANDS

In the past 20 years, swamps, marshes, and seeps have gotten an image makeover as they've been upgraded to wetlands. Over half of North America's freshwater wetlands have already been lost to agriculture or urban development, but these days natural wetlands are being preserved rather than developed. Bird counts in wetlands can be four to twelve times higher than in nearby dry sites. Insect eaters like swallows and pileated woodpeckers are well-represented on lists of birds found in wetland environments.

Different birds prefer different types of wetlands. Wood ducks, great blue herons, and kingfishers look for new wetlands with plenty of water, such as those created when beavers fell trees to dam up streams. Flycatchers, on the other hand, prefer older wetlands that have been colonized by cattails, sedges, and other bog plants.

Low-Maintenance Bog Gardens

Because many weeds grow poorly in wet soil that holds little oxygen, weed control is a modest challenge in a new rain garden compared to a traditional garden bed. If you like, you can even grow bog plants in plastic pots sunk into the ground.

EVERYBODY WINS

Rain Gardens for Birds

If you have a low spot on your property, you can easily transform it into a miniature wetland for bug-eating birds. Attach a length of pipe to a downspout on your house to deliver thousands of gallons of free water to your rain garden each year. Locate the output point of the pipe just above your rain garden and then bury the pipe to hide it from view. Each time it rains, the low spot will be flooded with sufficient water to turn it into a boggy retreat for birds—a far better option than letting it flow through your town's storm water runoff system.

Plants for your rain garden can include numerous native shrubs and wildflowers often found along stream edges, including those that grow in shallow water. A backdrop of tall ornamental grasses, sedges, or cattails will shelter the spot from wind while providing perching space for flycatchers and other small bug-eating birds.

Take a Closer Look

Wood Thrush *(Hylocichla mustelina)*

Male and female wood thrushes have brown heads, backs, and wings, contrasted with a buff-colored chest sprinkled with drops of chocolate brown. Their long legs have a pinkish color; stout bills have a dark brown tip. Adult birds are 7 to 8 inches (18 to 21 cm) long. Wood thrushes nest across the eastern United States and Canada, from southern Ontario to the Gulf Coast and northern Florida. Winter finds them in Central America. Like its American robin relatives, the wood thrush builds a large, cup-shaped nest of grasses, leaves, and weeds held together with mud.

Regional Relations

The slightly smaller hermit thrush (*Catharus guttatus*) breeds in the Far North, and several subspecies spend winter in mild areas of North America. Compared with wood thrushes, hermit thrushes have more muted colors. They're most likely to be seen in places with mature pines, hemlocks, and other conifers.

The varied thrush (*Ixoreus naevius*) lives year-round in parts of the Pacific Northwest and its breeding range extends throughout Alaska and westernmost Canada. Partial to mature conifer forests, the varied thrush is a large, robinlike bird with orange throat, chest, and wingbars and dark gray-blue back and markings.

Tempting Features and Treats for Wood Thrushes

- A ground-level water supply located near dense shrubs can help to draw wood thrushes out into the open.
- Green lanes (see page 114) attract wood thrushes because they resemble small open spaces within a forest.
- Migrating wood thrushes often stop to feed when they encounter a spicebush (*Lindera benzoin*), heavily laden with drupes, among other berry-bearing shrubs.
- Wood thrushes are unlikely feeder guests, but occasionally may patronize a low platform feeder serving crumbled suet, raisins, or mixed peanut butter and cornmeal.

The Magic of Moist Mulch

When scientists investigated the habitats most likely to host nesting pairs of wood thrushes, tall trees accompanied by a dense understory of shrubs proved important, but the most significant environmental factor was the presence of moist soil covered with a deep layer of decomposing leaves. To create similar hunting grounds in your yard, blanket a moist spot with a thick covering of chopped leaves every fall. If you pause for a moment while working in your yard in late summer and early fall, one of the first bird sounds you'll notice may be the rustling noise made by thrushes hunting insects in the dry leaves.

Did You Know?

- Wood thrushes migrate at night, often flying 1,200 miles (2,000 km) in a single shift. They spend winter in Mexico and Central America.
- Favorite foods gathered from leaf litter include beetles, moth pupae, spiders, ants, and centipedes.
- The wood thrush's song is often described as a flutelike version of "echo-lay" followed by a low trill.
- Wood thrushes often live to be 7 or 8 years old. Older birds often return to nesting places they got to know in previous summers.
- It's common to find one or more brown-headed cowbird eggs in a wood thrush nest, particularly if the thrushes are nesting in a sparsely wooded area.

LESSONS FROM BUG-EATING BIRDS

One of the reasons we watch birds is to connect to nature. We share an omnivorous hunter-gatherer view of life with bug-eating birds, so getting to know them better may illuminate the following bits of human wisdom that we've heard all our lives:

- **Stick with what you know.** As they fly long distances to breed in summer and rest up in winter, neotropical bug eaters carry with them knowledge of precise locations where they enjoyed successful past seasons. Rather than looking for someplace better, they stick with the sure thing.
- **Don't settle for second best.** Many migratory birds fly thousands of miles to breed in summer, because great habitats are worth long-distance travel. For these birds, only the best breeding grounds will do.
- **Stay flexible and roll with the punches.** A wood thrush prefers beetles, but will gorge on centipedes when they're available. When a nest fails for some reason, a wood thrush pair will quickly start a new one.
- **Plan ahead for tough times.** Woodpeckers and nuthatches often hide acorns and other nuts so they'll always have food to eat.
- **Learn from your mistakes.** In learning experiments, after naïve bug-eating birds were fed gut-wrenching monarch larvae one time, the birds refused to go near them again. A misidentified bug can lead to a bad bellyache, so paying attention to details is crucial for bug-eating birds.

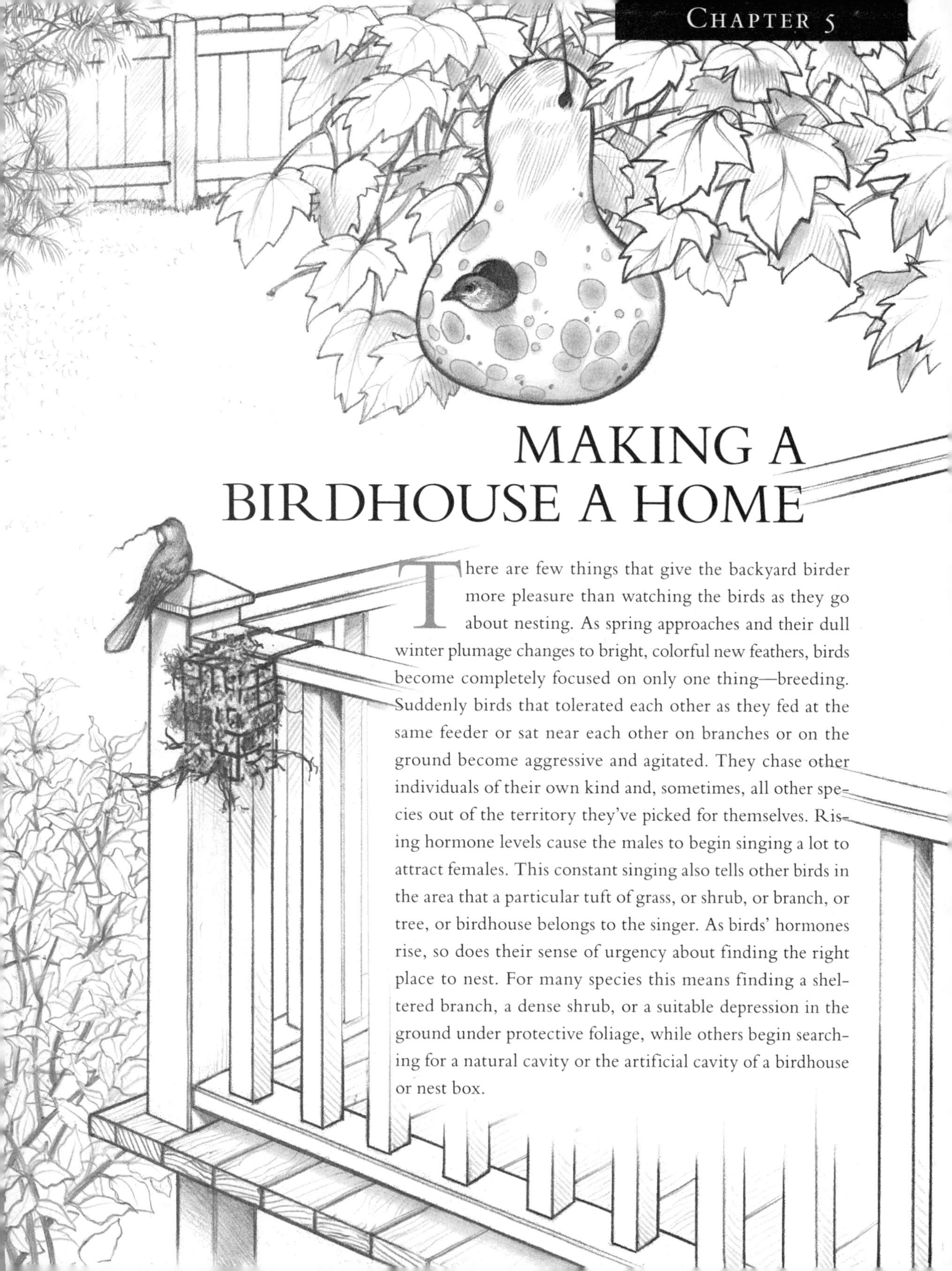

CHAPTER 5

MAKING A BIRDHOUSE A HOME

There are few things that give the backyard birder more pleasure than watching the birds as they go about nesting. As spring approaches and their dull winter plumage changes to bright, colorful new feathers, birds become completely focused on only one thing—breeding. Suddenly birds that tolerated each other as they fed at the same feeder or sat near each other on branches or on the ground become aggressive and agitated. They chase other individuals of their own kind and, sometimes, all other species out of the territory they've picked for themselves. Rising hormone levels cause the males to begin singing a lot to attract females. This constant singing also tells other birds in the area that a particular tuft of grass, or shrub, or branch, or tree, or birdhouse belongs to the singer. As birds' hormones rise, so does their sense of urgency about finding the right place to nest. For many species this means finding a sheltered branch, a dense shrub, or a suitable depression in the ground under protective foliage, while others begin searching for a natural cavity or the artificial cavity of a birdhouse or nest box.

WHEN BIRDS BEGIN NESTING

Most songbirds begin looking for suitable nest sites as spring approaches. Some early birds, such as chickadees, titmice, nuthatches, and bluebirds, start singing their courtship songs and searching for desirable real estate in mid- to late winter, even while snow still covers the ground. The timing that each species follows in choosing when to migrate, mate, and nest is determined by genetics and is triggered by the position and angle of the moon and sun, the length of day, and other natural signs.

For example, even though it's much warmer in winter in the southern parts of the United States, it's still winter and birds don't begin nesting until all of nature's signs tell them it's time to do so. Species like the house wren that nests all across the country still don't begin until early March in the most southern areas and later into June in the most northern climates. One of the earliest nesters in the eastern two-thirds of the country is the eastern phoebe. It's often found occupying a nesting territory in mid-March as early as St. Patrick's Day.

SIGNS OF NESTING SEASON

As birds attract mates and settle into their chosen territories, you may notice several indications that nest construction is underway. The singing that started when migratory males arrived and began staking out their space and advertising their desirability as mates continues as they guard their claims and tell other birds to keep out. If you hear a scolding call or feel the rush of air from wings passing near your head as you walk in your yard, you may have ventured too close to someone's nest site. Other signs of nesting include:

- Small sticks begin appearing here and there on the ground in your yard.
- Feathers, usually just one or two but in odd places, also begin showing up. All birds molt, replacing old worn feathers once, twice, or even three times a year, and a lot of them do this in spring when the shed feathers can be recycled into nest-lining material.
- Many species sing less once eggs are being incubated and until young birds have fledged, to avoid calling unwanted attention to the location of the nest.

As clutches of eggs begin to hatch, you may see:

- Broken eggshells appear in the middle of your lawn, on paved surfaces, or in places nowhere near trees or shrubs. When young birds hatch, the adults have to remove their shells from the nest, so they carry them away and drop them wherever they feel like it.
- Soft, white fecal sacs that aren't pleasant to look at or step on appear in random places. Young birds that can't fly still have to get rid of their waste material. So the adults remove these fecal sacs from the nest and fly off to drop them wherever it's convenient. Bird parents busy feeding a nest full of hungry hatchlings may catch a quick meal between food-gathering duties by eating the first few fecal sacs produced by their young.

Doves Don't Mourn These Feathers

When you see a mourning dove missing some tail feathers, a few wing feathers, or even its entire tail, it doesn't necessarily mean that something bad has happened to the bird. Missing feathers are especially noticeable on mourning doves because they're big, easily recognizable birds that spend a lot of time out in the open. If you watch a mourning dove that's missing all or some of its tail, you'll see that it doesn't affect its behavior or keep the bird from going about its daily business. It's these naturally molted feathers, and often the feathers from barnyard fowl, that other birds pick up and use in their nests.

GUARDING THE NEST

Once a bird or pair of birds has set up a territory and nesting is taking place, whether it's in a birdhouse, in a natural cavity, on a branch, or on the ground, the parents are extremely protective of the space around the nest. When both the male and female birds are involved in the nesting, the male sings from nearby perches to defend the territory from other birds. A female on a nest that's raising young on her own, as is the case with hummingbirds, becomes very quiet so as not to attract attention to the nest area, especially after the eggs are either already in it or about to be laid. When anyone or anything gets too close to the nest, the parent birds immediately react. They'll carry on and fly back and forth around the nest area. Sometimes they fly a long distance away to divert attention from the nest. They see everything as a predator, and that includes humans, all kinds of animals, reptiles, and other bigger birds.

When a nest's location is obvious, as it is when birds are using a birdhouse, the adult birds will fake attack on any perceived intruder into their territory. This is especially true of tree swallows and eastern bluebirds. If you get too close to their box, they'll continuously dive-bomb your head and loudly click their bills until you leave. Seldom do they actually make contact, but occasionally they will graze your hair or head. It's intimidating but not really dangerous. However, it's best not to bother them by getting too close to the nest unless you have to. You can observe a lot by sitting quietly nearby and watching. If you're monitoring a bluebird or other type of birdhouse trail, then you have to get close because you have to regularly check the contents of the boxes. You'll learn how to do this quickly and then move away.

Open a Nest-Builder's Supply

Just as each bird species has preferred foods that it relies upon, so does it have favorite materials that it looks for each year for nest building. Not every bird will use man-made items in constructing its nest, but a fair number will take advantage of a supply of nest-ready materials if you offer them. Cut natural fiber string, twine, or yarn into 4- to 8-inch (10 to 20 cm) pieces and drape them over a branch where birds are likely to find them. Or fill an unused wire suet cage or a plastic mesh berry basket with hay or straw, hair (yours or your pet's, gleaned from a brush or comb), shredded paper, or the feathers from an old pillow or down comforter, and hang it where you can see who comes to take items from your nest-builder's supply.

SOME BIRDS ARE SINGLE PARENTS

Many birds form mated pairs but not all of these pairings are permanent. Some species that raise more than one brood during the breeding season only stay a couple for the first nesting and then move on to other mates for the second nesting. Some species remain faithful for an entire breeding season but will change mates come the next year. And some species mate for life, however long that may be for both the male and female birds.

Then there are species like hummingbirds, in which the male and female birds only have contact with each other during the mating process. After mating is over the male goes off to look for other females, and it's the female alone who builds and attends to the nest and the young. In cases like this, when there's only a single bird attending to the nest, she won't make a lot of noise to drive someone or something off but instead will stay still and quiet so that you won't suspect there's a nest nearby. If the nest is discovered in spite of this tactic, she'll take aggressive defensive action, dive-bombing any perceived threat, chipping loudly, and making all sorts of scolding calls. When threatened, a nesting bird will do whatever it can to throw a predator off track.

BIRDS THAT USE HOUSES

Most of the birds you see in your backyard don't use birdhouses. But there are enough birds that do to make it worthwhile to install one or more birdhouses on your property. The kinds of birds you're most likely to attract to these boxes, the birds you want to encourage to nest in your yard, include wrens, chickadees, titmice, woodpeckers, flickers, bluebirds, tree swallows, purple martins, screech owls, and American kestrels. If you live near water or in the woods near a lake or pond, you may be lucky enough to attract wood ducks or even prothonotary warblers to a birdhouse.

When birds nest in your yard, they give you more opportunities to observe them and learn more about them. If a downy woodpecker chooses one of your birdhouses, you'll see that it lands vertically, not horizontally, on tree trunks or other surfaces and that it uses its stiff tail as a stabilizer. The black-and-white 6-inch (15 cm) downy woodpecker, the smallest and one of the most common woodpeckers in North America, will use a birdhouse if no appropriate tree cavities are available. Young downies often stick around for a while after they've left the nest, and the adults stay to feed them until they go off on their own. You may then notice something about them that you hadn't before. You probably already knew that the adult male downy has red feathers on the back of his head. But now you'll see that the juvenile male has red feathers on top of his head, while females, both young and old, don't have any red feathers at all on their heads. If you also have the similar but bigger hairy woodpeckers around, you'll see that the same is true for them.

Odd Birds in the House

Occasionally a bird that doesn't normally use a birdhouse will use one for reasons no one really understands. There's documented evidence of a chipping sparrow, a species that normally builds small grassy nests on branches, using a house wren box. Great crested flycatchers in the East and ash-throated flycatchers in the West normally nest in tree cavities, but once in a while they'll use a box. Putting out a birdhouse can produce all kinds of surprises.

BIRDS THAT NEST IN CAVITIES

There are many birds that nest in cavities. Some of them readily use birdhouses when they're available while others prefer natural cavities, although this is variable depending on the individual bird. It's even variable within a single species or genus. For example, although all chickadees nest in cavities, the ones that nest near populated areas are the ones most likely to use man-made houses or nest boxes. A black-capped chickadee is much more likely to use a birdhouse than a mountain chickadee is because of where they both naturally range. That doesn't mean, however, that a mountain chickadee wouldn't use a birdhouse if it were available. One cavity-nesting species, the purple martin, has become completely dependent upon man-made housing for its nest sites.

Birds That Readily Use Birdhouses

- Bluebirds
- Chickadees
- House sparrows
- Nuthatches
- Purple martins
- Screech owls
- Titmice
- Tree and violet-green swallows
- Wood duck
- Woodpeckers
- Wrens

Birds That Sometimes Use Birdhouses

- American kestrel
- Barn owl
- Common merganser
- Great crested and ash-throated flycatchers
- Prothonotary warbler

Not a Snag to Spare

For a host of reasons, the practice of leaving decaying trees and fence posts standing has gone out of style. Few people have space on their property to allow a dead tree to rot slowly away, and such snags, as they're called, are considered unattractive and dangerous. In some areas, zoning laws require the prompt removal of dead or dying trees. In terms of preventing injuries and property damage, clearing out snags makes sense, but such unnatural tidiness creates a tremendous lack of real estate for birds and other wildlife that make their homes in the spaces within decaying timber.

Where safety doesn't preclude it, leaving a dead tree standing is one of the best ways to help birds. Even if the top portion of a failing tree has to be taken down for safety reasons, if a part of it can be left in place it will offer nesting space for cavity-nesting birds as well as a buffet of wood-boring insects. If no cavities are immediately available in the snag, don't worry—woodpeckers will soon get the excavation underway.

TAKE A CLOSER LOOK

House Wren *(Troglodytes aedon)*

The house wren is a small, extremely active bird found in backyards everywhere. Other names for a house wren include Jenny wren, plain brown wren, or wood wren. The house wren is a dull brown bird with tan belly and breast, and horizontal dark stripes on its tail. Some individuals appear more gray than brown, while western house wrens may be rufous, a warm reddish brown color. A relatively long bill makes the house wren's head look big. Males and females look alike and measure 4½ to 5 inches (11 to 13 cm) long. During the nesting season, male wrens deliver seemingly endless performances of their loud, fast, and bubbly song. House wrens nest in cavities, tending five to eight white eggs that are heavily speckled with reddish dots.

What House Wrens Eat

- All kinds of insects, including caterpillars, bees, flies, wasps, crickets, and grasshoppers
- Crumbled suet
- Hulled seeds

Regional Relations

Eight other wren species may be seen in North America. In the East, the bigger and more rufous Carolina wren (*Thryothorus ludovicianus*) is plentiful. Its look-alike cousin, the grayish Bewick's wren (*Thryomanes bewickii*) is found primarily in the West. Both Carolina and Bewick's wrens will use birdhouses although they're more likely to nest in other man-made objects like old barrels, stone walls, or under the eaves of old buildings. Both species are about an inch bigger than the house wren and have louder and more varied songs. There's a very big wren in the Southwest called the cactus wren (*Campylorhynchus brunneicapillus*) that's 8½ inches (21 cm) long with a striped brown and white back and a speckled breast. Two other large western species are the rock wren (*Salpinctes obsoletus*) and the canyon wren (*Catherpes mexicanus*). The sedge wren (*Cistothorus platensis*) and the marsh wren (*C. palustris*) build pendulous grass nests near wet areas. The smallest is the winter wren (*Troglodytes troglodytes*), a dark, secretive bird with a complex, long tinkling song. It breeds primarily in the North and far into Canada.

Tempting Features and Treats for House Wrens

- Mixed plantings of shrubs, perennials, and annuals, as well as organically tended vegetable gardens, ensure that wrens will find a regular and varied supply of the insects that make up nearly all of their diet.
- Perches placed in and around a garden give wrens places to rest while they look for insects to eat.
- Natural cavities for nesting make wrens feel welcome, but they'll also nest in houses and hollowed-out gourds as well as in odd nooks and crannies like pipes, flowerpots, old shoes, mailboxes, old cars, or in laundry hanging on the line.

Did You Know?

- In spring, male house wrens return to their nesting territories before the females. The male builds one or more stick nests in cavities or birdhouses; after he finds a mate, she chooses the nest she wants to use.
- The female house wren finishes the nest by making a cup of grass, hair, and other soft materials on top of the sticks gathered by the male.
- The bond between a mated pair is often broken and reformed with a different bird for the second brood.
- House wrens winter in the southern United States, Central America, and down into South America.
- Some house wrens remain in the northeastern part of the country well into November.

House Wren Nest Box Specs

- Interior dimensions should be at least 4 × 4 inches (10 × 10 cm) and 6 inches (15 cm) deep.
- The 1¼-inch (3 cm)-diameter entrance hole should be 4 inches (10 cm) up from the floor of the box.

GOURDS AS BIRDHOUSES

The large, roomy fruits of the birdhouse gourd (*Lagenaria siceraria*) and other similarly substantial gourds may be converted into houses that many birds will accept readily. Here's how to turn one into desirable avian real estate.

1. Select a gourd with an inside cavity that's at least 4 × 4 inches (10 × 10 cm) at the bottom and 6 to 8 inches (15 to 20 cm) deep. Avoid gourds that are long and skinny, extremely large, or oddly shaped.
2. Put the gourd in a sheltered place to dry, leaving a portion of the stem on it. Drying could take a few weeks or a few months, usually the longer the better. Black moldy spots will appear on its outside as it dries. This is normal and a sign that the inside moisture is evaporating. The gourd is completely cured when you hear seeds hitting the insides when you shake it.
3. When the gourd is dried, cut into it at the spot where you're going to put the entrance hole. The finished round hole should be 1¼ inches (3 cm) in diameter, but don't cut it that big to begin with. Make a hole just big enough to get inside with a bent spoon, a piece of wire, or something else to scoop out the dried pulp and seeds. Make the right-size hole after you're done cleaning it out.
4. Put drainage holes in the bottom. Space them so that any water that gets inside runs away from the nest. A drill with a ⅛- or ¹⁄₁₆-inch (0.3 or 0.16 cm) bit works well for making the drainage holes; you can also use a hammer and a small nail to make them. Keep the holes small—only big enough for water to run out of them.
5. Push a long piece of sturdy wire through the base of the stem to make a hanger. Twist the wire around the stem a number of times to keep it securely attached. Make a loop at the top for hanging.
6. Treat the outside of the gourd with white or light-colored exterior latex paint or clear varnish, making sure it's completely dry before you hang it.
7. Hang the gourd from a branch or hanger, giving it minimal leeway to move in the wind. The house can move a little, but it shouldn't blow around so much that it stresses the bird using it. A bird may start to build a nest in a gourd that sways back and forth a lot, but will eventually abandon it. If possible, angle the gourd so the hole faces slightly downward to keep rain from getting in.
8. At the end of summer, bring in the gourd for winter. Store it in the same place you cured it and be sure to clean it out before you put it back outside in spring. If you choose to wash it out before you store it, use mild dish detergent and rinse it thoroughly. A properly prepared and cared-for gourd house can last for years.

Take a Closer Look

Eastern Bluebird *(Sialia sialis)*

One of the most recognized birds in our country is the eastern bluebird. The adult male is unmistakable with his intense deep blue back, head, and wings, red breast, and light underbelly. The female is the same size (7 inches; 18 cm) but drab compared to the male. She has a red breast but it's muted, and her head and back are a dull gray-blue. Young birds are the same size except for a short tail that quickly grows in once they're out of their nest box and able to fly around. They have white eye rings and spots on their breasts.

In early spring and sometimes even late winter, small flocks of bluebirds wander around checking out potential nest sites by going in and out of nest boxes. Eventually a mated pair travels alone, but it will still continue to explore new boxes. Sometimes the birds will spend a lot of time at one box and seem like they're going to use it, but then they move on to a different one. Even their removing old nest materials from a box doesn't necessarily mean that's the one they intend to use. You'll only know a pair has chosen a box for sure when they begin carrying nest material into the box, not out of it. Eastern bluebirds have a very distinct, soft, musical warbling song. They also chatter a lot, but it's not a sound you'd recognize as coming from a bluebird until you become really familiar with them.

What Bluebirds Eat

- All kinds of insects–grasshoppers, crickets, katydids, beetles—and spiders
- Berries, especially those from Virginia creeper and sumac, and wild grapes
- Mealworms
- Suet
- Occasionally tree frogs or earthworms
- Sometimes peanut butter/cornmeal mixture

Regional Relations

There are two bluebird species in the West, the mountain bluebird (*Sialia currucoides*) and the western bluebird (*S. mexicana*). The adult male mountain bluebird is almost entirely blue except for a white lower belly, but his color is more like the blue of the sky than the deep, dark blue of the eastern bluebird. The western bluebird looks a lot like the eastern bluebird but the western adult male has an entirely blue head and some chestnut red color at the lower edge of his back above the wings. The females of all three bluebird species look very similar; geography often is the best way to tell them apart.

Preferred Habitat

- Open, mostly rural areas with large fields; not in deep woods or densely populated areas
- Fences, small trees, or other perches from which they can fly down to the ground to grab insects
- Fields that are not chemically sprayed and that are close to woods or a stand of trees where young birds can take cover when they first leave the nest
- Areas away from a lot of traffic or human activity
- Viney, shrubby fencerows that provide lots of berries and insects

Did You Know?

- The eastern bluebird is the state bird of Missouri and New York.
- Eastern bluebirds are year-round residents in the South. Surprisingly, some of those that choose to nest instead in the North do not migrate south in winter. Many gather together in groups and spend the winter eating insects and berries in sheltered areas of northern woods where they can even be found in deep snow.
- It's primarily the female who builds the nest of grasses, animal hairs, and other plant material, and who does most of the incubating. Both parents feed the young birds once they've hatched.
- Normally it's not a good idea to open a nest box when birds are using it, but people monitoring bluebird trails have to do this on a regular basis. It doesn't seem to bother the birds too much so long as you do it quickly and efficiently. Just take a quick look and leave, being sure that the box is securely closed.

- The average number of light blue eggs is five, but sometimes there are more and the eggs are white.
- Bluebirds often begin nesting so early in spring that their first brood fails due to cold temperatures, lack of food, or other weather-related reasons. But parents almost always have two and sometimes three broods a summer, so when they lose a nest they'll build another one.
- If a nest inside a box is abandoned or destroyed, remove it so that the nest box will be used again.
- Preferred natural cavities may be from 3 to 20 feet (0.9 to 6.1 m) above the ground, but nest boxes are most successful when mounted 5 to 6 feet (1.5 to 1.8 m) high with their entrance holes facing away from the prevailing wind. Spacing boxes 150 to 300 yards (137 to 274 m) apart is typical on bluebird trails.
- Predators of bluebirds include house cats, snakes, raccoons, foxes, house sparrows, starlings, tree swallows, house wrens, blue jays, and other birds.
- Mounting nest boxes on metal poles helps reduce predation, as does adding a guard around the entrance hole and placing a metal or plastic baffle on the pole below the box.
- Special bluebird feeders with glass or clear plastic sides are available but the birds may be slow to use them. You place berries, fruit, or mealworms inside them and the bluebird has to go through an opening to reach the food.
- Mealworms are available from bird supply stores, pet stores, or through the mail. You'll find instructions for raising your own mealworms on page 82.

Back from the Brink

Human intervention during the past 30 years has brought back the bluebird population from desperately low levels. When suburban development began replacing farmland and woodlands began replacing fields that had been cleared for crops, bluebird numbers plummeted. At the same time, the populations of both house sparrows and European starlings exploded and took over most of the natural nest cavities that were left. With the ongoing expansion of the suburbs, old trees, fencerows, and stumps began to disappear. The bluebirds were in a lot of trouble.

Then, in 1977, the North American Bluebird Society (NABS) was formed and people began establishing and monitoring long lines of bluebird boxes called bluebird trails. This is what brought them back from the brink of disaster. Today NABS (at PO Box 43, Miamiville, OH, 45147, www.nabluebirdsociety.org) is bigger than ever and has affiliates all over the country. The society provides information on hosting bluebirds and detailed instructions on how to buy or build a proper nest box, erect it, and monitor a bluebird trail. Most states have a NABS chapter, and most chapters have annual or semi-annual meetings. Involvement with a bluebird organization is helpful for getting up-to-date information about bluebirds in your area and about how and where to set up and maintain a bluebird trail.

If you don't have enough space or the proper kind of space in which to create your own trail but you'd still like to monitor one, many local, state, and national conservation organizations and established parks are always looking for volunteers to do just that. Sharing this task with others and learning with and from them can be an enjoyable and rewarding experience that also gives you the opportunity to meet other like-minded individuals in your community.

BIRDS THAT NEST IN COLONIES

Most birds prefer to nest in pairs—or even singly, in some cases—within a chosen territory that they announce with song and defend against intruders, especially other birds of the same species. But some species take a more social approach to nesting, forming colonies that may range from a few pairs to hundreds of birds nesting in close proximity to one another.

Colonial nesting is more than just a whim or an inclination to be sociable, of course. The birds that gather in great groups for nesting typically do so in response to a combination of access to food and limited habitat. Seabirds are the most obvious examples of avian colonists—just like group-oriented humans on vacation, together they seek out undisturbed spots near the ocean. Since both natural geography and human activity limit the amount of suitable coastal real estate available for nesting, it wouldn't do for individual pairs of birds to claim extensive territories from which other birds were excluded. Out of necessity, these birds are programmed to share, nesting in colonies wherever they find that desirable combination of an ample food supply and suitable sites for nesting and raising young.

ADVANTAGES OF COLONIAL NESTING

Besides access to food and a suitable location, birds that nest in colonies enjoy a few other benefits of their association with a larger group. While a songbird pair may expend a lot of energy guarding its nest and fending off would-be predators, a colony may have dozens or hundreds of pairs of watchful eyes on the lookout for potential threats.

- Predators are less likely to raid the nests within a colony because they're more likely to be spotted and driven away by a group of adult birds than if they go after an individual nest.
- Young birds or adults that are sick or injured may receive protection and food from the group.
- Colonies tend to form on prime sites (from a bird's perspective) that offer plenty to eat and isolation from disturbances that would endanger their nests. Nesting in a colony increases birds' chances for survival and successful reproduction.

Common Colonial Nesters

- Gannets, puffins, and auks
- Great blue heron
- Gulls
- Terns

Other Birds That Nest in Colonies

A few species of land birds nest in colonies, for reasons very similar to those of seabirds and shorebirds. The formation of a colony usually is determined by the need for very specific nesting conditions, as in the case of cliff swallows, and proximity to a rich and reliable food supply.

- Brewer's blackbird
- Cliff and bank swallows
- Purple martin
- Swifts

Two Undesirable Householders

When you put up a birdhouse, there are two species for which you'll want to set out the "unwelcome" mat: house sparrows (page 324) and European starlings (page 320). These introduced species from Europe are opportunists that are well-adapted to a wide range of living conditions. Given half a chance, house sparrows and starlings will take over available cavities, leaving native bird species out in the cold. Since humans brought these too-successful transplants to this continent, it only seems fair that we lend a hand to native birds that are losing their nest sites to them. For example, simple nest box features can make a big difference: Offer boxes without perches (or remove existing perches)—native cavity-nesting birds don't need a perch to get into a nest box, but a perch makes access easier for starlings and house sparrows. Providing nest boxes specifically designed to accommodate native species while excluding "pest" birds is a way to help bluebirds and others that have been threatened by the double whammy of habitat loss and competition from adaptable aliens.

Tree Swallows May Take Over

Adult male tree swallows are smaller than purple martins and have dark blue-green backs and white fronts. Females have dark drab backs but also have white fronts. At times they're mistaken for purple martins because they'll occasionally nest in a martin house. Tree swallows will force bluebirds out of a nest box. To keep this from happening on some bluebird trails, two identical boxes are placed 15 to 25 feet (4.5 to 7.6 m) apart facing away from each other. The theory is that the swallows will use one box and the bluebirds the other, and it often works. In areas where the violet-green swallow's range overlaps with those of bluebirds and tree swallows, all three species may compete for the same nest cavities. Just as bluebirds and tree swallows will share a territory, provided nest boxes are placed at a suitable distance and facing away from each other, so will violet-green swallows nest in proximity to either or both of the other species. However, none of the three will tolerate nesting birds of their own species within the same territory.

This technique can't be used to keep tree swallows out of apartment-style martin houses because the nest holes are so close together. Tree swallows that occupy a unit in a martin house may be tempted to move by offering them a single-family nest box nearby. Meanwhile, plug up the holes in the martin house until the tree swallows have settled into other digs.

Take a Closer Look

Purple Martin *(Progne subis)*

At 8 inches (20 cm) long, the purple martin is the biggest North American swallow. From a distance the adult male looks purple but he's actually dark bluish black. Because of this and his size, purple martins are often mistaken for European starlings. The female is the same size but lighter in color. Her back is a dull blue-black, and she has a gray collar, gray breast, and speckles down her belly. Young birds, when they leave the nest, are as big as the adults and resemble the female but are even lighter in front. Martins sing a very distinct low-pitched gurgling song that doesn't sound anything like other swallows'. They also make a down-slurred whistle. Their wings are very long and pointed, much like the wings of barn swallows, but their tails aren't nearly as long or as deeply forked, and they don't fly as fast as barn swallows do.

What Purple Martins Eat

- Insects of all kinds, including moths, butterflies, and just about anything that they can catch with an open mouth as they fly around
- Grasshoppers
- Stinkbugs and other bugs on the ground

Regional Relations

Five other swallow species are found throughout North America, all of which are smaller than the purple martin. The two that are most likely to be confused with a martin are the barn swallow (*Hirundo rustica*) and the tree swallow (*Tachycineta bicolor*). Barn swallows don't use nest boxes but they often are found in the same habitat as purple martins are. Tree swallows are an eastern species that also uses nest boxes but usually prefers the kind that bluebirds use. In the West the violet-green swallow (*Tachycineta thalassina*) is sometimes taken for a martin even though it's much smaller with a white face, front, and rump. Rough-winged swallows (*Stelgidopteryx serripennis*) and bank swallows (*Riparia riparia*) look a lot alike and nest along or near riverbanks.

Preferred Purple Martin Habitat

- River valleys
- Lakeshores
- Open meadows or grassy areas near ponds but away from buildings
- Marshy coastline areas
- Occasionally in appropriate housing even in towns or cities far from water

Did You Know?

- Purple martin colonies range in size from a few pairs to hundreds of pairs.
- Martins begin moving north through North America in January and reach the Northeast in mid-April.
- Males arrive first and pick a nest site. When the females reach the breeding territory and select mates, they accept the sites the males have chosen.
- A typical purple martin nest holds four or five pure white eggs; the female may not lay eggs in the nest until a month or more after the nest site is chosen.
- Martins build a rim of mud at the front of the nest box to prevent the eggs from rolling out the opening.
- The female does all the incubating, which takes about 30 days, but the male guards the nest when she temporarily leaves.
- Martin colonies are very sensitive to bad weather. The lack of insects during sustained periods of rain or cold can wipe out whole colonies or even entire regional populations. Numbers of purple martins in some areas of the Northeast still have not recovered from a week of hurricane rain in June of 1972 that killed off all the martins nesting there.
- In 1947, a New Jersey man had a martin house with 379 holes.

Purple Martin House Specs

- Entry holes must be 2.15 inches (5 cm) in diameter and 1 inch (2.5 cm) above the floor.
- The inside dimensions of each compartment must be at least 6 × 6 inches (15 × 15 cm) wide and at least 7 inches (18 cm) tall.
- When natural gourds are used, each one must be more than 8 inches (20 cm) tall. Uniformly shaped and adequately spacious plastic gourds are available.
- Both martin "apartment" houses and gourds should be painted white to reflect as much heat as possible.
- Natural gourds should be treated with water sealant or copper sulfate.
- Natural or artificial nesting gourds may be hung up singly or in groups on poles.

Apartment-Dwelling Colonists

Purple martins have long enjoyed a cooperative relationship with humans. Native Americans in what is now the southeastern United States hung gourd houses around their gardens to attract the prodigious insect eaters. Over the years, the loss of natural cavities for nesting threatened the purple martin's existence, but populations of these large swallows began to recover as people started providing artificial nesting alternatives. As a result, purple martins in the eastern United States are almost completely dependent on man-made structures called martin houses for nesting. In the West, martin pairs nest in natural cavities in cacti and trees and don't often move into martin houses.

Martin houses used to be made of wood and mounted on tilted or pivoting poles, and you had to climb up a ladder to maintain them. Commercially available houses now are typically made of aluminum or plastic, making them lighter and less prone to toppling over in strong winds. Telescoping mounting poles now enable martin-house "landlords" to raise and lower the house for cleaning and maintenance, rather than having to raise and lower themselves on a ladder. Bottle gourds, both natural and plastic ones, also are widely used to provide martin housing.

Tending a purple martin condominium requires a commitment to proper siting, cleaning, monitoring, and more. Before you invest in a martin house, you'll want to learn more about what's involved in attracting and maintaining a colony. Two excellent resources on martin house management are the Purple Martin Conservation Association of North America, 301 Peninsula Drive, Suite 6, Erie, PA 16505 (www.purplemartin.org/main/info.php) and the Purple Martin Society of North America, 21250 South Redwood Lane, Suite 101, Shorewood, IL 60431 (www.purplemartins.com).

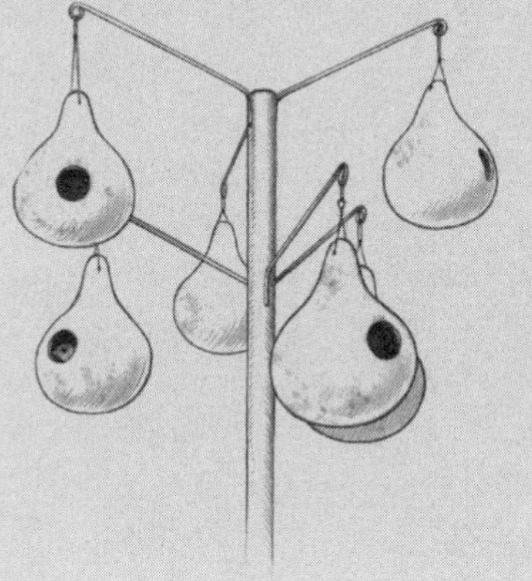

SELECTING THE RIGHT BIRDHOUSE

Matching the house you put up to the species you expect will use it is the first step on your way to a successful and satisfying experience as a landlord for nesting birds. If you approach birdhouse buying or building with your prospective tenants' needs in mind, finding and installing the right house need not be a confusing process.

Different birds have different nesting requirements. As much as the bird chooses the house, so the house, in many respects, "chooses" the bird. The size of the house's opening, its inside dimensions, and where you put it all contribute to determining which birds will use it. Before you build or buy a birdhouse, think about what kind or kinds of birds you'd like to host. Do some research to learn the recommended specifications for a nest box for that bird species. Since these sometimes change in response to scientific research and observations reported by backyard birders, it's best to seek the most up-to-date guidelines for a house that meets birds' needs and gives them the right conditions for successfully raising their young.

Organizations that focus on a particular bird species are the best place to start if you want to know what sort of house to put up for bluebirds or purple martins, for example. These groups can tell you where to buy a suitable house or can provide plans for building your own. Your local chapter of the National Audubon Society is another good starting point, especially if you plan to offer housing that may attract a few different species. By talking with people who have been tending birdhouses in your area, you can learn which kinds of houses are favored by local birds, which materials hold up best in your climate, and when to put up a house so prospective tenants will consider it during their search for a nesting site. Experienced bird landlords also can tell you what problems you may encounter, as well as creative ways to avoid common pitfalls.

You'll also find birdhouse plans and loads of practical information on placing and maintaining houses through the Web sites and publications of groups such as the Cornell Lab of Ornithology, the National Audubon Society, and the American Bird Conservancy.

Birdhouse or Nest Box?

Confused by the difference between what some people call nest boxes and others call birdhouses? Don't be. The two terms are interchangeable, and each simply means a type of artificial cavity made to provide a nesting place for birds. It's true that people who consider themselves avid birders are more likely to say "nest box" while those who are newly thinking about offering birds accommodations may refer to "birdhouses." Likewise, a more decorative unit may be dubbed a birdhouse while plain-but-functional structures tend to be tagged nest boxes. As long as a house/box supplies the features that birds need—shelter from the elements, protection from predators, and appropriate-size space for nest building—it doesn't matter what people call it. Birds looking for a place to raise a family will probably call it home.

TAKE A CLOSER LOOK

Eastern Screech Owl *(Megascops asio)*

The sound of a screech owl calling in the night has struck fear into the heart of many a person who doesn't know that the downward whinnying call is coming from a bird only about 8½ inches (21 cm) tall. Screech owls may be gray, rusty red, or brown, although gray birds are most common. They have prominent feathers called ear tufts on a large head with big eyes. A white X marks the screech owl's face, crossing above its greenish-yellow bill and angling up over its bright yellow eyes and down across its cheeks. Males and females look alike. Screech owl pairs do not make nests; they just lay four or five pure white glossy round eggs on the bottom of the cavity or box.

What Screech Owls Eat

- Small mammals, particularly meadow voles, other rodents, and sometimes bats
- Insects, including katydids, moths, and just about anything small that flies at night
- Small reptiles and amphibians
- Many different songbirds

Regional Relations

The western screech owl (*Megascops kennicotti*) is almost identical in habit, size, and appearance to the eastern screech owl except that the western has no red form. Its song, however, is different. It's a series of short whistles that go up the scale, not down. That's how you can tell the two species apart in the small crossover area along the Rocky Mountains where both are found.

Preferred Habitat

- Woods
- Residential areas with backyard trees
- Parks, even in big cities
- Farmland
- Just about any place that has trees with cavities in them

Did You Know?

- Small songbirds often give away a screech owl's location by mobbing the box it's in.
- Its eyes are immobile, but a screech owl can rotate its head 270 degrees.
- Screech owls—like other owls—regurgitate pellets containing indigestible materials like hair, skin, bones, and fur after they've eaten. Finding these pellets on the ground beneath a tree is a sure sign that an owl of some kind is using that tree on a regular basis.
- Like all owls, an eastern screech owl's ears are slits on either side of its head. The "ear tufts" aren't really ears, just feathers.
- Screech owls normally nest in cavities located 5 to 20 feet (1.5 to 6 m) up, but nests have been found as high as 80 feet (24 m) above the ground.
- Mating season for eastern screech owls is late winter through early spring.
- Even though its soft song makes it seem like it's far away, the screech owl can be very close.
- A screech owl will sit at the opening of a cavity during the day, especially if it's roosting there rather than nesting. Its eyes may be opened or closed.
- Owls see perfectly well in daylight.

Screech Owl Nest Box Specs

- Screech owl boxes should be at least 15 inches (38 cm) tall and 8 × 8 inches (20 × 20 cm) wide.
- Entrance holes should be round, 3 inches (8 cm) in diameter, and located 12 inches (30 cm) up from the bottom of the nest box.
- Cover the floor of the nest box with a 1- to 2-inch-deep (2.5 to 5 cm) layer of wood shavings.
- Mount the box on a tree, 10 to 30 feet (3 to 9 m) above the ground and below the leaf canopy.

ESSENTIAL BIRDHOUSE FEATURES

Whether you're making your own birdhouse or buying one already made, knowledge about what bird or birds may use it and what they require in a house is essential. Don't go into a store and just buy what looks good or catches your eye. Quality materials and construction are important, but they won't bring in the birds if a house's entrance hole is the wrong size or in the wrong place for the birds you're trying to attract. You'll also want to provide housing that will safeguard birds' health and well-being. A box that's inadequately ventilated, for example, may allow heat to build up to levels that are fatal for nestlings; a house that's hard to open and clean at the end of the nesting season may harbor harmful parasites. Choose materials and construction that welcome cavity-nesting birds and give them the best possible chance at successfully raising their young.

Wood is good. Although you can find birdhouses made of concrete or ceramic, most birdhouses are still made of wood because it can hold up through years of use. Red cedar and other naturally rot-resistant woods make particularly good, long-lasting houses, but chemically treated wood of any kind should be avoided in birdhouse construction. If you build your own house, use untreated wood that's ½ to ¾ inch (1.3 to 1.8 cm) thick. If you buy a house, look closely to see if you can determine what kind of wood it's made of. Well-made birdhouses typically provide relevant information about their features and construction; badly or cheaply built houses usually don't. You don't have to spend a lot to get a good-quality birdhouse, but one that seems cheap in terms of price probably is cheap in other respects as well.

Check the connections. Hardware matters in any structure that will be exposed to the elements. Houses that are glued together will eventually come apart as the wood warps and the adhesive degrades. Nails can rust, pull loose, and fall out. A house assembled with brass or other rust-resistant screws holds together longer and is easier to take apart, if needed, for cleaning and repairs.

Open and shut housecleaning. Since cleaning a house at the end of—or during—the nesting sea-

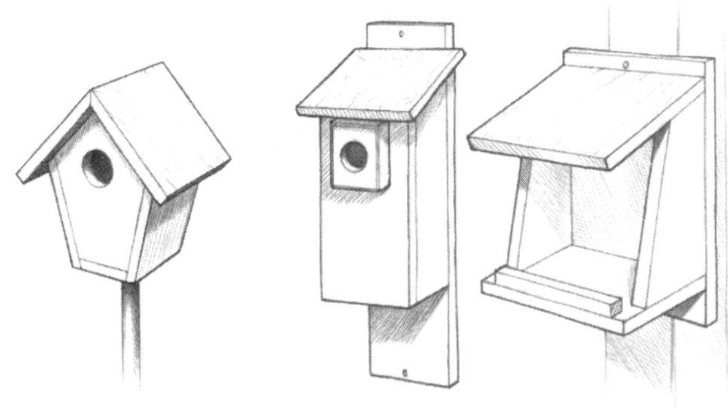

Rustic or modern, plain or fancy—looks matter little to birds seeking a place to make a nest. As natural cavities become ever scarcer, it's up to people to provide suitable alternatives that give nesting birds shelter from the weather and protection from predators.

son is important to the health of the next birds to use it, there must be a way to open the house so you can clean it out. Equally important is the ability to close the house securely after you've cleaned it. Look for durable fasteners and hinges or other features that will grant you the access you need without making the occupants vulnerable to dexterous predators such as raccoons.

Get the roof right. A slanted roof that extends out over the entrance hole helps protect the front door from the elements, but it shouldn't stick out too far. An oversize overhang might seem like a good idea, but it can make the house top-heavy and stress its attachment to the pole, post, or tree trunk on which it's mounted. Too long a roof also makes it prone to tipping over or forward in high winds or under a topping of snow. With a long roof to cling to, agile predators can hang upside down to gain access to the inside of the box, while birds inside may have their view of incoming hazards blocked.

Keep things dry and comfy. Drainage holes, preferably one in each corner of the floor, are a must to keep any rainwater that gets in from flooding the box. Adequate ventilation prevents the adult bird on the nest and the young birds in the nest from suffocating in the hot air that collects in the top of the nest box in hot weather. Drill small holes in the sides close to where they meet the roof to let hot air escape. Some birdhouses have a slit or multiple slits at the top where the sides meet the roof. Positioning these can be tricky if you're building a house because you have to make sure they don't affect the tightness of the joints where the roof and sides are connected. Drilling holes in a homemade house is easier.

Plain is preferable. Leave the wood around the entrance hole and on the inside of the house bare— it should not be painted or treated in any way. If you want to paint or seal the outside of the house to give it added protection from the elements, choose a clear sealant or an unobtrusive shade of paint that blends in with the surroundings. If you put the house in the right spot, a bird in search of a nesting cavity will find it, but brightly colored houses are more likely to attract unwanted attention and predators. Plain wood, with or without a coat of varnish, is best. Keep in mind, too, that the darker the color of the house, the more heat it will absorb.

Rough it—but just a little. The wood on the inside of the house should be slightly rough to give young birds a foothold to get to the opening to look out or leave. Except for the small area around the entrance hole, the outside of the box should be relatively smooth to keep predators from getting a hold.

Play the Angle

An opening that's cut at an upward angle through the front wall of the nest box helps to keep rain out of the box and is a sign of a well-constructed house. After you cut the entrance hole, use a planer or similar tool to make the bottom of the hole angle upward. To keep predators and unwanted bird species from gaining access, avoid enlarging the hole beyond the recommended size as you add a slant to it.

Take a Closer Look

Wood Duck *(Aix sponsa)*

Although the wood duck is small at 18½ inches (47 cm) long, it's one of the flashiest ducks around. The male has a round green head with a crest that falls down the back of his neck, an orange and yellow bill, a white bridle pattern on his dark face, a chestnut breast and rump, and a bluish gray back. The female is dull gray with spots on the sides of her belly and a big white patch around each eye. Wood ducks have unusual voices. The male makes a loud but squeaky whistling sound when he's disturbed or as he's flying around. The female makes an odd upward squeal.

What Wood Ducks Eat

- Aquatic plants
- Seeds and pinecones
- Tubers and seeds of sedges, grasses, and pondweeds
- Wild rice
- Acorns, beechnuts, hickory nuts
- Grapes and berries

Regional Relations

The mandarin duck (*Aix galericulata*) is an Asian species that sometimes escapes from zoos and private collections. It's slightly smaller than the wood duck but is often mistaken for one because of its general appearance and size. Unlike the male wood duck, the male mandarin duck has a wide white line above each eye that goes down the back of his head, and a head that's lighter in color. Female mandarin ducks look a lot like female wood ducks because they're gray with white around their eyes and have mottled fronts. There's a feral established population of mandarin ducks along the California coast, but escaped mandarin ducks are only occasionally found in the East.

Preferred Habitat

- Lakes and ponds bordered by trees or edges of creeks and slow-moving streams
- Suitable cavities in trees that can be a mile or more away from water

Did You Know?

- The female wood duck puts no nest material in the box or cavity except for her own down feathers.
- The normal clutch size is 10 to 15 creamy-white unmarked eggs. But sometimes two females will share a nest of up to 40 eggs. This is called a dump nest.
- The female lays one egg per day.
- When it's time for the young to leave the nest, the female calls to them from the ground. They use their sharp claws to climb to the opening and jump out. Once they reach the ground, she leads them to the nearest water, which can be a long distance away.
- Wood ducks have only one brood per year.
- In winter, large numbers of wood ducks congregate on ponds and lakes in the South.

Wood Duck Nest Box Specs

- Mount a wood duck box at least 10 feet (3 m) off the ground.
- The box should be at least 2 feet (60 cm) tall and 1 foot (30 cm) square on the floor.
- A door or side opening of some kind is essential so it can be cleaned out every year.
- Make the entrance hole oval-shaped and approximately 3 inches (8 cm) in diameter, 18 inches (46 cm) up from the bottom of the box.
- The roof should slant down over the entrance hole.
- Put a 3- to 4-inch (8 to 10 cm) layer of sawdust or wood shavings in the bottom of the box.
- Make drainage holes in the floor of the box.
- Attach this big, heavy box securely with long screws or metal brackets to keep it from pulling loose from its own weight and that of its occupants.

CRAFT-STORE CONVERSIONS

It's easy to find a store that has birdhouses for sale, but much harder to find one selling houses that birds would actually use. Often form has won out over function when it comes to the pricey and highly adorned birdhouses sold at gift shops, craft shops, and tourist attractions. As items of décor, these houses may be your cup of tea, but rarely do they appeal to avian occupants other than the rather undiscriminating house sparrows. A brightly painted and heavily decorated birdhouse may be attractive to humans, but it's not usually good for birds nor do they care what a prospective home looks like. If you've received one of these over-adorned structures as a gift (or purchased one yourself in a moment of weakness), don't despair: With some modifications, you may be able to convert it into a nest box that the birds actually will use.

Go for a (Single) Hole in One

- Check the placement of the hole and compare it with recommendations from reliable sources of bird information. If it's too high above the bottom of the house, young birds may have difficulty getting out when it's time to leave the nest. If it's too low, predators may be able to reach or crawl in. If everything else about the box is acceptable or can be made so, you may be able to fill in a pre-existing hole and drill a new one.
- Make any hole you have to redo at least 2 inches (5 cm) in diameter. Even houses made for small birds have to have an opening big enough for them to get through.
- No birdhouse, except for a martin house, should have more than one entrance, and even martin houses have only one opening per compartment. Many craft-store birdhouses have multiple entrance holes and often quaint signs advertising "bird apartment houses." Cover all of the holes except for the one that's in the correct place. Before you go to this trouble, check the inside to be sure that there aren't a lot of compartments. Only martin houses have multiple compartments but with only one entrance for each. A birdhouse for any other species should have only one hole and one compartment.

Birdhouses with bright paint jobs, perches, extra entrances, and other adornments may seem cute by human standards but birds have little use for such fanciful touches. If you choose to put out a decorative house, make sure its quaint features don't put your prospective tenants in harm's way.

Other Features to Fix or Refuse

- A gaily painted birdhouse looks cute to us but it may draw the eyes of predators—and even curious people—to a site that birds would rather keep private. If a house's other features are bird-friendly, it's easy enough to give it a fresh coat of paint in a more subtle shade and make it just right for birds to move into.
- You may also find houses that have one of their sides made of glass or clear plastic. The idea is for you to be able to see what's going on in there. While this may seem like a clever idea, it really isn't. Birds want and need privacy when they're nesting. Give them what they need—paint that side or cover it somehow and let your tenants nest in peace.
- Leave oddly shaped houses, especially tall, skinny ones, on the store shelf. A scaled-down outhouse replica makes a cute conversation piece but its shape is not for birds. Besides being unfamiliar to most birds looking for a nesting cavity, a tall, narrow house offers poor air circulation, especially in hot weather. The floor area is too small for young birds to move around properly, and insects are more likely to infest the unused space under its roof.
- Consider plastic birdhouses with extra care. Good-quality nest boxes made of durable recycled plastic "lumber" may be found at many bird specialty stores and from reputable catalog companies. These typically include all the features necessary to keep birds safe and healthy while they nest. But houses made of thin, rigid plastic rarely give birds what they need. Ventilation is lacking in a plastic house, which also may absorb more heat during hot weather than birds can tolerate. In extremes of heat and cold, rigid plastic houses tend to warp and crack, leaving gaps that expose nestlings to rain and predation.
- At the other end of the spectrum from cheap plastic models are high-priced houses made from the finest building materials and fitted with copper roofs and other high-end features. Such houses may be lovely and extremely well-crafted, but it won't matter to your would-be tenants. Birds don't care how much you've spent for a house, and nothing will keep it

BIRD MYTH-BUSTERS

Bypass the Perch

Although the songbirds we most want to attract to nest in our yards are known as passerine, or perching, birds, a perch at the entrance to a nest box is not the spot for sitting and singing. A perch just below the door used to be a common feature of birdhouses and was believed to help adult birds get in and out with ease. But cavity-nesting birds don't need perches to get in the door; their predators, on the other hand, do. A perch on a birdhouse enables predators to get too close to the opening and puts the nest and birds inside at great risk, especially during the night when they're roosting. If you have an old house that otherwise serves birds well, use a hacksaw to cut off the perch flush with the front of the house and return it to a likely spot in your yard.

from getting dirty and weathered. An expensive, elegantly constructed birdhouse will tempt you to put it in an exposed spot in your yard where other people can admire it, rather than in a secluded spot that's better for the birds. The best-built and most expensive birdhouse in the world will only become a display object if it's not put in the right place.

SELECT THE RIGHT SITE

The widely cited rule of thumb for real estate—location, location, location—holds as true for birdhouses as it does for human habitats. A well-tended nest box with all the right features will go unoccupied—or will attract only pesky house sparrows—if you put it in a spot that birds find unappealing or dangerous. While placement preferences vary somewhat from one bird species to the next, the following do's and don'ts will help you identify the prime birdhouse real estate in your yard.

House Placement Do's

- Build on your successes and learn from your mistakes. Start with one house in a spot that's near trees and shrubs. If birds other than house sparrows nest in it, then you know you've done things right. Look around and see if there are other similar places where you can put a second or even a third house.
- The best place to mount a birdhouse is on a metal pole securely anchored in the ground, because that limits the number of animals that can climb up to the house. Consider installing a baffle, too, for further protection against predators. Baffles work well at preventing predators from climbing up, but obviously they don't keep away predators that can fly or jump from nearby shrubs or trees. If you use a wooden pole to hold your house, try to keep it as smooth as possible. Sometimes, in spite of your best efforts, squirrels, cats, and other free-roaming predators get to the box. When that happens, try to figure out why and how it happened and make adjustments.
- Use sturdy hardware to attach a birdhouse to a pole, tree trunk, or limb. If the house is suspended in any way, be sure that it only swings back and forth a little bit in the wind and can't rotate 360 degrees. That's a surefire way to keep birds from successfully nesting in it.
- If you choose to fasten a hanger or bracket to a tree trunk to hold a nest box, do your best to find the right spot before you start making holes for the hardware. Multiple holes in the trunk put the tree at risk for diseases and insect infestations.

The combination of a baffle and a tall, smooth pole help to thwart predators that might climb up to raid a nest box. The right size entrance hole—just big enough for the intended residents—and a perch-free front make it harder for pest birds to disturb the nest.

Birdhouse Best Practices

- Pick a spot where there are trees, shrubs, and other plants nearby for shelter and protection from predators. The amount of nearby cover needed depends on which birds are using the box. Learn the needs of the species you're trying to attract. Bluebirds need a big open area near a box while most others prefer some nearby shelter. House wrens prefer a lot of shelter nearby.
- Think about whether or not this area will get overgrown or change a lot in the future.
- Choose a place where you can easily get to the box to check, clean, and maintain it in the off-season.
- Don't place a box where there's a lot of human activity.
- Avoid feeder areas.
- Take the time to erect the box securely, using good materials to keep it from falling or coming loose while birds are using it.

House Placement Don'ts

- Never put a birdhouse near bird feeders. Nesting birds are extremely territorial. If too many other birds come into their territory, or if there's too much activity in the area, the nesting birds will leave for quieter quarters.
- With the exception of houses for bluebirds or swallows (such as purple martins), avoid putting a birdhouse out in the middle of a large expanse of lawn all by itself where it bakes in the afternoon sun.
- If you hang a nest box from a tree, be sure that it's not too close to overhanging branches that offer hiding places where a predator can wait for a chance to attack the house and its occupants.
- Unless it's for an owl, don't put a birdhouse so far up on a tree trunk that you can't easily reach it. The harder it is for you to get to a box, the greater are the chances that you won't take care of it.
- In your enthusiasm, don't overdo it and put too many houses in a small yard. If things are too crowded, most of the houses will go unused. How many houses birds will use in a backyard or on any property depends on what the habitat will support. In a typical backyard, allow 25 feet (7.6 m) or more between boxes. If you have enough room and plenty of trees, shrubs, and shelter, you may want to put them farther apart. Where you live will help determine the right number of boxes to put out. In the typical suburban backyard, one or two pole-mounted houses, a wren box hanging from a tree, and a screech owl box are enough.

SHELF HOUSING

Many birds that won't use a nest box will sometimes build a nest on an open shelf. If a bird uses a properly built and placed shelf, you often have the opportunity to watch the nesting process from beginning to end.

The species that use shelves naturally nest on any available open ledge, including places such as under the eaves of buildings and bridges, on top of light fixtures, and on or in rain gutters. Sometimes the birds pick a spot where you don't want them. Discourage them from nesting in a troublesome spot by covering up the area, moving things around, or removing the beginnings of a nest before it's finished. If you do this as soon as the problem arises, the birds will relocate and make their nest elsewhere.

Bird shelves are structures that have at least one open side; some have all four sides open. The nest floor area tends to be bigger than that of most birdhouses, even though the shelves are meant for small songbirds. The birds that use them don't like being enclosed and generally build bigger, wider, and sometimes messier nests. Bird shelves, like other types of man-made bird housing, should be made with appropriate materials and sturdy, weather-resistant hardware. If you buy a bird shelf, check everything about it just as you would a birdhouse. Even in stores that specialize in bird products, nest shelves may be harder to find than traditional houses and boxes. Because consumer demand for shelves is less than for birdhouses, fewer companies make them.

Birds That Use Shelf Housing

- American robin
- Barn swallow
- Carolina and Bewick's wrens
- Eastern phoebe
- Gray catbird
- House finch
- Northern cardinal
- Song sparrow

Bird Shelf Specs

- The floor should be at least 8 × 8 inches (20 × 20 cm).
- Make the back 2 to 3 inches (5 to 7 cm) tall, unless you're going to attach a roof to it. Make the back 6 inches (15 cm) tall if the shelf will have a roof over it. Attach the roof securely to the back so that it won't come loose and fall down onto the birds or the nest.
- You can also put on a roof by placing 6-inch (15 cm) posts at the corners of the floor.
- Leave the sides and front of the shelf open.
- A shelf with a back may be attached to the side of a building, under the eaves, or against a tree trunk.
- A shelf that has only a roof and floor may be hung from a branch or fastened on top of a branch. Attach it securely to keep it from falling while in use.
- Once in place, the shelf shouldn't move at all.

ROOST BOX RULES

A roost box is a shelter into which birds go to sleep, stay warm, protect themselves from harsh weather, or all of the above. It's not the same as a birdhouse, even though birds sometimes will roost in clean, empty birdhouses outside of their breeding season or during cold weather. If you really think ahead when you're putting up a nest box, you'll make it so you can turn it upside down as winter approaches. It won't take the place of a box made specifically for roosting, but it's sure better than nothing. Sometimes in the harsh cold of winter, birds will use any birdhouse they can find as a shelter, even though no warm air is being trapped at the top as it would be in a roost box. Downy woodpeckers, in particular, will go into bluebird houses and hunker down for the night.

But a well-made roost box is much better for sheltering birds from cold weather. Birdhouses may be taken down in harsh winter weather if you want, but roost boxes are meant to stay outside during snow, sleet, ice, and whatever else comes along. Fall is the time to put up roost boxes. Pick a spot or spots where there's protection from winter weather. Put the boxes where they can be easily reached but high enough to discourage predators. Take them down in spring when it's time for the birds to begin nesting. Once the weather gets warm at night, the roost box is no longer needed, and it's best to take it down so rodents, squirrels, or other animals won't get into it.

If you build your own roost box, use durable materials that will hold up under prolonged exposure to the elements. Because durability is so important, a well-made roost box may be expensive, but the investment in quality usually pays off. You can also find nest boxes that are designed to be converted for roosting once the nesting season is over. A convertible nest/roost box has two holes on the front, one at

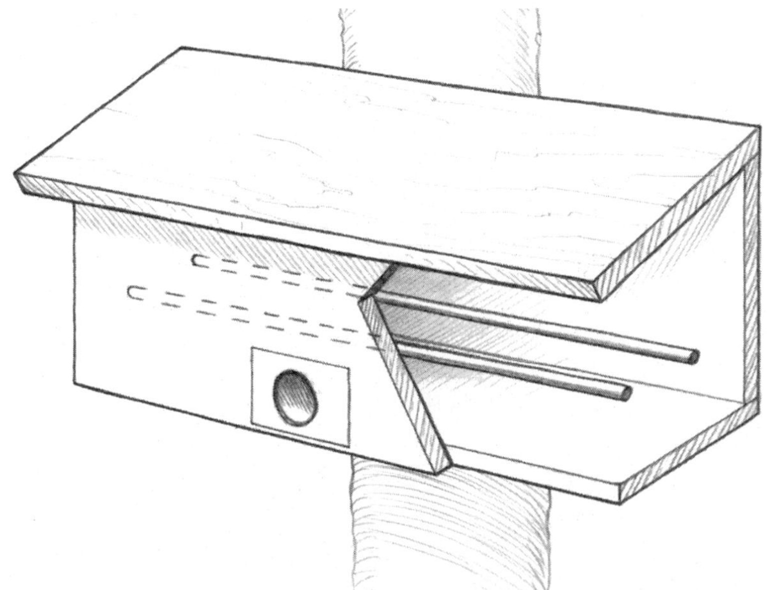

A sturdy roost box offers birds a place to take shelter during cold weather. A roost box typically has interior perch space for several birds, a tightly fitted roof, and an entry hole near the floor—this combination of features helps hold in the body heat of birds roosting within it.

the bottom and one at the top, one of which is always closed. When nesting is over, remove any nest materials from the box, place dowels for perching inside, and close up the top hole. If you buy a box meant to serve both functions, be doubly sure to check that it's well-made. Sometimes the more removable parts a box has, the more problems it can develop.

ROOST BOX FEATURES

- A roost box should be two to three times bigger than a birdhouse and taller than it is wide.
- The opening of a roost box is at the bottom, not at the top. It should be about 2 inches (5 cm) in diameter so that different size songbirds can use it.
- A roost box doesn't have ventilation holes near the roof like a birdhouse does, because it's meant to trap and hold the heat rising from the bodies of the birds roosting inside it.
- The inner walls should be rough so birds can grab onto them.
- Wooden perches inside the box are placed at different levels, not exactly opposite each other.
- You need to be able to clean it out when warm weather arrives, so its top, not its sides, should be hinged to allow easy access.
- Try to place a roost box where it gets the most winter sun or warmth. A southward facing position is best. Sometimes the microclimate around a house or other building is ideal because it stays warmer there.
- Because a roost box is big, make sure that it's securely attached wherever you mount it.
- Take the roost box down when you're sure it's no longer needed or else cover up the bottom opening of a dual-purpose box. All kinds of creatures, specifically rodents, can get inside and raise their young there. Wash it out with a mild detergent and check to see if it needs any repairs before storing it away. Then when it's time to put it back out, it will be ready.

ACCIDENTAL OCCUPANTS

Sometimes your birdhouses remain empty in spite of your best efforts, while birds instead decide to make nests in unexpected spots. Hanging baskets of flowers or plants are especially attractive to some birds and may be chosen as nest sites even though they weren't intended for that purpose. If you're unwilling to play host to a nest in this location, it poses a bit of a problem. If you catch the birds while they're still in the midst of nest construction, relocating the materials may do the trick. Sometimes, simply disturbing the nesting birds by watering the container will convince them to go elsewhere. Once a nest is finished, trying to move it may be less successful and possibly illegal. The birds may simply attempt to rebuild in the same spot. Also, the federal Migratory Bird Treaty prohibits the removal or destruction of any active songbird nests. Unless the plants in the container are particularly precious, it's usually best to let the birds go ahead and do their thing.

House finches, house wrens, Carolina wrens, robins, mourning doves, and some western hummingbird species have been known to successfully nest in hanging baskets. Mailboxes, even those being used, are sometimes chosen as nest sites. House wrens have been reported as nesting in all

An active nest in your hanging basket may be a delight or a nuisance. Protective parent birds may keep you from tending your plants, and the mess from adult birds and nestlings can be considerable. But if you're not too worried about the fate of your flowers and don't mind the extra chores, a nearby nest can provide hours of up-close bird enjoyment.

kinds of odd places, including laundry hanging on a clothesline. Barn swallows have been known to nest in old cellar ceilings even when the cellar door wasn't open all day. The swallows would wait until the door was opened, even if it was late in the day, and then fly in, build their nest, and raise and feed their young.

PREVENTING ERRANT NESTERS

If a bird chooses to nest in your favorite outdoor planter, there are ways to discourage it. But it's best to never let that happen at all, which is something you can do by checking the containers every time you water them. No matter how much rain normally falls, containers, especially hanging baskets, nearly always need supplemental watering at times. Be on the lookout for anything unusual showing up among the flowers. If you see sticks piling up, remove them. That's usually enough to make the bird go elsewhere. Feathers are another indication that a bird has at least been exploring the container, so remove them too. If it really becomes a problem, covering the soil of the container with a piece of wire mesh or similar material may be enough to make the bird go elsewhere. Oftentimes just the normal watering process will make the bird leave. Moving the basket or container, even just temporarily, to a spot where

BIRD MYTH-BUSTERS

Mom and Dad Don't Mind the Smell

If you handle a baby bird, your lingering scent does *not* doom it to certain abandonment by its parents—most birds don't have a sense of smell. That means it's safe to pick up a fallen hatchling and return it to its nest. But it's still best to maintain a hands-off policy when you do discover a nest filled with eggs or young birds. Why? Human activity around a nest may cause parent birds to abandon it; at the very least, they may use up a lot of energy defending their home at a time when they can ill afford to pause in feeding their hungry young. And even if the birds don't notice your scent, predators can and may follow it straight to the nest.

there's a lot of human traffic or other activity also can work. Most birds don't want to nest in heavily used areas.

It's a different problem when a bird chooses to use a spot or hole at a place it shouldn't, like under the eaves of the house or in the downspouts. Then it's not so easy to make the bird move elsewhere because the spot can be hard to reach. And unless you're extremely tolerant, you really should try to get the bird out of there because the nest may clog spouting or cause other structural problems. At the very least, the nesting site is an indication that perhaps you need to check that part of your house closely to see why the bird chose it. It almost always means that there's something that needs attending to. It may be a sign that termites have weakened or destroyed some of the wood there. It could mean that some boards or siding have come loose without your knowledge. Or there may be a tear in a screen that allowed a bird to get in.

SEASONAL SHIFTS IN BIRD BEHAVIOR

When nesting season is over, the activity in your yard slows down and may seem almost to disappear. It may seem like there aren't many birds at all around anymore, but that's not true. The young birds are out learning to do what adult birds do, and the adult birds are doing what they do when they're not breeding—surviving from day to day.

In late summer, birds take advantage of the abundant supply of food and move around a lot. As fall approaches, they eat more to pack on fat for a lengthy migration or to help them make it through winter. When you're sure nesting is over for summer, clean out all the nest boxes and check them thoroughly for any repairs that have to be made. Nest boxes should be left up until the cold weather hits and some can be left out year-round if you prefer. Boxes mounted on poles, as in the case of bluebird houses, usually are left out all winter because bluebirds or other species sometimes use them for roosting. Screech owl and wood duck boxes should be left out all winter because they often see use as roost boxes by these species. Hanging houses, especially any made from gourds, must be taken in during the cold months to preserve them for future nesting seasons.

In the long, cold months of the North, the birds eat constantly to keep their metabolism and body heat up. If they've migrated farther south, they have a plentiful supply of food and they're pretty laid back. When the days get longer and the sun moves higher in the sky, hormones once again begin to rise. Migrants know it's time to fly back north again and breed. Birds that never migrated at all feel that same breeding urge. They just don't have far to go to begin their nesting. Spring comes back and once again the birds in your backyard will be looking for the great nest box that they used there the year before.

CHAPTER 6

WATER FEATURES FOR BIRDS

What's more important than food, protective cover, and nesting sites? If you're a bird—or pretty much anything else, for that matter—the answer is water. Providing water year-round for visiting and resident birds is the single most important thing you can do for them. In this chapter, we'll review all the options, from a simple clay or plastic saucer to a solar-powered drip birdbath, heated birdbaths, and even water gardens. We'll tell you how to choose, set up, and maintain water features so they're safe and inviting to birds. We also will take a closer look at some water-loving backyard visitors, including belted kingfishers, great blue herons, red-winged blackbirds, and even mallards.

Birdbaths used to be one of the most boring and static of landscape ornaments—a (often empty) concrete bowl and pedestal sitting in a sea of grass. No longer! Now birdbaths can be as fun and lively as you like, suited to any style and budget, and super-simple or gizmo-riffic. And they're just the start! Read on to discover the wet, wild world of backyard water features. Your feeder birds will thank you, and we can guarantee that you'll be able also to attract species that wouldn't dream of coming in to a feeder (unless it was full of, say, frogs).

Let's start splashing!

BATHS FOR BIRDS

Does something as simple as setting out a birdbath really work? When we asked Pat Varner, co-owner with her husband, Will, of the Wild Birds Unlimited store in Allentown, Pennsylvania, to choose her favorite backyard bird-related product, she didn't hesitate: "I love the birdbath in my yard," she said. "It brings in all kinds of birds—even the ones that don't eat from feeders. Adding a birdbath heater in the winter really brings birds into the yard. There's not much water anywhere when the temperature goes below 32°F! We get tons of birds."

That's a strong endorsement. We all know how important it is to provide water as well as food, so everybody does it, right? Wrong. A survey of super-enthusiastic backyard birders—the Project FeederWatch participants—revealed that the only place where more than a tiny fraction had put out a source of water for their birds was in the arid Southwest, where it was obvious that water was a bigger draw than any amount of food. Even in the broiling heat of a Southern summer or the freezing cold of a Northern winter, FeederWatchers just hadn't felt compelled to provide water. (And you may recall from Chapter 2 that these folks averaged seven feeders apiece!)

Yikes. We want to stress this point because, in an increasingly developed landscape where natural water sources are literally drying up, it's more important than it ever was to provide birds with fresh, clean water. After all, they can't turn on the tap or drill a well! And birdbaths provide more than drinking water for birds—baths also allow them to bathe. For birds, bathing serves a much more important function than simple hygiene: It keeps their feathers in good condition so they can fly. No wonder water features are such incredible bird magnets!

In this chapter, we're going to show you that having a water feature—be it a simple saucer or an elaborate water garden—and having the incredible wealth of plant, bird, insect, and animal life that springs up in and around it (or stops by to visit) will be the best thing that can happen to your yard. It might turn out to be the best thing that could happen to *you*! That's because a water feature is interesting. It's ever-changing. Frankly, it's *fun*.

Where to Find Birdbaths and Supplies

Stores and Web sites that sell bird feeders usually sell birdbaths as well. We suggest that you review the resources in Chapter 2, "Seeds and Feeders," beginning on page 25, to find some of our favorites, including Wild Birds Unlimited, Wild Bird Centers, Duncraft, and more. There's also an Internet store that focuses on birdbaths: BirdBaths.com (www.birdbaths.com). It sells an unbelievable 530 birdbath models! It also offers free or low shipping costs (a big help when dealing with a heavy birdbath), lists of bestsellers and best-reviewed models, and a solar birdbath FAQ (Frequently Asked Questions). You should definitely put BirdBaths.com on your must-see list! But as always, we recommend comparison shopping, since you might find a lower price locally. (And besides, it's fun to look!)

And it's fun for kids, pets, and wildlife as well as for adults.

Let's start by looking at the amazing diversity of birdbaths you can buy or make yourself. If you're like us, you'll be outside setting out your first ground-level birdbath before you've even finished reading!

CHOOSING A BIRDBATH

Follow these tips when you select and site a birdbath so you can't go wrong.

- **Put it where you can see it.** When you're choosing birdbath locations, put at least one bath where you can enjoy the sight of birds drinking and splashing around. If you live in a cold-winter area, make sure it's the one you'll heat in winter for year-round enjoyment.
- **Choose the site before you choose the bath.** Where you want to put your birdbath may determine what kind of bath you want to buy (or make; see page 181): a pedestal, hanging, on-ground, or inground type; a solar or plug-in style; a stylish or pedestrian model. Clearly, a shady site is a bad choice for a solar birdbath, and a front-yard setting may call for a better-looking birdbath than one you're planning to place on the ground near shrubs in the backyard. And siting a birdbath under trees will invite a torrent of leaves into your birdbath in fall, and seeds and/or fruits in spring and summer. We don't need to tell you that means more work!
- **Choose a style that works for you.** With so many birdbath styles available, there's no reason to limit yourself. You can buy pedestal and ground-level baths in classic concrete, copper and other metals, ceramic, cast resin, faux stone, and plastic—as well as hanging plastic, ceramic, and metal models. Styles vary from the time-honored basin on a pedestal to a cascading recirculating fountain of bowls, a faux stone version that looks like it's been hewed from great slabs of granite, and even one that resembles an office water cooler. And those are just the more common versions! You can find artisan-made, sculptural birdbaths, cast "Victorian" birdbaths with flowers, birds, and other embellishments, and many other models. We recommend that you choose one that matches your landscape style (formal, informal, cottage, natural, etc.) and your own taste—you'll have to look at it every day, after all!—while still meeting the birds' basic needs. Let's take a look at what those needs are.
- **Keep it shallow.** First of all, songbirds avoid deep water—they're not ducks!—so if you choose a deep birdbath, don't fill it with more than 1½ to 2 inches (4 to 5 cm) of water. The flatter the bath, the more water surface it will present to the birds, while the more bowl-shaped the bath is, the smaller the amount of water you can add before it's too deep. And the more water surface you provide, the more birds you'll get; a flat-bottomed birdbath is best of all. But a shallow birdbath has another advantage, too: It's easier for the birds to get down to the water. Birds are cautious creatures and are less likely to plunge down steep sides than to wade confidently in from a wide, shallow rim.
- **Give birds some purchase.** Birds love water for drinking and bathing, but they need to be able to get to the water easily. They basically fly

down to the edge of the birdbath and then step in rather than plunging directly into the water, so they need something to step onto that's not slippery or they won't come in for a dip. A rough surface on the birdbath, such as concrete, textured cast resin, or even textured plastic, can give them enough of a foothold to feel confident about stepping in. Ceramic, glass, smooth plastic, and metal present slick surfaces that birds will avoid. You can compensate by adding some stones, pebbles, or pieces of brick in the bottom of the birdbath so birds will be willing to hop down onto them.

- **Get moving.** Moving water, that is. Many more birds will be drawn to your birdbath if they can see and hear water movement. Choose a birdbath with a fountain, spray, or drip already attached, or select a model that will accommodate a separate fountain or drip element. (See "Water in Motion" on page 185 for the many ways to provide birds with this enticing feature.)
- **Think seasonally.** Solar-powered fountains in summer, water heaters in winter: Consider how easy it is to accessorize the birdbath model you're considering before you make your final choice. Some models come with built-in heaters and/or solar components. (See "Here Comes the Sun" on page 205 and "Heating Up" on page 185 for more on these features.)
- **Get real.** Okay, it's time to get practical. Don't overlook the mundane maintenance aspects when you're choosing your birdbath, since they're the ones that make having a birdbath a pleasure or a pain. As you look at each birdbath model, ask yourself: Is it easy to lift? Is it easy to move? Does it come apart for easier moving and storage? Is it easy to clean? Is it stable? Is it durable? Will it crack or shatter if it gets knocked over? Is it weatherproof? Are its components easy to replace?

Install a Half Bath

Try this wonderful tip from Sally Roth, backyard birder and author of *The Backyard Bird Feeder's Bible.* Sally points out that, since many pedestal-mounted birdbaths are sold in two pieces—the basin and the pedestal—she'll often just buy the basin and use it as a ground-level birdbath. Great idea!

Many backyard birds prefer a low-level spot for drinking and bathing, and placing a basin on the ground avoids the risk that it will topple from its pedestal and break.

© Svetlana Larina/iStockphoto

© Rich Phalin/iStockphoto

Tempt orioles to visit your feeding station by serving up an orange half impaled upon a nail. These vocal, colorful birds also are fond of grape jelly and sugar-water "nectar."

Filled with black oil sunflower seed, a tube feeder quickly becomes a regular destination for finches and other small-to-medium-size seed eaters. A sturdy tube feeder can last for several years with little care other than refilling and cleaning.

Courtesy of Judit Bozsár

A well-stocked feeding station is almost guaranteed to attract a crowd on a cold, snowy day. Birds seek out feeders when winter weather makes it difficult for them to forage for seeds from natural sources. Several species may perch side by side or feed peacefully in mixed flocks on the ground. As the breeding season nears, squabbles may erupt as birds become more territorial and less tolerant of one another's presence at the feeder.

© Steve Maslowski/Visuals Unlimited

A downy woodpecker clings to the mesh of a feeder designed to protect suet from less acrobatic starlings and other would-be suet gobblers. Woodpeckers, nuthatches, titmice, and chickadees have no trouble reaching the feeder's contents and the roof protects the suet from exposure to the elements.

© Gary Meszaros/Visuals Unlimited

A rose-breasted grosbeak displays the brilliant red bib and sturdy bill described by its name. These seed lovers may visit feeders across the eastern two-thirds of the United States as they migrate to breeding sites in the Northeast, the Upper Midwest, and Canada. While the showy male bird is nearly impossible to miss, his drab, streaky brown mate resembles a large, heavy-beaked sparrow and may go unnoticed when she visits your feeder.

© Spectrumphotofile.com

A pair of red crossbills shows off the tools that let them extract seeds nestled between the scales of pine, spruce, and fir cones. Red crossbills are year-round residents of conifer forests across North America. Flocks of crossbills may relocate in search of abundant cones and will nest wherever food is plentiful.

© Norman Bateman

Mulberries attract a wide range of birds, including bright-colored scarlet tanagers. Tanagers occasionally may appear at feeding stations offering fruit, but a wooded landscape with mature trees is their primary interest. A flash of red high in the treetops may be the only sign of scarlet tanagers in your yard. Despite the male's eye-catching breeding plumage, tanagers are secretive birds that spend most of their time hunting insects up in the canopy.

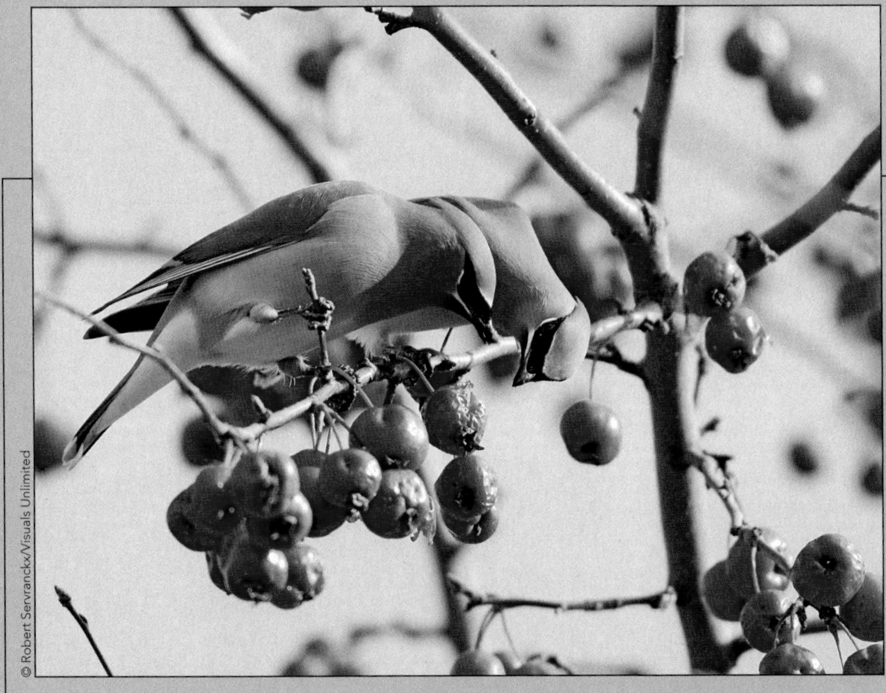

© Robert Servranckx/Visuals Unlimited

Elegant cedar waxwings often arrive in flocks to feast on crab apples, cherries, and other fruits. Dogwood berries may be eaten in fall as soon as they ripen, while crab apples and some types of berries may not attract hungry birds' attention until late winter after they've grown softer from repeated freezing and thawing. Waxwings swallow fruits whole and effectively distribute the seeds of many fruiting plants via their droppings.

Vocal red-eyed vireos are much more likely to be heard than seen as they glean insects from the foliage high in the trees. Caterpillars are a favorite food of these olive green songsters, although their winter diet may consist almost entirely of fruit. Brown-headed cowbirds often lay their eggs in vireo nests, but vireos nesting in the interior of a wooded area are less likely to be discovered by breeding cowbirds.

Numerous in eastern woods and shady suburbs, great crested flycatchers rarely venture down to ground level, spending most of their time among the treetops hunting insects. Great crested flycatchers are cavity nesters and will use a nest box placed 10 to 20 feet (3 to 6 m) above the ground at the edge of a wooded area. Snakeskin is a common nest-lining material for great crested flycatchers; in the West, ash-throated flycatchers prefer rabbit fur in their nests.

During the summer months, yellow warblers sing in the treetops from northern Canada and Alaska through nearly all of the lower 48 states. These small birds glean caterpillars and other insects and arthropods from trees and shrubs; their favored nest sites are brushy areas near water. When a brown-headed cowbird deposits an egg in a yellow warbler nest, the warbler often starts afresh, building a new nest right on top of the old one.

© Rick & Nora Bowers/Visuals Unlimited

Despite its size, you may not notice the well-camouflaged common nighthawk unless you spot one in flight as it hunts insects on the wing at dusk or dawn. Not hawks at all, nighthawks nest on gravel rooftops or rocky open ground where their coloring makes them almost invisible.

© Tom J. Ulrich/Visuals Unlimited

Courtesy of Duncraft

A roost box offers birds shelter in harsh winter weather. While a nest box entrance is high on the front panel of the box, the opening to a roost box is near the bottom. A convertible box like this one lets you flip the front panel to position the entryway for roosting in winter and for nesting in spring and summer.

© OlsonPix/Shutterpoint

Almost any relatively flat, elevated surface will do when robins are seeking a nest site. A broad beam with a supportive right angle suits these and other shelf nesters' purposes even if the messy nest's location proves inconvenient for human neighbors.

© Joe McDonald/Visuals Unlimited

Young wood ducks often must leap several feet to the ground when it's time to venture out of their nest.

The oriole's nest is an intricately woven pouch of stalks, bark, and string.

© Gerard Fuehrer/Visuals Unlimited

When temperatures fall below freezing, finding water is as important to wild birds as finding food. When winter weather makes fresh water scarce, a heated bath will bring plenty of thirsty birds to your yard. You can add a heater to an existing birdbath or choose a bath with a built-in heating element. Either way, place the bath where you can see it easily from indoors and where its cord won't interfere with other outdoor activities.

Courtesy of Duncraft

Courtesy of Duncraft

Turn your birdbath from boring to busy by adding a mist sprayer or dripper. The sight and sound of moving water is irresistible to most birds and, much like people, some birds seem to prefer showers to baths! Hummingbirds, in particular, are often seen flying through the fine mist from a sprinkler.

A male ruby-throated hummingbird shows off his colorful gorget as he sips nectar from a flower. Although hummingbirds often are seen visiting flowers or nectar (sugar water) feeders, their diet also includes tiny spiders and insects. Even plants with flowers that aren't shaped for hummer beaks can benefit the tiny birds by attracting small flies and other buggy treats.

The bright orange-red blossoms of trumpet vine (*Campsis radicans*), also called trumpet creeper, are practically guaranteed to invite hummingbirds to your landscape. Plant this vigorous woody vine in a spot where it has room to grow and a sturdy support to climb. Prune it annually to keep it from outgrowing its assigned space in your yard.

The tiny calliope hummingbird is the smallest bird in North America and the smallest long-distance migratory bird in the world. Calliope hummingbirds breed in the mountainous areas of the Pacific Northwest and spend the winter months in southern Mexico. Male birds are distinguished by wine-red stripes on their white throats.

Only slightly bigger than petite calliope hummingbirds, rufous hummers have the distinction of breeding farther north than any other hummingbird. These rusty orange birds spend summers along the Pacific Coast, from northern California all the way up to southern Alaska. Their migration path covers most of the Southwest as they travel to and from Mexico. They're also known to stray from their usual routes and frequently appear at feeders in eastern states and along the Gulf Coast.

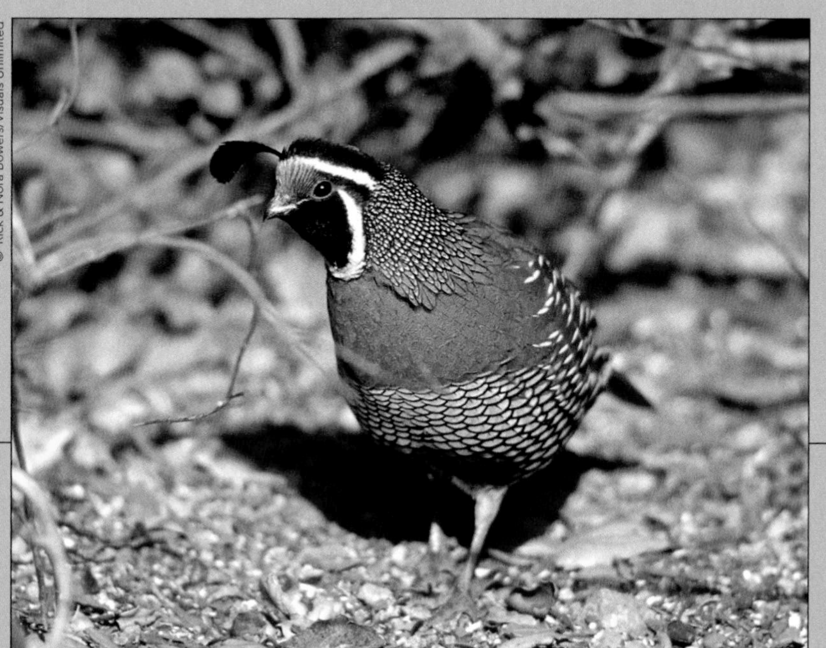
© Rick & Nora Bowers/Visuals Unlimited

The state bird of California wears a prominent black topknot as it forages on the ground for seeds and insects. California quail are tolerant of human activity and may feed in small coveys in suburban yards and parks. Offering scratch feed the ground or on a low tray feeder may bring them to your yard if you live within their range. Like most ground-nesting birds, young California quail are down-covered and ready to walk shortly after they hatch.

© Joe McDonald/Visuals Unlimited

The western screech owl ranges across the western third of North America, from south coastal Alaska and Canada's Pacific coast all the way to central Mexico and east to central Texas and Colorado. A small percentage of western screech owls are brown, but most are gray and look very much like the gray morph of the eastern screech owl. For a time, western and eastern screech owls were considered to be the same species. Hybrids sometimes occur where the two species' ranges overlap.

Eastern screech owls may have gray (*at left*) or red (*below*) plumage; these color variants are known as morphs, with gray birds outnumbering red ones. Brown morphs also occur, but are more rust-colored than brown western screech owls. Screech owls nest in cavities and will readily use suitably large nest boxes. Whether in a natural cavity or a nest box, screech owls lay their eggs on the bare floor without any cushioning material. The screech owl's descending, whinnying song is the stuff of horror movie soundtracks and has no doubt inspired terror in countless campers.

If you see this bird in your yard, it will probably be clutching a feeder bird in its talons. The handsomely marked blue-gray peregrine falcon is a fierce and successful predator that dives down upon its prey in high-speed stoops that may approach 200 miles per hour. Birds of all sizes make up a good portion of the peregrine falcon's diet, along with a variety of small mammals. Peregrine falcons live on every continent except Antarctica.

Majestic and graceful in flight, turkey vultures seem to soar effortlessly through the sky as they search for carrion. Encountering one of these large birds on the ground is awe-inspiring in a different way—the combined effect of its unattractive featherless head, its hooked beak, and its impressive 5½-foot (1.7 m) wingspan can be rather alarming.

Introduced to North America by European settlers, pigeons, also known as rock doves or rock pigeons, have a long history as domestic birds. Now resident throughout southern and coastal Canada, the United States, and Mexico, pigeons may display an extensive range of feather colors and markings, as a result of interbreeding between wild pigeons and escaped domestic birds. In some urban areas, efforts to promote nesting by peregrine falcons have had the added effect of helping to reduce burgeoning pigeon populations.

Habitat loss continues to jeopardize the existence of the Florida scrub-jay. These beautiful blue birds are found only in Florida in scrubby oak woods on sand dunes where they feed on insects and acorns. Even this required habitat becomes unsuitable without periodic burning, making it problematic for the human development that presses all around it. In spite of the threats that humans pose, Florida scrub-jays are relatively tame and are among the easiest birds to hand-feed.

© Neal Mishler/Visuals Unlimited

A flock of Canada geese flying in a V formation is one of the most visible examples of bird migration. Every year millions of birds travel from north to south in fall and from south to north in spring. Some species travel thousands of miles, while others relocate by only a few hundred miles. Some birds fly by night, stopping in daylight to rest and feed; some follow routes that require them to fly great distances over open water. With each passing season, the work of ornithologists, conservation groups, and interested backyard birders increases our understanding of this fascinating bird behavior.

Crows are entertaining, intelligent, and loud. A tree filled with crows rarely inspires the same delight as a feeder crowded with goldfinches. Roosting crows tend to awaken early, beginning their raucous cawing before dawn and carrying on for hours. The slightest disturbance sets off a cacophonous chain reaction. Although crows sometimes eat the eggs and nestlings of other birds, they also help to protect songbirds from predators, calling out loud warnings when they spot a hawk or a prowling cat.

© Steve Maslowski/Visuals Unlimited

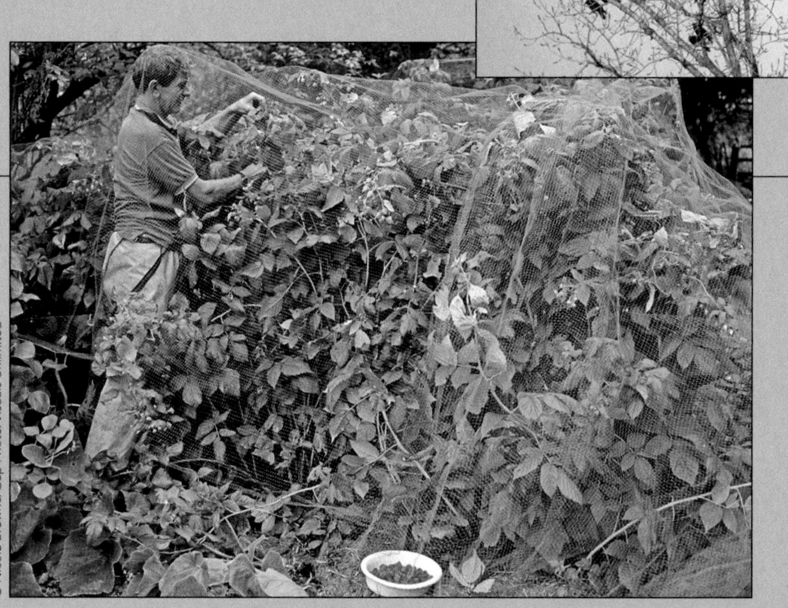

© Nicola Browne/Gap Photo/Visuals Unlimited

You can have birds and berries, too! It just takes a bit of planning and prevention. You'll find that, although scare devices are widely available, birds quickly become accustomed to all but the most elaborate tactics. Using netting to exclude birds from berries you want for yourself is an effective method, as long as you secure the net at ground level and support it above the berry plants—some birds will go under a net to dine, and others will perch atop it to gobble any fruit they can reach through the mesh.

© Chris Barton/photographersdirect.com

The grassy expanses of athletic fields and public parks are lush green welcome mats for Canada geese. Where conditions are to their liking, populations of these big birds may give up their migratory habits and become full-time residents, often to the dismay of humans who don't wish to share recreation space with large numbers of messy and sometimes aggressively territorial geese. Towns and corporations that find themselves hosting unwanted geese often must invest substantial resources to resolve the problem.

© Dr. William J. Weber/Visuals Unlimited

The brown-headed cowbird may be the least-loved bird in North America, at least among folks who know what this parasitic pest is up to. Rather than making a nest of her own, a female cowbird lays each of her eggs in a songbird's nest, leaving the unsuspecting nest holders to raise a young cowbird along with or in place of their own nestlings. Not all songbirds fall for this plot: Some evict cowbird eggs, some abandon parasitized nests, and some simply build a new nest atop the old one.

Birds may not be the only wild creatures to show up at your feeders in search of a meal. Squirrels might be the most evident and persistent mammalian feeder raiders, but raccoons, opossums, mice, flying squirrels, deer, and even bears are widely known to take advantage of a well-stocked bird feeder. If large quantities of seed and suet begin disappearing overnight, suspect something bigger and furrier than a bird. You may need to bring feeders in at night or take them down entirely for awhile until the four-legged bandits go elsewhere to dine.

BUDGET-WISE BIRDING

Begin with a Recycled Bath

One thing we'll say about birdbaths: Some aren't cheap. You can end up paying up to $300 for a birdbath *before* you add a heater or a drip attachment! Of course, not all birdbaths are in this league. You can find a lightweight cast-resin birdbath and pedestal for under $30. However, we admit that the sound of "free" is even more appealing.

So we suggest that you try a repurposed birdbath—one you recycle from something you already have at home or can buy for a dollar at the thrift shop or a local yard sale. For example, you may have large plastic plant saucers—the shallow dishes you set under plant pots—gathering dust in the garage, basement, or shed. We like the thick, terra-cotta-colored saucers ourselves, since they're attractive and almost unbreakable, but any color is fine. You can use clear plastic saucers as well, as long as they're thick and rigid, not the thin, flexible kind. Put your saucer on the ground near sheltering shrubs, or on a flat-topped tree stump or other support. Add a few stones to give birds a place to perch while they drink or bathe, pour in water, and you're in business!

Of course, if you have a *really* large clay saucer, you could use that as a birdbath, too. Just make sure you store it (and the clear plastic saucers) in a freeze-free place for winter or it will break. Thick plastic saucers can be left out over winter, but since you can't put a water heater in them, the water will freeze when temperatures plunge below 32°F (0°C). You can set out a second saucer of fresh water while the first one thaws, but we prefer to use flexible black rubber water dishes (see page 186) in winter.

We've seen recommendations that you set out old pots and pans in the yard as birdbaths, but we don't like the idea of turning your yard into a junkyard. Much as we love frugality and birds, we wouldn't try that tip!

However, there is one kitchen item that we enjoy for its decorative appeal—a stainless steel mixing bowl. You may have a few extras hanging around or you can always find them at thrift stores. Choose the ones with sloping sides rather than deep-sided bowls. Any size will do. You can even make a grouping of several sizes for a landscape feature! (Three bowls would look good in a cluster.)

If you have a silver gazing ball, setting it among the bowls would be an especially attractive touch. You could even put a small gazing ball in the middle of a large stainless bowl. Pebbles (such as the glass marbles or pebbles sold for aquariums and flower arranging) and/or a piece of brick in the bottom of each bowl will give it stability as well as giving the birds a safe place to stand, although they do make the bath harder to clean. And don't fill the bowls to the brim—1½ to 2 inches (3 to 5 cm) of water is plenty for backyard birds.

Not into shiny? An old ceramic mixing bowl can make a beautiful birdbath, especially if you add a fountain. If you're crafty, you can turn a metal or ceramic bowl into a piece of art by covering the outside with mosaic pieces of crockery, china, or glass set into an adhesive base. Bear in mind that if you choose any birdbath with slick, sloping sides—and that includes all kitchen bowls, stainless or ceramic—it's vital to give the birds something to perch on in the water and to keep the water shallow for their security and comfort. Otherwise, you're just setting out an oversize water dish for the dog!

So choose the castoff that works best with your landscape style and personal taste. And have a lot of fun seeing what you can come up with!

COOL TOOLS AND GREAT GIZMOS

Visiting a Wild Birds Unlimited store is always lots of fun, even before you get into the store, since store owners often display bird feeders and birdbaths outside the store so passersby can see the wild birds happily flocking to their offerings. But the last time we went to a Wild Birds Unlimited store, our attention was completely captured not by the birds, not by the feeders and birdbaths, but by a gizmo. It was in one of the birdbaths. It shimmied. It shook. It wiggled around. It looked like a small alien had fallen into the birdbath and couldn't figure out how to get out. We couldn't take our eyes off it!

When we finally did make our way into the store, we discovered that the gizmo was a Water Wiggler, a dome-shaped, plastic, battery-powered apparatus that sits in the center of your birdbath and stirs up the water. Moving water, of course, is attractive to birds, but unattractive to mosquitoes, a dynamic combination. Admittedly, we haven't gone for the Water Wiggler ourselves—it was simply too visually distracting. We'd like to keep our attention on the birds! But we note that it's one of BirdBath.com's customers' top-rated products. And we see that there's even a "natural pottery" version for folks who'd rather look at a mushroom in their birdbath than a spaceship!

The Water Wiggler may be the most attention-getting birdbath gizmo, but it's far from the only thing on the shelf. There are water heaters and cleaning brushes, as well as stoneware pebbles to give birds a foothold in the water. You'll find water-clarifying enzyme solutions and refillable filter inserts for birdbaths and fountains. There are birdbath covers that look like mini versions of the plastic covers people use on grills and lawn furniture in winter. Birdbath adhesives keep the bowl of the birdbath, which is usually a separate piece, firmly on its pedestal. You can find drippers that turn any birdbath into a bird magnet, solar-powered fountain pumps, avian misters, hooks for hanging birdbaths, even a specially-formulated adhesive to repair birdbath cracks.

Some of the pole-mounted feeder systems (see page 54 in Chapter 2 for more on them) are also designed so that you can attach a birdbath on top of the pole. (Of course, you'll need to buy a birdbath that's compatible with the pole system you have.)

Many stores and Web sites offer kits for birdbath cleaning or winter maintenance as well as individual components. In our experience, the kit components are always the same high-quality products that are sold individually rather than cheaper versions, so a kit is a good value if it has the components you're looking for.

We found what we think is the most practical gizmo of all in the Duncraft catalog (also online at www.duncraft.com): a birdbath leveler. (We don't know about you, but our yards are not exactly floorboard-flat.) Just set the concrete- or terra-cotta-colored disk under your birdbath or birdbath pedestal, turn to level it, and voilá! No more deep and shallow ends in your bath.

KEEPING IT CLEAN

There's no point in beating around the bush: If you're going to get a birdbath at all, you *have* to commit to keeping it clean. Dirty birdbaths are a hazard to birds, pets, and people (see "Why

Siting for Safety

Birds love bathing and playing in the water. But a wet bird is a vulnerable bird, since it takes a bit longer to escape from a predator's attack or another perceived threat than it would if the bird's feathers were dry and flight-ready.

Some authorities recommend placing a birdbath 10 feet (3 m) from the nearest cover—that birdbath-in-the-open-lawn tradition—to avoid providing hiding places for cats and other lurking predators. Other experts recommend that you put a birdbath near a brush pile or dense evergreen like a juniper, holly, or arborvitae so the birds can dive to safety if danger threatens. Confused? We were, too, so we asked Pennsylvania birding pro Rudy Keller for his advice.

"Not all species will come to a birdbath in the middle of a lawn," Rudy told us. "You might attract robins, but species like warblers like to be able to perch near the birdbath and scope out the area for potential danger, as well as to hop out of the bath and onto a perch to dry off. But you don't want to tuck a ground-level birdbath under an evergreen, either, especially if its branches go all the way to the ground. A cat can hide out beneath the branches and take the birds unawares. The best approach is to site the bath a few feet out from a deciduous shrub the birds can see into or an evergreen that's been pruned up from the ground so a skulking cat is easy to see. A brush pile is a good option, too, since a cat may hide behind it but is unlikely to hide inside it."

Virginia birder Cole Burrell agrees. He adds, "I like to landscape my ground-level birdbaths with ferns and other herbaceous plants as well as shrubs to give the birds a two-tiered escape route."

Cleanliness Matters" on page 184 for more on this). Better to have no water than dirty water. Having said that, it's easy to keep your birdbath clean—certainly no more trouble than cleaning a toilet bowl. (And we trust you do that, right?!) All you need to do is commit yourself to emptying and refilling the water every day and taking 5 minutes a week for scrubbing the birdbath basin.

The folks at Duncraft say that the best way to clean your birdbath is to scrub it with a solution of 1 tablespoon (15 ml) of white vinegar (to prevent algal growth) in a gallon (4 l) of water. Virginia birder Cole Burrell uses a weak bleach solution (also a tablespoon to the gallon) in his birdbaths and rinses them well with plain water to flush out any traces of bleach before refilling them with fresh water. Stephen W. Kress, author of *The Audubon Society Guide to Attracting Birds,* recommends a simple weekly cleaning with a stiff brush. And many backyard birders find that a daily blast from the hose is enough to keep their birdbaths clean.

None of these options is complicated or hard to do. So we say, don't sweat it, just do it! You can buy brushes that are designed specifically for birdbaths from wild bird stores and Web sites. (Duncraft even sells one that attaches to your garden hose, so you can rinse out the bath while you're scrubbing it.) And of course, you can always use a (new, please) toilet bowl brush. Choose a stiff-bristled brush to get algae, bird droppings, and other detritus off the surface of your birdbath.

Do you *really* need to empty and refill your birdbath every day? That depends on your goals. You can keep mosquito larvae from hatching if you empty and refill the birdbath every 3 days. But aren't you trying to provide drinking water for birds? You'll be providing fresh water for the birds to drink—water that's free of feathers, parasites, bird droppings, and other detritus—if you change it daily. And how hard is that? Perhaps you have feeders that you refill daily? Take the extra minute and refill the water while you're out there.

Provide for Puddles

Puddles are birds' first choice for bathing sites. If you want to really make them happy, scoop out a bare spot in the backyard (where it's not front and center but you can still enjoy the show) and prepare to see a bunch of grateful birds! When it rains, they'll splash in their puddle; as it dries, butterflies will flock to the mineral-rich mud. When it's dry, the birds will return for their other favorite: a dust bath.

Why Cleanliness Matters

We've said it before, and we'll say it again: Bird droppings carry disease, and some bird-borne diseases can affect people, including the serious lung disease histoplasmosis. Bird droppings aren't the only bad things that can end up in birdbaths, either: Bathing birds can leave lice behind, and birds can drop food (such as bread and other baked goods and even fruit, lettuce, and other greens) into the water, where they'll spoil if not promptly removed. And then there are mosquito eggs.

Our point is that, for the health of your backyard birds as well as your own, it's important to make sure your birdbaths are filled daily with fresh, clean water and cleaned once a week. Weekly cleaning will also keep algae from taking hold. And a daily refill will insure that, even if some misguided mosquito lays its eggs in your birdbath, they'll never have a chance to hatch and produce a new generation.

Let's talk about another safety issue while we have your attention: birdbaths that attach to deck railings. We realize that these are popular because they're convenient and bring bathing birds in close. But again, you'll be getting bird droppings all over the part of your deck that's beneath the birdbath. And the messiness and disease potential aren't the only hazards. The birds, too, are more at risk. As we discussed on page 183, wet birds aren't able to fly away as fast as dry ones. And a hunting cat can jump onto a deck railing faster than you could lift a hand.

Rather than put your birds—and possibly yourself—in the path of danger, we suggest instead placing birdbaths on the lawn or in garden beds, where the bird droppings will act as a natural fertilizer and birds can fly up into overhanging branches or into nearby cover to escape from danger. As with deck-mounted feeders, if you simply must have a deck-mounted birdbath, buy one that's half-moon-shaped and attach it to the outside of the railing so it's over the ground, not over the deck.

WATER IN MOTION

The sound of dripping or running water is the ultimate bird magnet. You'll be astounded by how many more birds will come in to a birdbath outfitted with a fountain, dripper, or mister—or, for that matter, even a common lawn sprinkler—than a static birdbath with still water. Try it—you'll like it! (And so will your backyard birds.)

Fortunately, companies that specialize in products for wild birds have been quick to pick up on this trend. It's easy to find drippers, misters, and fountains at any store or Web site that sells wild bird products. Many fountains now come with a dripper, mister, or fountain as standard equipment. You can also buy components to retrofit an existing birdbath. It's well worth it to see hummingbirds zipping through a mister or warblers splashing in the sparkling drops from a dripper.

Confused about the differences between fountains, drippers, and misters? Here's the deal: Fountains produce multiple jets of water. The fountain component is usually set in the basin of the birdbath and the water moves up and out before falling back down into the basin. A dripper, as the name implies, produces droplets of water much like a slow-leaking faucet. The basic dripper even looks like a faucet—a crook-shaped piece of copper tubing set on the side of the birdbath. Some models are set in a faux or real stone and can be placed at the bottom of the birdbath. And some fancy models resemble vines with flowers or even butterflies. A mister produces a fine mist spray and can either aim upward from the basin of the birdbath, sideways when attached to a stake, or even downward if attached to a branch.

What about that lawn sprinkler? We just have to remind you that it wastes water—much of the water it dispenses evaporates before it ever hits your lawn. Not to mention that choosing lawn grasses that are well-adapted to your area and practicing sound lawn-care techniques (see "Keep Your Lawn Chem-Free" on page 202) should mean that you never need to resort to a sprinkler. And of course, you should *never* use a sprinkler in an arid area! Instead, practice water conservation and choose a recycling fountain or dripper for your birdbath. If, however, you live in a temperate area and have and use a lawn sprinkler, keep an eye out when you turn it on—you may see birds, including hummingbirds, darting through the spray.

HEATING UP

If you live in a cold-winter area, it's especially important to provide water for birds once the natural sources of water freeze over. That means either exchanging frozen dishes of water for fresh ones every few hours or investing in a heated birdbath or water heater.

Wild bird stores and Web sites offer two alternatives: heated birdbaths and separate submersible heater elements. The heated versions come with a heater component already incorporated into the birdbath design. Some of these are detachable, so you can store the heater element in warm weather and attach it in winter, and others are integral parts of the birdbath assembly. One type of plastic birdbath has the heater component in a hollow cavity between the dish of the birdbath and the bowl-shaped base that holds the dish. You can lift the dish off for easy cleaning.

If you choose to add a heating element/deicer to an existing birdbath, make sure the birdbath will withstand a heater—some plastic and cast-resin models won't. Always ask before risking a meltdown or worse. Submersible heating elements are typically flat, U-shaped heating coils with short cords. (BirdBaths.com also offers a flat disk-shaped model especially designed for shallow birdbaths.) For birdbaths, 50- to 200-watt heating elements are recommended. Some birdbath models are designed with internal thermostats to conserve electricity. You can also find elements designed for livestock water tanks, but they may have more power than you need.

A submersible heating element lets you offer birds a drink of water all winter long. For safety's sake, secure the cord to avoid tripping over it and tipping the bath.

Note that term "deicer." When it's bitterly cold, a heater is unlikely to keep a birdbath completely free of ice, but it will keep some part of the surface open and the water from freezing solid. Don't worry—thirsty birds will "skate" out to the open area.

All birdbath water heaters, whether submersible or integral, have short cords. What's the deal? The answer, we found, is that you're not supposed to plug the cord from the heating element directly into an outlet. Instead, it's designed to plug into an outdoor extension cord, and *that's* what you plug into your outlet. The benefit is that it's much easier to store the heating units without having to coil and secure several feet of cord. (Some birdbaths even have compartments to store the cord out of sight when the heating element isn't in use.)

Of course, there are low-tech alternatives to heated birdbaths. For an inexpensive winter birdbath alternative for ground-level watering, we like the flexible black rubber dishes that are available from farm supply stores (such as Agway and Tractor Supply) for our winter birdbaths, because the black color holds heat longer and the dishes are flexible, so you can overturn them and stomp the ice out with a single step, then refill. They come in a variety of sizes, so you can choose one that works for you; just remember to keep the water shallow and add some stones for perching purchase.

Basic Is Better

The simpler your birdbath setup, the easier it will be to clean. If you have one or two stones in your birdbath, it's easy to lift them out to scrub them and the now-empty birdbath. Contrast that to a birdbath full of pebbles!

Take a Closer Look

Belted Kingfisher *(Megaceryle alcyon)*

Female belted kingfishers look like what you'd get if you crossed a blue jay with a robin: They have a robin-red band across their white bellies; a slate blue breast band, wings, and back; and a slate blue head with a ragged crest, a long, pointed gray bill, a white throat, and a white spot in front of each eye. Males resemble females but lack the rust-red on their bellies. Juveniles resemble adults. Adults are 11 to 14 inches (28 to 36 cm) long, with 19- to 23-inch (48 to 58 cm) wingspans. Females lay five to eight white eggs in burrows that they dig in stream banks or embankments along roadsides.

Regional Relations

Along the lower Rio Grande Valley in Texas, you might see the ringed kingfisher (*Megaceryle torquatus*), which at 16 inches (40 cm) long is larger than the belted kingfisher and fishes in larger rivers and ponds. Males have solid robin-red breasts, and even females have considerably more red on their undersides than the male and female belted kingfishers. Also in the lower Rio Grande Valley in Texas and in southeastern Arizona, the smallest kingfisher, the 8½-inch (22 cm) green kingfisher (*Chloroceryle americana*), sometimes makes a rare appearance. This species resembles a green-backed woodpecker; males have a band of red across the breast, and both males and females have spotted wings and undersides. Neither species is likely to turn up anywhere near a backyard.

Tempting Features and Treats for Kingfishers

- The best way to attract a kingfisher to your yard is to include a pond, large water garden, or stream in your landscaping.
- Unfortunately, if a kingfisher pays a visit to your water garden, it's probably planning to make a meal of your goldfish or koi. Dense surface vegetation like water lilies, rushes, and lotuses can help your fish hide out when a kingfisher threatens.
- If you have a stream on your property with mud banks, it's possible that a pair of kingfishers might decide to dig a nest tunnel there.
- Kingfishers will also eat small frogs and aquatic insects and snails.

Did You Know?

- Belted kingfishers are one of the few bird species in which the female is more colorful than the male.
- Kingfishers can hover over water to look for fish, then dive in headfirst to catch them in their sharp beaks. They kill their prey by pounding it against a tree branch.
- You will most often see kingfishers on tree branches or even telephone wires near lakes, ponds, and woodland streams and rivers. You'll usually see a single kingfisher rather than a pair, as they tend to fish alone and are generally solitary birds.
- Kingfishers are year-round residents across most of the United States. They also summer in Canada and the northernmost states and winter in Mexico and the Southwest.
- The call of a belted kingfisher is a loud, harsh rattling noise.
- Although there are only three species of kingfishers in the United States, there are 93 species around the world.
- The tunnel leading to a kingfisher's nest burrow may extend as much as 8 feet (2.4 m) into a mud bank.

BUDGET-WISE BIRDING

Install an Inground Water Feature

With nothing more than a shovel and a sack of ready-mix concrete, you can make an inground water feature that will bring birds running (or flying). Just ask Pennsylvania birder Joan Silagy, whose husband, Bob, created an inground drip bath that's become the focal point of their backyard. Here's how he did it.

First, Bob chose the location for his birdbath, siting it under trees in the backyard near the feeders, where the Silagys could watch birds from the picture window above their kitchen table. Bob dug a circular hole about 8 inches (20 cm) deep by 3 feet (.9 m) in diameter and filled it with a few inches of gravel. He shaped the gravel to form a bowl, with deeper gravel sides and a shallower center. Next, he poured in the concrete so it was 4 to 5 inches (10 to 12 cm) thick in the center of the gravel bowl, thinning to 1½ to 2 inches (3 to 5 cm) thick at the edges. Bob shaped the bath into a 2-inch (5 cm) deep basin with sloping sides so it would be easy for the birds to get in without slipping on steep sides. To make it even easier for them to get a grip, Bob roughed up the basin's surface a little to add more texture.

Joan notes that you can easily make a birdbath this size with a single sack of concrete and even have some left over for a second birdbath. The Silagys chose to leave their concrete its natural color and let it age in the landscape—its color now blends perfectly into its surroundings—but if you prefer, you can buy various shades of green, brown, and grey concrete pigment to color your birdbath. Because of the gently sloping, textured sides, the Silagys didn't add perching pebbles to their birdbath, but you could certainly put some in yours if you want them.

Adding movement. Experienced backyard birders that they were, Joan and Bob knew that to attract the most birds, they needed moving water. So they added a simple, ingenious drip system to their birdbath. Bob had built the bath beside an old tree trunk (dead trees are called snags and provide wonderful nesting opportunities for cavity-nesting birds like woodpeckers) with a branch extending out over the basin. Bob took a simple metal water bucket and punched a hole in the bottom with a nail, then threaded fishing line through the hole and secured each end by tying it through a button. He suspended the bucket from the branch over the basin, filled the bucket with water, and voila!: an instant "automatic" drip system. The water drips down the fishing line, beads on the button, and slowly but steadily drips into the birdbath below, to the delight of the birds (and observers).

Because Bob wanted to make the birdbath easy to operate, he ran a narrow hose through a pipe leading from an outdoor faucet to the tree trunk, then ran the hose up the trunk and out the branch so they could fill the bucket from the faucet rather than taking it down and hauling it back up each time it needed a refill. You could emulate this system or simply refill the bucket from a watering can or jug. Joan notes that if you don't have a tree trunk handy, a wooden mailbox post with its cross-arm would work beautifully to hold the bucket.

A year-round delight. We asked Joan if she'd ever had any problems with her inground birdbath. Did she heat it in winter? And if not, didn't it heave up out of the ground and/or crack when the ground froze? Joan told us that her birdbath has been going strong for 20 years now. "It's beginning to show a few surface cracks, but it still holds water perfectly," she reports. She says that you could add a heater if you wanted to, but she doesn't—instead, when it's cold outside, she refills the birdbath with warm water two or three times a day. "It works just fine," she says. Joan also points out that you can empty and cover the bath in winter if you're concerned about cracking, but she doesn't advise it: "Water is so important for birds in the winter."

What about predator protection? Joan's wooded landscape already provides plenty of cover, but she's a big believer in brush piles for songbird protection and has one set up near the birdbath. Surprisingly, it blends into the "forest floor" landscape she's created so well that we didn't even notice it until she pointed it out! What we *did* notice were the colorful birds playing happily in the water.

Are Joan and Bob pleased with their creation? You bet! A few years ago, they built a second one in a flower bed in the side yard that's full of hummingbird plants. The hummingbirds love it!

It's surprisingly easy to make your own inground birdbath. All you need is a shovel and a bag of quick-set concrete!

WATER GARDENING: BEYOND THE BIRDBATH

Picture a serene backyard pond filled with blooming water lilies and lotuses. Goldfish or their high-end relatives, koi, swim serenely beneath the surface, a frog perches on a lily pad, and a dragonfly or two drift just above the water.

How idyllic, right? For us, right. For birds, wrong. Following is the good, the bad, and the ugly about water gardens, at least as far as backyard birding is concerned. Do we have your attention?

First, let's talk about the typical water garden: It's a molded plastic form that's settled into a hole in the ground dug to accommodate its shape. Or it's a shallow concrete pool that's edged in stone. Or it's a shape dug in the ground, lined with old carpet or newspaper, and covered with a thick waterproof rubber or plastic sheet designed for water gardens, then bordered with stone. Typically, all of these water gardens are filled with water and some aquatic plants. Often, they're stocked with ornamental fish. And they do attract amphibians like frogs as well as water-loving insects and birds—including herons and, if the water garden's large enough, possibly ducks and geese.

So what's wrong with this picture? Nothing, as long as you don't install a water garden assuming that songbirds will come to it. Remember that songbirds love puddles, which are often less than an inch (2.5 cm) deep. They won't visit a birdbath that's deeper than 2 inches (5 cm) unless it has stones for them to perch on. Water gardens are typically 18 inches to 2 feet (45 to 60 cm) or more deep.

The good news is that you can add features to your water garden that will increase its appeal to songbirds. Thanks to pumps, tubing, and preformed fiberglass inserts with spillways, it's fairly easy to add moving water to your water garden. Check out the options, including solar-powered pumps and fountains, at stores and Web sites that carry water garden supplies.

A fountain or a shallow waterfall spilling down stones will attract the same songbirds, including hummingbirds, that would come to a drip or fountain feature on a birdbath. A shallow recirculating "stream" connected to your water garden will allow songbirds to perch, bathe, and sip, especially if you've added stones to the streambed. Adding sand, pebbles, and low-growing edging plants around the lip of the water garden rather than flat stones or other slippery surfaces will help thirsty birds get a grip. And if you tuck a birdbath bowl into the pebbles and plants at the water garden's edge, the birds can enjoy poolside bathing.

Plants can also help birds out. You can place potted water plants on bricks or overturned clay or plastic pots to raise them to the level of or just under the water's surface and then cover the planting material with decorative stones so birds can perch there. And you can choose plants with stems that rise out of the water, like rushes, cattails, or papyrus, so birds can cling to the stems while taking a drink or looking for insects. The plants don't have to be in the water, either. A plant near the water garden with branches that trail or extend over the water's surface provides a wonderful perch for birds.

WATER GARDENING DO'S AND DON'TS

Water gardening can provide more pleasure than just about any activity except backyard birding—as long as you take a few things into consideration before digging a hole and plunking a preformed pool into the ground. Use these "Do's and Don'ts" to avoid some all-too-common disasters and to make sure your water gardening experience is a success.

- **Do** think about where you'd like to have a water garden before rushing out to buy one and just plunking it in the ground. Site it where you can enjoy it from the house, deck, or patio, as well as the yard. But make sure you keep the next three "Do's and Don'ts" in mind when choosing the best place for your water garden.
- **Don't** site your water garden at the bottom of a slope. Runoff from higher ground could wash pollutants and toxic lawn chemicals (from the neighbors' yards if not from yours) into your water garden and kill or damage plants, fish, and birds. It can also carry debris down the slope and into your water garden. When possible, choose a level site.
- **Don't** site your water garden in heavy shade under trees, especially deciduous trees, unless you don't want to grow water plants and do want to spend tons of time fishing fallen leaves out of the pond. Leaves tend to be acidic and can change the pH of your water over time to levels that are unhealthy for plants, birds, fish, amphibians, and other creatures, so you have to clean them out regularly. And most pond plants prefer full sun; although they'll grow fine in partial shade, they may not bloom as well as in a sunny location.
- **Don't** site your water garden in full sun unless you include moving water and/or plenty of water plants. Full sun encourages algal growth, which can quickly transform your beautiful water garden into a vat of green, sludgy slime. Fortunately, water plants compete with algae for nutrients and light, so if you put in lots of plants, you're much less likely to have an algae problem. Moving water—a fountain, waterfall, recirculating stream, and/or pump—will also keep algae at bay. And you get an added benefit: By now you know that moving water will also attract more birds!
- **Do** make your water garden the right size—big enough to enjoy but small enough to maintain. Most experts say the No. 1 problem with water gardens is that the owners start too small, and then realize they can't have the plants, fish, and other water features they dreamed of. As a result, they tend to dot their yards with more small water gardens rather than starting from scratch and building a bigger one. Similarly, a really big water garden, stocked with fish and plants, can be a maintenance nightmare, especially if you don't know what to expect. For these reasons, we recommend that everyone start out with a half-barrel garden before moving on to an inground model. It's great fun and great practice, and after a year of caring for a half-barrel garden, you'll be much more confident about moving on to a full-size model if you find that water gardening is for you. (See "Roll Out a Half Barrel" on page 194 for more on setting up a half-barrel water garden.)
- **Don't** overstock or overplant your water garden. If fish and plants are happy, they'll grow—usually much more than you'd think. It's astounding how one tiny water lettuce, a single small water lily, or a half-cup of water fern can spread to cover the entire surface of your water garden well before season's end. And goldfish and koi both grow to fill up the space available, so that inch-long aquarium fish may be a foot long after a few years in a roomy pond.

Overcrowding leads to unattractive, unhealthy plants and fish. You won't go wrong if you start out with one plant or fish for every three you think you want. Once they're well-established, you can always add more if they're not enough.

- **Do** visit local water gardens and nurseries that stock fish and plants for water gardens. There are some great mail-order sources of water plants, fish, and equipment—you'll find some of our favorites included in "Resources for Backyard Birders," starting on page 340—but there's no substitute for seeing plants, fish, and equipment firsthand. Talking to the staff and making your own observations will also help you determine what does well in your area, and you'll be making helpful contacts who might have the answers if you run into trouble.

- **Don't** junk it up. With all the adorable statues and other accessories for water gardens, it's easy to fall into the "one of each" syndrome. This will quickly turn your water garden into a junkyard. Each piece may be great on its own, but a bunch of stuff will simply distract the eye rather than encouraging people to focus on each individual piece. Worse still, people will see the junk instead of the water garden. Even a "one of each" approach to water plants can make your water garden look like a nursery holding tank instead of a serene landscape. We recommend a "none of each" approach until you've had a chance to enjoy your water garden *au naturel* for at least a season. Then, if you decide to add a statue or abstract sculpture, wind chime, urn, or other

Moving water from a small fountain helps keep plants healthy by adding oxygen to the water, and it makes your water garden almost irresistible to birds.

feature, we suggest choosing one that's impressive and in keeping with the water garden, rather than taking the polka-dot approach.

- **Do** match your water garden to your house and landscape. The most successful water gardens suit their landscapes. A tiny water garden in a huge yard (or vice-versa), a freeform water garden in a rigidly formal landscape (or vice-versa), a water garden edged in a material that clashes with the house and/or walks and patio—these are definite don'ts. A formal square or rectangular water garden is perfect for a landscape with square or rectangular terraces, patios, flower beds, and garden rooms. A round or oval water garden is perfect for an informal landscape with island beds and connected groups of trees and shrubs. If you're not sure what shape would look best in your yard, think about what sort of swimming pool you'd choose—a concrete inground rectangle or an aboveground oval—for a hint.
- **Do** invest in maintenance from the outset. A water garden is like a huge outdoor aquarium. We've all seen hideous aquariums that have a few pathetic-looking fish and algae-covered plastic plants and ornaments. If we're lucky, we've also seen the occasional dream aquarium, full of gorgeous live plants, schools of healthy fish darting among rocks, and decorative snails, shrimp, clams, and other interesting creatures. These aquariums seem effortlessly beautiful and self-maintaining. But "seem" is the operative word. Owners of aquariums like these have spent years trying out combinations of plants, fish, and other creatures, as well as pumps, filters, lighting, and the like, before figuring out a combination that works for their conditions. You can bet they've spent a lot of time over the years reading about aquariums, fish, and plants, and visiting aquarium stores and Web sites. When you're planning your water garden, we suggest that you do the same—read everything you can, check out Web sites, visit stores. Ask about pumps, filters, and other essential maintenance equipment, and don't be afraid to work with store personnel until you're confident that you know how to operate your setup. Your area probably has professionals who will come to your yard to install and/or maintain water gardens. You might find it well worth the money to have them out for a consultation and, when your water garden is up and running, for a hands-on maintenance lesson.
- **Do** ask around. Don't be shy—people love to talk about their water gardens! If someone in your neighborhood has a water garden you admire, try to catch them outside and let them know you'd love to hear all about it at a convenient time. If your dental hygienist begins talking about her new water garden during your annual cleaning, ask for details—we know one water gardener who found a fabulous installation professional this way. If you hear people discussing water gardens while waiting in a checkout line, speak up (politely, please!). Look at each occasion as an opportunity to learn.
- **Do** get problems under control as soon as you notice them—it's usually much easier when you can catch them early. (See "Troubleshooting Your Water Garden" on page 201 for solutions to some common problems.)

BUDGET-WISE BIRDING

Roll Out a Half Barrel

Water gardens tend to be pricey projects. But you don't need a lot of cash to make a container water garden, and it will provide hours of entertainment and enjoyment. Use this step-by-step approach and enjoy the beautiful results!

1. **Choose a container.** You can use a traditional wooden half barrel with a liner insert or even a half-barrel liner insert (made from black plastic) by itself for your container water garden. If you choose a wooden half barrel, you *must* add a liner, both to prevent the water from leaking out and to keep substances in the wood from leaking in. Stores and Web sites that sell pond and water garden supplies carry liners. The liners are standard sizes but the barrels aren't, so make sure the liner you choose fits your half barrel before bringing them both home! If you opt for just a plain black liner rather than the rustic half-barrel look, you'll be pleased to know that for less than $20 you'll be choosing a container that lasts for many years. If you don't want to have fish, you can also buy a shallow liner for a low water garden that birds will enjoy.
2. **Set up the container.** Site the container where you want it—anchoring the corner of your deck or patio with a strong visual element, tucked into a flower bed, or at the center of an herb garden—and fill it with water. The water will need several days to warm up, and if it's chlorinated, it will need at least 24 hours for the chlorine to evaporate, so you should fill the water garden at least a couple of days before you add any plants or fish.
3. **Accessorize.** If you're adding a fountain, dripper, or mist feature, you can put it in while you're adding the water. The same is true of protective cover for fish: Drop in a short section of clay pipe (available from building supply stores) now to give them a hiding place from hungry birds, raccoons, cats, and other marauders.
4. **Add plants.** At least 24 hours to several days after filling your water garden, you can add plants. Choose some submersible plants like anacharis that grow underwater and aerate the water garden; some potted plants like arrowroot, canna, parrot feather, dwarf papyrus, and/or a miniature water lily; and some floating plants like water lettuce, miniature water hyacinth, duckweed, and/or water fern. A plant with upright stems such as papyrus will give birds a place to cling to as they take a sip. Bear in mind that happy water plants spread and grow very quickly, so resist the temptation to buy more than one water lettuce or water hyacinth or to pack the container water garden with plants. This is definitely a case where less is more!
5. **Add fish and snails.** Once you've added plants, you'll need to wait another week or two before you add fish and snails. Container water gardens are too small for koi, the gorgeous carp of the Orient that are prized by water gardeners worldwide. But containers are big enough for a few goldfish or golden orfe and water snails. The goldfish or orfe will add life and color and will eat mosquito eggs and larvae, and the snails will tackle any algae. Just don't overdo it!

A container garden can support fewer fish and snails than you might think. Three goldfish or golden orfe and two to five snails will be plenty.

6. **Keep it going.** Like an aquarium, a container garden requires regular maintenance. You need to feed the fish (less is more here, too), prune the plants, clean out debris from overhanging trees (especially fallen leaves), remove any algae, replenish the water, and so on. If you keep up, you'll keep problems at bay. Check up on your container garden daily.
7. **Winterize.** If you live in a cold-winter area, you'll need to prepare your water garden for the cold. You can take your plants and fish inside for the winter (see "Troubleshooting Your Water Garden" on page 201 for more on this), remove the fountain and all other accessories, empty out the water, hose out the container, and store it and the pond equipment in the garage, shed, or basement until the following spring. If the water garden is likely to freeze solid in your climate, this is probably the best approach. If only the top will freeze, you can remove the fountain (if you have one) and/or other accessories, including the pump, and store them for the winter, then put a pond deicer (available from stores and Web sites that sell water garden supplies) into the water and plug it in. It will keep an open area so the fish can breathe. Don't feed them once the temperature falls below 45°F (7° C)—they won't eat again until spring. You'll still need to take tropical plants indoors (or give them away or compost them), since they'll die if left out in cold-winter areas.

TAKE A CLOSER LOOK

Red-Winged Blackbird *(Agelaius phoeniceus)*

With their bright red epaulettes edged in buff yellow, male red-winged blackbirds are the military officers of the bird world. Or at least the leaders of the marching band! The plumage of the male is glossy black, setting off his brilliant shoulder patches. Females are brown with streaked undersides, resembling female house finches or sparrows. Juveniles fall somewhere between the adults in appearance; young males tend to be dark brown with rust-colored epaulettes. Adult birds are 7 to 9 inches (18 to 22 cm) long. Females lay three to four dark-splotched blue-green eggs in a cup-shaped, mud-lined nest of coarse grasses and vegetation, often woven among the stems of several rushes or weeds and even hanging over open water.

Feeder Favorites for Blackbirds

- Mixed seed
- Millet
- Cracked corn
- Sunflower seed, especially striped and hulled
- Milo, especially in sprigs

Regional Relations

In parts of California, red-winged males may lack the yellow-buff border on their red epaulettes; these birds are called bicolored blackbirds. Another look-alike, the tricolored blackbird (*Agelaius tricolor*), is a separate species of the California coast, with white rather than yellow-buff borders on their epaulettes. The male yellow-headed blackbird (*Xanthocephalus xanthocephalus*) displays a bold, bright yellow head and throat, a black body, and white wing patches; females are duller and browner. These 9½-inch (24 cm) birds of the prairies and marshes summer in southwest Canada and in the western and north central United States; they winter in the Southwest and Mexico. They will take cracked corn, mixed seed, and scratch grain, as well as whole grains, if offered directly on the ground.

The eastern and western meadowlarks (*Sturnella magna* and *S. neglecta*) don't look much like blackbirds, with their mottled brown backs and wings and their bold yellow throats and chests, separated by black V-marks resembling ribbons intended to hold medals of honor. But these 9-inch-long (23 cm) birds of pastures and meadows do occasionally turn up at feeders for black oil sunflower seeds and millet. Project FeederWatch participants have reported seeing far fewer western than eastern meadowlarks at their feeders. The two blackbirds most worthy of the name are the all-black Brewer's (*Euphagus cyanocephalus*) and rusty (*E. carolinus*) blackbirds, though even they are not coal black; the Brewer's has purple-green highlights and the rusty takes on reddish overtones in fall. Both are also 9 inches (23 cm) long and have summer breeding grounds in Canada (and in the Northwest in the case of the Brewer's blackbird). The rusty blackbird winters in the mid- to southeastern United States, while the Brewer's takes up winter residence in the Midwest to the Southwest and Mexico. Brewer's blackbirds often turn up at Western feeders, enjoying mixed seed and cracked corn, but rusty blackbirds, though not unknown at Eastern feeders, are not common visitors. When they do pass through, they'll eat cracked corn and hulled sunflower seeds.

Big black birds with heavy purple, green, bronze, or blue iridescence and showy keel-shaped tails are grackles, which are also in the blackbird family. The common (*Quiscalus quiscula*) and boat-tailed grackle (*Q. major*) appear at feeders from February well into spring and will stroll boldly up to your deck door, eating anything they can find. Common grackles are smaller at 12½ inches (31 cm) than boat-tails (16½ inches or 42 cm) and have a much wider range, appearing throughout the eastern United States year-round and through the Midwest and north central states and much of Canada through the summer. Boat-tailed grackles are birds of the East and Gulf Coasts and are a much rarer sight at feeders than their common cousins.

Tempting Features and Treats for Blackbirds

- Blackbirds love insects, and thankfully, they especially love some of gardeners' most dreaded pests: Japanese beetles, gypsy moth and tent caterpillars, grasshoppers, grubs, flies, weevils, ants, and a wide range of other beetles and caterpillars. So if you have a garden, offer a warm welcome to this natural pest patrol, and if you happen to find some grubs or beetle larvae as you're digging and weeding, set them out on a platform or tray feeder for your feathered allies.
- Grackles would rather eat dry cat food than any feeder food. A small dish of cat food placed away from your feeders will keep them occupied, so they won't empty the feeders.
- Since flocks of migrating blackbirds can wreak havoc on your feeders in spring, distract them with some cracked corn or scratch grain, a type of chicken feed made from cracked corn and grains including wheat; it's sold at feed mills and stores like Tractor Supply and Agway. Set the food out on a tray feeder away from your other feeders or sprinkle it directly on the ground, to keep the aggressive blackbirds occupied so they don't scare off your other feeder birds.
- Blackbirds enjoy fruit, including apple chunks, orange halves or slices, and berries, as well as bread and other baked goods and popcorn. Grackles and Brewer's blackbirds have been observed dipping bread and popcorn in water before eating them, presumably to soften them up rather than to rinse them off!

Did You Know?

- Not all blackbirds are black and they're not all called blackbirds, either. Meadowlarks, cowbirds, grackles, and even the bobolink are all in the blackbird family. So are orioles. Surprised?
- Blackbirds are observant and smart. They'll often watch their peers try a new food to see how they like it before venturing a bite themselves.
- The only blackbird to make the list of state birds is the western meadowlark, but it was chosen by six states: Kansas, Montana, North Dakota, Nebraska, Oregon, and Wyoming.
- Believe it or not, the bird with the biggest population in North America isn't the pigeon or starling—it's the red-winged blackbird, with a population in the hundreds of millions.
- Unlike many feeder birds, red-winged blackbirds are more likely to turn up at feeders in spring than in fall and winter. In fact, many bird-watchers consider the arrival of red-winged blackbirds at the feeder to be a sure sign that spring is on the way.
- Many birds are monogamous, but not blackbirds. Each male can have many mates—a marital state known as polygyny—and breeding tends to occur in large groups, as opposed to birds that form mating pairs and defend their territory from others of their species.
- Male and female red-winged blackbirds love to glean spilled corn and seed from harvested fields, but they have slightly different food preferences: Males prefer corn, females prefer weed seeds. That's why if you want to attract them to a feeder, you should set out cracked corn and mixed seed.
- Red-winged blackbirds are year-round residents along Canada's west coast, throughout the United States and Mexico, and into Central America. They also have summer breeding grounds in much of Canada and wintering grounds in Baja California and western Mexico.
- The piercing voice of the red-winged blackbird can be overwhelming when the birds flock together, especially because of its loud "check" call. It sings a melodic "o-ka-lee" and calls in a whistling "cheer" or "terr-eee."

MAKING THE MOST OF NATURAL WATER FEATURES

If you're lucky enough to have a natural water feature on your property, like a pond, stream, or spring, you can enjoy a diversity of wildlife (including wild birds) every day. You may see a family of ducks or geese at your pond, with deer drinking at the edge and perhaps even beavers at work in its depths—not to mention an assortment of fish, turtles, frogs, and water snakes. Herons, kingfishers, red-winged blackbirds, and numerous other birds will visit your pond and may nest nearby, or, in the case of red-winged blackbirds, even in the tall grasses or cattails in the pond's shallows.

You don't need a big expanse of water to draw wildlife, either. Hawk's Run, the little stream behind Ellen Phillips's Pennsylvania cottage, is not much more than a trickle during dry summers, averaging just 5 feet (2.25 m) wide with 3-foot-high (.9 m) banks. But she enjoys the sight of minnows, crayfish, water gliders, dragonflies, and the occasional water snake in her shallow stream, as well as a vast assortment of butterflies and birds. And every spring, a pair of mallards returns to the stream and floats happily behind her house for several weeks before heading downstream to nest.

Get Over It

We humans have a passion for order. We want everything around us to be spotless, neat as a pin, manicured—and that goes for our yards as well as our homes. Unfortunately, the result of our tidy landscaping is a sterile environment that's not just unappealing, it's actually harmful to birds and the other creatures who share the planet with us, since it destroys valuable habitat and exposes them to predation.

But, we can hear you saying, if we let the yard go "wild," what will the neighbors say? We get your point. Our suggestion: Keep the front yard, the public, on-display space, neat as you please. (But don't use toxic chemicals—not even there. See "Keep Your Lawn Chem-Free" on page 202 if you're wondering why.) Then help the birds out in the backyard. Grow a hedgerow—or at least a hedge!—of bird-friendly plants and resist the urge to shear them into stick-filled box shapes. (See Chapter 3, "Plants and Landscape Features for Birds," beginning on page 87, for some bird-friendly plant choices.)

Plant shade trees if you don't have them, and grow island beds of shrubs and shade-tolerant perennials, ferns, and groundcovers underneath them. Grow a small natural meadow of wildflowers and native grasses and let it stand over winter to provide seed and shelter for the birds. Choose at least some of your landscape plants with birds in mind. Rather than a sterile, scrawny tea rose, select a big, bushy, thorny type like a rugosa or eglantine rose. You'll be providing showy, vitamin-rich rose hips for the birds as well as excellent cover and nesting sites—not to mention

Needless to say, if you're lucky enough to have a natural water feature on your property, we suggest that you keep it as natural as possible. You may want to keep a sight line clear between the pond and your house, so you can see who's visiting, but otherwise let the vegetation grow up around your pond. The birds and other wildlife will thank you! (Except for geese—see "Troubleshooting Your Water Garden" on page 203 for more on this.) You may also want and/or need to add a bridge or two across a stream or creek, possibly with a deck or patio on one side where you can sit and watch the water and wildlife.

But for the most part, enjoying a natural water feature as it is will be much better than trying to tame it or dress it up with garden plants and artificial features. If you want those, add a water garden to your landscape and go for it!

Natural or man-made, water features can be all too easily contaminated by toxic chemicals that are dumped on lawns and other parts of the landscape. Chemical fertilizers, herbicides, and pesticides can easily end up in your pond, stream, or water garden, creating a toxic situation for birds and other wildlife. (See "Keep Your Lawn Chem-Free" on page 202 for more on this.) Nature and toxic chemicals don't mix, so please, if you're trying to attract birds to your yard, go organic or just hold off. Your landscape will survive without chemical intervention (and so will your birds)!

hundreds of highly fragrant roses for your own delight. Add some junipers and other dense evergreens for year-round shelter and seed-bearing cones. Even your flower choices can favor birds—black-eyed Susans, purple coneflowers, sunflowers, and many others produce seeds that many birds, including goldfinches, relish straight from the stem.

Tuck in a brush pile, one of the best sources of cover for birds, where it won't be an eyesore, and toss your Christmas tree on top when the holidays are over. Add a compost pile or open bin to your garden—it's amazing how many birds love to search piles for a tasty tidbit. If a tree dies and it's not near the house or another structure, consider leaving it up to provide food and nest sites for cavity-nesting birds like woodpeckers, owls, and bluebirds. Make sure you create several seating areas so you can go out with a book or magazine and coffee and enjoy the show. And of course, add some water features!

Let your bird-friendly landscape evolve slowly, so you (and the neighbors) can get used to it. You can add new plants and features each year rather than putting everything in at once, doing your back and your budget a favor. We think you'll love it when you see what a gorgeous, restful haven it is. What a great way to spend some time, sitting out under a shade tree or arbor, or on the deck or patio, and watching the birds and butterflies. And we bet when your neighbors see what you've achieved, they'll start adding plants to their own yards, too!

TAKE A CLOSER LOOK

Great Blue Heron *(Ardea herodias)*

In all the bird kingdom, the silhouette of the great blue heron—the long legs, long beak, raised leg, zeppelin-shaped body, and curved neck—is one of the most instantly recognizable. In flight, the big birds are equally distinctive, with their long legs trailed behind them like streamers. These large birds are 38 to 54 inches (0.9 to 1.3 m) long, with wingspans of 66 to 79 inches (1.6 to 2 m). They can weigh over 5 pounds (2.25 kg). Adult great blue herons are actually dark gray to blue-gray, with long, S-shaped reddish necks, yellow eyes and beaks, a white head, and sweeping black eye stripes. Males and females look alike. During breeding season, adults of both sexes have black plumes on their heads, necks, and backs. Juveniles are entirely bluish gray, but otherwise resemble adults. Females lay two to six pale blue eggs in a large platform nest of sticks built in trees high off the ground; great blue herons typically nest in colonies.

Feeder Favorites for Herons

- Mice or voles attracted to spilled seed
- Occasionally songbirds, if they can catch them

Regional Relations

An all-white form of the great blue heron, known as the great white heron, lives in coastal areas with shallow salt water from southern Florida through the Caribbean; it has yellow legs and was once considered to be a separate species. There is also the smaller snowy egret (*Egretta thula*), with white plumage, a black beak and legs, and yellow eyes and feet. It reaches 24 inches (60 cm) long with a 41-inch (1 m) wingspan and inhabits wetlands on both coasts as well as various parts of the interior United States; look for it in trees over marshy pastures. Like the great blue, the green heron (*Butorides virescens*) is a common visitor to ponds and water gardens throughout the eastern United States, the West Coast, and parts of the Southwest. A small (18-inch, 45 cm), stocky heron with short legs, the green heron sports colorful plumage: dark green crown and back feathers on its blue-gray body, a red-brown neck, and a white throat. Through much of the United States, south-central Canada, and Mexico, you could also be treated to the dramatic sight of a black-crowned night heron (*Nycticorax nycticorax*), with its black crown and back setting off its otherwise white plumage. You might even see a group of these short-legged, 25-inch (63 cm) birds roosting in a tree near a pond, lake, or marshy area.

Tempting Features and Treats for Herons

- Unfortunately, the most tempting treat you can offer herons is the assortment of goldfish or koi in your water garden. Try to protect the fish by heavily planting your water garden so they have hiding places.

Did You Know?

- Herons are primarily fish eaters, skewering their prey on their long, sharp bills. But studies have shown that voles and mice also form an important part of their diet, and they will eat amphibians (especially frogs) and reptiles, as well as the occasional songbird.
- These wading birds are expert fishermen, remaining statue-still in shallow water until they see their prey, then spearing it with lightning swiftness. That's why it's so hard to tell when driving by if the heron in someone's water garden is a statue or a live bird; the statuelike pose is entirely natural.
- The great blue heron is as large as a big raptor, but its silhouette in flight looks nothing like the birds of prey: It flies with its wings extended upward over its body, its S-shaped neck pulled in so it looks like a pouch or sac below its head, its long, straight beak out-thrust, and its long legs extended behind.
- Great blue herons live year-round throughout most of the United States; they also have summer breeding grounds throughout Canada and winter grounds in Mexico and Central America extending into South America.
- The call of a great blue heron resembles a hoarse croak, more froglike than birdlike.

TROUBLESHOOTING YOUR WATER GARDEN

Like any part of your yard, a water garden can develop problems. Some (like visiting geese) are more likely if you have a pond or stream on your property, while others (like leaks) apply to man-made water gardens. Here are some of the most common concerns and what to do about them.

- **Algae.** Algae is unsightly. It not only covers the water surface with green slime; it also uses nutrients that water plants and fish need to thrive and it reduces available water surface for birds. Prevent or get rid of it by adding more water plants to your pond or water garden; cutting back on the amount of food you feed your fish and/or the number of fish you have; or adding a fountain or other feature to keep water moving. Black Japanese snails (*Viviparus malleatus*), available from stores and Web sites that sell water gardening supplies, are valuable allies that will eat algae but *won't* eat your water plants; add some to your water garden for additional control.
- **Mosquitoes.** Keep these pests under control with the following tactics: Because mosquitoes lay their eggs in still water, where larvae hatch out, keeping the water moving with a fountain or other device will keep them at bay. If you have fish in your water garden, they'll eat the larvae and control the mosquitoes. And biological controls containing Bt (*Bacillus thuringiensis israelensis*), like Mosquito Dunks, will kill the mosquito larvae before they can mature into adult mosquitoes. (Use one doughnut-shaped Dunk for every 100 square feet, or 30 square m, of water surface and replace it with a new one every month during the growing season.)
- **Dead plants.** If your plants die when the weather turns cold, you've probably chosen tropical water lilies and other tender aquatic plants like cannas and papyrus rather than cold-tolerant native water lilies, cattails, and the like. You can grow tropicals and tender perennials in your water garden even in cold-winter areas, but bring them indoors for the winter. A greenhouse, sunroom, or glassed-in porch is ideal, but a basement or garage will do as long as temperatures don't fall below 55°F (12° C) and you keep a light over the plants you don't want to go dormant. (You can cut the tops off cannas and tropical water lilies after the first frost and store their tuberous roots indoors, wrapped in damp newspaper in loosely closed plastic bags.) The plants will live just fine in buckets or plastic half-barrel liners as long as you make sure they're in water (don't let it evaporate). Once the weather is consistently warm and the pond water has warmed up, set the plants back outside. They'll probably look pathetic after their winter indoors, but will soon perk up and grow luxuriant new foliage. Of course, some people simply treat their tropicals like annuals and let them die each year, replacing them with new plants each spring. But we say, what a waste of a water lily!
- **Dead fish.** Assuming that nothing's attacking them, if your fish are dying you probably have more fish than the oxygen in your water

garden will support. The poor things are suffocating! Add more oxygen by putting a fountain or waterfall into your water garden to move the water. You can also increase water oxygen levels by adding more plants, especially submerged oxygenators like anacharis. And don't add so many fish next time! For a small goldfish, you need 2 to 3 square feet (0.6 to 0.9 square meters) of water surface or 5 gallons (19 l) of water in your pond or water garden. And remember, those goldfish will grow to be 6- to 12-inch (15 to 30 cm) monsters. Less is more! (Because koi can grow to 2 feet (60 cm) long, they're best suited to very large ponds or water gardens.)

If something *is* eating your fish, try covering the water garden with black plastic netting, sold by stores and Web sites that carry water garden supplies, and make sure you give the fish a piece of clay pipe submerged horizontally or a flat rock balanced underwater on bricks to make a cave for them to hide in.

In regions where water freezes in winter, fish will die if they're frozen solid. Use a pond deicer (also available from water garden suppliers) to keep some surface area unfrozen so the fish can get oxygen, or transfer them to an indoor aquarium for winter. Stop feeding your fish when temperatures fall below 45°F (7°C) in fall; they'll survive in a quasi-dormant state 'til warmer weather returns in spring. (But be sure to feed them regularly once the water warms in spring! Give them a high-quality pelleted food developed especially for goldfish.)

Leaf buildup from falling autumn leaves can also kill fish by lowering the water's pH to levels that are too acidic and by reducing oxygen levels. Keep leaves out of your pond by diligently using a net or skimmer or covering the pond with black plastic netting in fall and clearing leaves off it as necessary.

Finally, if the fish die as soon as you put them into the water, you're probably shocking them with a sudden temperature change.

Keep Your Lawn Chem-Free

If you love birds, don't douse your yard with pesticides and other toxic chemicals. And if you have a wet meadow, boggy area, pond, stream, or other source of water on your property, it's especially important to avoid chemicals, including chemical fertilizers, since they can leach into the water or wash into it with runoff from rain and snow. According to Stephen W. Kress, author of *The Audubon Society Guide to Attracting Birds,* lawn chemicals used by U.S. homeowners are responsible for killing 7 million (yep, that's 7 *million*) birds every year. Lawns don't *need* artificial chemicals to grow well and look good: Choosing lawn grasses that are adapted to your area, letting grass grow 2 to 3 inches (5 to 7 cm) tall between mowings so its roots stay moist and shaded, and leaving the trimmings on the lawn to act as mulch and fertilizer is all you need to do to create a lush lawn. So please, please put those chemicals away! The birds and other wildlife will thank you—and so will your pets and kids.

Here Comes the Sun

One of the most exciting developments in birdbath technology is the increasing use of solar elements in birdbath design. Solar elements are used to power fountains in birdbaths. You can buy birdbaths with the solar-powered fountain included in the design—the solar panel sits in the birdbath itself and the pump and wiring are hidden in the pedestal or base. Some of these birdbaths even come with lights, so the water is illuminated at night, all thanks to the sun! Solar-powered birdbaths come in a wide assortment of styles. We suggest that you check out the selection at your local wild bird store and online at wild-bird specialty sites like BirdBaths.com.

Already have the birdbath of your dreams? You can retrofit any birdbath with a fountain and solar panel setup, in which case you'll have wires extending to the pump/fountain element. But you can hide them behind the pedestal or base. These retrofits are available from wild bird stores, Web sites, and catalogs like Duncraft.

Obviously, if you're using solar power, you need access to the sun. The birdbath must be in a sunny area if the solar panel sits in the bath, and the panel must be in the sun if it sits on the ground and is wired up to the fountain. But you're not running up electric bills or running ugly extension cords across the lawn!

The other thing to keep in mind about solar birdbaths is that they're not able to withstand freezing weather. If you live in a cold-winter area, remove and replace the solar element with an insert that comes with the birdbath and store your solar element out of the elements (so to speak) before winter arrives. Or if your solar component is freestanding, store the component and drop in a submersible heater for winter instead.

Always float the closed bag they came in on the surface of your water garden for 15 to 20 minutes before opening it and releasing the fish, so that the water temperature in the bag can gradually match that of the surrounding water.

- **Leaks.** Leaks are more likely to occur in water gardens made of PVC or rubber pond liners or of concrete than in preformed water gardens. If concrete cracks, it's a relatively simple matter to drain the water garden and patch the concrete. Patching a PVC or rubber liner is another matter! It's a lot easier to avoid sources of liner leaks to begin with than to try to repair them. Start with a thick liner material such as 32-mil, 2-ply PVC or a rubber liner with geotextile fabric bonded to the underside. Once you've dug and smoothed the hole for your water garden, make sure to remove any stones, roots, sticks, or sharp objects from its bottom and sides that could puncture the liner. Add a 2-inch (5 cm) layer of sand over the packed soil and cover that with old carpet, carpet remnants, or geotextile material before laying the pond liner into the hole. Make sure the liner extends at least 6 inches (15 cm) past the lip of the water garden and cover the extension with flat, smooth stones, bricks, or pavers.
- **Geese.** A few geese visiting at your pond might be exciting, but a whole flock is overwhelming. (And their droppings can encourage algae

Take a Closer Look

Mallard *(Anas platyrhynchos)*

If you've only seen one duck, the mallard was almost certainly it. Male mallards have the familiar dark green, iridescent head, yellow bill, white neck ring, chestnut chest, and pale grayish white back, wings, and underside. Wings have a brilliant blue "blaze" that's edged with white on both sides; these blue feathers flash when the birds are in flight. The tail is black and curled upward with white on the sides, and the legs and feet are orange. Males' color dulls down when the birds aren't breeding. Females are brown with white and buff streaking—though they too sport the blue wing blaze. Adults are 20 to 26 inches (50 to 66 cm) long with 30- to 36-inch (76 to 90 cm) wingspans and weigh less than 3 pounds (1.35 kg). Juveniles resemble the females. Females lay up to 13 creamy to greenish-buff eggs in a grass-and down-lined depression in the ground. Ducklings hatch bright-eyed, downy, and ready to follow Mom around.

Feeder Favorites for Mallards

- Mixed seed
- Cracked corn
- Whole corn
- Sunflower seed
- Whole oats, wheat, and other whole grains

Regional Relations

Because mallards breed freely with both escaped domestic ducks and other duck species, including the American black duck (*Anas rubripes*), hybrids are common. Mallards in Central Mexico were formerly considered a separate species, the Mexican duck. Another species, the mottled duck (*A. fulvigula*), is considered by some ornithologists to be a subspecies of mallard. All these ducks tend to resemble female mallards. Mottled ducks live in Florida and along the Gulf Coast, while the American black duck can be found throughout the eastern United States and Canada. Project FeederWatch participants have occasionally reported American black ducks at their feeders, as well as wood ducks (*A. sponsa*); see "Take a Closer Look" on page 166.

Tempting Features and Treats for Mallards

- Mallards may patrol your pond or stream in search of snails, aquatic insects, water plants, small fish, and other tasty tidbits.
- As every child knows, mallards love bread and will eat it or crackers if offered. However, wild mallards won't come up to you to take it, unlike their park-dwelling brethren. Instead, tear it in pieces and place it near your water garden, pond, or stream where the mallards will see it.

formation.) Geese are much less likely to land on a pond if it's surrounded by high plants like cattails or water rushes. If geese have been a problem in the past, add tall plants around the perimeter of your pond.

- **Herons.** You don't need a huge pond to attract herons to your property. Steve van Gorder, an aquaculturist who lives near Breinigsville, Pennsylvania, knows this all too well. Steve sank a spare aquaculture tank—a round pool not much bigger than a hot tub—in his backyard, landscaped it, and then added plants and fish to create a water garden. Unfortunately, the fish he added were expensive koi. Steve has often seen great blue herons in his pond with fish in their beaks—usually hastily departing when he and his dog Jackson dash out there. These days, Steve usually stocks his pond with inexpensive goldfish instead. If you have koi or just want to protect your

- Here's a shock: Mallards eat potatoes! Cut raw potatoes in chunks and leave them out with (or instead of) bread.
- Set out a little shredded lettuce or other fresh, shredded greens for your mallards.
- Surprisingly, mallards love acorns. If you don't have an oak tree in your yard, you can gather these tempting treats on a neighborhood walk and set them out for the ducks.
- Mallards also eat grains. Try setting out some scratch grains, a type of chicken feed available from feed mills and stores like Agway and Tractor Supply, containing grains like wheat as well as cracked corn.
- Mallards enjoy the occasional bit of dog kibble as a treat.
- Zookeepers and duck breeders recommend Mazuri Waterfowl Maintenance diet, the feed they give their ducks (check www.mazuri.com or call 1-800-227-8941 to find a source near you).

Did You Know?

- Mallards belong to a group of ducks called dabbling ducks or dabblers, because of the way they look for food. Dabblers filter-feed, using their beaks to skim food off or just below the surface of the water. They'll also upend themselves in search of underwater food, such as snails, aquatic insects, and vegetation—the familiar tail in the air display at park ponds.
- Mallards form monogamous breeding pairs and are tender and considerate towards their partners. But the males also engage in brutish behavior on the side, sexually assaulting unmated females that sometimes die as a result of their brutal attacks.
- With one exception—the Muscovy duck—all domestic ducks are descended from mallards.
- Female mallards are the ones that quack. Males grunt, whistle, and make a rasping noise.
- Mallards are year-round residents throughout much of the United States and Mexico. They also have summer breeding grounds throughout Canada and Alaska, and wintering grounds in the South and Southwest.
- Some experts believe that mallards were the first domesticated fowl, preceding chickens.
- Unlike other North American ducks, mallards produce two broods each year.

goldfish, keep visiting herons away with a trick used by fish hatcheries: a plastic heron statue. Putting a heron statue in the pond makes real live herons think the pond is already occupied, so they stay away. You may have seen attractive metal heron sculptures in catalogs, but pass them up. They may look like herons to you, but they look like scrap metal to live herons. Only the lifelike plastic herons will do.

Raccoons. These wily omnivores can scoop fish out with their hands and eat them like sushi. To keep raccoons out, put a section of clay pipe in the bottom of your water garden so fish can hide inside from predators, and plant the water garden with surface-covering plants like water lilies so your fish will have some protective cover to hide under.

CHAPTER 7

HOSTING HUMMINGBIRDS

Attracting hummingbirds to your backyard is easy—and addictive, as you'll soon see. It can be as simple as setting out a nectar feeder or planting a few flowering annuals, perennials, and/or vines that act as hummingbird magnets. Or you can go all-out and create an entire flower border designed to bring in hummingbirds (you and your family and friends will enjoy the beautiful flowers, too). In this chapter, you'll discover how to make your backyard more welcoming to the hummingbirds that call your area home, whether you live in the desert Southwest or the wooded suburbs of the Southeast, the West Coast or the East Coast, or anywhere in between. You'll find in-depth profiles of two beloved North American hummingbirds—the ruby-throated hummingbird of the East and the rufous hummingbird originally found in the West but now found practically everywhere in the United States—as well as shorter descriptions of other hummers you might see depending on where you live and whether some venture off course during migration.

ESSENTIALS OF GOOD HUMMINGBIRD HABITAT

The most effortless way to attract hummingbirds to your yard is to include features that make it appealing to them. True, you won't draw the numbers that would come to a nectar feeder, but you'll be enhancing the beauty of your property and making it more attractive to many other birds and butterflies, too. And you won't have to worry about making nectar and constantly cleaning and refilling hummingbird feeders!

Admittedly, most hummingbird lovers want the best of both worlds, so they hang out a few nectar feeders along with creating a more hummingbird-friendly landscape. (Don't worry, it's easy!) Get an overview of the options in the illustration on pages 206 and 207. You'll find more about great plants for hummers on page 236 and how to choose and set up hummingbird feeders on page 224. But first, let's look at the few essentials hummers really need.

5 THINGS THAT MAKE YOUR YARD A HUMMINGBIRD HAVEN

If you can provide the following five things, you'll have hummingbirds in your yard if there are any in your area. We're willing to bet that you already have four of the five items right now—and it's quick and easy to add the fifth (moving water). See for yourself!

1. **Trees** provide perches, shelter, nesting places, nectar, and insects. We think of hummers as nectar eaters, but they also love insects. Trees attract a whole host of insects to their bark, leaves, and blossoms. Fruit trees are especially good, as are trees with big, showy flowers like magnolias. Ripened and/or rotting fruit attracts all kinds of insects, and the hummingbirds will eat the insects and lap up the fermenting fruit juices. Softwood trees like those in the poplar family also harbor lots of insects that hummingbirds eat. But softwood trees are prone to being blown down in high winds, so you have to be careful where you plant them.
2. **Shrubs** also provide perches, shelter, nesting places, nectar, and insects, only at a lower level. Hummingbirds, like all birds, need to be able to seek shelter at all levels when they feel threatened.
3. **Flowers** provide both nectar and insects, vital to sustaining hummingbirds with their mile-a-minute metabolisms. Insects provide much-needed fat and protein, while nectar supplies fluid, calories (remember, unlike us, hummers need lots of these!), and nutrients. Most people think red when they think of hummingbird flowers, but there's more to it than that. See "Gardening for Hummingbirds" beginning on page 236 for the inside scoop—plus lots of options for trees, shrubs, and flowers hummers just love.
4. **Edges**—the areas where trees, shrubs, vines, and/or taller herbaceous plants meet lawns or meadows—are important for safety's sake. Hummingbirds love these large or small sheltered spots near open areas, which

let them nest, seek safety from predators, and get out of the way of aggressive or rival hummingbirds.

5. **Water** provides the moisture birds need to drink and bathe. Hummingbirds like to fly through moving water. Fountains, waterfalls, drippers, and even lawn sprinklers are especially relished. See Chapter 6, "Water Features for Birds," beginning on page 177, for ways to add moving water to your landscape.

Treat Hummers Like Birds

When you're creating a natural habitat for hummingbirds, the most important thing to remember is that they may look exotic, but they still need to have the same things all other birds need in a good habitat: food, shelter, water, and places to nest. The most welcoming habitat for hummingbirds also will be attractive to other birds in the area.

Warning: Hummingbirds Are Addictive

Once you see your first hummingbird, you may suddenly find yourself thinking about ways to improve your yard and plantings so you can see more of them. For some people, putting out hummingbird feeders or planting masses of nectar-rich flowers is a natural next step after they've been feeding various kinds of birds for a while. But for other bird-watchers, attracting hummingbirds to their yards is where they begin and where they stay. These folks don't put out seed or suet feeders—they just want to see hummingbirds. They become so fixated on these tiny birds that they become obsessed with them. They'll do everything they can to attract more hummingbirds to their yards, even if it's only for 3 or 4 months during the year.

There's something so addictive about hummingbirds that once people become involved with them, they want to attract more and more. This fascination often leads people down a path they never thought they'd take. Maintaining just one backyard feeder and a few flowers in the beginning may eventually lead to five or six feeders and extensive hummingbird gardens.

Hummingbird enthusiasts want to learn as much as they can about their favorite birds. This often leads to becoming involved with other hummingbird aficionados, checking daily Internet Listservs dealing with hummingbirds, and becoming members of local or even national birding or conservation organizations. In some cases, an obsession with hummingbirds even propels someone to become a hummingbird bander, something that takes years of work and study.

More than one casual backyard birder has turned into a knowledgeable hummingbird authority who conducts workshops, gives lectures, and/or writes articles just because he or she began watching these amazing little birds. Who knows? You may end up joining them!

WHERE THE BIRDS ARE

As you plan your hummingbird garden or think about hanging feeders, you're probably wondering how many kinds of hummingbirds you might see. There are a whopping 339 species of hummingbirds in the Americas, but only eight hummingbird species with widespread breeding ranges in the United States, and eight more that breed in very limited areas. All of them are found in the West or Southwest except for two: the ruby-throated hummingbird, *the* hummingbird of the East, and the rufous hummingbird, a western species that's now often found in the South and on the East Coast.

Other species have been seen or have shown up on extremely rare occasions—vagrant tropical species like the cinnamon hummingbird (*Amazilia rutila*), which has only been seen in the United States once or twice. When an unexpected hummingbird is found in the States, it's usually close to the Mexican border or in Florida. The exception is the green violet-ear hummingbird (*Colibri thalassinus*), a large dark species that breeds as far south as Peru. There are more than 40 recorded sightings of them in the States, including some from Michigan, Maine, and New Jersey.

Actually, there are probably many more hummingbirds going off course and temporarily visiting backyards where they're not supposed to be. But unless they're adult males, they usually go undetected because it's hard to tell the difference between female birds and juvenile birds even in the common species you're used to seeing. And the females of many species look incredibly alike. Size is a very important identifying characteristic. If you're not used to seeing different

Do Just One Thing

Can't wait to get started bringing hummingbirds buzzing to your yard? Then it's time to set out your first nectar feeder. Go to your nearest wild bird specialty store such as Wild Birds Unlimited or a Wild Bird Center—or anywhere with a great selection of bird feeders—or online to a great bird product Web site like Duncraft (www.duncraft.com) or eBirdseed.com (www.ebirdseed.com). The Hummer/Bird Study Group (www.hummingbirdsplus.org) also offers a selection of feeders that it has used successfully and recommends highly. Look for a simple, disk-shaped "flying saucer feeder" (you'll find out why when we talk about feeders on page 224). You can buy ready-made nectar to put in it or mix up your own at home. (It's easy! Just dissolve one part plain white table sugar in four parts hot water, cool the solution, and fill the feeder.) Hang your feeder where you can easily see it from your favorite chair, but not too close to a window or screen. Now sit back and enjoy the rest of this chapter while you wait to see who's going to turn up!

kinds of hummingbirds, though, you don't have much to work with. Even if you live where there are many different kinds, the size difference from one to another can be a quarter of an inch or less.

Hummingbird banders—people who put numbered bands on hummingbirds' legs so they can be tracked for scientific purposes—will be the first to tell you that sometimes the only way to tell the species of an adult female or young bird for sure is to have it in hand. The measurements of the bill, wings, and tail, an examination of the feathers, its weight, and an overall general close look all have to be done before someone can positively determine what the bird is. Sometimes the difference between one species and another or even determining a bird's sex depends on something as small as the presence or absence of a notch in a tail feather.

HUMMERS ON THE MOVE

Most hummingbirds that breed in the United States leave their breeding grounds and go south to the tropics when they've finished nesting. Depending on the species, this can begin as early as late June. But the peak migration time for most of them is late July through August. Not all hummingbirds that migrate, however, leave the continental United States for winter.

It's common knowledge these days that some hummingbirds spend the cold months along the Gulf Coast or in the warmer parts of the country. A few, in fact, may even spend some or all of the cold months in the northern or eastern states. Conventional thinking in the past held that all hummingbirds, except for a few species known to breed and live year-round in southern California or the Southwest, left the country after they'd finished nesting and spent the winters in Mexico or Central America. And while this is certainly true for the bulk of the migratory species, more are being found every year as winter inhabitants in warm parts of the United States. This means that instead of migrating south, some hummers go east, southeast, or even northeast, crossing the Rocky Mountains in the process.

Scientists aren't sure why this is happening. Some think it always happened, and we just didn't know about it. Others believe a change in migratory patterns is occurring due to warming and changing conditions in the atmosphere. Still others think that once a bird goes off course, it becomes genetically imprinted and passes that knowledge on to the next generation. Lending some credence to that belief, some off-course birds come back to the same yard and feeders for many years in a row. There's a record of a buff-bellied hummingbird (*Amazilia yucatanensis*) returning to a backyard in Louisiana for more than 10 years.

Today we know more than we ever did about how many western hummingbirds go off course during migration and end up spending the winter where they're not expected, due to three simple things: First, of course, when a banded bird is recaptured, it tells scientists where it has gone. Second, a lot of people now look closely at the hummingbirds in their yards instead of just assuming they're the normally expected species. And third, people now leave feeders out much longer than they used to. In the North, this can even mean leaving a feeder out until it freezes.

Band of Birders

Believe it or not, backyard birders like you are responsible for a lot of what we now know about hummingbirds. It's thanks to homeowners' early observations of unusual species appearing in their backyards that the new awareness of off-course migrants and returning "exotics" was ultimately accepted as scientific fact. And of course, this change in behavior stirred up even more interest in these amazing little birds.

The increased interest in watching and learning about hummingbirds has led to a dramatic increase in the number of trained hummingbird banders. When a hummingbird is caught, banded, and then released, there's always the chance, small as it may be, that the same bird will be seen, found, or caught elsewhere. When this happens, dates and data from the bird are taken and compared, and this data reveals how far the bird has traveled, the direction it went, and how long it has lived. Banding operations along traditional migratory routes in the northern parts of the country are conducted from late July into early September. In the South, banding takes place from October through early February. Occasionally, banding operations for other types of birds catch hummingbirds in their nets in spring.

Hummingbird banders put a nectar feeder inside a cage equipped with a remote-control closing device. If there are other feeders around, all but the one in the cage are taken down. When a bird goes in to feed, the door of the cage closes. If a lot of birds are being caught, as sometimes happens at spots along migratory routes, banders put them in mesh bags until they can measure and band them. The banders weigh them and check for fat deposits, then measure their wings, tails, and bills. At times, these measurements are the only things that positively determine the bird's age and/or sex.

In the East it's not unusual for 20 to 30 birds to be caught in a single morning during late July and August in a backyard with good habitat. There are even some places east of the Rockies where hundreds of birds congregate as they migrate south, but they're few and far between. On the western side of the Rockies down through the Southwest, multiple species of hummingbirds migrate along the same paths, so banders there may catch hundreds of birds a day.

Many people have played a big part in promoting banding efforts, including master bander Nancy Newfield of Metairie, Louisiana, who was the first to call attention to the phenomenon of unusual hummingbird species turning up in unexpected places. In early winter of 1974, Nancy found a rufous hummingbird in her yard where she'd have expected only ruby-throats. Soon more unexpected species turned up in birding reports.

When it became public knowledge that individuals of eight or more species of hummingbirds spent the winter months along the Gulf Coast, more people became interested, and some of them went on to become banders, including master banders Bob and Martha Sargent of Clay, Alabama. Every year they and other master banders train more banders. Bob trained with Nancy and then went on to form and head the Hummer/Bird Study Group. He and Martha travel the country giving very entertaining lectures and workshops about hummingbirds. Check the group's Web site, www.hummingbirdsplus.org, for its calendar of events.

Many unusual species that show up in the Northeast don't do so until October or November. Most of them don't stay long, but some do, and some may even return to the same spot the following year. In warm-winter areas, the annual winter occurrence of multiple hummingbird species means that many people look forward to a period from September through March as the time when they have the most (or, at least, the most interesting) hummingbirds around.

GET TO KNOW YOUR HUMMINGBIRDS

All this talk about random hummingbirds showing up in unexpected places is probably confusing. Maybe you're wondering how you'll even recognize the hummingbirds that are *supposed* to be in your area, much less the oddities that just might turn up. Luckily, there are some great resources available to help you with hummer ID. Two recommended photo guidebooks are the Peterson Field Guides' volume *Hummingbirds of North America,* by Sheri Williamson, and Steve Howell's *Hummingbirds of North America: The Photographic Guide.* Both contain all kinds of information previously not known by or available to the general public. In addition to full-body photographs of both adult and juvenile hummingbirds of all species, the books offer close-up photographs of wings, tails, and heads. All of these guides are excellent starting points!

For more in-depth discussion of how to attract hummers to your backyard, it's impossible to beat Sally Roth's wonderful book, *Attracting Butterflies & Hummingbirds to Your Backyard.* If you're inspired by this chapter to make the beautiful little hummers part of your life, then you owe it to yourself to find her book! If you live in the eastern half of the country, where the hummingbird you're most likely to see is the ruby-throat, buy Robert R. (that's our friend Bob) Sargent's Wild Bird Guides volume, *Ruby-Throated Hummingbird.* Other good choices are Sheri Williamson's *Attracting and Feeding Hummingbirds,* Donald and Lillian Stokes's *Stokes Hummingbird*

The Hummingbird ID Secret: Adult Males

The best way to learn how to tell one hummingbird species from another is to begin by learning to identify the adult males. Start with the species that are found where you live. The adult males are the most colorful and distinctly marked, and it's not hard to tell one species from another based on the males. Even in two very similar-looking species, such as black-chinned and ruby-throated hummingbirds, it's easy to tell the males apart by the color of their throats. Such is not the case, though, with adult females and immature birds, because they look so much alike. So start out by studying the males in your field guide or hummingbird book and you can't go wrong!

Book, and Marcus Schneck's *Creating a Hummingbird Garden*.

But right now, you don't have a specialist's book. What to do?! Never fear, we're here to help you identify your brilliant little buzzers with confidence. Read on . . .

HEADS OR TAILS?

It takes time and a lot of experience to be able to tell young hummingbirds from the adult females of the same species. And it takes even more time and experience to be able to differentiate between them and the young and female birds of a *different* species. Closely looking at their heads, faces, and throats sometimes helps a lot, but even in species in which only the males have red throats, there are times when adult females may show a few red throat spots. If you see one like this, you'll wonder if that means the bird's an adult female with a few colored feathers or a young male just beginning to get his throat feathers.

Confronted by an issue like this, it's time to turn tail. Learning to look closely at the shape and color of their tail feathers can be more helpful in identifying female and juvenile hummingbirds than just looking at their heads. Unlike adult males, whose tails are colored or dark and often forked or distinctly shaped, the tails of young and adult female hummingbirds usually

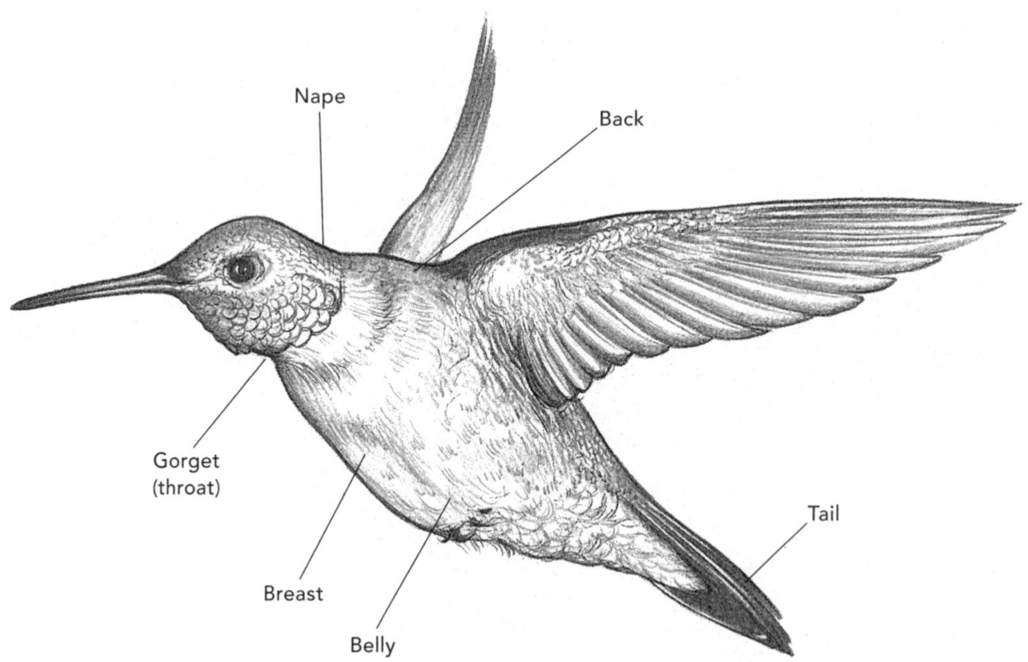

While hummingbirds are distinct from other types of birds, it takes careful observation to sort out different species of hummers. Head, gorget, nape, back, breast, and belly color all may give clues to a bird's identity, along with the shape of its tail and wings. These features are most helpful when you're looking at an adult male hummer; female and juvenile birds often look very similar from one species to the next.

Operation RubyThroat

Hilton Pond Center for Piedmont Natural History in York, South Carolina, hosts Operation Ruby-Throat: The Hummingbird Project (www.ruby-throat.org). Founded in 1999 by the center's director Bill Hilton, Jr., an enthusiastic naturalist and bird bander, Operation RubyThroat gathers information on the behavior and distribution of ruby-throated (and other) hummingbirds throughout North and Central America. It involves students and teachers from kindergarten on up in hummer-related projects, including establishing schoolyard hummingbird habitats, and its Web site is nothing less than fantastic. If you want to see spectacular photos, find out more about hummingbirds, and/or participate in the project (which is open to everyone), you owe it to yourself to check out this site! (The parent site, www.hiltonpond.org, is wonderful, too. You'll enjoy some of the weirdest and most amazing wildlife photographs ever!)

have white tips on some or most of the feathers. Above the white tips is black, and above that is usually either green or rufous (orange) coloring, depending on the species. The shape and size of the white tips combined with the width of the black area are what helps to determine if the bird is an adult female or a young bird of either gender.

There's no easy way to learn this, but having a good book on hummingbird identification, like the two field guides we recommended earlier, really helps. Both of them have detailed drawings or close-up photographs of the heads and tails of different species side by side for easy comparison between similar birds. If you look at the tail photos closely, you'll see the difference in the tails of immature female black-chinneds and immature female rubythroats. The white tips on the tail of the immature female black-chinned hummingbird are much smaller and rounder than the white tail tips of an immature female ruby-throated hummingbird.

This might seem like an impossible task to master, but it's worth the effort if you live in an area with multiple species or where multiple species migrate through. If you get frustrated, remind yourself that even the experts don't always get the age and sex right! Just enjoy your backyard identity guessing game and leave the positive IDs to the banders.

Throat Color May Vary

It's often easiest to identify adult male hummingbirds by their throat color—but not always. Because hummingbirds' throat feathers are iridescent, they don't always show their color. This is true of all hummingbird species, and it's because the color is created by the microscopic arrangement of the feathers rather than by pigment, as is the case with most birds. A lot of things determine whether the throat will just look dark or show color, including the angle from which it's seen, the amount of sunlight and natural light, and weather conditions.

Take a Closer Look

Ruby-Throated Hummingbird *(Archilochus colubris)*

If you took the United States and cut it down the middle, more or less, the only hummingbird that you'd find breeding in the eastern half would be the ruby-throated hummingbird. Many people who've never traveled to the West have never seen any hummingbird except for this one. If you live in the East—from southern Canada down to Florida, over to central Texas, or north to the eastern end of the Dakotas—this is the hummingbird that you're most likely to see in your backyard. Because of their abundance, Bob Sargent, head of the Hummer/Bird Study Group, wrote a book, *Ruby-Throated Hummingbird,* which deals only with this species. If you really want to know everything about this bird, this is the book to have!

Like many other hummingbird species, the rubythroat, as it's often called, is small, measuring only 3¼ to 3¾ inches (8 to 9.5 cm) long. And like all the others, it moves fast and often, making it hard to get a good look at it unless it perches somewhere in plain view. The adult male rubythroat is easy to identify: It has a green back and head, a greenish-gray belly, dull white breast, and a fiery, ruby-red throat, or gorget. The gorget color can vary from almost yellow through the color spectrum into deep red. There's a black patch below each eye and its bill is black. Its dark green and black tail is deeply forked.

The female is muted in color compared to the male. She's got an all-green back, a green tail with black and white tips, a white or whitish gray front, and a light throat that's sometimes marked with stippling or small dots. Occasionally, an older female may show a few flakes of red on her throat, but her throat is never all red. All the rubythroats you see in spring have matured to the adult stage during the winter months.

What Ruby-Throated Hummingbirds Eat

- Nectar from flowers (favorites include trumpet vine, jewelweed, bee balm, cardinal flower, and fire pink)
- Sugar-water solution ("nectar" for feeders)
- Tree sap, especially from "wells" made by sapsuckers
- Tiny insects and spiders

Regional Relations

The differences between the ruby-throated hummingbird and its western counterpart, the black-chinned hummingbird *(Archilocus alexandri)* are subtle. Overall, the black-chinned is a duller green and lighter on the face than the ruby-throated. While males of both species have black chins, the male rubythroat sports a red gorget, the male black-chinned a black one with a thin band of purple at its base. The black-chinned nests in the western half of Texas, north along an angled line through Idaho, and then farther west. Apart from geography, a surefire way to tell the difference between a black-chinned and a rubythroat is to look at the shape of the tips of its outermost wing feathers—*if* you can see them! On a black-chinned, they're broad and rounded; on a rubythroat, they're pointed. The black-chinned pumps its tail a lot, but rubythroats pump their tails too, just not as much, so it's not a reliable way to distinguish between the two species.

Preferred Habitat

The ruby-throated hummingbird nests in trees and shrubs in woods, orchards, backyards, parks, and along the edges of big tracts of forested land and clearings. Its walnut-size nest is usually, but not always, built in a deciduous bush or tree where a skinny branch begins to slope down. The nest must be easily accessible from below or from the side but sheltered above. Rubythroats don't commonly nest in cities or other highly urbanized areas, but once in a while one will fool you. Males and females have different territories that they choose because they have an adequate supply of food. They like places with lots of perches, the males especially, so that they can guard their territory when they're not busy eating and chasing other rubythroats.

Did You Know?

- In spring, male rubythroats arrive at their territories first, and the females follow a few weeks later. In fall, the males depart first to make the return trip ahead of the females.

- In the morning, the males patrol their territories by flying around the perimeter and vocalizing.
- The wings of a rubythroat beat from 75 to 200 times per second, depending on how it's flying.
- The average weight of a rubythroat is 3 grams (0.11 ounce) or a little more. When it packs on fat to migrate, it can bulk up to between 4 and 5 grams (0.14 and 0.18 ounce). (By comparison, a nickel weighs 4.5 grams.)
- Rubythroats have a very long migration period. In the Northeast, spring migration extends from mid-April through early June and autumn migration can begin as early as mid-July and last through late September, sometimes extending as late as November!
- The female rubythroat will sometimes rebuild the same nest she used last year. At times, she may actually build a new nest on top of the old one.
- There's no pair bond between male and female rubythroats. The only contact the two have, other than chasing each other away from a good food source, is when mating occurs. The female has a completely different territory than the male. She builds the nest and raises the young on her own, while the male goes back to looking for more females to mate with.
- In addition to carbohydrates from sucrose in the nectar they consume, rubythroats eat protein in the form of tiny insects that they pick out of spiderwebs or snatch out of the air flycatcher-fashion.
- The female covers the outside of her nest with lichens that often come from the tree she has chosen for the nest. Using them makes the nest blend in well with the tree's branches.
- At times during the nesting season, it may seem at times like there are no rubythroats around. They're really just out of sight, doing what they came north to do, mate and raise young. The males constantly look for females. The females don't go far away from their nests until their young are gone.
- Once the young birds are out on their own, there's no further bond between them and the female who raised them. The birds you see chasing each other away from food sources may in fact be a mother and the young she raised.
- Rubythroats take dust baths to help get rid of mites and other pests in their feathers.
- Rubythroats begin to migrate by the middle of July. The birds you see in your backyard by the end of August are almost certainly not the same ones that were around earlier in the summer.
- Ruby-throated hummingbirds migrate during the day, although they may also fly during the night when they're crossing the Gulf of Mexico.
- By late August or early September, almost all the adult males are gone from the northern and central parts of their breeding territories. Females and young will continue migrating for another month or so.
- Rubythroats can fly hundreds of miles nonstop over the Gulf of Mexico.

Torpor's No Trouble

At night, when necessary, rufous and ruby-throated hummingbirds will go into torpor, a sort of suspended animation that slows down bodily functions to conserve heat and energy. That's how they're able to withstand very cold temperatures. So if you see a hummer in your yard in winter, don't worry: It doesn't need to be captured and brought inside and taken care of. And it's illegal to do that anyway unless you're a licensed hummingbird rehabilitator. Instead, enjoy watching your tiny visitor while it's with you!

A WHO'S WHO OF NORTH AMERICAN HUMMINGBIRDS

The most common hummingbirds in North America, the ones found across the largest geographical areas, are the ruby-throated, black-chinned, and rufous. As we've mentioned, if you live in the eastern part of the United States—at least, north of the Gulf Coast—you'll generally see only ruby-throated hummingbirds and would be lucky to see a rufous hummingbird. But if you live in the West—especially the Southwest or on the West Coast—you might see quite an assortment of hummers. See our list below to find out more about the species that occur where you live.

COMMON BUT LOCALIZED SPECIES

The five species that follow are common in the areas where they're found, but they breed in smaller areas than the three most common species (ruby-throated, black-chinned, and rufous). For example, Anna's and Allen's hummingbirds are year-round residents of coastal California, and are the dominant species in the areas where they live.

- The **Anna's hummingbird** (*Calypte anna*), 3½ to 4 inches (9 to 10 cm) long, is a year-round resident along the California coast. It's often described as being stocky, chunky, or looking like it has a big head. Its gorget (throat) is coppery red and it has the same color on its forehead and around its eyes. Its back is blue or bluish green, its tail is deeply notched, its front is gray, and its bill is black.
- The **Costa's hummingbird** (*C. costae*), 3 to 3½ inches (8 to 9 cm) long, is also considered to be a year-round resident and is found in the southern parts of California, New Mexico, and Arizona. It's really small, but is easy to identify because of its purple-violet gorget, which has long extensions of colored feathers down both its sides. The Costa's has white feathers under its eyes, a white breast, and a gray belly. Its back is deep green, and its bill is slightly down-curved and dark.
- The tiny **Calliope hummingbird** (*Stellula calliope*), 2¾ to 3¼ inches (7 to 8 cm) long, is the smallest hummer in the country. It breeds in the Pacific Northwest and travels primarily to the southwestern part of Mexico in winter. It's easily identified by its gorget of long, skinny, wine-red to reddish purple stripes of colored feathers over a white background. Its back is green, its front is white with green along the sides, and the base of its tail feathers is a rufous (orange) color. Its bill is short and dark.
- The **Allen's hummingbird** (*Selasphorus sasin*), 3¼ to 3½ inches (8 to 9 cm) long, breeds along the Pacific coastline from Oregon down through southern California. It migrates to south-central Mexico in the winter months. It's a green and rufous bird. Its head and back are green, it has a scarlet-orange gorget, and there's a lot of rufous coloring on its tail and along the sides of its front. Its bill is dark.

(continued on page 222)

Fairy Nests

Hummingbird nests are so small and so well-disguised that you may never see one, even if a hummer is nesting in your yard. The golf-ball-size round cups are made from materials the female gathers from the area, usually from the tree she's nesting in. She uses strands of spiderweb to hold the nest materials together and lines it with the softest filler she can find—including fluffy plant material from seedheads and animal fur. Then she coats the outside with bits of lichen and bark, so the nest visually disappears into the branches of the tree it's built in.

In general, hummers tend to choose native trees and other plants to nest in—conifers in the Northwest, palm trees in Florida and southern California, cacti in the Southwest. Pretty much any native tree is fair game, and the little birds also often choose vines, brambles, shrubs, and even man-made objects like ropes and cords to nest in. The tiny size of the nest and its secure spiderweb attachment makes all sorts of locations possible, but remember, unless they're in a very exposed place—which is unlikely!—they'll still be very hard to spot.

Fortunately, there are lots of wonderful photos of hummingbird nests and birds in the nest, even eggs in the nest, in the books and on the Web sites we've recommended. If you'd like to try to see a real "live" nest, the best way is to keep an eye out for females in your yard in spring and summer. If a female turns up regularly at your feeder or flowers, try to watch discreetly to see where she goes once she's eaten.

Once you've pinpointed the general area, scan it with binoculars to see if you can find a nest. Don't go over and look—you'll disturb the female, who may become so upset she'll even abandon the nest. Instead, continue to check with your binoculars and make a note of the location. In fall or winter, when the family is long gone, you can walk over and check the area thoroughly. If you find the nest, great! But please leave it where it is—remember, some hummingbirds recycle their nests.

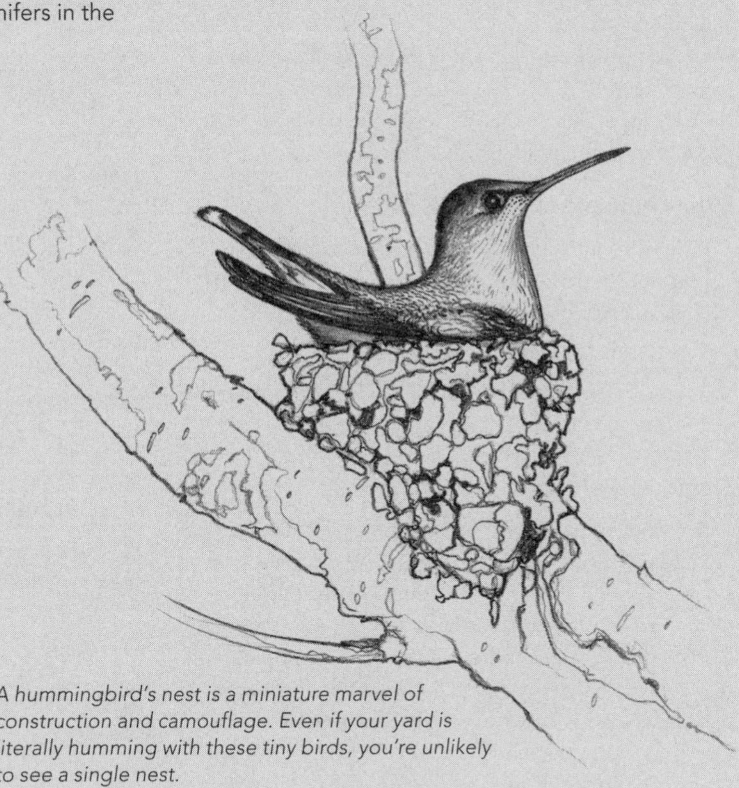

A hummingbird's nest is a miniature marvel of construction and camouflage. Even if your yard is literally humming with these tiny birds, you're unlikely to see a single nest.

Take a Closer Look

Rufous Hummingbird *(Selasphorus rufus)*

Although the rufous hummingbird, which is 3½ to 4 inches (9 to 10 cm) long, breeds in the Pacific Northwest up through southeastern Alaska, it's a bird many people all across the country have become acquainted with. Of all the hummingbird species in the country, this is the one most likely to be found out of its range. There are, in fact, so many records of rufous hummingbirds being found in the eastern states and along the Gulf Coast from late summer through early March that they're now expected annually.

The adult male has a rufous (orange) head, back, and tail. The sides of its white belly are also rufous. The top of its head is green. Whenever anyone reports an odd-looking orange hummingbird, this is almost always the one they're talking about. Female and young rufous hummingbirds aren't as easily identified. You have to look closely at them to be able to see the rufous color on the tops of their tail feathers and above their eyes.

What Rufous Hummingbirds Eat

- Nectar from flowers (favorites include cleome, larkspur, Indian paintbrush, penstemon, crimson columbine, and delphinium)
- Sugar-water solution ("nectar" for feeders)
- Tree sap, especially from "wells" made by sapsuckers
- Tiny insects

Regional Relations

The Allen's hummingbird (*Selasphorus sasin*) that breeds along the Pacific Coast looks a lot like the rufous hummingbird except that its back is green, not rufous. However, don't automatically assume that a hummingbird that's mostly orange but has a green back is an Allen's, because a small percentage of adult rufous hummingbirds have green backs. Note that Allen's are slightly smaller than rufous hummingbirds. Unless you live in the Allen's limited territory, however, what you're seeing is almost certainly a rufous hummingbird.

Preferred Habitat

Because the rufous hummingbird breeds in the Pacific Northwest, it's more likely to be found nesting in conifers than other hummingbirds would be. But, like others, it also nests in deciduous hardwood forests, along the edges of clearings, and in large shrubs and second-growth woods where there's an abundant supply of food and water. It's also found in the temperate rain forest along the Pacific Coast.

Did You Know?

- The rufous hummingbird is very aggressive and territorial, even during migration.
- It can withstand temperatures as low as 0°F (-17.8°C). There are many records of rufous hummingbirds visiting feeders and surviving for long periods of time in the dead of winter.
- Rufous hummingbirds begin arriving on their breeding grounds as early as late February through March. They also begin moving around, in a movement known as post-breeding dispersal, and migrating south before most other species do. Some individuals begin showing up in backyards along the Gulf Coast as early as August.
- Rufous hummingbirds, which breed as far north as the Yukon and winter in Mexico, make the longest migration of any bird when measured by body lengths flown.
- Of all the hummingbird species that spend part or all of winter "out of place" along the Gulf Coast or in the Southeast, rufous hummers are the most plentiful.
- Like other hummers, rufous hummingbirds can scoot sideways when perched, but they can't walk.

Is It a Bird? No, It's a Bug!

Beginning bird-watchers sometimes mistake sphinx moths and hummingbird moths for baby hummingbirds. But when young hummingbirds are able to fly around on their own, they're already as big as the adult birds. And no hummingbirds have antennae! But it's easy to make this mistake, since several of these moths are named for their resemblance to the little birds, and their behavior—hovering by themselves over nectar flowers while their wings are moving so fast they're a blur—also mimics hummers'.

Sphinx moths may be as big as hummingbirds and are often seen feeding at flowers before it gets completely dark, around the same time hummingbirds make their last feeding trip before settling down for the night. These moths are abundant throughout the country and active during the same seasons as hummingbirds. But if you look closely at the two that are most commonly mistaken for hummingbirds—the snowberry clearwing (*Hemaris diffinis*), which resembles a bumblebee and is often called the "bumblebee moth," and the hummingbird clearwing (*H. thysbe*)—you'll see that they have beige backs with black stripes and, of course, antennae. Hummingbirds don't have beige backs with stripes and they're bigger than these sphinx moths.

Here's another way to tell the difference: Even though these moths eat nectar, they almost never go to feeders. If they did, you'd see how small and different-looking they are. You can find photographs of some of these moths in the Peterson Field Guide, *Hummingbirds of North America*. If you have online access, go to a Web site like Hummingbirdmoth.com (www.hummingbirdmoth.com), where you can read all about them, see great photos, find lots of links, and even watch video of the moths in action!

So-called hummingbird moths (right) look a lot like their avian namesakes as they hover over flowers and feed on nectar. Although you're unlikely to see bird and moth side-by-side, there are significant differences to help you distinguish between them. Even the biggest moths are generally smaller than most hummers, and anything with antennae is clearly an insect. Finally, moths suck up flower nectar through a slender, straw-like proboscis that looks nothing like a hummingbird's beak.

- The **broad-tailed hummingbird** (*Selasphorus platycercus*), 3¾ to 4¼ inches (9.5 to 10 cm) long, breeds from central Idaho down through Central America. It has a green back and head, a white breast, and rufous coloring at the base of its long tail feathers. Its gorget is dark pink to rose-red and very showy. One way to know for sure that it's a broad-tailed hummingbird is to listen for the loud wing trill that the adult male's wings make when he flies.

UNCOMMON OR RARE BREEDING SPECIES

The following species also breed in the United States, but only in small, highly specialized areas. They're not species that you'd automatically expect to see, even if you went to their breeding areas at the right time of year. To see them requires planning, traveling to places off the beaten track, and often a lot of luck. If and when any of these species regularly visit a backyard feeding station, the news travels fast in the birding community. Check Web sites like Birdingonthe.Net (www.birdingonthe.net), the HUMNET Listserv of Louisiana State University's Museum of Natural History (search for HUMNET via Google or another search engine), and the Hummer/Bird Study Group (www.hummingbirdsplus.org), as well as Rare Bird Alerts (www.birder.com has an extensive selection), to find out which species are turning up where.

- The **white-eared hummingbird** (*Hylocharis leucotis*), 3½ to 4 inches (9 to 10 cm) long, is a rare but regular breeder in the Huachuca Mountains of southeastern Arizona. It's easily recognized by a big white stripe back from its eyes, black cheeks, bluish violet crown and chin, and turquoise throat. Its front is a mottled green, its back is yellow-green, and it has a red bill tipped with black.
- The **broad-billed hummingbird** (*Cynanthus latirostris*), 3½ to 4 inches (9 to 10 cm) long, only breeds in the area where southeastern Arizona meets New Mexico and western Texas. Although it's rare, in some places it's becoming more common. It's a dark, distinctive-looking bird. Its breast is dark green, its gorget is blue, and its tail is dull black and forked. Its bill is orange with a black tip and, as the bird's name implies, is wide at its base.
- The **blue-throated hummingbird** (*Lampornis clemenciae*), 4¾ to 5¼ inches (12 to 13 cm) long, is one of the largest hummingbirds in North America. It breeds sparsely in the mountains of western Texas and in similar habitat in southern New Mexico and southeastern Arizona. It has prominent white stripes on its face, a large blue gorget, a green back, a gray front, a big black-and-white tail, and a dark bill.
- The **magnificent hummingbird** (*Eugenes fulgens*), 4¾ to 5¼ inches (12 to 13 cm) long, is another large, dark hummingbird that only breeds in the mountains of western Texas through southeastern Arizona. It's dark green on the back, dull and dark on the front, and has a dark green notched tail. Its head and face are unmistakable, with its turquoise gorget and violet crown. Its dark bill is very long.

- The **Lucifer hummingbird** (*Calothorax lucifer*), 3½ to 4 inches (9 to 10 cm) long, breeds from western Texas to southern Arizona. It's easily recognized by a bright magenta-purple gorget with feathers that go down onto its white breast at the corners. It's dark green on its back, has a deeply forked dark tail, and is dark on its belly below its breast. Its bill is dark and noticeably down-curved.
- The **violet-crowned hummingbird** (*Amazilia violiceps*), 4 to 4½ inches (10 to 11 cm) long, is chiefly resident in southeastern Arizona and southwestern New Mexico. This hummingbird is easy to identify. Its crown is a bright blue-violet, its back and tail are gray-green, its front is white, and its bill is coral red with a black tip.
- The **buff-bellied hummingbird** (*A. yucatanensis*), 3¾ to 4¼ inches (9.5 to 10 cm) long, is resident along the Gulf Coast of Texas. Its head, face, and back are apple-green, it has a metallic green to turquoise throat and breast, a buff belly, and a notched rufous tail. Its bill is red with a black tip.
- The **berylline hummingbird** (*A. beryllina*), 3¾ to 4 inches (9.5 to 10 cm) long, is resident mostly in the mountains of southeastern Arizona. It looks a lot like the buff-bellied hummingbird, but its tail isn't as bright, and its metallic green throat speckling extends farther down its front. It has rufous coloring at the base of its wings and a violet rump. Its bill is black on top and orange-red underneath.

Help! There's a Hummer in the House!

Every so often, a hummingbird will accidentally fly into a house or other building. One will sometimes fly into a garage that's been left open. Once a panicked hummingbird is in your house, shed, or garage, it's not easy to coax it back out. Sometimes hummingbirds caught inside get so stressed that they sit still and even appear to be dead! Help your trapped hummer find its way back to the great outdoors with these techniques. And remember, be patient! It may take several hours for the poor little hummer to calm down enough to fly off.

- Open as many doors and windows as you can, and turn off all the lights so the only bright spots are the open doors and windows.
- Put a feeder or something red near the spot where you think the bird flew in.
- Try quietly shooing it toward an escape route with a soft object, being careful not to hurt it.
- If you can't get the bird to go outside on its own, you may have to try to temporarily capture it. Try using a pillowcase strategically placed so the hummer is likely to fly into it. Once the bird flies into the pillowcase, fold the case gently around it and take it outside as quickly as you can. Set the pillowcase on the ground and open it carefully. Don't try to pick up the bird and be especially careful of its bill. If a hummingbird's bill gets seriously damaged, it's usually an automatic death sentence.

FEEDERS AND NECTAR SOLUTIONS

These days, there are so many hummingbird feeders on the market that it's hard to decide which ones to use. But as long as the feeder is built well, easy to clean, and not too big, it really doesn't matter what it looks like. You just need to be sure to put the right kind of sugar-water solution into it and put it in the right place. Timing is also important.

The right time to put out a hummingbird feeder is in spring a few weeks before the first males are expected to arrive each year. In the southern and southwestern parts of the country, this can be as early as March 1st. The dates gradually get later as the birds move up the continent. An exception is at places along the West Coast as far north as Washington, where rufous hummingbirds breed. This species begins moving back north to breed earlier than other species. Someone living in Maine may not need to put out a feeder for a rubythroat until early May, but at the other side of the country at about the same latitude, you'd need to put out feeders for rufous hummingbirds much earlier.

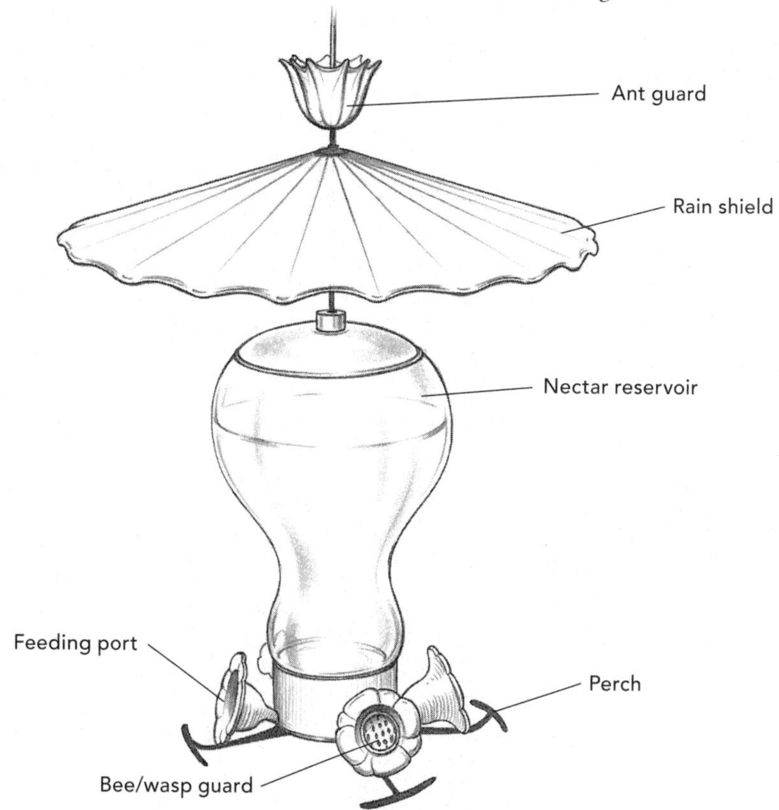

A hummingbird feeder may be as simple as a container of nectar and a single tube or opening for birds to drink from, or it may include guards to keep insects out of the nectar, a cover to protect it from the rain (more important for flat, saucer-style feeders), red plastic "flowers" to attract hummers to the ports, and perches that hummingbirds may or may not use.

In the North, feeders should stay out until at least Thanksgiving or even until their contents freeze solid. Any vagrant western species that shows up may come to one after all the flowers have been killed by frost. The farther south you go, the longer you can leave feeders out. Some people in the Deep South never take their feeders down at all.

NECTAR FEEDER FEATURES

Choosing a good hummingbird feeder is easy, if you bear three things in mind: durability, capacity, and ease of cleaning. Here are key features to look for in a good feeder.

- A feeder must be easy to take apart, clean, and put back together again.
- Bigger feeders require less frequent refilling, which is great if your yard hosts dozens of hummingbirds. If you just have a few hummers, though, you may find that most of the sugar water in a big feeder will go bad before it's consumed, and one or more small feeders will work best for you. (See "How Many Feeders Should You Have?" on page 228 for more on this.)
- A feeder should be simply shaped and not indented or dimpled on its surface. Go with a simple design, not something that's cute with a lot of nooks and crannies, or you'll end up with a cleaning nightmare.
- A well-made plastic or combination plastic/glass feeder is preferable to one made mostly of glass.
- Check to make sure the plastic is thick, not thin and flimsy.
- Feeders with flat feeder ports are a lot easier to clean than the ones that have protruding ports (usually in the shape of flowers). Imagine having to brush out all those "flowers" every time you wash your feeder!
- Choose a feeder with red parts on it—for example, a red top. There are two reasons for this: Hummingbirds are attracted to colors like red, orange, and pink at the long-wavelength end of the color spectrum; and bees, which can become nuisances at nectar feeders, don't see red very well.
- Check to make sure the metal hardware or hanger is securely attached and can be easily taken out for cleaning if it's removable.
- It doesn't matter if the feeder does or does not have perches. Some hummingbirds prefer to sit and drink while others prefer hovering. Almost all of them will do both.

Clean Easier with "Flying Saucers"

The easier a nectar feeder is to clean, the less time and effort you'll have to put into feeder upkeep. That's why Virginia birder Cole Burrell insists on disk-shaped hummingbird feeders, or as he says, "flying saucers." The top comes off of these feeders for easy cleaning, unlike tube feeders that require special brushes. No matter how carefully you clean your tube feeders, Cole says, "tube feeders always get gnarly, and eventually hummers stop using them." Make feeding easy on yourself and your hummers with a saucer feeder, such as one of the HummZinger models that are readily available from stores, catalogs, and Web sites that specialize in wild bird products.

What about Glass?

Some people prefer glass feeders over plastic ones because they find them more attractive. Unlike plastic, glass will not fade and deteriorate from extended exposure to sunlight, and four-legged critters seeking a sugary treat will not gnaw through a glass feeder—although they might knock it down and break it. Glass is fragile. If a glass feeder is your choice, keep these drawbacks and precautions in mind:

- Don't put a glass feeder where it will easily fall and break in high winds.
- Don't put hot sugar water in a glass feeder because it can crack.
- Be extra careful when cleaning glass feeders. They may or may not be dishwasher-safe. Check the tag to see if it mentions this.
- The sugar-water solution inside a glass feeder will heat up faster—and consequently will spoil faster—than in a plastic feeder if you put it in full sun.
- Glass feeders usually aren't designed to work with a pole mount.

Feed Them, and They Will Come

There aren't a whole lot of people with the problem of having so many hummingbirds in their backyards that they can't keep up with the feeders, but there are some. In the West, there are feeding stations maintained by wildlife and conservation organizations, usually on federally or state-owned lands, where the number of hummingbirds coming to feeders in a single day at the peak of migration is in the *thousands.*

Even in the East, there are places where hundreds of rubythroats are caught and banded daily. The places in the eastern half of the country that get big numbers of rubythroats are normally, but not always, located on a migration route somewhere near a ridgeline or coastline. In the West, mountain ridge migration corridors concentrate many different species in a central location. In all interior parts of the country, hummingbirds tend to gather in large numbers at feeding stations in valleys next to mountains.

That's not to say that there aren't big hummingbird concentrations at some places far from mountainous areas, but the biggest numbers are always found near large and mostly uninhabited forested areas. You may be surprised to learn that these areas don't contain an abundance of flowers or even many nectar sources at all. But if you're lucky enough to live on or near a hummingbird migration route, you can encourage them—sometimes dozens or even

Keep Replacement Parts Ready

If your feeder has removable feeding ports that need to be cleaned periodically, know where you can get replacements in case some of them get lost or broken. Ditto for bee guards. To save time during feeder cleaning, keep a full set of replacement ports and install them in place of dirty ports when you clean and refill your feeder. You can soak the dirty ports in the cleaning solution of your choice, rinse, and let them air-dry; they'll be ready to return to service at the next cleaning session.

Make 'Em See Red

Most feeders have red on them somewhere because the color attracts hummingbirds; we recommend that you choose a feeder with red on it for that reason. (Some people like to add even more red by tying red bows on branches or hanging red Frisbees near feeders to lure in hummingbirds; some birders even paint the feeders' roofs red!) But even if a feeder has no red parts, most birds will find and use it anyway if it's put in the right place. Hang it near an area with flowers or natural shelter.

hundreds of them—to make your backyard a regular stop on their route by setting out nectar feeders, water features, and/or hummingbird plants.

The ultimate feeding frenzy. Twenty-six years ago, Gerry, a woman who had recently moved to rural West Virginia from California, hung out one feeder, hoping to attract one hummingbird. Sure enough, one hummingbird showed up. The following year, she added another feeder, and as more hummers turned up, she kept adding feeders each year. Now Gerry has more than 30 16-ounce (473 ml) feeders hung close together under the protection of her deck, and she uses more than 3 gallons (11.4 l) of sugar water each day! The buildup of birds at her place was gradual, but has now reached incredible numbers from the end of July through August. Not too far from Gerry's home is another backyard feeding station in the same rural area where hummingbirds arrive by the dozen at the same time they turn up at Gerry's feeders.

Both Gerry and her neighbor live near a large forested area that's part of a major migration route for ruby-throated hummingbirds. The first hummingbirds to find these feeders years ago almost certainly began coming back year after year. Their offspring did the same, other birds then began coming, and the numbers just kept climbing. For such tiny creatures, hummingbirds have amazing memories. They're as loyal to their migration routes as they are to nesting territories and backyard feeders.

If you're like Gerry and want to have a backyard full of hummingbirds, before you put out a bunch of feeders, remember that they take a lot of work. The big numbers of hummers all come during a 6-week to 2-month period beginning in midsummer, during which time you're going to be very busy mixing gallons of sugar water and washing out feeders. The old saying, "Be careful what you wish for because you may get it," is very applicable here. If you find yourself bitten really hard by the hummingbird bug, try to make sure your family shares your enthusiasm. Maintaining more than a couple of hummingbird feeders is a lot easier if the task is shared. (On the plus side, at least sugar water is cheap!)

HOW MANY FEEDERS SHOULD YOU HAVE?

Unless you live in the West where many species of hummers migrate at the same time, you don't need a big feeder. Several small 8-ounce (236 ml) feeders placed among flowers, shrubs, and trees are enough for most backyard situations. According to Sheri Williamson, author of the Peterson Field Guide *Hummingbirds of North America,* just one 8-ounce feeder is sufficient to meet the daily energy needs of 40 to 60 hummingbirds! Not all hummers even use feeders. Some hummingbirds will never use feeders, regardless of where you put them or how many you have. Some birds love them and some birds ignore them. It's also a mistake to think that just having a lot of feeders will bring more birds into your yard. For that to happen, you need good habitat in addition to the feeders. (We'll talk more about making your landscape hummingbird-friendly in "Gardening for Hummingbirds, beginning on page 236.)

So why even bother to put out more than one feeder? Actually, there are several good reasons.

- The biggest reason to set out multiple feeders is because of male hummingbirds. Males are territorial, and they'll defend their territory from all comers, including female and juvenile hummers. If you just set out one feeder, a male may decide it's his and keep other birds away. But even territorial males can't defend three or four feeders at the same time. So setting out more than one nectar feeder means you'll host more hummers, and the feeders may even bring in more of the colorful males, since each male hummer can claim one feeder as part of his territory.
- Multiple feeders not only bring in more birds, they give you more places to watch them. You can set up feeders where you can see them from all your favorite vantage points.
- Multiple feeders bring hummingbirds out into the open in areas where previously they weren't thought to be.
- Hummingbirds can come in to feed from all directions.
- It's easier to clean and maintain several small feeders than one really big one, and you can clean and refill multiple feeders on a rotating schedule so one or two are always available when a hummer stops by for a sip.
- Unless your yard hosts lots of hummers, most of the sugar water in a big feeder will go bad before it's eaten.

Just how much sugar water does it take to keep several feeders filled? Pennsylvania birder Rudy Keller has four standard feeders at his home. He says he typically feeds a quart (0.95 l) of sugar water a week, though during peak migration, the hummers may consume a quart 5 every 3 days. Rudy makes his own sugar-water nectar (find out how you can, too, in "What's on the Menu" on page 231). Like most serious birders, Rudy never puts dye in his sugar solution.

Leave a Little Room

No matter how small your hummingbird feeder is, resist the temptation to cut down on refilling chores by filling it all the way up to the top. If the solution expands at all, you'll wind up with a leaky, drippy feeder and an insect-attracting mess on the ground below. Leave a little space for the sugar water to expand and contract.

How Nectar Feeders Help Hummingbirds

Birders often are surprised to learn that bird feeders, including hummingbird feeders, aren't the primary source of food for backyard birds. Instead, they're more like a backup. Birds typically survive just fine on the foods that are naturally available where they choose to live, breed, or winter over. (In fact, water is more likely to be a critical issue to birds' survival than food.) So why set out a feeder?

First of all, feeders make it easy and fun to watch hummingbirds (and, of course, the same is true of setting out seed and suet feeders for other birds). Setting out a nectar feeder gives you the opportunity to bring hummers in where you want them, so you can watch them from the comfort of your kitchen or deck. A feeder can bring them in close so you can enjoy their beauty and their antics every day, as opposed to catching a rare glimpse. And the nectar in feeders definitely gives the birds a calorie boost—the most calories for the least work. This is especially helpful in spring, when hummers are returning from migration and before there are a lot of flowers in bloom; while the females are nesting; as well as late in the year when the occasional bemused juvenile might make its way to your yard, or an unusual cold snap kills nectar-producing flowers in a normally warm-winter area.

But there's more than food and fun to feeders. Backyard birders who set out feeders are helping ornithologists learn more about birds. As we discussed in "Band of Birders" on page 212, some of the most important discoveries about changes in hummingbird migrations were initiated by backyard birders watching their nectar feeders. Whether you participate in an organized effort like Project FeederWatch (see page 28 for more on this) or Operation RubyThroat (see page 215), or simply learn as much as you can about the various hummingbird species and keep an eye on your feeders, you *can* make a difference.

Professionals have found nectar feeders valuable as well. Because hummingbirds readily use the feeders, they've made it possible for banders to catch hummingbirds to track them. The banders put a feeder inside a cage and wait for a hummingbird to go in. It's a direct result of feeders that vagrant species never before known to have been in certain areas have been found.

Enjoyment, assistance, education: three good reasons to put up feeders in your yard!

Provide Places to Perch

Support your flowers . . . and hummers too! Hummingbirds like to sit and watch what's going on around them when they're not feeding. A place to perch close to feeders or near flower beds makes them comfortable and brings more hummingbird activity into an area. Metal poles, dead branches, fence posts, clotheslines, tomato cages, and almost anything sturdy that they can sit on will get used. Wire cages or frames that garden centers and catalogs sell to support perennials are especially good because they hold flower stems upright so you can see hummingbirds feeding at each blossom. They also give the birds a place to sit after feeding, when they preen and work their tongues in and out to clean them off.

SITING YOUR FEEDERS

Of course, you want to hang your hummingbird feeders where you can see them easily from inside the house as well as wherever you enjoy sitting when you're outside on the deck or patio or out in the yard. And you want to put them close enough so they're easy to maintain—you're less likely to refill and clean them regularly if it feels like you have to walk miles from the house to check on them. But apart from these commonsense measures, there are some special considerations to take into account when choosing a spot for your hummingbird feeder. Here are a few do's and don'ts to keep in mind.

- Hummers are even more prone to crash into window or deck-door glass than other birds because they're so aggressive. When a territorial male is chasing off other hummers, nobody's really paying too much attention to where they're going—they're all just trying to get away and/or fight back. If a feeder is too close to the glass, fatalities are inevitable. And if it's too far from the glass, the same thing can happen because of reflection. If you're putting a feeder where birds can see a glass surface, site it just over 3 feet (0.9 m) away from the glass. You can also put decals on your glass windows and doors—many hummingbird and other wild bird stores, Web sites, and catalogs offer special ones that are shaped like hummingbirds—or use protective bird netting as an extra precaution.
- Because of hummers' distinctive flexible, needle-shaped bills, glass isn't the only hazard that windows, doors, and screened porches present. If a hummer flies into a screened surface face-first, its bill can become caught in the screen. The best advice is simply to keep feeders away from screens.
- Don't put a feeder out in the middle of a big, grassy area all by itself. The sun will heat up the sugar water, and as a result, the birds won't use it except in the morning and late in the day. In really hot weather, the solution will get cloudy, begin to ferment, and mold will form in only a few days' time.
- Put feeders high enough to keep cats and other animals from jumping up to them, but not so high that you can't reach them. They can be as low as 3 feet (0.9 m) in the middle of a flower bed if there are no cats around, but 5 to 6 feet (1.5 to 1.8 m) is the recommended height.
- Feeders in, around, or above flower beds usually attract hummingbirds to them relatively quickly, because where there are flowers there are bugs. But you may have to move the feeder as the flowers grow. A hidden feeder is an unused feeder.
- Feeders placed near the shelter of shrubs or trees shouldn't be so close that predators can easily hide in the leaves. Praying mantises are especially fond of camouflaging themselves in leaves near hummingbird feeders and then grabbing the bird as it feeds.
- Make sure there are bare branches near your feeder so the hummers can perch and see oncoming rivals. This doesn't mean that you have to site your feeder near a dead plant! But hummers will feel much more confident about

patronizing your feeder if you have a tree or shrub with open branches, such as a redbud, willow, butterfly bush, or naturally shaped (not sheared) privet nearby.

- Some people believe that putting five or more feeders only a few feet apart in a cluster arrangement enables more birds to feed. Hummingbirds—males, females, and young—all instinctively chase each other from food sources. Having a lot of options close together seems to allow more birds to feed at the same time.
- A popular arrangement is to put one feeder on each corner of a deck. Unlike seed feeders, there's no problem with messy spilled seed or bird droppings, and the deck is a great place to view hummers while relaxing with your own favorite beverage!

WHAT'S ON THE MENU

After you have a feeder and decide where to hang it, you need to put a nectar solution in it. You can buy ready-made nectar from the same sources that sell feeders, but fortunately, it's really easy to make your own.

Analyses of natural nectar sources preferred by hummingbirds show that most of them contain 20 to 25 percent sucrose. To make a solution that mimics the nectar concentrations found in flowers, combine ¼ cup (57 g) of white granulated sugar (ordinary table sugar) with 2 cups (473 ml) of water. Stir until the sugar is completely dissolved. For extra convenience, you can make a bigger batch of this nectar than you need and store it in the refrigerator, but don't keep it for longer than a week.

Here's more good news: You don't have to sterilize the solution by boiling it. The second a hummingbird puts its bill into the solution, it's no longer sterile anyway. Boiling can even affect the concentration by evaporating some of the water. There's no problem with heating the water a little to make sure that the sugar completely dissolves. But if you do heat the sugar-water solution, be sure it's completely cooled off and at room temperature before you put it into the feeders. If it's too hot, it may warp plastic and break glass.

One warning: *Never* use honey, brown sugar, or artificial sweeteners to make the nectar solution. Brown sugar contains molasses products, honey is thick and heavy, and artificial sweeteners aren't natural sucrose. The digestive systems of hummingbirds are well-oiled machines that process the sucrose they get from natural sources through their bodies in about 20 minutes. They're not designed to handle additives or heavy, viscous solutions.

Once you've mixed up your sugar water and it has reached room temperature, add the solution to a clean feeder, leaving a little room in case the liquid expands a bit—and it's ready for hungry hummingbirds.

MANAGING YOUR HUMMINGBIRD CAFÉ

Tending to hummingbird feeders shouldn't be a full-time job. By choosing a simple, durable feeder and putting it in an easily accessible spot, you've already made things easier on yourself. Keeping a feeder or feeders clean and filled with unspoiled nectar is the most important thing you need to do. With the right planning, maintenance won't take up much of your time. Except for during the hottest weather (when nectar in feeders in the sun may get cloudy and have to be changed every other day), you won't need to change the sugar water in most feeders more often than every 3 or 4 days. This is especially true if the feeders are in the shade most of the day.

Some people prefer to serve up fresh nectar every other day or even every day. If that makes you feel better, do it, but it's completely unnecessary and doesn't keep the hummingbirds healthier. In the wild, hummingbirds eat from fermenting fruit that's been rotting on the ground for days or even weeks. And changing the nectar daily may be more harmful in other ways: You may get so tired of doing it that you stop taking care of the feeders altogether during the periods when visits to the feeders are low. The one time you *would* need to replace the nectar daily is if the hummingbirds have consumed it all—a sure sign that it's time to add a feeder!

BIRD MYTH-BUSTER

The Solution Is Clear

It's well-documented that hummingbirds come to the color red, but the color that attracts them need not color what they eat. A spot of red on the feeder is enough to attract hummers' attention to a feeder's clear, sweet contents, but the solution inside needn't be—and many say shouldn't be—red. There are many products for sale that are processed with red dye already in them. People use them because they're convenient. But it's still unclear as to whether or not this dye is harmful to the digestive systems of hummingbirds, even though it's not the same red dye that was used years ago and taken off the market because it was found to be harmful to people.

Studies at some feeding stations have even shown that hummers will feed more if the nectar solution is clear than if it's colored red, but there haven't been enough studies to make this data a hard-and-fast rule. However, many birders are emphatic about avoiding nectars with red dyes; some even claim that the dye causes cancer in hummingbirds. Why take a chance? It's even more practical to make your own nectar: A simple homemade sugar-water solution is much easier and cheaper to make than buying a ready-made one with red dye in it.

In addition to products produced with red dye, there are many kinds of clear, pre-made nectar products for sale. A lot of them are flavored or advertise that they contain nutrients and vitamins that the hummingbirds need. This isn't true. Hummingbirds get all the nutrients they need from natural sources. Putting added ingredients into what should be a simple sucrose solution just makes the product costlier. Plain sugar water is just fine at your feeder—there's no need to pay more for unnecessarily enriched nectars.

Feeder Cleaning Options

You should clean your feeders every time you change the solution in them. They need to be thoroughly washed with water and mild detergent. You should clean them out with a soft bristle brush or pipe cleaner. (Many brushes designed especially for hummingbird feeders are available from wild bird specialty stores, Web sites, and catalogs). Don't forget to clean out the feeding ports, too! If you use a pipe cleaner, use a new one every time.

Why all the bother? Just rinsing them with water won't get rid of the beginnings of mold that you may not even know is there, or the buildup of particles on the inside of the feeder.

One exception to complicated cleaning is the disk or "flying saucer" feeder, which is one reason we recommend it. Because the top lifts off and the flat surface is easy to clean, you can rinse it out with water for the first and second refill, sterilizing it with a 1:10 bleach-water solution every second or third change. But don't try this with a tube feeder!

Different birders have different ways of cleaning feeders. Using bleach is the most foolproof method and the one most people use, but it's not an exact science as to how much to use. Other people swear by other methods. Here are a few feeder-tending options.

- After emptying the feeders and brushing them out, immerse them in a mild bleach-water solution for at least an hour. Commonly used concentrations vary, but 1 cup (237 ml) of bleach in a 2-gallon (7 l) bucket will do a satisfactory job. Thoroughly rinse the feeders after they come out of the cleaning water, making sure they don't feel slippery to the touch. Then let them air-dry before refilling them. Scientific studies and chemical analyses have shown that a small amount of water-bleach solution remaining in the feeders won't harm the birds.
- You can substitute distilled white vinegar for the bleach in the solution to make a more natural cleaning product. The cleaning procedure is the same.
- Some people treat their feeders like dentures. After they empty the old nectar from them, they rinse them out and put them in a clean bucket. Then they fill the bucket with water, making sure the feeders are completely immersed, and drop in one or two denture-cleaning tablets. They leave the feeders in the bucket for at least half an hour after the fizzing stops. Then they rinse them thoroughly and let them air-dry.
- You can also use a mild dish detergent solution to clean feeders. But if you choose this option, be extra sure that you rinse away all the sudsy soap before drying and refilling them.
- Make sure you wash your brushes every time you clean your feeders. Use the same solution you use for the feeder to clean and sterilize the brushes.
- Some feeders or parts of feeders can be put into the dishwasher, but you need to be very careful about doing this. If the feeder's label doesn't specifically say it's dishwasher-safe, don't try it.
- To avoid leaving hummingbirds waiting while you wash and refill their feeders, keep more feeders than you put out at one time. When one feeder needs to be washed, replace it with a clean, full feeder and take the time you need to clean, soak, and air-dry the first one before swapping it with the now-dirty one.

TROUBLESHOOTING HUMMINGBIRD FEEDERS

Unless a predator is eating your hummers, there are usually only two main troubles with having hummingbird feeders: nectar problems and insect problems. Let's take a look at what might happen and how to prevent or resolve each issue.

Nectar Problems

Weather conditions, especially air pressure and very hot temperatures, can affect sugar-water levels in all feeders. The heat expands the sugar water and can make it drip out. Sometimes the heat even causes air bubbles to collect and prevent the solution from flowing into the ports. Feeders with a single feeding tube extending down are especially prone to dripping if they're not properly stabilized to keep them from swinging back and forth in the wind.

In extreme heat, check the feeders daily by gently moving them back and forth to stabilize them and to make sure the sugar water's freely flowing into the feeder ports. Also check the ground beneath the feeder. If it's wet and sticky, you need to reposition the feeder.

Shield Flat Feeders from Rain

Flat feeders, the disk or "flying saucer" types that look like plates with lids on top of them, are extremely easy to clean, but need protection from the rain. Install a plastic or metal rain guard over the top of the feeder to keep rain from diluting or washing away the sugar water. They're readily available from the same sources that sell feeders and often are shaped like umbrellas.

The other problem with sugar solutions is that they can mold or even ferment in hot weather. Siting your feeders out of the sun, choosing smaller feeders, changing the sugar-water solution every 3 days, and diligently cleaning your feeders should prevent either problem. (See "Managing Your Hummingbird Café" on page 231 for specifics on cleaning.)

Insect Problems

Wasps and bees are a problem around hummingbird feeders from summer, when the higher temperatures bring them out, to frost. There aren't many insects or even bigger birds that hummingbirds won't chase, but even one wasp on a feeder will keep a hummingbird from feeding, because they instinctively know it will harm them. Bees are a problem too, but mostly because they're usually around in large numbers. Wasps and bees also drink sugar water.

Here's the bad news: There are no surefire ways of keeping them away from nectar feeders, any more than there are surefire ways to keep squirrels out of seed feeders. But there are some options. Try them and see what works for you. Some people have success with putting a dish of 2:1 sugar-water solution on the ground near the feeder once the insects start showing up in summer. If the bees and wasps find it, they'll usually go to that instead of the feeders. But it doesn't always work.

Many feeders have yellow guards ("bee guards") on the feeding ports to keep bees, wasps, and other insects out of the openings. But some people believe that the color yellow actually draws in the bees and wasps, so they remove the guards completely. Sometimes that keeps them away, but at other times, it just gives them free access to the sugar water. Others paint the bee guards red. The only real solution to this problem is not to buy a feeder with yellow bee guards—if you want to try them, choose one with red bee guards instead.

Bees and wasps aren't the only insects that "bug" feeders. Ants pose a problem because they'll clog feeder ports. Fortunately, all kinds of ant guards are commercially available, and most of them work pretty well. These guards are placed on the hanger above the feeder to keep the ants from climbing down the hanger and into the sugar water. Most of them are cup shaped, and you put water in them to make a moat. The ants go down the hanger into the cup, then fall in the water and drown. People don't like seeing ants on feeders or in the sugar-water solution, but unless there's a lot of them or they're so big that they clog the feeder ports, they're not nearly the problem bees and wasps are. And sometimes hummingbirds will eat the ants on a feeder—one-stop dining!

Whatever you do, don't use Vaseline or cooking spray on the feeder ports to keep insects off them! Although you may have seen this recommendation, it's not a good idea. These materials will get on hummingbird bills and feathers, and the birds may even swallow some of it. Anything on a hummingbird's strong but tender bill may keep it from feeding correctly. Why take a chance on having a hummingbird eat something it's not supposed to? And if Vaseline or any other foreign substance gets on the birds' feathers, it may make it hard for them to fly.

Other Birds That Sip Sweet Stuff

Hummers aren't the only birds that enjoy a little shot of sugar water now and then. You're probably aware that orioles enjoy sugar water—you may have even seen special oriole nectar feeders for sale—but we'd bet you'll be surprised by these other nectar fans!

- Orioles eat a lot of nectar and are major pollinators of certain flowers. Feeders specifically made to hold a 3:1 water-sugar solution for orioles are available, but sometimes orioles like the big, flat hummingbird feeders better. They don't usually visit hanging vertical hummingbird feeders. You'll find more tips on satisfying orioles' taste for sweets on page 80.
- House finches eat seeds, but they probably take advantage of the sugar water in hummingbird and oriole feeders more than any other seed-eating birds.
- Many kinds of woodpeckers occasionally visit hummingbird feeders and drink the sugar water, but this is an opportunistic rather than a regular behavior. Downy woodpeckers do it more often than others, because they're small and the feeders can support them. But even bigger species like the red-bellied, acorn, and hairy woodpeckers will drink sugar water from feeders if given the chance.
- Northern mockingbirds are big, brash, loud birds that will take advantage of just about any good fruit source. They don't seek out sugar-water solutions, but they will drink some if they can find them.
- A lot of birds you wouldn't expect to see drinking nectar or sugar water sometimes do. They include many different kinds of warblers, including the northern parula and orange-crowned warbler.

GARDENING FOR HUMMINGBIRDS

Whether you live in the western part of the country or the East, when you're establishing a flower garden for hummingbirds, you have two goals: to grow plants with nectar-rich flowers and/or plants with flowers that attract the insects that hummers need; and to grow plants that will either bloom in succession from early spring through frost, or will bloom all season long, or both.

Besides having abundant nectar, the second most important thing a flower needs to have to be good for hummingbirds is a shape that makes it easy for the bird to get to the nectar. Long, tubular blossoms are ideal. So are flowers with big open lower lips. If it's hard to get to the nectar, the birds will pass up that flower in favor of another one. They quickly learn which ones are good food sources and which ones aren't, and they'll constantly come back to the good ones.

Pluck Spent Posies

Hummers bypass faded flowers. As flowers age, their nectar production dries up, and both hummers and insects (which might also attract hummers to blooms) stop visiting them. One essential chore for any hummingbird gardener is deadheading—removing the old or spent blossoms. You need to regularly deadhead any hummingbird flowers you grow to keep them producing new, nectar-rich blossoms. That's because when the old flowers set seed, the plant no longer needs to produce blossoms to attract pollinators. From the plant's perspective, its job is done for the season!

Plan for a supply of nectar that will be available to hummingbirds throughout the season. That means you need a lot of different flowers, both perennials and annuals. Perennials are plants that come back every year and bloom at a certain time, like hostas (a shade-tolerant hummingbird favorite), but not always for a long time. Annuals are flowers like impatiens and petunias that bloom all summer but die when winter comes.

Books like *Hummingbird Gardens: Turning Your Backyard into Hummingbird Heaven* (Stephen W. Kress, editor), Sally Roth's *Attracting Butterflies & Hummingbirds to Your Backyard*, Marcus Schneck's *Creating a Hummingbird Garden*, or Sheri Williamson's *Attracting and Feeding Hummingbirds* will help you learn when and how long different plants bloom, and where they'll grow best.

Of course, like any other kind of gardening, you need to pay attention to the basic needs of your plants as well as the hummers you hope they'll attract. For example, if you plant a shade-loving plant where it gets sun most of the day, it's not going to do well. Some plants that need full sun will do all right in the shade for a while, but eventually they'll stop blooming. And it goes without saying that you need to have good garden soil and an adequate supply of water.

Unless you grow nothing but annuals, which only live for one growing season, you also need to know which plants do well in the area of the country where you live. When you read about something in a nursery catalog that's supposed to attract hummingbirds, make sure that you know two things. First, identify which plant hardiness zone you live in (consult the USDA Plant Hardiness

Zone Map on page 356). And second, find out in which planting zone and where in that zone the plant does best. A plant that does well in Zone 6 in the East may not do well at all in the western end of Zone 6. Talk to local gardeners and pay attention to plants that grow well in your neighborhood.

The Internet can be a great source of information. There are several Listservs that deal only with hummingbirds and plants that attract them. Two of the most useful ones are HUMNET, which we discussed on page 222, and the Hummingbird Forum (www.hummingbirdforum.com). You have to sign up for them, but they're free, and every day you get postings from people all over the country. There are also a lot of trees, shrubs, and flowers that hummingbirds visit but you'll never see on hummingbird planting lists. Go to as many local public gardens and nurseries as you can, and if you're lucky enough to see hummers at a plant there, add the plant's name to your list.

BIRD MYTH-BUSTER

Nectar, Not Color, Brings Hummers to Flowers

Think you have to grow red flowers to attract hummingbirds? Think again. It's not the color but the nectar the little birds are after. They'll flock to the white, pink, and lavender blossoms of rose-of-Sharon bushes, stems of blue salvia flowers, orange and yellow jewelweed, and multicolored columbines. Do they love red flowers? You bet. But a successful hummingbird garden includes much more than a collection of red flowers.

The red color will attract hummingbirds, but red flowers with little or no nectar won't keep hummers coming back for more. It's mistakenly believed by a lot of people that all red flowers have nectar, but that's untrue. Geraniums are a good example of this. The bright red color of many geraniums will draw a hummingbird in, but the bird quickly learns that's there nothing there to eat.

So remember: The color of the flower doesn't really matter. Some of the best nectar-producing flowers you can grow have purple, blue, pink, coral, yellow, or even white flowers.

That brings us to another myth we can bust while we're at it: Hummers only come to tubular nectar flowers. It's true that hummers love nectar-producing blooms, and it's also true that many flowers evolved tubular shapes specifically so hummingbirds, which are excellent pollinators, could probe them with their long, slender bills. But the reality is that hummers will enjoy nectar from any nectar-producing flower, regardless of shape. There's more to flowers than nectar, anyway—they also attract the insects that hummers need to feed their young and to meet their own protein requirements. Hummingbirds, especially young ones, explore all kinds of flowers looking for food.

Pennsylvania birder Rudy Keller says it best when he points out that "hummingbirds will visit *any* flower, for insects if not for nectar." So expand your hummingbird plant horizons with the plants we recommend in this chapter, and watch your garden, well, hum.

Hummer Flower Quick Picks

There are so many hummingbird plants to choose from when it comes to narrowing your selection. What's a backyard birder to do? We opted to help you out by asking a couple of birding pros for their recommendations. You'll find descriptions of most of these plants in the lists that follow. Use them as a starting point for your own hummingbird garden, along with the recommended salvias on page 240 ("You Can't Go Wrong with Salvias").

Pennsylvania birder and professional horticulturist Rudy Keller likes to recommend native plants to people who want to grow a hummingbird garden. "The native columbine (*Aquilegia canadensis*) is the first to attract rubythroats in my area," he says. "Later in the season, trumpet honeysuckle (*Lonicera sempervirens*), bee balm (*Monarda didyma*), and trumpet vine (*Campsis radicans*) are favorites." Rudy warns that trumpet vine is aggressive, so you shouldn't grow it on the house or up a chimney, but trumpet honeysuckle makes a great porch vine and has a long season of bloom. He also recommends the salvias, especially the self-sowing Texas sage 'Lady in Red' (*Salvia coccinea* 'Lady in Red'). "Even the common annual scarlet sage (*Salvia splendens*) will attract hummingbirds," he says.

Virginia birder and landscape architect Cole Burrell has many bird-friendly plantings at his home, Bird Hill. "Hummingbirds just love the garden phloxes," he says. "They can't get enough of them!" Like Rudy, Cole recommends salvias, columbines, and monardas (both bee balm and wild bergamot, *M. fistulosa*), as well as catmints (*Nepeta* spp.), fire pink (*Silene virginica*), and cannas (*Canna* spp.). ("But only the small-flowering species of cannas," he says. "Hummingbirds don't like the big hybrid blossoms.") He also recommends goldenrods (*Solidago* spp.) and early-blooming asters (*Aster* spp.) to attract lots of insects in fall, just when the hummers are trying to bulk up for their migration. Cole emphasizes the importance of growing a wide variety of insect-attracting plants if you want hummingbirds to nest in your yard, since hummingbirds feed exclusively insects to their nestlings and are likely to nest where insects are abundant.

Abundant whorls of tubular flowers make bee balm and other species of monarda highly appealing to hummingbirds, as well as to bees, butterflies, and moths. Unlike insects, which drink through a proboscis, hummers use their serrated tongues to lap nectar from flowers and feeders.

A BOUQUET OF HUMMER-FRIENDLY FLOWERS

When we say flowers, we mean flowers that appear on every kind of plant, from trees and shrubs to annuals, perennials, and vines. Hummers don't care what plant the flower grows on—they love 'em all! The plants in the lists that follow are top choices for hummingbirds.

Trees

Trees are an essential part of any good hummingbird habitat, even if they don't all have big, showy flowers. They can be deciduous, meaning they lose their leaves in winter, or they can be evergreen—hummingbirds like both. Here are some of their favorites.

- **Red buckeye** (*Aesculus pavia*). This small tree has red spikes of flowers in spring. It's found mostly in the Southeast but will grow in the North and West and in just about any kind of soil. Zones 5 to 8
- **Tulip poplar** (*Liriodendron tulipifera*). The tulip poplar is found in the eastern part of the country and can grow to be 100 feet tall. It grows rather fast and thrives in any decent soil where it gets a lot of sun. Hummingbirds, as well as many warblers, visit its blossoms for the insects they attract. Zones 5 to 9
- **Desert willow** (*Chilopsis linearis*). This western tree has orchidlike blossoms that bloom for a long time in the sometimes harsh weather conditions of the Southwest. Zones 8 to 9
- **Mimosa, silk tree** (*Albizia julibrissin*). The flowers of this fine-textured Asian tree look like pink powder puffs. Hummingbirds and butterflies love them for their abundant nectar. Zones 6 to 9

Shrubs

You can't go wrong with shrubs, and most of them are easy to grow in average to good garden soils. Even if a shrub doesn't have blossoms that produce a lot of nectar, hummingbirds usually make good use of it anyway for shelter and the insects it attracts. There are countless good shrubs available in every part of the country, so pick ones that are suited to your climate.

- **Flowering quince** (*Chaenomeles japonica*). This is one of the first shrubs to flower in spring. It has coral-orange blossoms. Zones 5 to 8
- **Honeysuckles** (*Lonicera* spp.). There are many kinds of honeysuckle shrubs with yellow or white blossoms and they all produce a lot of nectar. Species and varieties suitable for most North American hardiness zones are available.
- **Viburnums** (*Viburnum* spp.). There are even more viburnums available than there are honeysuckles. Hummingbirds like them for their shelter and insects. They're especially drawn to the native varieties. You can find species and varieties for almost every hardiness zone in North America.
- **Flowering currant** (*Ribes sanguineum*). This shrub does well in the Pacific Northwest. It blooms early in spring, with long, showy trusses of hot-pink/red flowers. There are varieties suitable for different parts of the country. Zones 6 to 8

- **Butterfly bushes** (*Buddleia* spp., including *B. davidii, B. alternifolia,* and *B. lindleyana*). All of the butterfly bushes have spires of flowers that hummingbirds love as much as do the butterflies for which the shrubs are named. Zones 6 to 9; some species Zones 8 to 9
- **Firebush** (*Hamelia patens*). Although it's primarily a plant for southern gardens, this Caribbean native shrub has orange tubular flowers that hummingbirds love. Zones 9 to 11

Vines

Hummers often nest in vines as well as enjoy their flowers, so you might get an extra treat from growing one. We're just giving you a "top three" list here to get you started.

- **Everblooming trumpet or coral honeysuckle** (*Lonicera sempervirens*). This is one of the two most recommended vines for hummingbirds. In warm climates, it blooms almost all summer.

You Can't Go Wrong with Salvias

If you've been reading along with us this far, you know that hummingbirds love salvias. The problem is that there are a lot of salvias to choose from. The best thing to do when you're trying to choose one kind of salvia over another is to consult world-renowned salvia expert Betsy Clebsch's *A Book of Salvias.* One glance at the photos and you'll see that a lot of the salvias that produce large amounts of nectar don't have red flowers.

If you're not quite ready for a whole book on salvias, the salvias in the list below are readily available at any good nursery or sometimes even in the garden sections of big chain stores. They're all relatively easy to grow. They all need at least half a day of sun, good garden soil, and adequate rainfall. For landscape impact, plant big patches of the same plant. It's easier to take care of them that way, too.

- **Scarlet sage (*Salvia splendens*).** This is the bright red salvia some people call "gas station salvia" because it's commonly planted with marigolds at gas stations along heavily traveled roads. It's almost indestructible, thrives even in harsh conditions, and will bloom all summer.
- **Texas sage (*S. coccinea*).** This plant has small red flowers and drops seeds freely at the end of each growing season. Even if you live in the colder parts of the country, it will come back for you the next year wherever it was planted. It's also available with pink, white, and coral flowers.
- **Black and blue sage (*S. guaranitica*).** This is a tropical plant, but it will come back from the roots as far north as Zone 6 if it's mulched in the winter. It gets big—up to 5 feet (1.5 m) tall—and its flowers are deep blue. Hummingbirds love it.
- **Pineapple sage (*S. elegans*).** This is the salvia that's known for attracting vagrant rufous hummingbirds in fall in the North. It doesn't even begin to form blossoms until the days shorten, but once it begins blooming, it's spectacular, with beautiful sprays of vivid fuchsia-red blooms. In spring it's often sold in the herb sections of nurseries. An extra bonus: Rub the leaves and you'll find that they *do* smell like pineapple!

Even in the North, it blooms in spring and sporadically right up until fall. Zones 4 to 9

- **Trumpet vine, trumpet creeper** (*Campsis radicans*). This is the other vine recommended for hummingbirds by just about everyone. Hummingbirds seek out its big, orange, tubular blossoms wherever they bloom. But be careful. It's woody and can get huge, and it spreads by runners. In a small yard keep it under control by yearly pruning. Zones 5 to 9
- **Cardinal climber or cypress vine** (*Ipomoea quamoclit*). This is a small but showy red annual morning glory that often reseeds itself.

Annuals and Perennials

There are so many nectar-producing flowers that attract hummingbirds, it's difficult to list only a small fraction of them here. However, these are some that are the backbones of a good hummingbird flower garden. And don't forget to add at least one salvia to your garden (see "You Can't Go Wrong with Salvias" on the opposite page.)

- **Bee balm** (*Monarda didyma*). The bright red blossoms of bee balm are one of the premier hummingbird lures in the country, especially in northern climates. This perennial blooms just as the first young hummers are leaving their nests. Zones 4 to 9
- **Columbine** (*Aquilegia canadensis*). Many columbine hybrids are available and hummingbirds use them all, but the one that attracts the most hummingbirds is this native red-flowered perennial. Zones 3 to 8
- **Cannas** (*Canna* spp.). These large tender perennial plants grow from rhizomes, or pieces of root, that have to be dug up in fall if you live in the North. They produce big flower spikes in many colors and sizes and can grow in water as well as soil. Zones 8 to 11
- **Penstemons** (*Penstemon* spp.). Hummingbirds will go to penstemon flowers regardless of their color. You can find species and varieties for almost every hardiness zone in North America.
- **Cardinal flower** (*Lobelia cardinalis*). The red flower spikes of cardinal flowers are found in wetlands and along stream banks. This is a short-lived perennial that doesn't do well in normal garden soil. Zones 3 to 9
- **Flowering tobacco** (*Nicotiana* spp.). This is an annual in most parts of the country. It doesn't require a lot of care and has hummer-friendly tubular blossoms.
- **Standing cypress** (*Ipomopsis rubra*). The showy scarlet flower spikes of this upright southeastern native perennial are covered with small, tubular blossoms. Some varieties have flowers in other colors. Zones 6 to 9
- **Bleeding heart** (*Dicentra spectabilis*). This old-fashioned perennial favorite often gets overlooked as a hummingbird plant, but it's one of the first ones that the birds visit each spring. Zones 3 to 9
- **Crocosmias** (*Crocosmia* spp.). Long, arched wands of tubular red or orange blossoms grace this perennial in early summer. It grows from small bulbs that multiply each year, even in some northern areas. Zones 6 to 9

CHAPTER 8

HAWKS, OWLS, AND OTHER BIG BIRDS

For a bird lover, few sights are as thrilling as seeing a red-tailed hawk soaring high in the sky. Or watching a barn owl sweep silently across a secluded road, its white wings ghostly in the dusk. Or seeing a flock of wild turkeys in a golden autumn field. Or watching a majestic ring-necked pheasant strut proudly beside a wooded lane.

Sounds good, doesn't it? But here's something that sounds even better: You can see all these birds in your own backyard! In this chapter, you'll meet some hawks and owls that you're likely to see (or at least hear, in the case of the owls) from your backyard, including the red-tailed hawk, Cooper's hawk, and great horned owl. You'll encounter that legendary speedster of the West, the roadrunner. And you'll learn all about the wild game birds, including the bobwhite, wild turkey, and ring-necked pheasant, who might visit your yard if you offer them their favorite treats.

You'll also learn how to get the most enjoyment from hawk-watching, which birds of prey are likely to use backyard nest boxes, how to make your yard hawk-friendly (and how to protect your feeder birds from predation if you'd rather watch hawks somewhere other than in your yard!), plus some fascinating facts about hawks, turkeys, and the other "big guys."

HAWKS AND OTHER BIRDS OF PREY

For most of us, hawks, eagles, and falcons are the royalty of the bird world. They're big, they're bold, they're smart, and best of all, they're easy to see—when they deign to show themselves. No wonder they're the birds of choice for heraldry and romance. Then there are the other birds of prey—the wise old owls, a reputation they've held since the days of ancient Greece, where the owl was the bird of Athena, goddess of wisdom.

It's always exciting to see a hawk, whether it's sitting still or flying overhead. But what about seeing, say, a thousand hawks, all on the same day? It's possible to see hawks, falcons, and eagles at the same spot, then go at dusk to check out a nearby area where an owl's been seen recently. But to see them, you have to find the places where they go, especially during fall and spring when large numbers of birds are on the move. Fortunately, lots of other people want to see them as well, so there's a lot of information available to help you find them. We'll take a look at some of the best viewing sites.

Significant Silhouettes

Since hawks and other raptors are high-flyers, you usually see them from below. They're easier to identify if you can recognize their distinctive silhouettes.

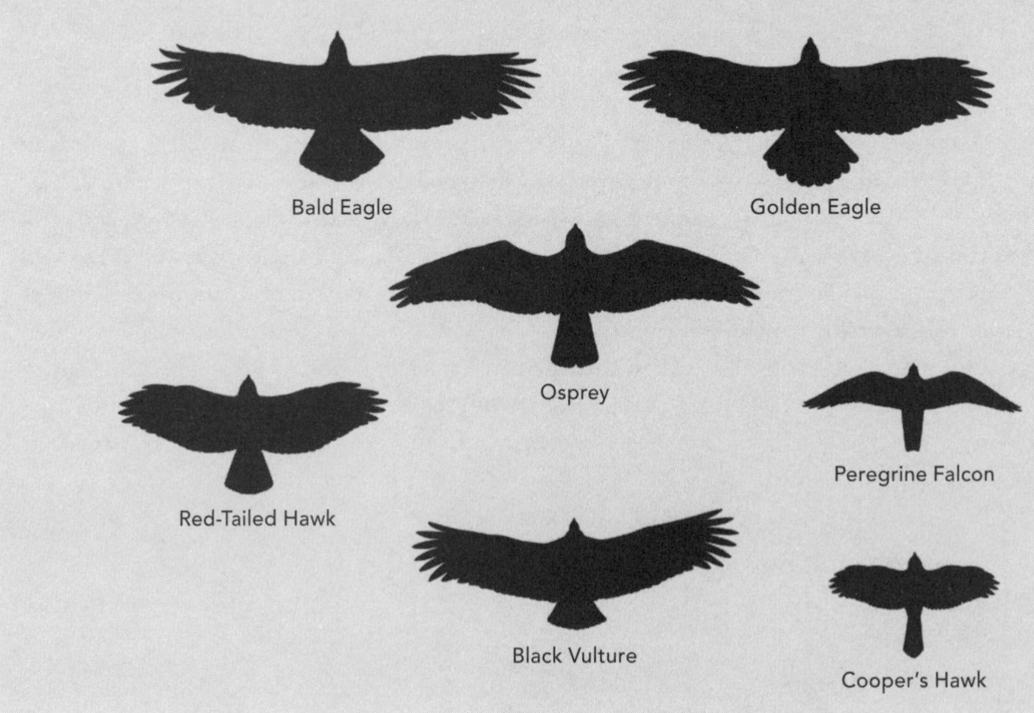

Take a Closer Look

Red-Tailed Hawk *(Buteo jamaicensis)*

If you see a big hawk in the sky and catch a flash of red, you've almost certainly seen a red-tailed hawk. At 18 to 26 inches (45 to 66 cm) long, with a 45- to 52-inch (1.1 to 1.3 m) wingspan, these hawks are hard to miss. They have short, broad tails and thick, chunky wings. Males and females are similar, though females are larger; plumage looks the same year-round. Adults have dark brown heads and backs, and their backs often have white mottling; their undersides are paler, often white with brown streaking or banding, especially across the belly. Darker variations are also common. The famous red tail is brick red, with a dark bar near the end when seen from above, but a solid brick red from below. Juveniles lack the red tail color (their tails are brown) and have more heavy streaking than adults. Females lay one to five white eggs with brown blotches in a large nest built out of sticks high in a tree.

Feeder Favorites for Red-Tails

- Mice and other rodents attracted by spilled seed
- Suet

Regional Relations

Harlan's hawk, a very dark form of Alaskan red-tail without the red tail, was once considered its own species; it winters in the Great Plains. There are many other color variations as well. Another big hawk that looks somewhat like a red-tailed hawk but actually is a separate species is the red-shouldered hawk (*Buteo lineatus*), which inhabits forested areas in the eastern half of the United States and the California coast. Red-shouldered hawks are somewhat smaller than red-tails, with black-and-white bands on their tails and reddish or barred breasts. You won't see the red shoulders unless you're looking down on the bird—they're only visible from the back.

Did You Know?

- The red-tailed hawk is the most commonly seen raptor in North America.
- In the bird world, red-tails are relative heavyweights, weighing up to 3¼ pounds (1.47 kg). A chickadee, by contrast, weighs an average ⅓ to ½ ounce (9 to 14 g), while a bald eagle can weigh over 13½ pounds (6.1 kg).
- Red-tailed hawks can live to be over 20 years old.
- The eyes of red-tailed hawks are almost the size of human eyes!
- Red-tailed hawks and kestrels have the widest ranges of any North American raptors.
- The soaring aerial courtship displays of red-tails are breathtaking as the pair circles each other in flight. Like most raptors, red-tailed hawks are monogamous and are believed to mate for life.
- While you're unlikely to see a red-tailed hawk at your feeders, you might often see one perched on a telephone pole along the road or soaring over an open field, pasture, or grassy area in search of prey. That's because the red-tailed hawk has adapted more successfully than any other bird of prey to human disruption of the landscape.
- John James Audubon called the dark form of the red-tail, called Harlan's hawk, "the black warrior."
- Most red-tails spend winter in the United States, but they do migrate through the country. Fall (southward) migrations are heaviest in November, and spring (northward) migrations can begin as early as February. Over 4,000 red-tailed hawks have been recorded in a single day's fall migration over Duluth, Minnesota.
- Red-tailed and red-shouldered hawks sometimes form groups ("kettles") and migrate together.

HAWK-WATCHING NEAR AND FAR

When you stop to think about it, you'll realize that you're already a hawk-watcher. You see vultures and hawks soaring in the sky, red-tails and other hawks (and even falcons, the colorful little kestrels) perched on telephone poles and wires, and, of course, the ubiquitous vulture flying awkwardly off a roadside carcass. But hawk-watching becomes a lot more fun when you start intentionally looking for hawks and other birds of prey, both at home and at places where hawks are known to gather, especially in fall and spring when they migrate to and from their wintering grounds.

We'll talk about hawks at home on page 251. But first, let's talk about hawk-watching itself. And in order to do that, we need to introduce you to a few specialized terms. Bear with us here—once you start reading about hawks and talking to knowledgeable hawk-watchers, trust us, you'll be glad you did!

Must-Know Words for Birds of Prey

As you expand your knowledge of birds of prey—by talking with fellow birders, by using field guides, or by exploring online resources—you'll encounter a number of frequently used terms. You'll find it easier to understand the things you learn about hawks, falcons, eagles, owls, kites, and vultures if you start by becoming familiar with these raptor-specific words.

- **Raptor.** Another word for a bird of prey. Hawks, falcons, eagles, owls, kites, and vultures are all raptors.
- **Buteo.** A group (actually a genus) of North American hawks that includes red-tailed, red-shouldered, broad-winged, rough-legged, Swainson's, and ferruginous hawks. You can identify a buteo by its short, stubby, fanned tail, hefty body, and broad wings. When flying, they're more likely to soar than flap.
- **Accipiter.** A second group (genus) of North American hawks, including Cooper's hawks, sharp-shinned hawks, and northern goshawks. Accipiters have long, narrow tails, as well as more slender bodies and shorter wings than buteos. In flight, they're more likely to flap than soar.
- **Falcon.** Falcons are yet another group (the genus *Falco*) of raptors, including some of the most dramatic of all birds of prey. The peregrine falcon is the fastest raptor, and the American kestrel is the most colorful. The elusive merlin, the prairie falcon of the western United States, and the majestic gyrfalcon of the Arctic complete the list of North American falcons. (You could also include the crested caracara of Mexico, which is related to falcons despite its vulturelike appearance and behavior, but most guides list it separately.) Like accipiters, falcons have long tails, but they taper rather than flare slightly at the tip. But the real giveaway is the wing shape—falcons' wings are long and sharply pointed at the tips, with prominent shoulders. In flight, the wings form an open M, with the bird's body running up the center.
- **Vulture.** In the South, you may hear a vulture called a "buzzard," but birders discourage this, since a buzzard is actually a type of European hawk. Instead, call a black or turkey vulture (distinguished by its naked black head or, in the case of a turkey vulture, pink head and

neck) by its true name, at least when you're in birding circles. Though they look ungainly on the ground, especially perched on roadkill, few birds look more majestic than a soaring vulture. And here's a "Did you know?" for you: The biggest North American vulture is the California condor!

- **Nocturnal/diurnal.** Most people know that nocturnal means active at night, like an owl. But did you know that diurnal means active during the day? There's even a special word for creatures (like deer) that are most active at dawn and dusk: crepuscular. You probably won't hear that one too often, but you might

(continued on page 250)

EVERYBODY WINS

The First Raptor Refuge

It's a beautiful autumn day on Pennsylvania's Kittatinny Ridge, but the hunters are only marginally aware of the weather. A long line of them stands practically shoulder to shoulder, their rifles aimed skyward as they fire round after round at the hawks, eagles, and falcons migrating majestically over the mountain ridge. Because of the vast numbers of birds, hitting a raptor is as easy as shooting fish in a barrel. Already, the ground is covered with dead and dying birds of prey, and the bodies are piling up. In a single day, hundreds fall to the guns, as the hunters congratulate each other on ridding the land of these "worthless varmints."

Such was the grim picture day after day, autumn after autumn, year after year, until one woman's vision put a stop to the slaughter. In 1934, Rosalie Edge bought 1,400 acres on Blue Mountain along the Kittatinny, including the hunters' hangout, and Hawk Mountain Sanctuary—the world's first raptor refuge—was born.

Today, beautiful autumn days still bring people to the mountain lookouts—60,000 a year, in fact—but now they're armed with binoculars, not guns. A visitor center provides exhibits, environmentally appropriate refreshments, educational materials, and raptor-themed gifts, as well as an assortment of first-rate optics (such as binoculars and spotting scopes) and field guides. A permanent staff of 17, assisted by 12 to 14 interns selected from around the globe and a dedicated corps of 220 volunteers, helps make visitors' hawk-watching experience enjoyable and rewarding.

Hawk Mountain sponsors lectures, field trips, classes, and weekend workshops, as well as annual native plant and wildlife art sales. Its quarterly publication, *Hawk Mountain News*, is free with membership in the Hawk Mountain Association (members also have free access to the sanctuary's trails). The sanctuary now encompasses over 2,500 acres, with 8 miles of hiking trails open daily from dawn to dusk, and is adjacent to the Appalachian Trail. Besides seeing hawks and raptors of all kinds, you can get views of spectacular scenery (some vistas extend for 70 miles), including the River of Rocks, an amazing Ice Age boulder field.

Visit the Web site, www.hawkmountain.org, and click on "Visiting Us" for a virtual tour of the trails with their views. The site also provides daily hawk counts, so you can see which raptors have been spotted on any given day (and in what numbers), an events calendar, and educational materials about raptors and conservation. You also can call Hawk Mountain Sanctuary's information line at 610-756-6000.

Hawk-Watching Hot Spots

The best times to look for hawks, falcons, eagles, and other raptors—especially in large numbers—is when they're migrating north to south in fall and back north from their wintering grounds in spring. The autumn migration can start as early as late August and run through December, while spring migration can start in February and continue through June. Different species tend to migrate at different times, so you can time your visit to try to catch a glimpse of a favorite species, or you can return often during migration to see as many different raptors as possible.

Note that some sites have greater migrations in fall, while others see the greatest numbers of migrants in spring. So do your research before you go!

Here are some great places to catch the show. But this list is only the beginning, focusing on some of the best-known migration sites.

These four sites are probably the most famous.

- **Cape May Bird Observatory,** Cape May, New Jersey
- **Golden Gate Raptor Observatory,** San Francisco
- **Hawk Mountain Sanctuary,** Kempton, Pennsylvania
- **Hawk Ridge Bird Observatory,** Duluth, Minnesota

Don't miss these hawk-watching hot spots.

- **Audubon Pennsylvania's Hawk Watch** at Waggoner's Gap, near Harrisburg
- **Bake Oven Knob,** Germansville, Pennsylvania
- **Braddock Bay Raptor Research center** on Lake Ontario, New York
- **Cape Hatteras National Seashore,** Manteo, North Carolina
- **Derby Hill Bird Observatory,** Mexico, New York
- **Florida Keys Raptor Migration Project** at Curry Hammock State Park
- **Gateway National Recreation Area,** Sandy Hook, New Jersey
- **Goshute Mountain Watchable Wildlife Area,** Elko, Nevada (near the Nevada/Utah border)
- **Holiday Beach Migration Observatory,** on Lake Erie, Essex County, Ontario
- **Kiptopeke State Park,** Cape Charles, Virginia
- **Laguna Atascosa National Wildlife Refuge,** Rio Hondo, south Texas
- **Militia Hill Hawkwatch** at Fort Washington State Park
- **Point Pelee National Park,** on Lake Erie, Essex County, Ontario
- **Santa Ana National Wildlife Refuge,** Rio Grande Valley, south Texas
- **Snake River Birds of Prey National Conservation Area,** Idaho
- **Southeastern Michigan Raptor Research sites** at Lake Erie Metropark and Pointe Mouillee State Game Area
- **Sulphur Springs Valley,** Elfrida, southeastern Arizona
- **Wachusett Mountain State Reservation,** Princeton, Massachusetts
- **Whitefish Point Bird Observatory,** Paradise, Michigan (on Lake Superior)

Take a Closer Look

Cooper's Hawk *(Accipiter cooperii)*

Cooper's hawks are classic accipiters, with the short, rounded wings and long, narrow tail that distinguish them from the buteos (like the red-tailed hawk) that have short tails and longer wings. Coopers are crow-size birds that range from 15 to 20 inches (38 to 50 cm) long, with a 24- to 32-inch (60 to 81 cm) wingspan. They are gray-brown to dark gray above and white with red-brown barring below. Adults look alike, though females are larger; plumage looks the same all year. Juveniles are red-brown above with fewer red-brown bars below. Females lay an average of three to five white to bluish white eggs in a stick nest built in the crotch of a tree trunk.

Feeder Favorites for Cooper's Hawks

- Mourning doves are their preferred avian fare.
- European starlings, house sparrows, and dark-eyed juncos are also taken.
- Chipmunks, squirrels, and other rodents attracted by spilled seed are fair game, too.

Regional Relations

The sharp-shinned hawk (*Accipiter striatus*) is the original "mini-Cooper," looking like a smaller version of the Cooper's hawk. Just 9 to 13 inches (22.5 to 33 cm) long with 17- to 22-inch (43 to 56 cm) wingspans, sharp-shins (also called sharpies) are the smallest accipiters, about the size of a blue jay. Like Cooper's hawks, you can recognize them in flight by their long, narrow tails and short wings.

Did You Know?

- Cooper's and sharp-shinned hawks are the hawks most likely to be seen in backyards—and attacking birds at your feeders! They're originally forest birds, but have adapted well to landscaped backyards with lots of trees and shrubbery. Cooper's hawks eat chipmunks and other small mammals, reptiles, and amphibians as well as birds, but sharpies dine exclusively on birds.
- Cooper's hawks may build their nests directly on top of old hawk, squirrel, or crow's nests.
- Cooper's hawks are year-round residents of the United States and Mexico; they also breed in southern Canada. Sharp-shins breed from Canada down through the Northwest and Northeast; they are winter residents throughout the United States, Mexico, and Central America.
- Cooper's hawks and sharpies are reckless hunters, crashing through trees and bushes, swooping down on their prey from above, and even running along the ground to snag a victim. Sharpies have been observed reaching into shrubbery to extract escaping prey. As a result, the hawks are often injured by branches as they hunt. According to the Cornell Lab of Ornithology, a recent study found that almost a quarter of the Cooper's hawks examined had healed bone fractures, presumably from hunting accidents.
- Cooper's and sharp-shinned hawks have been observed bouncing up and down on top of brush piles, attempting to flush out birds hiding in them.
- Cooper's and sharp-shinned hawk populations declined dramatically during the 1940s through the 1960s because of DDT, but have since rebounded.
- Sharp-shinned hawks can migrate in huge numbers; hawk-watchers can occasionally see a thousand birds at a time. Cape May, New Jersey, holds the daily and seasonal record, with 11,000 sharp-shins counted in one day and 61,000 counted in one fall migration season.
- Rather than biting their prey or killing it on impact like many birds of prey, Cooper's hawks use their feet to squeeze victims to death!
- Sharp-shinned hawk females may weigh twice as much as the males, the greatest male-female difference of all American hawk species.
- Cooper's and sharp-shinned hawks have a distinctive flight pattern, combining a series of wing flaps with a gliding movement. This is more pronounced in sharpies; their characteristic flight pattern is three flaps followed by a glide, with the pattern repeated as they fly.

find it in a description in your field guide. Now you'll know what it means!

- **Thermal.** A bubble or column of warm air that forms over land as it heats up. Raptors, including broad-winged and Swainson's hawks and eagles, take advantage of thermals to soar effortlessly, often quite high—a phenomenon called "riding the thermals."
- **Updraft.** These are the wind patterns that form along ridges, which is why migration routes often follow mountain chains—it takes a lot less energy to travel long distances when the wind is carrying you!
- **Kettle.** In bird terms, a kettle is a group of raptors flying together. When you see a cluster of vultures circling over a field, that's a kettle—they're all being carried on the same thermal. During migration, literally hundreds of broad-winged hawks may fly together in a kettle, an unforgettable sight. Why is it called a kettle? We can only speculate that the sight of all those raptors boiling upwards must have reminded someone of bubbles rising up through a kettle of boiling water.

HOW TO WATCH A HAWK

It doesn't take much to start watching hawks: a field guide, binoculars, and directions to the nearest hawk-watching hot spot are really all you need. See "Hawk-Watching Hot Spots" on page 248 and "Raptor Resources" on page 254 for our recommendations, and Chapter 9, "Sharing Space with Birds," beginning on page 269, for tips on choosing the best field guide, binoculars, and other equipment for your family's particular needs.

Warm up for hawk-watching by using your field guide to familiarize yourself with the various raptors that are likely to be in your area, both during breeding season and during migrations, as well as any year-round residents. Notice what they look like from below, while they're in flight, as well as when they're sitting still.

Once you're familiar with what you're likely to see—as well as what you might be lucky to see—at a given time of year, practice using your binoculars if you're not used to using them regularly. Checking out a Cooper's hawk on a branch in the backyard or a kestrel or red-tailed hawk on a telephone line is straightforward: Focus the binoculars, look; check your field guide, look.

Beginning raptor-watchers may be unprepared for the experience of supporting binoculars for long stretches of time while hawk-watching during a migration—your best chance to see the most, and most kinds of, raptors. Work on trying to keep a bird in view and in focus as you follow its flight with your binoculars. (It isn't easy.) Practice on whatever's flying overhead—even airplanes—until the motion becomes second nature. (You'll be strengthening those binocular-supporting upper-arm muscles at the same time.) When a raptor finally comes along, you'll be glad you did!

Because you need to hold your binoculars steady to watch for hawks, many raptor-loving birders eventually opt to buy spotting scopes, which are much heavier than binoculars, but have their own tripods so you don't have to keep holding them once you reach your hawk-watching destination. After getting started with binoculars, you may ultimately decide to upgrade to a scope.

Whatever your choice, we recommend that you start by watching hawks in the company of experienced raptor-watchers who can give you some pointers.

Birding hot spots like Hawk Mountain Sanctuary usually have experienced volunteers who will call out the type and location of passing raptors. Clay and Patricia Sutton, expert raptor-watchers, have a great piece of advice to offer in their excellent book, *How to Spot Hawks & Eagles:* Familiarize yourself with the names and locations of various features of a hawk-watching hot spot before you arrive (or at least before you head out to the spotting area). Many of these well-known spots will provide maps online or at the visitor center with their features marked. Then when a spotter calls out "bald eagle at No. 5," you won't waste precious time trying to figure out what he or she means!

If no staff members or seasoned birders are at a hot spot when you arrive and so you're on your own, start by scanning the clouds with your binoculars. It will be easier to see a soaring bird of prey when it's framed against a backdrop of clouds than as a tiny speck against a dazzling sun or, even worse, a moving target below the tree line. Those big birds don't look so big when they seem to be (and occasionally actually are) miles up in the air, and it's amazing how easy it is to lose sight of them against a backdrop of trees!

Also remember that a flying raptor will try to conserve as much energy as possible, so it will let the wind, an updraft along a ridge, or a warm thermal carry it along. If you see vultures soaring upward in their familiar spiral, it signals an updraft or thermal that may bear other birds of prey as well. The same holds true of vultures soaring along in what appears to be a straight line—they're riding the wind, and hawks, falcons, and other raptors also might be going along for the free ride. Focus your binoculars on the vultures and see what else you might see!

Explore Your Hawk-Watching Options

Want to see if there's a hawk-watching hot spot close to home? A fantastic resource is the Web site of the Hawk Migration Association of North America (HMANA). Go to its Web site (www.hmana.org) and you'll find a tab for Hawkwatch Sites. Click on that and it will take you to a map of North America. Click on any state or province and you'll find a list of hot spots, with maps, contacts, directions, and bird counts for each site.

You can also check with your local birding club or Audubon Society, or go online to Birding.com and take a peek at its list of the Top 200 North American Birding Hot Spots. The list is alphabetical by state and province, but it gives the latitude and longitude of the hot spots rather than their addresses and locations! However, once you have the names, you can do an online search for more information. Most will have their own Web sites. While you're visiting Birding.com, check out its list of Top 25 Birding Sites (Web sites) as well. It's outstanding and makes a great jumping-off place in your search for hawk-watching hot spots—and/or fellow birders to see them with!

HAWKS OUT BACK

Seeing hawks in flight is exciting. But what if you want to attract hawks to your backyard so you can watch them from the comfort of your kitchen table or deck? Unfortunately, attracting hawks—at least sharp-shinned and Cooper's hawks—is easier than most backyard birders would like.

"Just put out a bird feeder," says Virginia birder Cole Burrell. "As soon as mourning doves discover the birdseed, you'll have hawks." Sad but true, mourning doves are one of the favorite foods of Cooper's hawks, though the hawks will also take care of your squirrel, chipmunk, and mouse problems. And virtually any feeder birds are fair game as far as sharpies are concerned. The fierce (or just hungry) hawks will stop at nothing to capture their prey, running across the ground, diving into trees and bushes after escaping birds, and even reaching into the foliage with their feet to seize their prey. Birds that opt for a late dinner at your feeder are especially likely to become a meal for a Cooper's hawk or even an owl—both like to do their hunting late in the day, especially as dusk begins to shade into nightfall.

What's a bird lover to do? One way to protect your feeder birds is to site feeders near dense evergreens or shrubs so the birds can get away if they see a hawk. Or take the advice of Pennsylvania birder Rudy Keller and put a brush pile beside your feeder. "Brush piles provide excellent protection for feeder birds," he says. "If birds spot trouble, they can zip in there and get out of harm's way." Choosing tray and platform feeders that are roofed rather than open will offer feeder birds some protection as well, since the roof will provide a hawk-deterring barrier.

Of course, you could adopt the attitude that it's all part of nature's cycle and let a hawk take the occasional dove or starling. Backyard bird enthusiast Ellen Phillips has a pair of resident Cooper's hawks at her rural home, Hawk's Haven, near Kutztown, Pennsylvania, and has never seen them take a bird at any of her feeders. But she also has a densely planted landscape so her feeder birds can quickly duck for cover!

Some hawk lovers even try putting out food for hawks in winter, setting big hunks of suet high in a tree, on a tall platform, or out in a field. While it's true that red-shouldered hawks, ravens, and other carrion eaters will come in for suet, unless you live way out in the country and far from any neighbors, this isn't the best idea. "Hawks aren't the only things that like suet," Rudy Keller points out. "You could end up attracting raccoons or even rats." Not to mention vultures!

CREATURES OF THE NIGHT: OWLS

Most of us don't have much trouble spotting a hawk, a vulture or two, or a colorful kestrel as we go about our daily commute. But an owl is another matter. Because owls tend to blend into their surroundings—their plumage provides perfect bark-like camouflage (or snowlike camouflage, in the case of the snowy owl)—and they generally roost high and well-hidden in trees—to see one is almost an accident.

If you *are* lucky enough to see one, the memory tends to stay with you for life: Pennsylvania bird lover Ellen Phillips will never forget driving to a remote country inn one evening and having a barn owl sweep across the road directly in front of

Take a Closer Look

Great Horned Owl *(Bubo virginianus)*

The original "hoot owl," the great horned owl is named both for its size and its prominent ear tufts. Great horned owls are cryptically colored—they look like sections of tree trunk, with mottled or barred rust-red, black, white, brown, and gray feathers. But their gigantic red-feathered feet, large yellow eyes, white eyebrows, and black beaks give them away—if you can see them! Also look for a white throat and rust-red facial disks around the eyes. Adults are 18 to 25 inches (45 to 63 cm) long, with 40- to 57-inch (1 to 1.4 m) wingspans; they can weigh up to 5½ pounds (2.5 kg). The females are larger than the males, but otherwise the sexes look alike. Juveniles resemble adults. Females lay one to five (typically two) spherical white eggs in a nest built in a tree hole or a stick nest that was built and abandoned by a red-tailed hawk, eagle, heron, crow, or even a squirrel.

Feeder Favorites for Great Horned Owls

- Mice and other rodents attracted by spilled seed
- Crows
- Game birds
- Hawks attracted to feeder birds

Regional Relations

Other owls you're likely to see (or at least hear) are the eastern screech owl (see "Take a Closer Look" on page 163) and barn owl (*Tyto alba*). Screech owls have gotten a bad name; it's actually barn owls that screech, while screech owls have whistling and trilling calls. Barn owls are best known for their white, heart-shaped faces and black eyes; males are white below, rusty brown above; females are similar but larger, with spotted cinnamon-brown rather than white underparts. These midsize owls are 13 to 16 inches (33 to 40 cm) long, with 39- to 49-inch (1 to 1.2 m) wingspans. Named for their tendency to roost in barns and their fondness for the mice and rats usually abundant there, these ghostly predators are on the decline due to loss of open fields that are their traditional habitat.

Did You Know?

- The ear tufts of the great horned owl are not horns and have nothing to do with hearing, either. (Its ear slits are on the sides of its head.) Scientists think the prominent feather tufts are camouflage, making the owl look more like the tree it's sitting in by breaking up its profile.
- Great horned owls will eat pretty much whatever they can catch, from mice, voles, squirrels, and rabbits to frogs, snakes, fish, and crayfish to young foxes, skunks, porcupines, waterfowl, other raptors, and crows. The University of Minnesota's Raptor Center describes them as "the most voracious of all raptors."
- Like all owls, great horneds are able to see and function during the day. They prefer to hunt at night, but will hunt during the day if they're hungry and prey is present.
- Most great horned owls are year-round residents of their territory.
- You can often locate a great horned owl because crows will mob it—fly near it and scream imprecations—as it rests on its perch. Crows hate great horned owls because crows are on the owls' menu.
- Great horned owls can live for almost 30 years; the chief cause of great horned owl death is shooting.
- The great horned owl has proved very adaptable in the face of habitat destruction. It can usually be found in stands of trees or woodlots near open fields, meadows, or large yards, but has also adapted to public parks in urban areas, and even to industrial parks.
- Great horned owls are distributed throughout the Americas, from the Arctic tundra to the desert Southwest and the tropical rain forests of Central and South America.
- Great horned owls will begin their characteristic hooting calls in fall, when they begin courting. Like the bald eagle, they begin courtship and nesting activities long before spring.

her car and disappear into a small, dilapidated barn across the street. Though she has driven this route at dusk almost weekly for years, this was the only time she ever saw the barn owl. Expert birder Rudy Keller recalls heading out to the Allentown, Pennsylvania, airport to see a snowy owl that had inexplicably taken up residence there one winter, seemingly unperturbed by the sound of aircraft. And those who have seen the great gray owl—the largest and most elusive of the owls of North America—are among the birding elite.

OWL-SPOTTING SUCCESS

There are ways to increase your odds of seeing owls. You can go on an owl watch at a local birding hot spot. (Many sponsor nighttime owl watches once or twice a year.) You can monitor local bird

Raptor Resources

Books for Hawk- and Owl-Watching

Hawks from Every Angle: How to Identify Raptors in Flight, by Jerry Ligouri. The ultimate photographic guide to field identification. The one must-have book for hawk-watching. Highly recommended!

Hawks in Flight: The Field Identification of North American Migrant Raptors, by Pete Dunne, David Sibley, and Clay Sutton. An excellent guide by some of the foremost birders and birding authors of our day.

Hawks of North America, 2nd edition, by William S. Clark and Brian K. Wheeler. Vinyl-bound so it holds up in field conditions, this volume in the famous Peterson Field Guide series provides an excellent overview.

How to Spot Hawks & Eagles, by Clay Sutton and Patricia Taylor Sutton. A great guide to the behavior, distribution, and field identification of hawks, eagles, falcons, kites, and vultures, with fabulous photos and lots of firsthand information about where to go to see them and what to expect when you get there.

How to Spot an Owl, by Patricia Taylor Sutton and Clay Sutton. Like their book on hawks, the Suttons' guide to owl-watching is fantastic. You'll learn how to find and identify owls (even at night), all about owl behavior, even how to attract them to your yard.

North American Owls: Journey Through a Shadowed World, by Jim Burns. As its title implies, this hardcover book is more than a field guide—it's a series of profiles drawn from the author's vast firsthand experience watching owl behavior in the wild. If you really want to know owls, this is the book for you! Lavishly illustrated with outstanding photographs.

The Book of Owls, by Louis Wayne Walker. First-person account of owl behavior, a one-volume owl education, including nearly 100 photos. Currently out of print, but worth looking for in libraries, used-book stores, and on the Internet.

Raptor-Related Associations

These associations and Web sites will give you a strong start on your hawk- watching adventures.

- **Braddock Bay Raptor Research's site (www.bbrr.org)** features a strong online community, including discussion forums and photo galleries.

hotlines and set off in pursuit if owls are listed. You can ask the most experienced birders in your local bird club or Audubon Society to take you along on an owl watch, if they happen to know where any owls are roosting. Or you can keep your eyes and ears open and check for signs or sounds of owls around you.

If you decide to strike out on your own, do your research first: Check your field guide and/or contact your local bird club or birding hot spot to see which owls are likely to be in your vicinity and what types of habitat they prefer. (Consulting a reference such as *How to Spot an Owl* will also give you tons of tips.) Listen to owl calls on a CD, cassette, or online at a site like the Cornell Lab of Ornithology's "All About Birds Bird Guide," since you're much more likely to hear an owl than see it. Then plan a daylight hike to look for signs of owls.

- **Cape May Bird Observatory's Web site (www.njaudubon.org/Centers/CMBO)** is considered one of the best by serious hawk-watchers.
- **Cornell Lab of Ornithology (www.birds.cornell.edu)** provides terrific profiles of hawks, owls, falcons, eagles, vultures, and other raptors on its site. Go to its "All About Birds" section and click on "Bird Guide," then "Species Accounts" to access the profiles.
- **Golden Gate Raptor Observatory's site (www.ggro.org)**, like the other Web sites connected to hawk-watching hot spots, has a complete listing of programs and events. It also has a great raptor "ID Help" feature to help you make sure you actually saw what you thought you saw.
- **Hawk Migration Association of North America (HMANA) (www.hmana.org)**, as its name implies, monitors raptor migration throughout North America, collecting data from hundreds of hawk-watching sites all over the continent.
- **Hawk Mountain Sanctuary Association (www.hawkmountain.org)** is an excellent all-around resource from America's premier raptor-watching site.
- **Hawk Ridge Bird Observatory (www.hawkridge.org)** offers excellent raptor profiles and photos, with plenty of other helpful information as well.
- **HawkWatch International (www.hawkwatch.org)** goes beyond local, regional, and North American raptors and sites to provide a central collection point for data about raptors the world over. Its focus is on education and conservation.
- **The Owl Pages (www.owlpages.com)** provides numerous resources and links for owl lovers.
- **Raptor Center at the University of Minnesota (www.raptor.cvm.umn.edu)**, sponsored by its College of Veterinary Medicine, focuses on promoting raptor health through education. It offers excellent links to other hawk-related sites; raptor information by species; and programs about (or benefiting) raptors, such as the "Recycle for Raptors" program.
- **The Virtual Birder (www.virtualbirder.com)** has an excellent hawk-watching section, including a list of hawk-watching hot spots by state, raptor-related resources, virtual tours of Hawk Mountain Sanctuary and the Cape May Bird Observatory, photo galleries, and links.

Great horned owls live in a wide range of habitats throughout the United States and nearly all of Canada. Their call is a deep "who hoo-hoo hooo oo."

What do we mean, a daylight hike? Aren't owls nocturnal? Mostly, yes. But *we're* not. And it might be easier to locate an owl when it's resting and we can see it, right? Here's what to look for.

- **Whitewash.** Owl droppings form white streaks down the trunks of trees where owls are roosting. Birders refer to these streaks as whitewash. If you see a streaked trunk—especially a heavily streaked trunk—look up. But not before you've looked down.
- **Pellets.** Owl pellets typically litter the ground beneath trees where owls are roosting. They're not droppings—that's whitewash. Instead, they're more like cat hair balls. Owls swallow prey whole, then cough up undigested parts like fur and bones in a compacted pellet. The bigger the prey, the bigger the pellet—a definite hint as to which kind of owl you're dealing with. Lots of pellets under a tree indicate that the owl has been there for a while. You can get some practice recognizing owl pellets (and even dissecting them) by visiting raptor centers like Hawk Mountain Sanctuary in Pennsylvania, which sells owl pellets in its gift shop, or by purchasing a book, *Owl Puke,* by Jane Hammerslough, which comes with an owl pellet. Whether you find or buy an owl pellet, you can dissect it to see what the owl has eaten. Hours of entertainment!
- **Silhouettes.** If you find whitewash and/or pellets, look up. Try to see an owl silhouette in the tree above you. Remember that owls are pros at camouflage, hiding deep in the foliage or blending into the trunk of the tree where they're roosting. Relax and look for anything that might be an owl shape, first with your naked eyes, and then with your binoculars. Looking at photos of roosting owls and knowing which ones you're likely to see will be a big help here.
- **Open space.** Owls may like to roost in tall trees or dense growth, but they need to hunt over open ground. Look for hiking trails, logging roads, areas that have been cleared for power line or pipeline right-of-ways, railroad tracks, riding trails, natural meadows, streams, ponds, or lakes, burned-over ground—anything that cuts an opening into the woods is ideal owl-hunting territory. Check it out.

- **Owl calls.** Owls may be hard to see, but they're not hard to hear. The unearthly hissing scream of a barn owl, a pair of hooting great horned owls (the male's voice is deeper), perhaps a trio of screech owls whistling or trilling in the woods, each in a different tree: Listen and try to follow the sound.
- **Other calls.** It's a fact that other birds don't like owls. Some birds, such as crows, absolutely hate owls. So if they spot an owl, they try to make it as miserable as they can with an action called mobbing, when they swoop at the owl while screaming at the top of their lungs. If you hear a huge racket in the woods, or see a bunch of crows or other birds screeching their heads off while circling a tree, there's a good chance an owl is perched there.

Once you've located an owl, you can return at night when it's more active and try to see it in flight. The best times are from the hour before to the hour after dusk. But don't be disappointed if you fail—even the most experienced birders rarely see owls in action.

Whatever you do, don't disturb an owl by making a racket, rushing toward it, shining a flashlight in its face (a good reason to plan an owl outing when the moon is full), or approaching its nest. Owls are serious predators that can hurt you if they think you mean them harm. And if there's too much racket around these secretive creatures, they might abandon their nests. Since many owls are already rare or endangered, shame on you if you cause them to do that! So behave yourself if you discover an owl nest or roost and approach quietly and with caution.

LANDSCAPING FOR OWLS

Besides going to owls, you can bring owls to you. One way is to set up a nest box (see "Raptor-Ready Nest Boxes" on page 258 and "Take a Closer Look: Eastern Screech Owl" on page 163 for more on this). Another way is to create an owl-friendly landscape. The first thing to remember is that owls tend to be cavity nesters (along with woodpeckers and many desirable feeder birds). So if you have an old tree trunk or dead branches on your property, don't be in a hurry to take them down. You may find that a pair of owls has adopted one for a nest site.

As with hawks, setting up bird feeders is likely to attract owls. But unless your birds have decided on a late snack, the owls will most likely be drawn to mice and other rodents scarfing up spilled feed at night rather than to feeder birds. (Whew!) If you attract big critters like opossums and skunks (usually by setting out pet food or failing to secure trash can lids), you may bring in great horned owls as well.

Bear in mind that a lawn with a single kind of grass is as boring to birds as it is to us (if you stop to think about it). You'll always attract the most wildlife—including owls—if you create a mixed lawn of many different grasses, clover, herbs, and other species, and break it up with lots of island beds, clumps of trees and shrubs, and other features. Mixed hedgerows at your property line and a source of water will make your landscape irresistible.

Borrowed scenery is fantastic, as well. If you have woods or fields—or, say, a park—near your yard, you and any nearby owls are in luck. You'll draw many more kinds of birds to your feeders and landscape than you ever would, no matter how many types of feeders you set out, with absolutely no additional effort on your part. Lucky you!

Raptor-Ready Nest Boxes

Populations of North America's smallest and most colorful raptor, the American kestrel (*Falco sparverius*), have been declining in the East, prompting concern among scientists and birders. Biologists at Hawk Mountain Sanctuary in Kempton, Pennsylvania, reported a 50 percent drop in the number of kestrel breeding pairs between 1998 and 2004. It's believed that destruction of the kestrel's preferred habitat—open meadows, pastureland, and permanent hay fields, with hedgerows and other brushy boundaries—in favor of row crops and housing developments has caused this precipitous drop.

Hawk Mountain responded to the crisis by launching an "Adopt a Kestrel Nest Box" initiative in 2004, creating educational programs for students and rural landowners, distributing more than 20,000 copies of instructions for building your own kestrel nest box, and encouraging individuals and organizations to contribute to the establishment, monitoring, and maintenance of more than 200 kestrel nest boxes by Hawk Mountain staff. (Contact the Sanctuary at 610-756-6000 or online at www.hawkmountain.org to find out more about the program, purchase a kestrel nest box, or request a free brochure with kestrel facts and nest box plans.) Hawk Mountain biologists have found that kestrels willingly use nest boxes, and that kestrel populations are growing where nest boxes have been set up.

Kestrels aren't the only raptors that will gladly take advantage of nest boxes. Eastern screech owls will use the same boxes as kestrels, in the same locations. The eggs of these diminutive owls are roughly the same size as kestrel eggs, but screech owl eggs are white, while kestrel eggs are covered with red-brown speckling. (Bluebirds and starlings may also lay eggs in a kestrel nest box. Their eggs are much smaller—half the size for starling eggs, less than a quarter the size for bluebird eggs—and are pale blue to bluish or greenish white.) Other owls like nest boxes, too, including barn, barred, and saw-whet owls.

Want to set up your own kestrel or owl nest box? You can buy one ready-made from Hawk Mountain Sanctuary or build your own from its free plans. BestNest.com (www.bestnest.com) sells both pre-assembled and kit houses for kestrels, kestrels and screech owls, saw-whet owls and screech owls, barn owls, and barred owls. To find more links to owl and kestrel nest box plans and ready-to-use nest boxes for sale, check out the Owl Pages (www.owlpages.com).

Note that these are hefty boxes—a kestrel/screech owl box is typically almost a foot (30 cm) wide and 2 feet (60 cm) tall in back (the box interior is 14 inches (36 cm) tall in front, 16 inches (40 cm) in back, and 10 inches (25 cm) deep, with a sloping roof and a 3-inch (7.5 cm) round entrance hole situated an inch (2.5 cm) down from the top of the box). The front or side panel of the nest box is designed to swing open for annual cleaning and maintenance and latches shut. The roof is designed with a ventilation space, and there are drainage holes in the corners of the nest box floor. Some models also have a ladder or perch on the inside face of the front panel to help fledglings climb up to the entrance hole when it's time to leave the nest. (There are no perches outside in order to discourage starlings and other undesirables.)

Boxes are typically made of untreated pine or cedar and have nail holes for mounting. They can be screwed or nailed (twopenny nails are recommended) 10 to 20 feet (3 to 6.1 m) from the ground onto the side of a building (such as a shed or barn) or onto the trunk of a large, isolated shade tree surrounded by a large, open lawn or near a pasture or meadow (for kestrels) or open woodland (for screech owls). Squirrels may take over the nest box if it's located 50 yards (45 m) or less from a wooded area. Site the box so it faces away from roads and is out of the path of human activity if possible, but position the opening so you can observe it. One box is enough—because these birds are territorial, nest boxes should be no closer to each other than half a mile (.8 km).

Maintenance is simple. At the end of February or in early March, open the front panel and clean out any old nesting material and debris. Check to make sure the nest box is holding up; replace any worn-out parts. Put 2 inches (5 cm) of coarse wood shavings in the bottom of the box, latch or nail the lift-up panel closed, and voila! You're ready to watch for new signs of life. Kestrel nesting usually takes place in mid-March, and fledglings are ready to leave the nest and strike out on their own in June. Look for the jay-size, colorful male, who sports dark gray and bright orange plumage with the classic falcon's black-and-white facial markings and dramatically dappled breast, arriving at the nest with food for the somewhat larger and drabber female and their young.

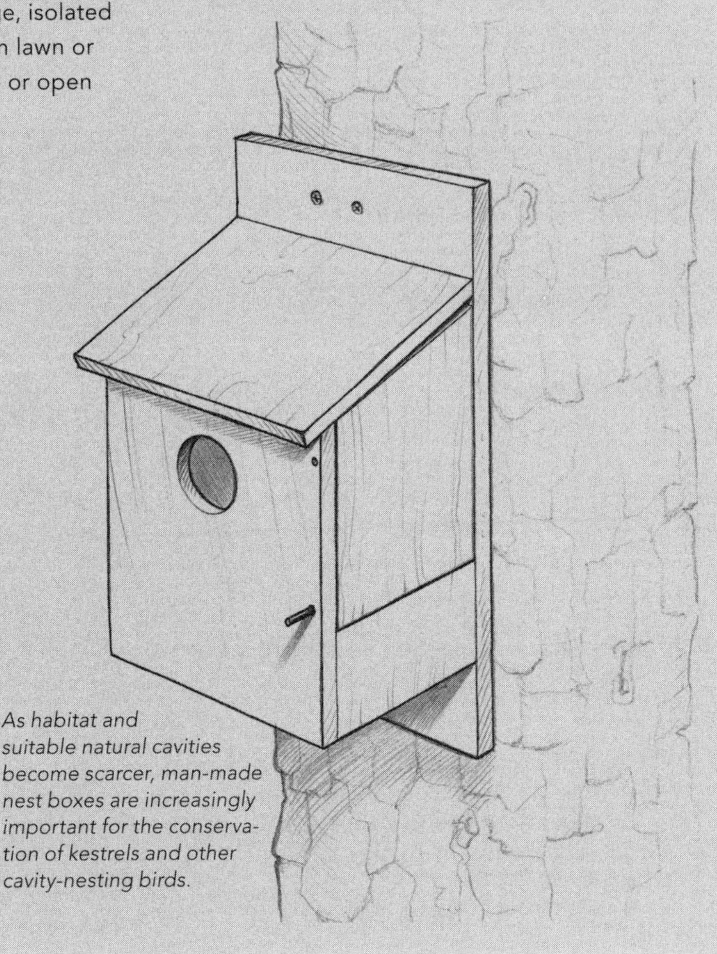

As habitat and suitable natural cavities become scarcer, man-made nest boxes are increasingly important for the conservation of kestrels and other cavity-nesting birds.

Take a Closer Look

Greater Roadrunner *(Geococcyx californianus)*

With their long legs and blue-black, caplike crests, roadrunners are distinctive birds—especially when they're racing along a roadside or hot in pursuit of prey. This bird is light brown with darker spotting and streaking on its head, back, and wings; its belly is all buff brown. Adults sport a bronze gloss on their feathers. Their bills are slightly curved and prominent. Males, females, and juveniles look alike, but males are larger and juveniles are less glossy and their markings are less distinct. Adult birds are 20 to 21 inches (50 to 53 cm) long, with 19-inch (48 cm) wingspans, and can weigh over a pound (0.45 kg). Females lay two to six white eggs with a yellowish dusty coating in a platform nest built of thorny branches in a thorny bush, small tree, or even a cactus.

Feeder Favorites for Roadrunners

- Songbirds
- Mice and other rodents attracted to spilled seed
- Apple pieces and other juicy fruits

Regional Relations

Despite its name, there is no lesser roadrunner. The greater roadrunner reigns supreme—and alone—in its home territory. You're more likely to hear than see its eastern relatives, the secretive, forest-dwelling black-billed cuckoo (*Coccyzus erythropthalmus*) and yellow-billed cuckoo (*C. americanus*); neither are backyard birds.

Tempting Features and Treats for Roadrunners

- Roadrunners will appreciate prickly pear (*Opuntia* spp.) fruits offered on a tray feeder or directly on the ground.
- Roadrunners are often drawn to backyards by the presence of water. A birdbath placed on the ground or on a very low pedestal or a pond will bring the big guys in.

Did You Know?

- The roadrunner is the state bird of New Mexico.
- Like us, roadrunners enjoy sunbathing. You may see one in the morning, warming up with its back turned to the sun and its back feathers fluffed to give the sun a chance to warm its dark skin.
- Roadrunners have patriotic markings: There's a red, white, and blue stripe extending beside each eye.
- A pair of roadrunners may cooperate to take down a large snake. A roadrunner will also repeatedly dash larger prey against rocks or the ground to kill it.
- Roadrunners' feet have two toes forward and two toes back, like all members of the cuckoo family, as opposed to three toes forward and one back like most birds.
- The song of a roadrunner is a series of hoarse cooing noises; it also has a whirring call.

The Wily Roadrunner

Beep-beep! If you live anywhere from California through the Southwest to Missouri and Louisiana and down into Mexico, you may encounter this big, brazen speedster zooming along at over 18½ miles per hour (30 kph), head down and tail held horizontally for maximum speed with minimum wind drag. A resident of arid and semi-arid regions, the roadrunner has a natural diet of scorpions, rattlesnakes, centipedes, tarantulas, rodents, lizards, and even carrion.

Unfortunately, these speedsters relish a different type of food when they happen upon your feeder: songbirds dining there. Roadrunners will also readily take birds' eggs and nestlings right out of the nest.

On the plus side, roadrunners will also eat mice that are attracted to spilled seed around feeders, as well as big insects like grasshoppers.

TALKING TURKEY

Most of us probably picture a grocery case full of Butterballs when turkeys are mentioned—or maybe those same birds stuffed, roasted to perfection, and served up proudly on Thanksgiving platters across the country. It's easy to eat turkey at today's Thanksgiving celebrations, but the Pilgrims would have had a much harder time bagging one of the big birds. That's because wild turkeys, unlike their domestic descendants, are smart and wary—and very well-camouflaged in their native woodland habitat.

The reintroduction of wild turkeys after their near eradication due to hunting and habitat loss is one of the great conservation success stories of the 20th century. (See page 263 for more on this.) Thanks to these efforts, you can now see wild turkeys in every state but Alaska. Look for them in open woods, marshy fields, and pastures, especially in fall when groups of females and their broods begin to congregate into winter flocks. They're a beautiful sight against a golden field. You can also watch them along rural roads, or even crossing the road after emerging from the surrounding woods, often with a small squad of turkey chicks in tow. And if you live in turkey territory and feed birds, you may look out one day and see them in your yard!

TURKEYS AT THE FEEDER

Wild turkeys are no dummies. With widespread and growing populations—more mouths to feed—and shrinking habitat, they've adapted to new sources of food, such as tray and ground feeders. You're unlikely to see a turkey at your feeder unless there are turkeys in wild areas near

ACORN EFFORT, OAK TREE RESULT

Stuff Wild Turkeys with Acorns

This time, we're taking our title literally! Turkeys *love* acorns. If you want to attract these fantastic fowl to your yard and you don't already have oak trees, go out and plant one. It's that simple: Visit a nursery in your area and see which oaks are native to or thrive in your region, grow most quickly (all oaks are pretty slow growers), or produce the heaviest acorn crops. Or—if you're willing to wait a decade or two for your first acorn crop—take a walk during acorn season, find an oak that's dropped lots of acorns, pick up a few, take them home, and plant them. Note that some oaks, such as red, white, and scarlet oaks, have glorious fall foliage color; many mature into majestic shade trees (read: they take up a lot of space and aren't for small yards). Beautiful species like willow oaks and live oaks are well-suited to the South, even the Deep South. Planting an oak is definitely an investment in your landscape's future. The turkeys (and other acorn lovers like titmice) will thank you!

your home, but if there are, you can attract the big birds with nothing more complicated than dried corn. Set whole or cracked kernels out on the ground, preferably at a wooded edge of your property, or on a tray feeder. Turkeys are most likely to come to your feeders at dawn and dusk (remember that word "crepuscular"?), so make sure you take a look as you prepare the morning coffee and before you turn on the floodlights in the evening.

Turkeys will also eagerly accept scratch grains—a type of chicken feed available from grain mills and stores like Agway and Tractor Supply. And these birds are fond of nuts, especially acorns. So if you have an oak tree in your yard, you may be able to attract turkeys when the acorns fall without doing a thing (except, of course, leaving the acorns on the ground rather than raking and bagging them). If you want to attract turkeys, consider planting an oak if you have plenty of room—like turkeys themselves, these beautiful shade trees get quite large. Turkeys are also fond of fruit, seeds, and buds. With a source of water plus some salt and calcium chips or crushed oyster shells, your turkey buffet will be complete.

But before you rush out and begin scattering corn across the lawn, hoping to attract these big, smart, fascinating birds, let us remind you: Turkeys are big. Turkeys are hungry. Turkeys form winter flocks. All this translates into a lot of running to the store for feed, and it—and the turkey population—can sometimes become overwhelming.

A Tale of Two Turkeys

Dolores Merrell lives on a wooded property near Pennsburg, Pennsylvania, overlooking the beautiful Unami Creek. Her home is surrounded by woods owned by a local Boy Scout camp. Dolores loves wildlife, and in this setting, she attracts a lot of it, from hummingbirds to deer. For the past few years, a trio of turkeys, two females and a male, has appeared in her front yard almost nightly to see what's on the menu. She loves watching them and, of course, has named them all. If one or more don't show up, she worries about them until they reappear a day or two later.

Not 50 miles away, Barbara Ellis and her husband, Peter, also had a trio of turkeys appear one autumn on their large property, which is surrounded by farms and patches of open woodland. Barbara thought it would be fun to feed the turkeys, too. She wasn't so sure the following fall, when a flock of 25 turkeys turned up for a handout. By the following year, the flock had grown to 75, and Barbara stopped feeding not just the turkeys but all her feeder birds until the flock departed for greener pastures (or filled feeders). A few turkeys are great, but unless you're a commercial turkey farmer, a flock of 75 is overwhelming. And what a mess!

Why did Dolores's flock remain stable while Barbara's exploded? Perhaps it was the difference in vegetation—Dolores's home is surrounded by woods, while Barbara's is surrounded by open fields, with just occasional patches of wood. Also, Dolores has a small yard, while Barbara and Peter have 10 acres. Maybe the turkeys just had more room to spread out, maybe there was a bigger turkey population in Barbara's area, maybe Barbara set out more food, maybe Dolores's turkeys were youngsters who hadn't started multiplying . . . and maybe we'll never know the reason. Before you feed wild turkeys in your yard, at least bear this cautionary tale in mind.

Take a Closer Look

Wild Turkey *(Meleagris gallopavo)*

With their plump bodies and naked faces, wild turkeys resemble a cross between a chicken and a vulture, at least until the male fans out his magnificent tail. They may not be able to compete with a store-bought Butterball, but these are *big* birds: 43 to 45 inches (1.09 to 1.1 m) long, with a 49- to 57-inch (1.2 to 1.4 m) wingspan, and a weight of 5½ to over 24 pounds (2.5 to 10.9 kg). Males are larger than females. Chestnut-brown plumage has darker bars and may be tipped with bronze or green iridescence. Males have a naked bluish head, a pendulous pink wattle, a brilliant red throat, and a "beard" of hanging feathers; females are drabber. Both have fan-shaped tails and black-and-white-barred wings. Juveniles resemble adults, and like chicks (and unlike baby songbirds), hatch from the egg bright-eyed, mobile, and covered in down. Females lay 7 to 14 tan to buff white eggs with tiny reddish dots in a leafy or grassy depression in the ground.

Feeder Favorites for Turkeys

- Corn, whole or cracked
- Scratch grains ("chicken scratch")
- Nuts
- Apple pieces and other fruit

Regional Relations

A subspecies of wild turkey native to Mexico was the ancestor of our domestic turkey. Unlike the wild turkeys of the East, these Mexican turkeys have white tail tips. (Eastern wild turkeys have chestnut-brown tail tips that match the color of the rest of the tail.) Today, wild turkeys in the East have brown tail tips while western wild turkeys have white-tipped tails like the Mexican subspecies. But if you see a turkey with a white-tipped tail in the East, it's probably an enterprising escapee from a nearby farm.

Tempting Features and Treats for Turkeys

- Turkeys are nut lovers who especially enjoy acorns. If you pass an oak tree on your walks or know of another good acorn source, collect some and set them out on a tray feeder or directly on the ground as a treat.
- Turkeys appreciate a salt block or a saucer of coarse salt set on the ground. A sprinkling of ground oyster shells or calcium chips in a saucer will give them a mineral boost and help them digest their food.
- Fruit-loving turkeys will appreciate offerings of berries—everything from mulberries to cherries—on a tray feeder or on the ground.
- Don't forget water! A birdbath, pan, or bucket set directly on the ground where the turkeys feed will help these big guys stay hydrated.

Did You Know?

- Once abundant in the United States, wild turkeys were almost wiped out by 1900. Conservationists first tried introducing domestic turkeys into the wild, but they were unable to survive on their own. Next, small populations of wild turkeys were released into new areas, and this proved highly successful. Today, wild turkeys are found in 49 states.
- Turkeys, native to North America, were first domesticated by the Aztecs. They were introduced into Spain by the Conquistadores, then made their way into commerce in northern Africa and Turkey before returning to Europe. They reached England in the 1520s or 1530s, complete with a name reflecting their supposed place of Middle Eastern origin, and were brought back across the Atlantic by colonists.
- The only New World birds that have been domesticated are the wild turkey and the Muscovy duck.
- The turkey vulture, another large bird with dark brown plumage and a naked pink head and neck, was named for its resemblance to the wild turkey.

Take a Closer Look

Ring-Necked Pheasant *(Phasianus colchicus)*

Once you've seen a ring-necked pheasant—or even a picture of a ring-necked pheasant—you'll never mistake it for anything else. That's because, since it's an import, nothing else in North America looks like it. (A peahen—a female peacock—does look something like a female pheasant, but unless one's escaped from a nearby estate, you're unlikely to encounter a peahen in the wild!) Ring-necked pheasants are 20 to 28 inches (50 to 71 cm) long, with wingspans of 22 to 34 inches (55 to 86 cm) and long tails, often held at an upward angle. Pheasants can weigh anywhere from just over a pound (.45 kg) to more than 7 pounds (3.1 kg); males are larger than females. A male ring-neck is a showy bird, with a gold-and-black back, copper-and-black underside, maroon breast, prominent white "ring" at the base of the throat, iridescent green neck and head, and a naked, bright red face. By contrast, the females are cryptically colored and patterned to blend safely into the scenery, with buff to brown mottled feathers (feathers are mottled with black on the wings and back). Juveniles resemble females. Females lay 7 to 15 olive-brown eggs on the ground in tall grass or other dense vegetation, including weeds. Like other game birds, chicks are born with their eyes open, covered in protective down, and ready to leave the nest almost as soon as they've hatched.

Feeder Favorites for Pheasants

- Cracked or whole corn (cracked is preferred)
- Sunflower seed, especially black oil, also hulled
- Mixed seed
- Safflower seed
- Millet

Regional Relations

There are many sub-types of pheasant in their native Asia—at least 34—and a number of these have been introduced in the United States. But if you encounter a pheasant that doesn't look like the typical ring-necked pheasant, it's most likely to be a show breed specimen that's escaped from captivity rather than a wild form.

Tempting Features and Treats for Pheasants

- Give pheasants a thrill by providing berries and other fruits in tray feeders or directly on the ground. Pheasants love berries!
- If you have a bare, dusty patch where grass just won't grow, don't despair. Like chickens, pheasants enjoy dust baths, and you'll enjoy the sight of them rolling around luxuriating in the little dust clouds they stir up.
- Treat your pheasants to some scratch grains, either on a tray feeder or directly on the ground. These mixed grains, a type of chicken feed available at grain mills and from stores like Agway and Tractor Supply, contain two pheasant favorites—cracked corn and wheat.

Did You Know?

- The ring-necked pheasant is the state bird of South Dakota and is pictured in flight on the South Dakota state quarter.
- Ring-necked pheasants were first introduced into the United States in Oregon in 1881.
- Pheasants separate into flocks of males and females in winter, reuniting and pairing off in spring. (Actually "grouping off" is more like it, as dominant males chase off other males and attract harems of females to their territory.)
- Pheasants, like most birds that prefer open fields and meadows with hedgerows or brushy zones between them, have not thrived since the advent of row-crop, monoculture-style farming. Their numbers have been steadily declining.
- The loud, piercing call of the male pheasant resembles the crowing of a rooster more than the song of a bird. It has been described as a harsh "koork-kork." Like roosters, pheasants are most likely to sound off early in the morning.
- The tail feathers of male ring-necked pheasants are fly-tying staples for those making flies for fly-fishing.

BOBWHITE AND OTHER NATIVE GAME BIRDS

The wild turkey's not the only native game bird that might show up in your yard. Depending on where you live, you might be lucky enough to see bobwhite, grouse, or quail at your tray feeder or eating cracked corn and seed you've scattered on the ground, especially if you've put up a rough lean-to over the ground-feeding area.

Why feed these portly fowl? If you're a hunter, the answer is obvious—for the same reason you'd feed deer or turkey, in anticipation of hunting season. But if you don't hunt, there are two great reasons to feed bobwhite, quail, and grouse: First, because bobwhite and quail are just so darn cute. And second, for the thrill of seeing elusive birds like bobwhite and grouse in your own yard. These forest birds specialize in remaining undetected, so to see them at all is a real coup.

If there are indoor-outdoor, outdoor, or feral cats (or loose dogs) in your neighborhood, resist the temptation to set out food for game birds. Cats in particular can wreak havoc on a covey of quail, since the birds prefer to run rather than fly away, and cats are faster.

LANDSCAPING FOR GAME BIRDS

You'll have noticed throughout this chapter that birds that prefer a combination of open spaces, such as meadows and pastures, and brushy areas, like hedgerows and weedy tree lines, have suffered habitat loss as farming has become mechanized. Most fields are now devoted to row crops and monocultures of a single kind of crop, and the hedgerows that once separated fields have become a thing of the past.

Fortunately, yards are basically open grassy meadows that are often separated by hedges or trees. You can help game birds, kestrels, and other species that prefer this type of habitat by enhancing your landscape's allure. Even a quarter-acre yard, landscaped to provide cover, shelter, a source of water (such as a ground-level birdbath) and food, is enough to attract a covey of quail or a bobwhite family to your yard. Tall trees (or a woodlot) and open lawn (or an adjoining meadow) will create perfect conditions for a kestrel or screech owl to

5-MINUTE MAKEOVERS

Set Up a Simple Shelter

If you know bobwhite, quail, or grouse live in your area, but they're not coming in to your tray feeder or even to where you toss cracked corn, scratch grains, and other favorites directly on the ground, try this quick trick: Set up a lean-to over your feeding area. Because game birds are prey species, they're naturally cautious and will feel more confident about approaching a sheltered feeding area where they're more protected from predators.

You don't need to make an elaborate structure: A sheet of plywood held off the ground in front with two sturdy stakes and attached in back to two shorter stakes will make enough of a shelter for these birds to feel more at home. Boyertown, Pennsylvania, birder Carolyn Reider simply leans sections of branches against a rustic fence to make her lean-to, then covers them with evergreen branches for a snug shelter. Fellow Pennsylvania bird lover Joan Silagy uses an old picnic table to make a lean-to, setting branches against one side to make a shelter. (She uses the top of the table as a platform feeder!) Toss your cracked corn and other grains and seeds directly on the ground under the lean-to to lure in shy bobwhite and other game birds.

move in and raise a family, especially if you add a nest box (see "Raptor-Ready Nest Boxes" on page 258 for more on nest boxes for kestrels and owls).

Hedgerow Havens

If you don't already have a hedge on your property, consider planting one. Rather than planting a hedge of a single species and shearing it into a rigid geometrical shape, consider doing wild birds a favor and mix things up. Planting shrubs like privet (songbirds love the fruits), rugosa and eglantine roses, and rose-of-Sharons (hummingbird favorites), plus favored shelter- and fruit-providing plants like blackberries, raspberries, and wineberries, will create a paradise for game birds and songbirds. In the South, heavenly bamboo (*Nandina domestica*) forms lovely bamboolike clumps with huge clusters of scarlet berries and scarlet-red fall foliage. The lovely flowers of native azaleas, which are deciduous, will also attract hummingbirds. Add some hazelnut bushes for nuts and perhaps some witch hazels for late winter-early spring color and buds, blueberries for succulent fruit and blazing fall color, the deciduous winterberry holly (*Ilex verticillata*) with its bright red berry clusters, and perhaps some fruiting viburnums such as American cranberry bush viburnum (*Viburnum trilobum*), and you and your birds will enjoy delights year-round.

If you shear an existing hedge regularly, let it grow out; it may surprise you. Privets form beautiful rounded shrubs, with colorful clusters of small navy-blue fruits and yellow-and-purple fall color. Forsythia will also form beautiful rounded bushes with yellow-purple fall foliage.

Add Some Evergreens

Evergreens provide dense, year-round cover and shelter for birds. Red cedars (*Juniperus virginiana*) are beloved by songbirds for their dense branches and for their waxy blue berries, which are actually cones. All conifers provide cover, winter shelter, and seeds or pine nuts. You can also mix shorter evergreens such as mugho pines (*Pinus mugho*) and the smaller, shrubby Japanese hollies (*Ilex crenata*) into your hedgerow to add more winter cover as well as pine nuts or berries. And don't forget rhododendrons, azaleas, and mountain laurels (*Kalmia latifolia*) for year-round cover if your landscapes's soil is naturally acidic and you have shade trees casting partial shade over your hedgerow.

Plant a Game-Bird Garden

If you really want to do local game birds a favor, plant a plot of favorite food crops just for them. Blocks of corn, brown-top millet, milo (sorghum), sunflowers, peas, and beans would provide food. Soybeans, clovers, buckwheat, alfalfa, cowpeas, sesame, Bahia grass, lespedeza, vetch, and native wildflowers such as tickseed sunflowers (*Bidens* spp.), coreopsis, purple coneflower (*Echinacea purpurea*), and black-eyed Susans (*Rudbeckia* spp.) are other good choices. You can actually purchase preblended seed mixes to grow for quail and other game birds from sources such as Wildlifeseeds.com (www.wildlifeseeds.com).

Prepare your plot just as you would any garden plot—site it in a sunny or partly sunny area, till and rake the soil smooth, and broadcast your seed mix or sow blocks of seed at the recommended spacing. Water the plot regularly if it doesn't rain often to give your plants the best chance to germinate and grow. These plots will attract all game birds, including pheasants and turkeys, as well as doves, quail, and waterfowl.

Take a Closer Look

Northern Bobwhite *(Colinus virginianus)*

Bobwhite are plump game birds with beautifully marked plumage. Both males and females have dramatic black-and-white breasts, with glowing red-brown joining the black-and-white patterning on the sides, wings, and back, and short gray tails. The male bobwhite has a broad white eye stripe and white throat; females have buff stripes and throats. Juveniles look like less colorful females. Adult birds are 9¾ to 10½ inches (25 to 27 cm) long. Females lay from 7 up to 28 (usually 12 to 14) white eggs in a nest built of dead grasses and weeds in a depression in the ground.

Feeder Favorites for Bobwhite and Other Quail

- Cracked corn
- Mixed seed
- Millet
- Sunflower seed, especially black oil
- Whole corn
- Milo

Regional Relations

In the West, quail are frequent feeder visitors. California quail (*Callipepla californica*) on the West Coast and Gambel's quail (*C. gambelii*) in the Southwest are the most commonly seen, but mountain, Montezuma, and scaled quail will also turn up at feeders in their ranges. These plump little birds appear readily at suburban as well as rural feeders. California quail are beautiful 10-inch-long (25 cm) birds, with blue-gray backs and throats and white streaks on their brown wings and undersides; males have black faces with white outlining and a black comma-shaped plume on the top of their heads. Gambel's quail are a little larger, with a pale buff belly and chestnut sides and crown; otherwise, they resemble California quail. Ruffed grouse (*Bonasa umbellus*) in the North and Far North, spruce grouse (*Falcipennis canadensis*) in the Far North, and dusky grouse (*Dendragapus obscurus*) in the Northwest may all appear at your feeders, if you live in a forested part of their range.

Tempting Features and Treats for Bobwhite and Other Quail

- Quail are especially fond of legume sprouts. For a special treat, offer sprouted mung beans or other beans. Sprout your own or buy a bag wherever sprouts are sold for human consumption.
- Project FeederWatch participants report that Gambel's quail have been known to eat baked goods at their feeders. If bobwhite or other quail are visiting your yard, try setting out pieces of doughnut or muffin or a slice or two of bread.
- Water is appreciated by all game birds, but is especially important in arid environments. Place a birdbath on the ground or on a low pedestal.
- Give your small game birds some scratch grains, either on a tray feeder or directly on the ground.

Did You Know?

- Our smaller native game birds have received their due from three states: The ruffed grouse is the state bird of Pennsylvania, the willow ptarmigan is Alaska's state bird, and the California Valley quail is the state bird of California.
- Bobwhite are named for their call, which does indeed sound like "bob-white."
- Bobwhite are a species of quail. There are 22 subspecies of bobwhite, each with different characteristics.
- Quail tend to form flocks or groups, called coveys, except during nesting season. If you see one quail at your feeder, you're likely to see the whole covey. Once quail discover your feeder, they're likely to be frequent winter visitors.
- Quail are crepuscular feeders, preferring to eat their fill at dawn and/or dusk and spend the rest of the day concealed from predators.
- Quail like to stay close to the ground, but they've been known to visit feeders in comparatively high places, including feeders on decks.

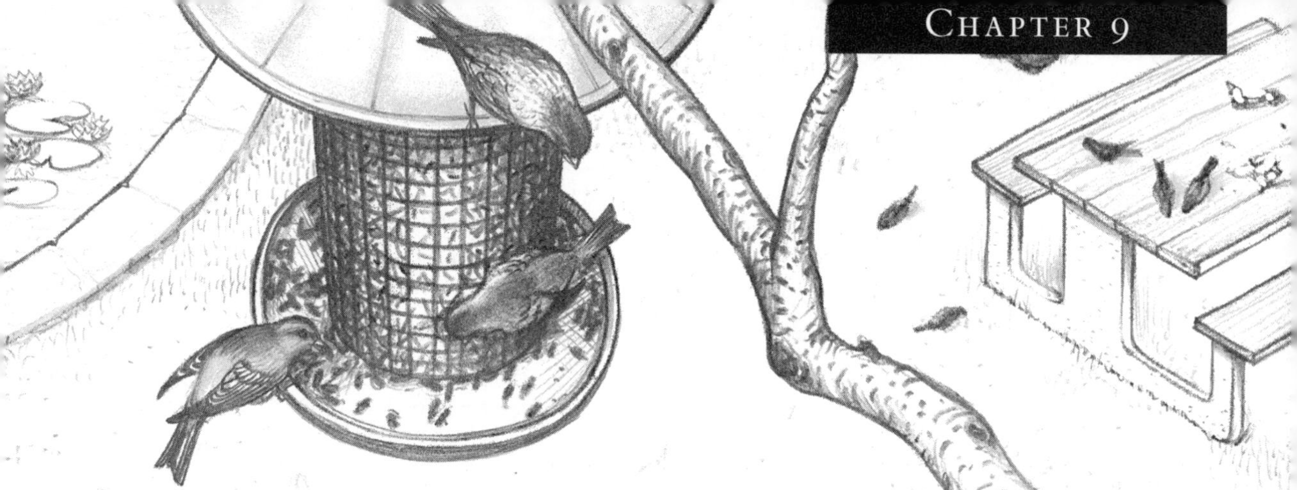

CHAPTER 9

SHARING SPACE WITH BIRDS

As more and more birds begin visiting your yard, you'll go from being a bird-watcher to actually interacting with your winged friends. It's natural and good to feel a sense of responsibility for the well-being of wild birds that share your territory, yet there are situations in which the living habits of humans and birds collide. Birds can't see large expanses of clear glass, are confused by mirrorlike reflective surfaces, and sometimes don't distinguish between a hollow tree and a seldom-used chimney. In this chapter, you'll learn how to handle these problems as well as how to draw birds so close that you can feed them by hand.

Many people love many different animals, including cats, dogs, and other pets that are natural predators of birds. As you develop your yard in ways that benefit birds, you're probably also benefiting yourself, your family, and your pets. This chapter includes dozens of tips that tone down conflicts among all those concerned, along with how to handle injured or dead birds. By taking a few steps to protect birds from hazards that come from sharing space with people and pets, you can help them live longer, healthier lives.

CREATE A CUSTOMIZED VIEWING STATION

Birds are always on the lookout for danger, and they're easily spooked by the noise and sight of people and pets. If they sense a threat, birds will fly away from feeders or might not even come to them at all. But you don't need to build a hunting blind or load up on expensive equipment to enjoy watching or photographing the birds in your yard. You can maximize viewing with just a little planning.

Select your viewing station with the best feeding times and weather situations in mind. Birds visit feeders most often in the early morning and again just before dusk. They use feeders less often in the afternoon and during rainy or inclement weather.

In winter, snow may force wintering birds to change their feeding habits. For example, sparrows, jays, and juncos may congregate at feeders in snowy weather if their typical feeding area, bare ground, is covered.

Indoors, find a place with a clear view of feeders and the ground below, plus surrounding trees and shrubs. Ideally, there should be a spot where you can sit still and watch, out of plain view of skittish birds.

As birds get used to your watchful eyes, avoid unnecessary noise from TVs and stereos.

Situate a comfortable chair or stool to maximize your viewing angle. A swivel chair is best, because you can change your angle without moving your body.

Have a table or flat surface nearby to hold your coffee or tea along with binoculars, bird identification books, and a paper and pen for making notes.

Sit as Still as a Scout

Unless you have a high-powered telephoto lens or use the magnification of a spotting scope to augment your camera's zoom abilities, getting good pictures of birds requires getting close to them. But getting close can be difficult, since most birds survive by staying far away from anything they perceive as a threat. Take a page from the original Boy Scout manual and try what scouts still call Seton sitting when you want to observe or photograph birds at close range.

Named for artist and author Ernest Thompson Seton, a naturalist who helped establish the Boy Scouts of America and who wrote the group's first manual, "Seton sitting" is the practice of sitting motionless in nature. In studying wildlife for his drawings and paintings, Seton found that remaining completely still for at least 20 minutes rendered him almost invisible to birds and animals. As time passed, the creatures around him seemed to forget he was there and accepted him as part of the environment, coming quite close to him until movement startled them away.

ENJOY HIGH-DEFINITION REALITY

"Window-watching" a busy feeding station may be the perfect pastime for a cold winter day. From the comfort of your home you can observe your hungry guests and become familiar with their

When a Bird Gets into the House

One of the hazards of feeding birds near windows or entryways is that they sometimes venture into your house. When a sparrow or hummingbird accidentally flies into your house, it can turn into an exciting day! Instead of panicking and trying to shoo the bird out through an open window or door, try these steps to help the bird get itself back outside where it belongs.

1. **Stay calm.** The bird is already frightened and disoriented, and loud voices and waving arms will only make the situation worse. Clear the area of pets and people and avoid sudden motions.
2. **Next, quietly close all the curtains or blinds.** Turn off lights and darken the room as much as possible. Then, open a door or large window, letting in plenty of natural light from only one source.
3. **Go to another room and be patient.** Once it calms down, the bird should head toward the light and fly to freedom.

likes and dislikes. Learn which foods each bird favors, count the species that frequent your feeders, and see which birds share nicely and which ones insist on having the feeder all to themselves. The little dramas that unfold over the course of an afternoon are as entertaining as any daytime soap opera and are much more real than the so-called reality shows on TV. No matter how much you're spending keeping your feeders filled, chances are good that it's less than a month's worth of cable or satellite television service, and probably at least as enjoyable. And the price of a crystal clear LCD TV will pay for several season's worth of birdseed!

BUDGET-WISE BIRDING

Try a See-Through Solution

Siting your feeders so you can see them clearly from the windows of your home simply makes good sense. You're much more likely to spend time watching the birds that come to your feeders if you can be warm and dry while doing it. It also makes sense to keep that view as clear as possible by cleaning the windows you're watching from.

Don't spend your (bird)seed money on bottles of colorful window cleaner. Mix a simple solution of ½ cup (118 ml) white vinegar in 1 quart (1 l) cool water. Wipe or spray your windows with this nontoxic mixture, then use a squeegee to wipe off the liquid. Keep a rag or paper towel handy to clean the squeegee between passes and to wipe up any drips. For a few cents' worth of vinegar and a light application of elbow grease, you'll get a crystal clear, streak-free view of the scene at your feeder.

DETERRING INTRUSIVE NEST BUILDERS

Sparrows, swifts, wrens, and several other birds sometimes prefer nesting in chimneys and attic vents to trees and nest boxes. To prevent bird intrusions, place wire mesh over your chimney opening. Be sure the mesh material is fireproof. If you've had birds nesting in your eave vents before, screen them with ¼-inch mesh hardware cloth or tough nylon netting. It's best to remove the vents, tightly stretch the mesh under them, and then reattach them.

In addition, check wall and roof openings for gaps near wires or pipes. Seal any gaps with caulk or foam sealant. If you don't want to climb, call a professional to do the job.

Never light a fire to get birds out of a chimney. Open the damper and follow the steps in "When a Bird Gets into the House" on page 271. If you have chimney swifts nesting or roosting, by federal law you cannot remove them. They'll leave after their breeding season, which usually goes from June through August. In the meantime, place insulation on the damper to muffle noise. Get a chimney sweep to clean up in September, after the swifts move on; be sure to ask the sweep to install appropriate screening to prevent future bird occupancy of your chimney.

Graceful chimney swifts may delight you as they dart through the air eating flying insects, but their charms can fade if they take up residence in your chimney.

CHOOSING AND USING BINOCULARS

Even if you never watch birds anyplace other than at your windowsill or from the chaise lounge on your patio, you should still have binoculars. A decent pair of binoculars will improve your ability to ID birds in your yard, and it will increase your understanding and appreciation of those birds. From a distance you can admire the bright red feathers of a male cardinal, for example. With binoculars, you can truly appreciate the subtle color variations of his mate's more muted but arguably more beautiful plumage.

Binoculars let you see birds that don't visit your feeders, too. Insect-eating warblers may sing loudly from the treetops without venturing close enough for you to see what's singing. Bird parents won't make you feel welcome if you come close to

Learn from Others' Experiences

Shopping for binoculars presents a bewildering array of sizes, features, and prices that can leave your head spinning. Porro prism or roof prism? 8× or 8.5× magnification? Coatings? Waterproofing? $100 binocs or $1,000 ones? There's so much to consider—and of course, every manufacturer says its product is best. Before you hit the stores, do a little research, preferably in the company of an experienced birder or two. Ask people who spend a lot of time looking through their binoculars what they like best and what's most important to them. Find out what your local Audubon Society recommends.

"Buying binoculars these days is like deciding which new car to buy," says Arlene Koch, a past president of the Lehigh Valley Audubon Society. "There are that many good ones on the market." When Arlene is tallying migrating birds in the counter's pit on the North Lookout at Hawk Mountain Sanctuary in Kempton, Pennsylvania, she uses 10×42 binoculars that let her see raptors coming from a great distance away. But she recommends a lower magnification for birders who are just getting started, noting that 10× magnification gives you a smaller field of view in exchange for greater magnification. "Most backyard birders would be more than satisfied with 7× or 8×," Arlene suggests. "I always tell beginners to start there and work their way up."

Tirah Keal, Hawk Mountain Sanctuary's bookstore manager, echoes Arlene's views on magnification, noting that 7× or 8× is plenty for most backyard situations. Tirah recommends checking the close-focus abilities of any binocs you're considering, to allow you to look at details of birds and objects right outside your windows. Look for binoculars with close focus to about 6 feet (1.8 m) she suggests, adding that more powerful binoculars may only focus to about 15 feet (4.5 m). While top binoculars may cost upward of $1,000, Tirah says there are good optics available in the $100 to $200 price range. If you're buying binoculars for window-watching from indoors, she says, spend money on optic quality instead of features such as waterproofing and image stabilization. At any price level, she adds, "Avoid bells and whistles and spend on optic quality and personal comfort instead."

Tips for Binocular Success

Use both hands. Innovations in optics have produced binoculars that are big enough—in both magnification and objective diameter—to use for birding and also light enough to support with one hand while you use them. But one hand can scarcely keep your binoculars steady enough to give you a clear view, especially on a caffeine-powered early morning watch or after you've been watching for awhile and begin to get tired.

Try before you hit the trail. Don't wait until you're out scanning the sky for birds before learning how to focus your binoculars or how to adjust the zoom. Practice at home by focusing on and following birds at your feeders and avoid the frustration of missing a bird that others saw while you were fiddling with your lenses.

Use the strap. Walking an uneven trail while looking upward—because that's where most of the birds are—creates ample opportunities for tripping and stumbling. Obviously, no one wants to go crashing to the ground, but if that should happen, it's better to have your binoculars around your neck than in your hand that you might extend to break your fall. If you find the pressure of a neck strap unbearable, consider a harness-type strap that distributes the weight of the binoculars over your shoulders.

their nest to get a look, but binoculars will let you follow their activity as they build a nest and incubate their eggs, and you don't have to risk being dive-bombed by an anxious father.

If you have an unlimited budget, you can choose from a wide range of top-quality binoculars, but most of us need to balance the price of binoculars with the features we value most. That said, price is not the only consideration. Although you'll want to buy the best binoculars you can afford, a big price tag is not a guarantee of quality nor is it the only indicator of first-rate optic equipment. In addition to your budget, here are other binocular features to consider.

- **Magnification.** This first number in a binocular's specifications indicates how much the object being viewed is magnified. A magnification of 7× to 8× is a good place to start for basic bird-watching.
- **Objective diameter.** The second number used to describe binoculars, this is the diameter of the "outgoing" lenses in millimeters. The larger this number, the more light the lenses admit and the brighter the image you see.
- **Image quality.** Quality includes depth of field (the focused area before and beyond an object) and field of view (the horizontal width of the view) as well as brightness, and is a function of magnification and objective diameter, plus lens coatings and other enhancements.
- **Durability.** Most binoculars on the market are sufficiently durable for moderate use and will withstand the occasional bump. Water resistant or waterproof binoculars are desirable for outdoor use, as are binocs filled with dry gas, such as nitrogen, to keep them from fogging up when you're out in the cold.
- **Weight.** Bigger lenses give you a better view, but do add weight to your binoculars. Much has been done, however, to make binocs that offer good objective diameter without being too heavy to hold.

- **Ergonomics.** How easy it is to hold your binoculars probably matters more than how much they weigh. Try before you buy: Binoculars should fit into your hands, be easy to focus, and fit your face—particularly the distance between your eyes. Seemingly minor features like indentations for your fingers can make a big difference in your comfort when you use binoculars.
- **Eye relief.** Adjustable eyecups accommodate eyeglass wearers and allow all users to hold the binoculars at a comfortable distance from their eyes.
- **Focusing.** Birding often requires quick adjustments in focusing to bring a moving bird into clear view. Be sure focus rings move smoothly and are easy to reach without being too easily knocked out of position.

EVERYBODY WINS

Be a Respectful Birder

In the excitement of spotting a bird species you've never seen before, it's easy to stray from designated pathways and into potentially fragile wildlife habitat. The thrill of locating a hidden nest may make you forget your nest-viewing manners (see page 301). Whether you're watching birds in your own yard or from the paths of a wildlife sanctuary, it's important to remember that birds are wild creatures that deserve to go about their lives undisturbed by human activity.

To help remind birders of their responsibilities to birds, the environment, and other people, the American Birding Association (ABA) has created a Code of Birding Ethics that begins with this statement: "Everyone who enjoys birds and birding must always respect wildlife, its environment, and the rights of others. In any conflict of interest between birds and birders, the welfare of the birds and their environment comes first."

The ABA's code consists of the following key elements:

1. **Promote the welfare of birds and their environment.** This includes protecting bird habitat and exercising restraint during observation, photography, sound recording or filming birds, as well as limiting the use of recordings and other means of attracting birds, and keeping a respectful distance from nest sites and other sensitive areas.
2. **Respect the law and the rights of others.** Do not enter private property without the owner's explicit permission. Follow all laws, rules, and regulations governing use of roads and public areas, both at home and abroad. Practice common courtesy in contacts with other people.
3. **Ensure that feeders, nest structures, and other artificial bird environments are safe.** Keep dispensers, water, and food clean, and free of decay or disease. Maintain and clean nest structures regularly. If you are attracting birds to an area, ensure the birds are not exposed to predation from cats and other domestic animals, or dangers posed by artificial hazards.
4. **Group birding, whether organized or impromptu, requires special care.**

To read the complete Code of Ethics, visit the ABA's Web site: http://americanbirding.org.

FEEDING WILD BIRDS FACE TO FACE

Snow White did it, and so did St. Francis of Assisi. Once you notice that your resident birds are watching you as you schlep bird feed to empty feeders, perhaps scolding you for taking so long, you might wonder about taking the next step toward getting birds to eat from your hand. This is easier than you may think if you're patient and dedicated to the goal of having a chirping bird standing in your palm, lifting your spirits as it pecks up seeds.

Some birding purists get their feathers ruffled by hand-feeding of wild birds. They say it may make birds overly dependent on human contact, but in fact very few people are likely to stick with the time and patience needed to establish such dependence. To most wild birds, hand-feeding is as much a folly for them as it is for you!

Don't attempt to begin the process in summer, when birds are preoccupied with mating and rearing young. It's best to start in autumn or early winter, when most birds are free from family obligations and have become habitual visitors to your feeder. Don't try hand-feeding if your bird feeding setup is new. Instead, wait until birds are accustomed to the feeding environment and have had plenty of time to get to know nearby shrubs, hedges, and trees that offer quick cover. If other household members want to watch, find a spot where they can see or take photos without spooking the birds. Finally, keep cats and dogs away from the scene and out of sight. A cat pawing at the window or a dog barking at birds will instantly undermine your efforts.

EASING INTO HAND-FEEDING, STEP BY STEP

1. Fill bird feeders at the same time each day. The best time is morning, when most birds are actively looking for food.
2. After filling feeders, stand calmly, 10 to 12 feet (3 to 3.5 m) away, for several minutes. Or use a chair or stool to sit very still (use the same chair or stool from then on). It's okay to talk or sing softly; birds will associate your voice with feeding time.
3. Wait patiently until the first bird comes to the feeder. Don't move; soon others will come, then a bunch will start feeding. Keep still. After about 10 minutes, slowly walk away and go indoors.
4. After repeating this for a few days, wearing the same clothes whenever you can, move 1 foot (0.3 m) closer to the feeder each day. Repeat your standing/sitting routine. Taking days off

Got Gloves?

To protect yourself from minor scratches, don gloves and long sleeves before starting a hand-feeding session. A gloved hand won't accidentally get clawed or pecked, and you won't have direct contact with mites or other parasites. Use the same gloves—or a pair of the same color—each time, so their appearance remains the same. Once birds become accustomed to taking seeds from your hand, add a hat to your bird-feeding wardrobe, because sooner or later the birds will start landing on your head!

Birds in the Hand

As resident birds grow accustomed to your presence in the landscape, you may be surprised by how many of them are willing to accept a treat offered in the palm of your hand. Even so, some wild birds are more likely to perch on your thumb for a peanut while others will never venture anywhere near you no matter how tempting the food may be. The list of possibilities varies, of course, depending on where you live, how patient you are, how much food is available, and so forth. In most of the United States and Canada, the following birds are the most likely candidates for hand-feeding:

Chickadees	Titmice
Jays	Woodpeckers
Nuthatches	

Other birds that may come to feed from your hand include white-throated sparrows, cardinals, evening grosbeaks, mockingbirds, grackles, and house and purple finches.

A chair may make it easier for you to remain still while you wait for birds to accept you as part of the normal scene. Choose a seat that's weatherproof, portable, and at least reasonably comfortable and incorporate it into your feeding routine.

is okay; just resume the familiarization process from the same spot where you stopped, as long as birds still come to your feeder freely.

5. Once you've made it right next to the feeder and birds still come to eat, place your open hand, protected with a glove, on or next to the feeder. Repeat for 3 or 4 days, until birds at least land on your gloved hand.
6. To achieve your goal, mime your usual feeder-filling routine, but remove all food from the feeder. Take some birdseed, or bits of nuts—walnuts, pecans, peanuts—into your palm and hold it out, keeping your hand steady. This may take several minutes, but remember that they're watching you, so make no sudden movements, even with your eyes. Eventually, a single bold bird will land on your shoulder, head, or arm. It will probably study you, so be still and . . . finally . . . it will take some food from your hand. If a bird takes food and flies away to cover, that's okay. It will soon come back, or other birds will. Refill your feeders for general feeding when your hand-feeding routine is done for the day.
7. Keep the same routine—clothing, gloves, and all—and soon you should have birds lining up to feed from your hand. In time, you can move about a little more freely, but always avoid sudden movements. Eventually, when you go outside for other reasons, the hand-trained birds may flock around you, looking for handouts.

Take a Closer Look

American Robin *(Turdus migratorius)*

One of the first species most people learn to recognize, robins are medium-size birds often seen in small flocks in fall and spring, or as pairs during the summer breeding season. The male robin has a dark, nearly black head, gray-brown back and wings, and a distinctive red-orange breast and underparts. A thin circle of white makes his eyes stand out against his dark head feathers, giving him an alert look. Females are smaller and have paler coloring than males. Adult birds are 8 to 11 inches (20 to 28 cm) long. Both male and female robins take part in nest building, although the female does the bulk of the construction work while the male spends part of the time singing in defense of his territory. A typical clutch consists of three to seven eggs that the female incubates; she may raise two or three broods during a single breeding season.

Feeder Favorites for American Robins

Robins eat mostly insects in summer, supplemented by whatever fruits they can find. You'll have the best luck attracting them to feeders in winter by offering these foods.

- Sunflower seeds
- Apples and other fruit, especially in winter
- Bread crumbs
- Dried blueberries or cherries
- Grapes

Tempting Features and Treats for Robins

- Robins love to scratch through deep leaf mulch in search of beetles and earthworms.
- Fruiting trees and shrubs including wild cherries, barberries, grapes, blueberries, and blackberries will keep robins close to home.
- Newly mowed lawns are favorite feeding grounds for robins.
- Robins prefer to nest and roost in dense shrubs and trees.

Did You Know?

- Robins have a whistlelike "cheerup cheerily cheerup" song, which males sing loudly around dawn, especially during nesting season. A robin calling "cheep cheep" is calling out a danger warning.
- Females build cup-shaped nests from grass and small twigs—and sometimes string, cloth, feathers, and paper—all held together with mud and finished off with a soft lining. A young female may spend a week making a so-so nest, while a more experienced bird can build a fine nest in 2 to 3 days.
- Robins' eggs are an unmistakable pale blue, and both whole and broken eggs often fall from nests during storms. Nests are usually made in a branch crotch in a tree that offers good shelter, or occasionally on window ledges or nooks in city buildings.
- Robins hunt in a distinctive way. They hop for a few feet, stand still, then cock their heads, as if listening for movement. Studies indicate that instead of listening, they're scanning the ground for any sign of movement. If they see the tip of an earthworm sticking out of the lawn, or see a slither in the leaf litter, they grab it. Robins also feed on beetle grubs, caterpillars, and weevils in lawns, leaf litter, and soil.
- In fall, robins form small flocks that wander about in search of good food supplies. As winter begins, most leave cold climates to spend the cold season where they can find a few insects during periods of mild weather.
- Because of their size and abundance, robins were once considered winter game birds in Sunbelt states. Today, it's illegal to hunt robins—a law that extends to sharp-eyed kids with slingshots!
- Mature robins often return to familiar breeding grounds, so it's likely that the same individuals that stole your blueberries (and ate thousands of Japanese beetle grubs from your lawn) last summer will be back again this year.

BIRDS AND WINDOWS

One day you hear an odd "thunk" from outside. A falling branch? Newspaper delivery? Better check around your windows, because in yards where birds busily come and go from feeders, collisions between birds and windows are extremely common. In the United States and Canada, estimates of bird mortality from collisions with windows range from 100 million birds to a staggering 1 billion birds annually.

Research shows that most birds crash into windows because they see a reflection of safe sky or landing sites. The window glass is invisible to them, so they head full-steam into what they think is a safe space. Sometimes the bird is just stunned, and may recover in a short time if left alone. Too often though, a window crash will result in serious

Move Feeding Closer to Home

Moving feeders close to your house—within 2 to 3 feet (0.6 to 1 m) from windows—can actually reduce window collisions. The birds will perceive the house's structure better, and at such a short distance they can't build up enough flight speed to get seriously hurt if they take off from a feeder in the wrong direction.

No More Knockouts

You'll find far fewer dazed or dead birds on your patio—or mysterious smudges of feathers on your windows—if you help birds perceive when glass is present. If one window is struck often while others are not, walk around outside to see what the birds are seeing when they look toward that window.

1. **Install a series of vertical strings on the outside of the window, spaced 4 inches (10 cm) apart.** The birds see the pattern created by the strings and recognize it as a barrier.
2. **Use thin pieces of colored tape to make a pattern on the window.** Be as creative as you like, but be sure to include all parts of the window.
3. **Use stencils and soap paste to create seasonal decorations on the window.** This is a great project for kids!
4. **Install sheer or lace curtains inside the window.** Keep the curtains closed unless you need them open to watch birds.
5. **Install a very taut, durable screen on the outside of the window.** With luck, it will cushion the blow when a bird flies into it.
6. **Cover the window with an awning.** Birds find shaded windows much less attractive than those that are bathed in natural sunlight.
7. **Check with retailers of wild bird supplies for "invisible" decals for your windows.** These decorative decals of leaves, butterflies, hummingbirds, and hawks look almost colorless to us, but they're bright blue to birds, because they reflect ultraviolet light that birds can see but we cannot.
8. **If you're building or remodeling your house, prevent the reflection problem from the start.** Design your windows so they tilt down a bit to avoid reflecting the sky or nearby food sources.

Better Architecture for Birds

Many birds die when they fly into windows of skyscrapers, office buildings, and classroom buildings. Many fatalities occur at night, when migratory birds are attracted by lights and end up dead on the sidewalk. In response to this problem, several college campuses and some cities have reduced unnecessary nighttime lighting. As new buildings are planned, architects often suggest tilting windows downward slightly, so that they reflect the ground rather than the sky.

internal damage and death. All kinds of birds are at risk, including songbirds like finches, cardinals, robins, doves, and many others.

OTHER STRUCTURES THAT TAKE A TOLL

In most home landscapes, windows are the biggest source of unwanted bird-structure interactions. Fortunately, as just described in "No More Knockouts" on page 279, there are several easy ways to minimize the risks that your home's windows pose to wild birds.

Other sorts of human construction can be much more difficult to manage in ways that prevent injury to birds and other wildlife. How much responsibility you accept for the existence of such structures is entirely up to you. Although you're unlikely to have a skyscraper or a tall communications tower literally in your backyard, perhaps you work in a tall building. Bird strikes against the upper stories of skyscrapers are common during spring and fall migrations and are much more likely to cause fatalities than the occasional bird colliding into a single-family home.

If you listen to the radio, watch television, or use a cellular phone and expect it to work wherever you may roam, you're among the millions of contributors to the growing network of tall communications towers spreading across the landscape. Tall towers—and the long guy wires that may support them and keep them from swaying—have been recognized for more than 50 years as a cause of bird mortality, particularly among migratory species. As cell phone and digital television networks expand, so will the number of communications towers and, without careful consideration for their effects on wildlife, so will the number of bird species threatened by these towers.

Lights Out Make Skyscrapers Safer

If you live or work in a tall building, there's a very simple way to reduce bird collisions with your windows: Turn out the lights. Birds that migrate at night may become confused by the light coming from the windows of tall buildings, increasing the risk that they'll crash into those lighted windows. Close curtains or shades to keep light from escaping from your 12th-floor apartment; do the same at your office or, better still, save energy and birds by promoting a building-wide lights-out policy during hours when offices are empty.

The Trouble with Towers

According to estimates from the U.S. Fish and Wildlife Service, at least 5 million birds die each year as the result of collisions with communications towers in the United States. With the number of tall towers increasing at a rate of more than 7,000 per year, the looming structures that bring us our phone calls and TV shows may well cost us several species of birds. An American Bird Conservancy report on the numbers and species of birds killed in tower collisions indicates that, of the more than 200 documented species, 52 are bird species that are known to be declining.

Since cell phones and other communication technologies are unlikely to disappear, conscientious bird lovers who also enjoy the benefits of technology need to support research into ways to make communications towers less deadly for migrating birds.

Write to your elected federal officials and ask them to direct the Federal Aviation Administration and the Federal Communications Commission to adopt bird-safe lighting and tower construction at new and existing installations. When tower construction is proposed in your area, find out if it will be in the path of known bird migration routes. Ask the company planning the installation to follow the voluntary guidelines from the U.S. Fish and Wildlife Service for construction of towers designed to minimize the effect on migratory birds.

HANDLING CONFLICTS BETWEEN CATS AND BIRDS

Many of us love feeding birds, but we love our cats, too. This is a serious problem, because any cat with intact claws is likely to become a lifelong killer of birds.

Like purring and prowling, a cat is born with a built-in instinct for hunting birds. Aside from bird deaths caused by cats, cats' mere presence near feeders may keep birds away and discourage them from nesting nearby. Jays, mockingbirds, and other bossy birds will sometimes attempt to herd cats by swooping down to harass them, but small skittish birds may move on to other places rather than share living space with a cat.

In most towns and cities, dogs must be kept fenced or leashed, but cats are allowed to roam free. We humans tend to accept this as the natural way of things as far as cats are concerned, but in truth it makes for a high-risk lifestyle for both cats and birds. Outdoor cats are prone to attacks from predators and competitors, including owls, hawks, other cats, dogs, and other animals. They're in danger of being run over by cars, they can get sick from eating rodents, reptiles, or dead or sick birds, and they can pick up fleas, ticks, mites, and other nasty parasites. In terms of life expectancy, indoor cats often live 10 years or more, while free-roaming cats have an average life expectancy of less than 5 years.

When cats are kept indoors, they can actually enhance your bird-watching pleasure. As they station themselves near a window or glass door to watch birds feeding outside, cats often click their teeth while clacking their tongues, perhaps in an attempt to imitate the chipping, clucking sounds of the birds.

Take a Closer Look

Blue Jay *(Cyanocitta cristata)*

Blue jays are slightly larger than robins, with a white face and a bluish crest, wings, tail, and back. They have a black necklace and sport a crest, which is an elongation of feathers at the top of their heads. Males and females are similar in color and size. Blue jays have a large bill, which they use to break open acorns, nuts, and even tent caterpillar cocoons. Adults are 11 to 12 inches (28 to 30 cm) long. The jay's nest is a large, loosely built cup of twigs, leaves, paper, string, and other readily available materials, which holds three to seven brown-spotted yellowish to olive-green eggs.

Feeder Favorites for Jays

- Sunflower seeds
- Peanuts or hazelnuts
- Fruits and berries
- Cracked corn
- Suet
- Crumbs or small pieces of bread

Regional Relations

Steller's jay (*Cyanocitta stelleri*) is the western counterpart to the blue jay, and the two species interbreed where their ranges overlap. Usually found in pine forests from the Pacific to New Mexico and up into Alaska, Steller's jays are big, bold birds up to 13 inches (33 cm) long, with purplish blue bodies and a blackish crest and front.

Also in the Mountain and Pacific West is the western scrub-jay or California jay (*Aphelocoma californica*), which is about the same size as the blue jay but without a crest. Florida is home to the rare Florida scrub-jay (*A. coerulescens*). Both western and Florida scrub-jays are easily tamed to the point at which they can be fed by hand (see page 276).

Tempting Features and Treats for Jays

- Jays stick close to good food sources, so yards that include oaks, hazels, and other nut-bearing trees are especially attractive.
- Berry-bearing shrubs including hollies, sumacs, and viburnums always get plenty of visits from blue jays in fall.
- Jays are more likely to feed on the ground or to visit suspended platform feeders where they can move about freely without feeling cramped.

Did You Know?

- You can sometimes tell what a jay has on its mind by looking at its crest. When surprised or agitated, it points its crest forward, and when excited, it holds its crest erect. When resting, quietly feeding, or about to fly off, it flattens its crest.
- Jays often stock up on surplus food by burying it. They especially like to cache large seeds and nuts, including peanuts. Most caching is done in autumn, when food is plentiful. In cold climates, blue jays dig in the snow to uncover cached acorns, beechnuts, or hard-shelled seeds.
- The individual blue jays you see at your feeder may be the same ones you've seen for years.
- Birds rarely use tools, but jays in captivity were observed using paper strips to corral pellets of food and pull them toward their cage.
- Jays are aggressive defenders of their nesting territory and feeding areas. They will dive-bomb cats, dogs, and people who come too close. Jays will fight a multitude of predators, including hawks, owls, falcons, and of course, cats.
- Like flickers, robins, grackles, and several other birds, jays sometimes groom themselves by combing through their feathers with live ants, which may help kill lice and other parasites.
- Blue jays are short-distance migrants. Small roaming flocks form when breeding season ends. Many jays in mild winter climates hold their territories year-round.
- With an average lifespan of 7 years in the wild, blue jays live longer than many other songbirds. One banded wild jay lived to be 17 years old!

A BIRD LOVER'S CATALOG OF FELINE FACTS AND FIGURES

Research studies paint a sobering picture of bird mortality caused by cats.

- Cats are populous, non-native predators of birds. There are more than 90 million pet cats in the United States and millions more stray and wild cats.
- Cats account for about 30 percent of birds killed at feeders.
- Studies show that cats kill hundreds of millions of birds each year. Scientists in Florida estimate that cats kill 68 million birds there each year.
- Cats prey on many common songbirds we attract, including cardinals, robins, juncos, chickadees, bluebirds, and song sparrows. A cat on the prowl for prey doesn't distinguish between common birds and endangered species.

Avoid attracting birds into a dangerous situation like a feeder or bath that's frequented by a cat. Keep birds (and pets) safe by keeping kitties indoors.

PROTECT YOUR FEEDER GUESTS

Putting up a bird-feeding station in a site that puts visiting birds at risk of becoming prey for cats is hardly sporting, to say the least. The American Birding Association puts it even more strongly, characterizing such behavior as unethical. In the ABA's Code of Birding Ethics, the organization recommends that birders "ensure that feeders, nest

EVERYBODY WINS

The Semi-Indoor Solution

Individual cats vary in how willingly they adapt to indoor life, and many young, healthy cats rebel when restricted to the indoors. One solution is to turn an enclosed or screened-in porch into an indoor-outdoor cat room, or to build a cage-type enclosure so your cat can get out in the fresh air and nap in the sun. Several companies, including Doctors Foster and Smith (www.drsfostersmith.com, 800-381-7179), Pet Solutions (www.petsolutions.com, 800-737-3868), and Petfavors (www.petfavors.com, 888-660-PETS), offer products and enclosures designed to allow cats to enjoy the outdoors while preventing them from indulging their bird-hunting habits. You'll never need to worry about a beloved cat that goes missing, and your birds can feed and breed without risk of being cat-nabbed.

Dealing with Other People's Cats

Even if you don't have a cat, predation on feeder birds can be a problem. Lots of birds regularly feeding in your yard may attract neighborhood cats.

- **If your neighbor's cat visits frequently,** or stray cats show up, don't encourage them with food. They'll become spoiled and treat your place as a second home. Instead, keep a water gun handy and squirt them when they come into your yard.
- **Talk with cat-owning neighbors about keeping their cats at home,** preferably indoors. To keep this from becoming a personal confrontation, obtain copies of the "Cats Indoors!" brochure published by the American Bird Conservancy (www.abcbirds.org) and hand them out.
- **To keep random cats from prowling around feeder areas,** spread chicken wire or hardware cloth on the ground beneath feeders. Cats don't like to walk on this springy, uneven metal grid; their paws get snagged. Fasten or weigh down the edges of the mesh so it won't trap small birds.

structures, and other artificial bird environments are safe." More specifically, the Code states, "If you are attracting birds to an area, ensure the birds are not exposed to predation from cats and other domestic animals . . ." As we've already noted, cats kill millions of songbirds each year, but they're less effective hunters when feeding areas are designed with this problem in mind.

Place your feeders well away from dense shrubs and trees, where cats like to lurk. This is especially important if you attract ground feeders like doves, phoebes, and pigeons. At the same time, locate feeders near upright trees and bushes that offer high branches where ground-feeding birds can escape from earthbound cats. Mow down nearby stands of tall weeds or grasses to eliminate cover for predators.

Space multiple feeders at different heights and distances from each other to avoid concentrating birds in one spot. In addition to frustrating predators, having multiple feeders reduces competition for food among wild birds.

Place birdbaths, water dishes, or pools in open areas, away from dense, brushy predator cover. As with feeders, birdbaths should have nearby trees or shrubs that offer branches that are too high and too flimsy for climbing cats, but are just right for birds to perch on post-bathing to preen their feathers back into top-flight condition.

BIRD MYTH-BUSTERS

Cat Collars with Bells

For years, bird-loving cat owners have attached bells to their cats' collars to make them less effective hunters. But does it work? Yes and no. When researchers at the University of Glasgow attached bells to the collars of 41 cats with strong track records as successful hunters, they found that the bells reduced bird and rodent catches by half. Although significant, that still leaves a lot of rodents—and birds—in cats' clutches. Other observers have noted that cats adapt to wearing bells and can move with enough stealth to avoid jingling a warning to their intended prey. In short, to ensure the safety of birds in your yard, a door is better than a bell.

Take a Closer Look

Mourning Dove *(Zenaida macroura)*

Mourning doves are slate-gray to grayish brown birds, with long, pointed tails featuring black and white stripes. Compared to males, females are slightly smaller and more brownish, but both genders have black bills, pinkish faces, and reddish legs and feet. Adult birds are 8 to 13 inches (20 to 33 cm) long. Two to four white eggs are laid in a nest of loose twigs built on a horizontal branch; mourning doves also lay their eggs on the ground or in old nests made by grackles, jays, or robins.

Feeder Favorites for Mourning Doves

- Nyjer seed (spilled by goldfinches)
- Millet seed
- Cracked corn
- Hulled sunflower seed
- Buckwheat kernels
- Occasional fruit and berries

Regional Relations

The range of the common ground dove (*Columbina passerina*) stretches across the Sunbelt states, and the Inca dove (*C. inca*) inhabits the Southwest. Often seen in ground-level nests or bobbing around roadside areas, fields, and beaches, these species are smaller and stockier than the mourning dove, being seldom more than 7 inches (18 cm) long. These diminutive doves do repeat a patient cooing song similar to that of the mourning dove. They often feed on the ground or at low platform feeders, eating millet, sunflower seeds, cracked corn and other grains, berries, and insects.

Tempting Features and Treats for Mourning Doves

- Provide native food sources by leaving some stands of weeds and grasses unmowed. Weed and grass seeds are diet staples for doves.
- Doves often clean up softer-shelled millet seeds found in birdseed mixtures and tossed aside by other birds.
- Doves much prefer feeding on the ground to competing for space at busy feeders.
- Provide water in low birdbaths or basins. Doves visit water mostly at dawn and dusk, so be sure to keep pets indoors during these times.
- Set out low pans of sharp sand, washed gravel, or crushed egg or oyster shells for doves to use as grit. This helps them grind and digest the multitude of seeds they eat.

Did You Know?

- When a dove takes flight as you walk by it hidden in a bush, it can make you jump! The mourning dove's large wings "whistle" or "whir" as air rushes through their feathers. The sound serves as an alarm to nearby doves.
- Mourning doves mate for life. Males and females take turns incubating eggs and feeding babies.
- Although slow-moving on the ground, mourning doves fly strongly and swiftly to escape predators, or to migrate in fall and spring. Doves fly many hundreds of miles to reach warmer winter sites.
- Mating males make soft calls of "coo-ah, woo-oo-oo" that can go on for hours. This plaintive song gives them their "mourning" moniker.
- The ever-cooing mourning dove is one of our most widely seen birds at feeders and in yards. You'll see them in all 48 contiguous states, southern Canada, and most of Mexico.
- Mourning doves (as well as pigeons and other dove species) are legal to hunt during specified seasons (usually September and October) in many states. Because their small size relative to other game birds makes them more challenging targets, dove hunting is a popular sport.
- With fewer good places to feed and nest, mourning dove populations are declining in many states that permit dove hunting.

Don't Feed Feral Cats

As we've already said, cats are hunters by instinct. They're programmed to go after small prey animals and no amount of food you offer them from a can or kibble bag will rewrite their internal code. Serving as a soup kitchen for the homeless kitties in your neighborhood may seem like a kindness that would keep feral cats from making their meals out of the birds at your feeders, but this is not the case.

A well-fed cat is simply a more successful predator, as millions of free-ranging and well-loved pets have proven ad infinitum by proudly presenting their owners with small carcasses covered in fur or feathers. Putting out food to ease the hunger of ownerless cats not only doesn't stop them from preying on birds but also invites more feral felines into your neighborhood.

More cats, as you can guess, likely will lead to still more cats, as nature takes its course. This, in turn, increases the risk of disease problems in the growing cat population, as well as increasing the number of nights when you'll be awakened by the sounds of cats fighting—with other cats or with dogs or other critters also attracted by the free food you're supplying.

Help Track Bird Predation

Through programs such as Project FeederWatch and holiday weekend bird counts, backyard birders have contributed substantially to our knowledge of wild birds. By simply observing birds and reporting their observations, citizen scientists across North America have increased our understanding of species distribution, migratory movement, courtship and nesting behaviors, and much more.

Now you can help further scientific study of the effects of predation on wild birds by participating in the American Bird Conservancy's "Project PredatorWatch." According to the ABC's Web site, the project is meant "to investigate the impact of free-ranging cats and other predators on wild birds in the U.S. and Canada." In its first year of gathering information, Project PredatorWatch collected more than 850 survey responses, "the majority of which were cat related," says Steve Holmer, director of public relations for the Conservancy.

By reporting any predator/wildlife interaction that you observe, you will help identify birds that are most affected by cats and other predators, as well as help scientists determine whether predation is more common in certain areas or at certain times of the year. To report incidents of predation, go to the ABC's "Cats Indoors!" Web site (www.abcbirds.org/cats) and follow the link to the Project PredatorWatch online survey.

TAKE A CLOSER LOOK

Pigeon *(Columba livia)*

Wild pigeons are mostly gray, but colors vary greatly among familiar pigeons of parks and large landscapes. Most pigeons have two black wing bars and rounded tail feathers with dark tips. The male typically has a larger, more iridescent neck than the female.

Adult birds are 10 to 13 inches (25 to 33 cm) long. Pigeons nest on loose, shallow piles of twigs, grasses, and similar materials; they tend only one or two white eggs at a time, but may raise three or more broods in a single breeding season.

Feeder Favorites for Pigeons

- Cracked corn
- Milo (sorghum) seeds
- Currants and other berries
- Fruits
- Crumbs and pieces of bread
- Oats and other soft grains
- Hulled peanuts

Regional Relations

North America's native passenger pigeons became extinct in 1914, and today's familiar urban pigeons are thought to have originated in caves and cliffs in North Africa, the Middle East, and southern Europe. Pigeons were reportedly brought here in the early 1600s by European settlers, probably as livestock meant to serve as food. Today, pigeons occupy such man-made cliffs and caves as buildings, roofs, ledges, and eaves throughout North America. Closely related to doves, pigeons are also called rock doves or rock pigeons by birders.

Tempting Features and Treats for Pigeons

- Pigeons eat lots of weed seeds and grains, so keeping a mixed-vegetation area unmowed will provide food and cover.
- A water source, such as a low birdbath or pool, will keep pigeons nearby, especially in the morning.
- Pigeons prefer to feed on the ground or on low platform feeders.
- When accustomed to being fed by people, pigeons will eat almost anything offered, including popcorn, bread crumbs and crusts, cake, peanuts, and fruit.

Did You Know?

- Pigeons' well-known song is a soft "coo-rooktoo-coo."
- A male pigeon courts by doing a little dance. First he circles around, bowing while fanning out his tail. He puffs his neck, holds his head erect, then high-steps around the courting area, strutting and showing off to the ladies.
- On land, pigeons shuffle about with their heads bobbing up and down, but in flight they're strong and steady (hence their longtime use as messengers and racers).
- Pigeons will peck at the heads of intruders that get too close to their nesting area.
- Compared to other birds, pigeons are sloppy housekeepers. They often build their flimsy nests, which are crude stick platforms, on top of previous ones.
- So-called homing pigeons are the same species as wild pigeons, but they've been bred for generations to quickly return home as soon as they're released. All pigeons can use Earth's magnetic field to orient themselves, and this talent is highly refined in homing pigeons.
- Homing pigeons often are used in races, and members of more than 700 clubs in North America compete to see whose bird makes it home fastest.
- Pigeons are widely used in scientific research, including studies of metabolism, color variation, genetics, behavior, and flight mechanisms. (They can fly up to 60 miles per hour.)

Take a Closer Look

Common Grackle *(Quiscalus quiscula)*

Grackles appear black at first glance, but they're really an iridescent dark purple, purplish green, or dark bronze, depending on region. Grackles' yellow eyes stand out against their dark plumage, and they have long, keel-shaped tails. Females are duller in color and slightly smaller than males. Adult birds are 11 to 13 inches (28 to 33 cm) long. The female grackle builds a cup-shaped nest and lays four or five greenish white, brown-marked eggs. In the East and South, both parents sit on the eggs; in the rest of the country, the female handles incubation by herself.

Feeder Favorites for Grackles

- Sunflower seeds
- Bread crumbs and scraps
- Kitchen vegetable scraps
- Fruit
- Cracked corn
- Other grains and seeds

Regional Relations

Boat-tailed grackles (*Quiscalus major*) and great-tailed grackles (*Q. mexicanus*) are bigger birds with distinctive larger-keeled tails. They're less iridescent; females are tannish. Both share the aggressive nature of common grackles and often are considered pests. Big boat-tailed grackles live along the Gulf and Atlantic Coasts, often rasping their song on telephone poles and power lines. They can grow to 15 inches (38 cm) long. The great-tailed grackles of the South and Southwest are even larger, sometimes up to 18 inches (46 cm) long.

Tempting Features and Treats for Grackles

- Colonies of grackles usually nest in evergreens or shrubs.
- Oaks and other nut-producing trees attract grackles, which will compete with jays and woodpeckers for acorns and nuts to eat.
- Grackles eat frogs and small fish, so they're often attracted to water features.

Did You Know?

- Grackles have long, sturdy, black bills. Sounding as musical as a rusty gate, they emit a "weedle-eek" song and a grating "ack," "chuck," or "swaak" call.
- Native to the wetlands and woods of the Midwest, grackles love farms! These enterprising birds thrive wherever humans cut down forests to make farms instead. Irrigation water, waste grain, and exposed soil make many farms dreams come true for grackles. Grackles will follow tractors to grab grain, insects, and field mice unearthed by the plow.
- Unlike most birds, which hop when they're on the ground, grackles walk.
- When grackles appear at feeders, other birds fly away. To deter persistent raiders, keep a squirt gun handy to douse aggressive grackles.

Birds of a Similar Feather

Grackle relatives include blackbirds, cowbirds, and starlings, which have a shorter tail and yellow bill. But don't be surprised to see mixed flocks of grackles and blackbird cousins feeding together in cold weather. Should such a flock take over a feeding station like a shipload of pirates, you can deter them using the techniques described in Chapter 11, "Less-Wanted Guests: "Pest" Birds and Other Wildlife at Your Feeders."

Look but Don't Feed

Taking stale bread to the park to feed the pigeons is a family tradition in many communities, but public health officials often discourage feeding pigeons anything at all. Leftover food may lead to problems with rats and mice in urban parks, and pigeon droppings require cleanup when large numbers of birds are fed in one place. Sometimes pigeon feeding is restricted to protect water supplies, too, because waste from big flocks can contaminate water with dangerous bacteria. In many cities, droppings are a major problem on houses, cars, and sidewalks. The uric acid in the droppings can eat away the finish on cars and corrode buildings, so it should be rinsed away often. See page 322 in Chapter 11 for tips on preventing pigeon poop problems at your house.

This Means You: Birds and the Law

Before migratory birds were protected by law, it was common for them to be slaughtered, poisoned, captured, sold, or harassed by anyone who wanted to. The Migratory Bird Treaty Act of 1918 (MBTA) changed all that. It makes it unlawful to pursue, hunt, kill, capture, possess, buy, sell, or barter a long list of birds ranging from cardinals to robins. Currently about 800 species are on the protected list.

The law prohibits you from shooting a woodpecker that pounds on your house and bans killing irritating but protected birds such as grackles and blackbirds. Federal laws do not apply to three nonnative birds—house sparrows, starlings, and pigeons—but state and local laws often further define what you can and cannot do about these pest birds. Always check with your local wildlife authorities before you take any steps to address nuisance wildlife. See Chapter 11, "Less-Wanted Guests: 'Pest' Birds and Other Wildlife at Your Feeders," for more information on dealing with birds that sometimes become a pesky presence in your landscape.

When Environmentalists Collide

An interest in the well-being of birds may be just one aspect of a greater interest in the well-being of the environment in which birds—and you—coexist. At the crossroads of bird conservation and the need for sources of clean, sustainable energy, you'll find wind turbines. These gigantic propellers loom over the landscape on poles that rival the heights reached by communications towers. Their spinning blades convert wind into electricity—and pose a collision risk for birds and bats traveling on those same breezes.

As with communications towers, it seems possible to build and manage wind turbines in ways that serve the human population without threatening wild species. Careful site selection is the first step to ensure that "wind farms" aren't placed in the paths of migratory birds or in the habitats of species that would be adversely affected.

DEALING WITH BIRD EMERGENCIES

Sooner or later, every backyard birder encounters a bird that has been injured, orphaned, or is very much dead. There are two simple rules to follow when deciding what to do in these situations. First, be prepared. Second, do no harm.

In terms of being prepared, have several pairs of disposable gloves in an easy-to-reach place, along with a few old towels and rags. Along with these supplies, have the phone number of a nearby wildlife rehabilitation facility handy. Local veterinarians can direct you to area experts who specialize in treating injured or sick wild animals.

BIRDS IN SHOCK

When a scary situation develops, your first step is to secure the area. For the safety of the bird and your pets, remove any cats, dogs, or other animals from the area. The next step is to wait, because birds that fly into windows or appear sick or injured may simply be in shock. Our impulse is to pick up the bird and take it to safety, but don't be too hasty. Sometimes birds in shock make miraculous recoveries by taking a hop or two and then gliding off into the air.

Above all, don't feed baby birds people food. In a pinch, you can make "bird stew" to feed to birds that normally eat insects and seeds by mixing together 1 cup (225 g) canned dog food and ½ cup (113 g) unflavored instant oatmeal. Feed the mixture in an eye dropper, or offer little nuggets with a pair of tweezers. As soon as possible, switch the bird to its normal diet, which may mean catching lots of beetles and earthworms!

Special Disaster Relief

If you find a dead bird with a band on one of its legs, contact the U.S. Geological Survey Bird Banding Laboratory at 800-327-BAND (327-2263) or visit www.pwrc.usgs.gov/bbl. You may be helping a bird behavior study or a study that tracks how long birds live and how they die.

If you find many dead birds at once, call your local or state wildlife agency or health department. Pesticides often are to blame when birds eat seeds that have been treated with insecticides or gorge on insects that have recently been sprayed.

IS IT AN ORPHAN?

We sometimes find baby birds out of their nests. The first thing to do is to move your pets inside. Then before you take further action, watch the young birds closely while looking and listening for cues from their parents. There's a big difference between an orphaned bird and a juvenile out exploring in the company of one or both of its parents.

Is the bird feathered? If so, it's probably a young bird out learning how to walk, feed, and fly. Jays, robins, towhees, and some other songbirds train their young on the ground, while others work with their young in shrubs and thickets. Usually the parents are watching nearby, making plenty of noise to deter intruders and reassure their young ones.

Once you get animals and people into the house, the parents can probably round up the little birds and move them to safety.

If a young bird has no feathers, it's probably a hatchling that has fallen from its nest. If you look up and locate the nest in a place you can reach, gently return the baby to it, wearing gloves if you wish to avoid direct contact with the bird and its nest. The parents may scold you, but they'll take over care of the little guy. Contrary to folklore, handling a bird will not cause the parents to abandon it.

SICK, INJURED, OR DEAD BIRDS

Be very cautious around a bird that appears sick or injured. The survival instinct of a frightened bird is to use its claws and beak, and being held and handled by a human is about the most alarming thing that can happen to a bird. Suit up with long sleeves and gloves, and try to pick the bird up from the rear, cupping it in both hands. Cradle a larger bird in a towel, rag, or T-shirt for transport. Instead of trying to rescue a large bird in distress, such as a duck, goose, heron, or pelican, call your state or local wildlife office, or local wildlife rehabilitator, for assistance.

Casual burial of dead birds is fine if you live in a rural area and can cover the little grave with a stone to deter digging by dogs and other animals. If burial is not an option, wear disposable gloves and roll the body onto a piece of newspaper with a stick. Wrap up the bird in the paper, slip it into a plastic bag, and place it in an outdoor garbage can with a tight-fitting lid.

WEST NILE VIRUS: A THREAT TO BIRDS AND PEOPLE

West Nile virus (WNV) is now permanently established in North America. Transmitted by mosquitoes, WNV can affect humans, birds, horses, and other mammals.

Birds have been particularly hard-hit by WNV, which has been found in about 200 species of dead birds. Crows and robins have been particularly affected, but many other songbirds including blue jays, wrens, chickadees, tufted titmice, and eastern bluebirds have fallen victim to this disease.

Although birds can carry—and die from—West Nile virus, the only way you can become infected is by being bitten by an infected mosquito. Mosquitoes also transmit WNV to birds, so everything you do to control mosquitoes will benefit birds, too.

- Drain any standing water in your area, including water in puddles, tires, trash lids, barrels, gutters, and basins. Dump, clean, and refill your birdbaths at least every 5 days. Under perfect conditions, mosquitoes can transform from egg to adult in about 7 days.
- Work with your neighbors to remove sources of mosquito breeding. Standing or slow-moving water that hosts mosquitoes can be treated with beneficial bacteria (*Bacillus thuringiensis israelensis*) that kill mosquito larvae but are harmless to birds, pets, and people.
- Get involved with local mosquito control programs once you question and are reassured that they're conducted properly. Spraying of mosquito-prone areas should be done at dusk—when the air is still, mosquitoes are active, and most birds have found a place to roost for the night.

While outside, take steps to protect yourself from female mosquitoes in search of a warm body (they must have a blood meal before they can reproduce). Use insect repellent when outdoors or wear long sleeves and pants, socks, and other protective clothing. Take special care early in the morning or just after sundown, when mosquitoes feed most intensively.

Chapter 10

UNDERSTANDING BIRD BEHAVIORS

Providing feeders and nest boxes while adding plants to create great habitat for birds will triple the number of birds that visit your yard. Each day you'll witness scenes that will make you wonder: What are those birds doing? And why? This chapter explores common and not-so-common bird behaviors and the motives behind them, which might be related to courting a mate, holding a territory, or rearing a successful family in less than 6 weeks.

From singing at dawn to funny face-offs at the feeder, few things that birds do are random events. Most are related to the most important task in any bird's life, which is to raise healthy offspring. Breeding activities run in seasonal cycles, so one of the best ways to track bird conduct is to consider various manners and their meanings at different times of year. The more you know, the less likely you are to disapprove of the bossy attitudes of goldfinches or mockingbirds, and you'll surely admire the leadership of chickadees, who are often followed by titmice, sparrows, and other birds because of their superior talent for finding food. As your understanding of birds deepens, so will your fascination with the private lives of the winged characters that call your yard their home.

BIRD BEHAVIOR THROUGH THE SEASONS

Experiments with wild birds raised in captivity have shown that birds are born knowing many of the motives and skills they'll need to get through life. Even when reared in cages, migratory birds know when to fly north or south, as well as the right direction in which to go. Males know the basics of their species' most popular territorial and mating song, and females have definite notions on the best way to build a nest. Still, birds accumulate crucial knowledge as they gain experience, and it's this drama that makes backyard bird-watching so interesting. By watching bird behaviors change through the seasons, you can come to understand not only what birds are doing, but why.

Powerful themes such as claiming and defending a territory in spring or forming flocks in fall are explored in the pages that follow. If you're a beginning birder, use this brief overview of seasonal changes in the bird world as an introduction to the private lives of your backyard birds.

Spring

- The northward spring migration begins in February and lasts into early June in the Far North. In mild southern climates, birds present all winter may suddenly disappear. See page 136 for maps of the most heavily used migratory highways in the sky.
- The intensity of birdsong reaches its annual high as resident and migrant species establish territories and form partnerships with new or old mates.
- Nest building becomes fervent by late spring. Birdsong quiets a bit as females incubate their first clutch of eggs.

Summer

- Parent birds work from dawn to dusk to feed their young. Most make more than 50 trips each day to gather food for their nestlings.
- Hummingbirds find flower gardens and vie for airspace with insects and other hummingbirds.
- Chipping or scolding sounds heard in shrubs and thickets indicate the presence of parents teaching fledglings how to feed and take care of themselves. As soon as fledglings can hop from branch to branch, the nests of most species are abandoned. After a few weeks, the nests may be reused for a second brood.
- Birds often continue to visit feeders as pairs or in small flocks. Small flocks of adults and juveniles are likely to be family groups.
- When their parenting duties ease, mated pairs become more visible as they expand their feeding ranges.
- Numerous birds use birdbaths or other water features for grooming, drinking, or cooling off on hot days.
- In late summer, most birds molt by shedding old feathers and growing new ones.

Fall

- Migratory species seek out high-fat foods to accumulate energy reserves. Most neotropical migrants leave their summer breeding grounds by late August.
- Bird behaviors change as individuals leave their families and assemble in flocks. Some flocks include birds of different species that share similar tastes in food and habitat.

BUDGET-WISE BIRDING

Keep a Calendar

When calendars go on sale in January, buy one to keep near your favorite bird-watching window. Jot down notes when you observe birds courting, fighting, or gathering nesting materials, as well as dates when summer or winter birds make their first appearance in your yard. In future years, you can use this information to fine-tune your feeding practices, or to put up new nesting boxes or clean out old ones.

- As trees shed their leaves, you can see the locations of formerly hidden nests. Roosting spots for year-round birds become easier to spot, too.
- In mild-winter areas, short-distance migrants arrive from colder climes. Some may claim territories, while others wander widely in search of food.

Winter

- Flocking behavior continues through the cold season for most species, though woodpeckers and a few other birds stick together in pairs.
- Prime activity areas move from treetops to low shrubs or dense evergreen branches, which offer superior protection from frigid weather.
- As days lengthen in February, birds begin singing again, tuning up for the breeding season ahead.

SECURING SPACE IN SPRING

Imagine a world in which every spring, most of the homes in your town are left vacant. You're anticipating a summer caring for three small children, so you all need a safe place to live where you won't have to run yourself ragged keeping your brood healthy and well-fed. As long as you get there first, you can claim any house in town. Which one will it be?

This is precisely the challenge birds face in spring, when males strike out as early as they can in search of a summer home. Just as the early bird gets the worm, the first birds to arrive in promising breeding grounds get first choice of homesites. When the ladies show up a week or so later, they'll be checking out the males based on how they look, sound, and conduct themselves, yet the females will also be looking beyond the flashy feathers at the home grounds the males have claimed for the season. Male birds select their territory, but females make the choice to accept a male and his real estate as a package deal.

The Advantages of Coming Home

Numerous birds from robins to warblers do their best to return to nesting sites where they reared healthy young the year before—which might be certain trees or thickets in your yard. By reclaiming a territory they already know, birds face fewer territorial challenges from other birds and spend less time looking for food and shelter. Plus, they have friendly relationships in place with the neighbors, because individuals of different species often share territorial rights. Studies have shown that many birds recognize the songs of other species that nested nearby in previous years and can tell the difference between old acquaintances and new arrivals.

Sing for Your Supper

Birds use song to court mates, but the most important purpose of singing is to maintain territories. Individuals that hold prime territories must sing longer and stronger than other birds, but all that singing is worthwhile if it safeguards a good food supply or discourages rivals. In studies of mockingbirds and song sparrows, birds with the largest repertoires did a better job of attracting mates, holding valuable territory, and avoiding direct conflict with rivals. Birds are born knowing the basics of their species' song, but they become better singers after a year or two of practice.

Track Cancelled Flights

During spring and fall migration seasons, watching the weather forecast can help you guess when you'll see flycatchers and other migrants on the move. Most migratory birds fly at night, but they come down from the sky when storms or strong winds make flying impossible. Have your binoculars ready for action the morning after a nighttime storm. In the first few hours after daybreak, you may see species that found overnight accommodations in the trees and shrubs in your yard. After spending the day resting up, they'll likely resume their travel agenda as evening falls.

Check for Birds on Radar

In spring and fall, so many birds may be using the major migratory flyways (see page 136) that the flocks show up on weather radar. If you look carefully at a radar map of your area just after nightfall on a clear evening and see scattered pixels moving faster or in a different direction from the wind, they're probably "clouds" of migrating birds. Once they're aloft, migratory birds typically travel between 30 and 50 miles (48 and 80 km) per hour.

EVERYBODY WINS

Keep Your Distance

Birds already expend huge amounts of energy defending their territory from other birds, and keeping your distance saves them from feeling that they have to defend themselves from you, too. By watching nesting birds from afar, the birds in your yard won't waste time and calories heckling you with scolding calls or frantically swooping from branch to branch in an attempt to make you go away.

Take a Closer Look

Northern Mockingbird *(Mimus polyglottos)*

Large gray birds with light gray breasts and charcoal wings with white wing bars, mockingbirds often show off their white tail feathers when they want to attract attention. Males and females look alike. As fledglings mature, their eyes change from black to yellow. Adult birds are 10 inches (25 cm) long. Mockingbirds build a bulky, cup-shaped nest of thorny twigs and other plant and man-made materials and line it with fine grass, hair, and soft plant matter. The female lays three to five blue-green, brown-spotted eggs.

Feeder Favorites for Mockingbirds

- Suet
- Peanut butter
- Dried tart fruits
- Stale doughnuts

Tempting Features and Treats for Mockingbirds

- Mockingbirds often forage for insects in freshly mowed lawns.
- In winter, mockingbirds eagerly gather the shriveled hips from multiflora rose, which is an invasive plant. Plant noninvasive roses that produce small hips to attract mockingbirds.
- Mockers are so territorial that it's best to give them their own suet feeder in winter. Once they claim a feeder, they often chase away other birds that attempt to stop in for a bite.

Did You Know?

- Mockingbirds often flash their wings as they hop along the ground or when they return to their nests. A sudden flash of white wing bars may help startle insects or it might get the attention of hatchlings that are ready to be fed.
- Most mockingbirds mate for life, but should a nearby female lose her mate while she's rearing young, a neighboring male may take on the responsibilities of guarding and feeding two nests.
- Both male and female mockingbirds sing, but males sing the most. Each year they learn new songs, often borrowing sounds from other birds. A 6-year-old male mockingbird may know as many as 200 short songs.
- The northern mockingbird is the state bird of five southern states: Arkansas, Florida, Mississippi, Tennessee, and Texas. Mockingbirds are year-round residents in the South, but in recent years many have begun flying a few hundred miles northward to breed. They also may have moved north and west to follow the spread of one of their favorite foods, the invasive multiflora rose.

Dive-Bombing Birds

Mockingbirds often nest rather close to the ground, in shrubs or small trees, within easy reach of cats, snakes, squirrels, and other predators. But when mockingbirds are taking care of their young, the male becomes so assertive that pets and people quickly learn to avoid the area. His usual method of attack is to fly a short distance upward and then swoop down so close that you can hear the rush of air as his wings stop just short of your head. Cats or dogs may be pecked. Some backyard birders have noticed that mockingbirds can even tell the difference between strangers and the person who stocks the bird feeders. With humans they deem less threatening, mockingbirds are more likely to fuss and scold than to dive-bomb people who get too close to their nests.

HOLDING TOP TERRITORIES

For birds, holding a fine territory is more about health than power. Studies have shown that birds in control of their territories' food supplies can cut their food foraging time by 20 percent or more. Most importantly, males who successfully hold their territories with strong song or intimidating flight displays never have to risk their lives in beak-to-beak combat.

Female birds will actively defend their nests (see page 305), but in the world of birds, maintaining territorial boundaries is a man's job. Most of a male's territorial actions are intended to discourage birds of the same species that might be after his mate or his food supply. The action escalates when an intruder crosses the resident male's property line.

Defense Strategies

- Long-range defense consists mainly of songs or calls that can be heard over a wide area. Potential rivals know that only strong, experienced birds produce loud, polished songs. Challenging such a property holder would involve risk of serious injury.
- A tough-guy routine commences should a male decide a rival is too close for comfort. Intense singing may be accompanied by piercing, scolding calls and showy aerial displays, as if the defending bird is saying, "You want a fight? Come on, I can take you!"
- In many species, direct conflicts are handled with face-offs, in which male birds stand a short distance apart, waving their beaks and showing their wings. These displays often settle conflicts, but when they fail, the birds may violently peck or claw at each other as a last resort.

THE NEED TO BREED

By the time males arrive at their summer breeding grounds and claim a territory, hormonal changes will have caused their sexual organs to grow to 10 times their normal size. You know what's on their minds! By the time the ladies arrive, the males are ready to sing, strut, and show off their agility as fliers. While females check out the territory for nest sites and convenient food and water, they're constantly distracted by males trying to get their attention. Kingfishers may offer a gift of fish, but a male song sparrow may suddenly fly in and knock over a female he wants to impress. Pigeons sometimes establish pair bonds by touching beaks. Birds that are mainly monogamous often get reacquainted with old mates, often in old, familiar territory. In a high quality territory where males are vying for dominance, a female may begin building a nest before she has finished choosing a mate.

Flirtatious Floaters

If they were human, you might call them gigolos or home wreckers, but flirtatious unmated male birds are called floaters. In most species, these guys hang around the edges of the territories of mated pairs, hoping for a morning when one of the resident males fails to sing. When an undefended territory or a nesting female becomes available, the floater moves in and stops his wandering ways.

Take a Closer Look

Northern Flicker *(Colaptes auratus)*

Large, sturdy birds with spotted breasts and brown wings barred with black, both male and female flickers have gray heads, black throat patches, and red patches on their cheeks or on the backs of their necks. Adult birds are 12 inches (30 cm) long. Like other woodpeckers, flickers nest in cavities that the male excavates. The nest holds five to eight unmarked white eggs on a bed of wood chips or sawdust within the cavity. Both parents sit on the eggs.

Feeder Favorites for Flickers

- Suet
- Cracked corn
- Shelled peanuts
- Dried fruits
- Sunflower seeds

Regional Relations

Flickers are sometimes sorted into sub-species, which often interbreed. In the East, the wings of the yellow-shafted subspecies have a golden cast, and the red patch is on the back of the head. In the West, the red-shafted form shows rosy color on the undersides of its wings and has its red patch on its cheek.

Tempting Features and Treats for Flickers

- Dead trees, or large trees holding thick dead branches, are the main feature flickers seek when looking for nesting or roosting sites.
- When dead trees aren't available, flickers will accept nesting boxes that are 7 inches (18 cm) square and 16 to 20 inches (40 to 50 cm) tall. The entry hole should measure 7½ inches (19 cm) across.
- Adding several handfuls of coarse wood chips will make a nesting box more appealing to flickers.
- In winter, flickers love to eat poison ivy berries. They also often peck up the fallen fruits of bayberries, grapes, and wild cherries.

Did You Know?

- The northern flicker is the state bird of Alabama, where it's known as the yellowhammer. Like other woodpeckers, flickers like to drum on resonant surfaces.
- Flickers are devoted mates during the summer breeding season, but most alliances end in fall, with flickers taking new mates the following year.
- A flicker's diet is about 60 percent animal and 40 percent vegetable. Most of the animal portion is ants, and the vegetable portion is berries.
- Flickers live year-round in most parts of North America. Some migrate a few hundred miles to breed in the Far North and return to more temperate climates in winter.

Check the Buzz

Should a flicker seem so interested in your house that it starts pecking at exterior woodwork, check for appliances on the inside wall that emit humming sounds. Flickers may mistake the hum of a computer or fan for the sound of wood-boring insects, especially carpenter ants. Moving the sound source may bring relief from unwanted flicker activity. If there's no obvious hum inside your home that's attracting the birds, consider the possibility that pests may be lurking within exterior wood.

Doing the Wic-Ka Dance

Most birds engage in show-off courtship behavior, but few performances are as sophisticated as the body- and beak-waving "dance" done by two competing male—or female—flickers. While a flicker of the opposite sex watches, the two competitors sit facing each other on a branch, waving their beaks back and forth in a figure eight pattern while calling "wic-ka wic-ka" in unison. The flashing of wing and tail feathers may accompany the dance. If you see the 10-second display once, keep a sharp eye out for repeated performances. The same dueling pair may repeat the dance several times, take a break, and then move to another branch to continue the dance.

THE SPRING NESTING SEASON

Almost all birds devote spring and early summer to raising a family. As soon as a pair is formed—or sometimes before—the female takes the lead in building a nest. In some species the male is an active participant, but it's the female who dedicates her life to the task. She arranges twigs, grasses, mud, string, spiderwebs and other materials just so and pauses frequently to press her breast into the bowl or cup-shaped bottom to make sure it's an exact fit. While the female works, the male often sings from a nearby branch or bush, drawing attention away from the location of the evolving nest.

Researchers have found that nest-building is instinctive behavior. Wild birds reared in captivity build the same style of nest typical of their species. Yet birds do learn through doing, because experienced females build stronger, tighter nests than first-timers. A few birds, such as large crows, spend a month or more building a large domed nest with front and back doors. Smaller species usually manage to build a sturdy nest in less than a week. Then there are ground nesters like killdeer and ducks, which gain camouflage for their eggs by laying them in a minimally prepared nesting spot.

Make Some Mud

Swallows, robins, and a few other birds shape their nests with mud. If there isn't a pond or stream nearby, you can provide mud by mixing soil and water together in a shallow plastic bin placed in an open area.

HOW TO SPOT A NEST

Many people think birds need nests in which to live, but many species use nests for only as long as it takes to rear their young. Birds that produce more than one brood each season may add a fresh layer to an old nest and reuse it, but not until the first group of fledglings is out and on its own. The best seasons for nest spotting are late spring and early summer. Abandoned nests become visible when trees and shrubs shed their leaves in fall.

Watch for female birds carrying bits of grass, twigs, or other fibers in their beaks, and watch where they go. Most female birds make hundreds of trips to and from their nests as they build them.

As you walk around your yard, listen for scolding calls and watch for the showy flapping of wings—two common ways birds tell you (or your dog) that you have come too close to their nest.

Once you've located a nest, find a nearby spot with good visibility for nest watching, but don't go too close to the nest. There will be little to see for a few weeks, and female birds need peace and quiet while they incubate their eggs.

MIND YOUR NEST-WATCHING MANNERS

If you've located a nest, it's fine to take quick looks inside as long as you mind your manners and avoid doing anything that would interfere with adult birds tending the nest or put the nesting birds in danger.

- Check nests at midday, the quiet break between morning and afternoon feeding times.
- Instead of climbing a ladder or tree to look into a nest, attach a small mirror to a pole to enhance your viewing.
- Never touch a nest and avoid touching nearby vegetation. Your scent won't drive away parent birds but it could attract predators to the area.
- Don't prune off branches that may be blocking your view, because doing so will expose the nest to the eyes of more dangerous predators.
- When going to watch a nest in the woods, include it in a loop trail rather than walking directly to it and back again. That way, your scent trail won't lead straight to the nest.

Stop Hubcap Attacks

Sometimes male birds become convinced that their archrivals are waiting to fight them every day—only their adversaries are their own reflections in gazing balls, or more often in car mirrors, bumpers, or hubcaps. In normal life, birds do not often engage in direct physical confrontation, but during breeding season (which sets their manly hormones on high), male birds can't tolerate the idea of a rival in their territory—even if it's just a reflection. To keep the bird from bloodying its beak in such futile battles, cover car mirrors or other small objects with paper bags for a few weeks. To help birds lose interest in a hubcap or bumper, tape plastic wrap or opaque paper over it. You can also protect the affected surfaces by "painting" them with a soupy mix of water, flour, and soap. Wash away the residue after a few weeks, when nesting season is over and most birds lose interest in the fight.

THE BIRD MATERNITY WARD

Once a nest is built—or an appropriate tree cavity or nesting box made ready—bird couples waste no time filling them with eggs. Most birds lay two to three eggs, though some species may lay six or more. Females typically lay one egg each day until the clutch is complete and then they may take a day or two off before they begin sitting on the nest.

Meanwhile, hormonal changes associated with nest building and egg laying cause a patch of feathers to fall from the female's breast, exposing a bare spot called the brood patch. Each time a female bird returns to the nest after feeding, she will carefully arrange herself so that the brood patch is in direct contact with the eggs. In addition to warming the eggs with direct skin-to-egg transfer of her body heat, the mother bird uses the patch as a sensing device to tell her if her eggs become too warm. To make sure the eggs receive even warmth, most species turn their eggs at least once a day. Males of many species help incubate eggs or bring the female food so she can stay in the nest for long periods of time.

Are They Warm Enough?

Normal body temperature for most birds is above 104°F (40°C), but the best incubation temperature for eggs is just above 98°F (36.6°C). Adequate warmth from the mother's brood patch keeps incubation moving along at a steady pace, but there's no need to worry if a mother bird leaves her nest for several hours—or even an entire day. Cooling of eggs is much less dangerous than having them overheat, which is probably why most bird species rear their young early in the season, before the onset of summer's heat.

Handling Fallen Nests

Birds abandon nests after their fledglings learn to fly, or sometimes even before they lay the first egg! Technically, it's illegal to collect any type of bird nest, but you can make an exception with nests that are torn from trees by storms. Do wear gloves to avoid contact with parasites, and let the nest dry thoroughly in the sun before bringing it indoors. The following spring, keep a close eye on the tree or shrub near where you found the nest. With luck, the same birds will return to build a new one.

THE IMPORTANCE OF GOOD HOUSEKEEPING

Birds carry a number of parasites, including mites, ticks, flies, lice, and fleas. These parasites naturally flourish in the nest, though parent birds do their best to keep conditions as clean as possible. Fecal pellets often are collected and removed, and some birds use their wings to keep the nest dry during heavy downpours. Parasites are a good reason to get the new family moved out of the nest as quickly as possible. Species that raise more than one brood of young each year usually build a second nest rather than reusing one that's crawling with parasites.

WATCHING THE WONDER

Bird species vary in how long eggs take to hatch and how long parents feed hatchlings in the nest. In the table below, days for egg incubation is the average time between when the last egg is laid and the first egg hatches. Then comes the intense period of feeding, as the parents raise their young until they're ready to leave the nest.

Bird Species	Days for Egg Incubation	Days from Hatching to Fledging
Barn owl	32–34	45–58
Barn swallow	14–16	18–23
Blue jay	17	17–19
Bluebird	12–18	16–21
Brown thrasher	12–14	9–12
Cardinal	12–13	9–11
Cedar waxwing	12–16	14–18
Chickadees	12	16
Downy woodpecker	11–12	21
Goldfinch	12–14	11–15
House wren	12–15	16–17
Indigo bunting	12	10–12
Kingbird	14–16	14–17
Mockingbird	12–13	10–13
Mourning dove	14–15	12–14
Nighthawk	19–20	21
Nuthatch	12	14
Phoebe	16	18
Pileated woodpecker	15–16	28–35
Purple martin	15–16	27–35
Red-eyed vireo	11–14	10–12
Robin	12–14	14–16
Ruby-throated hummingbird	16	30
Sparrows	11–12	9–10
Towhee	12–13	10–12
Tufted titmouse	13–14	17–18
Warblers	10–13	9–11
Wood thrush	12–13	12–14

Take a Closer Look

Killdeer *(Charadrius vociferus)*

Snow-white below and rich brown above, killdeer sport two black rings around their necks and a third black streak over their foreheads. In flight, an orange patch above their tails becomes visible. Male and female killdeer look alike. Adult birds are 10½ inches (27 cm) long. Ground-nesting killdeer do not build true nests. Instead, they scrape away a comfortable place for their three to five tan speckled eggs, which look like stones. A nest would ruin the eggs' very effective camouflage. Unlike most songbirds, killdeer young hatch wearing down, which they quickly exchange for feathers resembling those of adult birds. Within hours after hatching, they follow their parents away from their birthplace to begin learning how to forage for insects.

Regional Relations

Although you can find killdeer living far inland, their closest relatives are the mostly shore-dwelling plovers also in the genus *Charadrius*. The loss of habitat and disruption of beach nesting areas by people, pets, and vehicles have dramatically reduced populations of piping plovers (*C. melodius*), Wilson's plovers (*C. wilsonia*), and snowy plovers (*C. alexandrinus*). Some beach communities now fence off known plover nesting areas in hopes of helping the birds to make a comeback. Like its cousin the killdeer, the mountain plover (*C. montanus*) often lives in dry fields, far from water.

Tempting Features and Treats for Killdeer

- Water features with shallow edges may be visited by killdeer in search of aquatic insects and larvae.
- Patches of tall grass that are mowed once or twice a summer offer plenty of grasshoppers and beetles—mainstays of a killdeer's diet.
- In cities, killdeer often nest on gravel rooftops.

Did You Know?

- Killdeer can live to be 10 to 11 years old. Mated pairs often stay together for many years.
- Killdeer fly south in fall to avoid cold northern winters. In climates where the ground does not stay frozen through winter, killdeer can find food year-round.
- Newly hatched killdeer chicks are "precocial," meaning they wear a covering of down and can walk—unlike most songbird hatchlings that are naked and helpless (known as "altricial").
- Like other plovers, killdeer run from place to place as they feed, rather than hopping or flying.
- Although they often run along the ground like their shorebird relatives, killdeer are excellent fliers and may reach speeds of more than 50 miles per hour (80 kph) in the air.
- Killdeer eat some seeds and berries, but they're insatiable consumers of grasshoppers and other insects. Although killdeer are rarely seen at feeders, they often nest in open areas in parks, playgrounds, and ball fields. Surprisingly tolerant of human activity, killdeer pairs often return to suburban sites where they successfully reared young in the past.

Everybody Wins

Leash at the Beach

Killdeer and other plovers love life at the beach, but the lively way they draw attention away from their young (see "Protective Parenting" on the opposite page) often backfires when the predator is a dog. Even well-behaved dogs can't resist the urge to go after a large, apparently injured bird, so keep your dog leashed at the beach and avoid walking Rover in areas designated as shorebird nest sites.

PROTECTIVE PARENTING

Killdeer are famous for their "broken wing" drama, in which a parent bird runs in front of a potential predator, dragging a wing so that it looks injured. The idea is to lure attention away from the nest, and it's a ruse that works almost every time. When the adult leads the predator far enough away, it flies off to safety.

Many other ground-nesting birds such as quail, grouse, cranes, and even roadrunners use the broken wing display, and in some species it's more often done by the female than the male. Instead of feigning injury, a male bird may fluff up his chest, flap his wings, and call out to attract attention, or fly in front of an unwanted intruder. On woodsy hiking trails, wild turkeys may make quite a show of leading you away from their nests. In your own backyard, mourning doves that suddenly seem chummy may be doing their best to keep you disinterested in their nest. Should you hear a strange hissing sound coming from a tree, it could be an owl trying to pass itself off as a snake—a sure way to discourage visitors near its nest.

Because birds are so protective of their young, some biologists think that it was one of the main motivators for birds to develop and refine the ability to fly. Once they became equipped with wings, they could make use of nesting sites that had far fewer predators than those close to the ground.

An adult killdeer that appears to be hurt is more likely to be acting than injured. Most ground-nesting bird species have a well-rehearsed performance that they put on whenever a predator threatens their nest.

MYSTERIES OF THE EMPTY NEST

Most birds continue to feed their young for 3 weeks or so after they leave the nest. Juveniles follow the parents as they feed, watching and learning how it's done, yet pausing often to beg for food. Like many other species, flicker parents encourage independence among their offspring by making them go hungry when it's time to take a scary step. About 26 days after hatching, the parents reduce the food they provide, so that the fledglings are motivated to take their first hops. Within a month after leaving the nest, fledgling flickers that are able fliers are turned away when they ask their parents for food.

TAKING SECOND CHANCES

Meanwhile, bird parents have other things on their minds. Urban birds in particular rear more than one brood during summer, sometimes by adding second or third stories to their original nest so that the new clutch of eggs sits in a clean bowl. Sometimes pairs build new nests altogether. Song sparrows rear up to four broods each summer, house wrens and bluebirds often rear three, and cardinals seldom stop before they've finished rearing two groups of young.

When you notice adult birds of any species gathering nesting materials in midsummer, you're seeing evidence that your yard is developing into a high quality bird habitat. Landscapes that provide birds with safe places to nest and a dependable supply of food support multiple brooding of wild birds. Warblers and other species that typically rear one brood per summer may invest their time and energy in a second one in very high quality habitats.

MARRIED TO THE MOB

When small birds gang up to harass larger ones, it's called mobbing. Some birds are much more likely to mob or be mobbed than others. Owls, for example, run such a high risk of being mobbed that they remain hidden and still during daytime hours. To bring out mob-minded birds so their pictures can be taken, some wildlife photographers play a tape of owl or hawk calls. If they're in a responsive mood, secretive warblers and other small birds will quickly come out of the trees, ready for a fight. Fight is not quite accurate, because mobbing irritates and drives away potential predators, but mobbers usually stop short of actual attacks. The group harassment strategy works, and carries with it several more remarkable advantages.

- Mobbing usually begins with a distress call from a single male as he takes to the air in pursuit of a predator, which might be a larger bird, a snake, or perhaps even you!
- Birds are most likely to mob during nesting season and are least likely to mob when they're passing through unfamiliar territory.
- Hawks and other birds of prey are more likely to be mobbed in flight than while perching.
- Jays, gulls, terns, and blackbirds often mob together in a single-species group, but many other birds band together into temporary mobs. The "we need to mob" call made by chickadees is understood by a number of small songbirds, so they often lead impromptu mixed-species mobs.
- Yearling birds, especially males, may be led into mobs by older birds in order to give them a close-up education on common predators.

- When challenged by a mob, a large bird usually changes direction and flies away. It has nothing to gain by fighting back and could sustain a serious injury. When mobbed by mockingbirds, thrashers, or robins, cats seek shelter or ask to come indoors.

HE'S GOT A FISH! MOB HIM!

When you see smaller birds mobbing a larger one, and the big bird is holding something in its talons, don't jump to the heartbreaking conclusion that the predator has made off with a baby bird. It's more likely that the large bird is simply carrying nest-building materials or another type of prey, such as a small rodent or fish. The sight of a predator carrying prey often triggers the mob response, or it could be that blackbirds, swallows, and other birds that are quick to form mobs know there's a reduced risk of retaliation if the mobbed bird's dangerous talons are busy holding something it wants to keep.

Every individual involved in mobbing exercises some restraint, because the cost of a high-speed injury might be death. A peregrine falcon diving for prey can reach speeds in excess of 100 miles (161 km) an hour, but birds of various sizes often fly between 20 and 30 miles (32 and 48 km) per hour (imagine the head-on collision of two racing bicyclists at top speed). Wing to wing midair collisions are avoided using the rear-end approach. Most mobbing moves come from above and behind, the safest approaches for open-air "get out of town" chases.

Mob Magnets

- **Hawks are mobbed by a huge range of smaller birds,** from crows to other hawks. Hawk mobbing is so popular among red-winged blackbirds and swallows that it may be done for sport.
- **Crows usually leave an area (under loud protest)** before they're mobbed, though a trail of jays or robins may dart and chatter behind them.
- **There's no size limit on mobbing,** which is even done by hummingbirds should they feel that their nests may be threatened by another type of bird.

Finding safety in numbers, smaller birds often join forces to drive away a crow that is perceived as a threat to their nests.

THE LATE SUMMER MOLTING SEASON

By the time they're finished building nests, incubating eggs, and rearing their young, parent birds are tired, and it shows. Like human hair, feathers are comprised of dead tissue that breaks and becomes shabby with wear. Rather than go into winter with a worn set of feathers, birds shed the old ones and grow new ones. This process, called molting, takes 5 to 12 weeks for most species. Long-lived raptors, however, may take 2 years to gradually grow a new set of feathers.

Molting season is the most challenging time to identify birds, and sorting out the species is made even more confusing because so many juveniles are flitting in and out of the picture. Although young birds share their parents' silhouettes, they often resemble other species in the colors of their plumage. In their first year of life, young male birds may look more like Mom than Dad until they mature and develop the breeding plumage that's meant to help them attract a mate.

Mopey Molters

Growing a new set of feathers takes a lot of energy, so molting birds often reduce their activity levels, staying in a quiet, restful state until the process is complete. They still need plenty of food, and berry-eating birds tend to develop their brightest colors when they consume dark-colored fruits that are rich in anthocyanins (red-blue pigments). Birds that reared more than one nest of offspring may appear especially lethargic. Multiple broods delay molting, leaving just enough time for new feather development before summer turns to fall.

Why Molting Matters

In most birds, new feathers push out the old ones, in much the same way that human baby teeth are replaced by permanent ones. How and when molting proceeds varies with its season and purpose.

- **In spring,** male birds become more colorful as old, worn feathers are shed, revealing brighter feathers beneath. In buntings, tanagers, and warblers, this is called the prenuptial molt.
- **Migratory birds go through a complete molt after they finish rearing their young.** A fresh set of feathers serves them well on their long southward journeys.
- **Juvenile birds cross the bridge to independence as they molt in late summer.** The new feathers of yearling birds often show dull colors, which become brighter the following spring when worn feathers are shed.
- **Because woodpeckers use their rigid tail feathers to balance as they feed,** they're replaced in pairs rather than all at once.

Take a Closer Look

American Crow *(Corvus brachyrhynchos)*

Large jet black birds that travel about in pairs or small groups are usually crows. You can also identify crows by their loud "caw" calls. Adults are 17½ inches (45 cm) long. Crows build substantial platform nests out of sticks, grass, bark, feathers, and other coarse materials to hold their four to six brown-spotted blue- to gray-green eggs. Great horned owls sometimes claim crows' nests for their own.

Regional Relations

If you live near Puget Sound, you may see the northwestern crow (*Corvus caurinus*), which looks much like an American crow, but is slightly smaller. Throughout mid-Atlantic and southeast regions, the fish crow (*C. ossifragus*) is quite common. It has a longer tail and slightly longer wings compared with the American crow. With a wingspan of 53 inches (1.35 m), the common raven (*C. corax*) is bigger than even a large crow, and its beak is noticeably sturdier, too. While American crows are widespread across the United States and southern Canada, ravens range over the western third of North America from Mexico into Alaska and throughout northernmost Canada; in the eastern United States, they live mainly along the Appalachian Mountains.

Did You Know?

- If a crow can't crack a nut, clam, or egg, it may fly up and drop it onto a hard surface in order to get at what's inside.
- Grasshoppers and beetles are important foods for hatchling crows. Parents may feed each baby twice an hour for over a month!
- On cold winter nights, crows may lower their body temperature to 100°F (38°C)—about 3 degrees lower than normal.
- Crows are omnivores that feed on everything from grain and garbage to roadkill and small reptiles. They also cache food, storing it away in hiding places to eat later.
- Crows, jays, magpies, and other blackbird relatives waste no time moving their young out of the nest, and for the rest of the summer they may stick together in family groups. If the parents raise a second brood, the new generation's older brothers and sisters may even help feed and defend them. In winter, both sets of offspring may stay with the family group or meld with a larger flock.
- In summer, crows live in extended family groups of a dozen or so related birds. In winter, they often join mass roosts, where thousands of birds converge in a tree during the night.
- According to the Cornell Lab of Ornithology, West Nile virus has taken a heavy toll on crows, which typically die within a week of being infected by the disease.
- Crows are frequent predators of smaller birds' nests, often eating eggs and young hatchlings.

The History of Crows

Fossil records indicate that crows have been around for nearly a million years and have benefited from North America's transition from forest to farmland. Crows often eat newly planted corn seeds and pull up vegetable seedlings, so millions of birds have been killed for trespassing onto farm fields. Now grain farmers will tolerate a few crows because they consume so many insects. In summer, the crow's diet includes many pests such as snails, grasshoppers, and caterpillars.

In the past, crows' intelligence led them to be kept as pets. Thomas Jefferson's pet crow is reported to have even learned a few human words. It's now illegal to keep crows in cages.

WHEN CROWS COME TO TOWN

Cities and towns from Kansas to New York share a serious problem every winter. Flocks of crows ranging from 1,000 to 75,000 individuals establish winter roosts in street-side trees, drenching cars and sidewalks with their droppings, and making sleeping late impossible for people. Beyond being messy, these roosts may pose a public health hazard. But getting roosting crows to disperse is far from simple. Trained wildlife control professionals typically use a combination of harassment techniques including exploding shells and firecrackers and playing tapes of crow death cries and hawk screams at earsplitting volume. To be effective, crow hazing must be conducted several days in a row, in early evening or just before dawn, the times when crows are naturally mobile. The plans may backfire when crows forced to abandon a roost next to the county courthouse find a new roost near a church or school. To avoid such failures, some crow control specialists use trained hawks and falcons, broadcasted distress calls, high-powered spotlights, and fireworks to move crows to places where they can safely be allowed to wait out winter.

How Smart Are Crows?

Captive crows have learned to mimic the human voice, match symbols with numbers, and solve simple puzzles. Wild crows often hide caches of food, and though they can't spend money or drive cars, they often collect shiny things including coins, car keys, or even jewelry. Crows look at everything with a sharp omnivore's eyes, and it's possible that their flexible food habits and lack of migratory commitments simply leave them time to indulge their natural curiosity.

Add Sparkle to Your Scarecrow

A scarecrow is an interesting piece of garden art for many people, but you'll need a working scarecrow to actually scare away crows.

- Construct a scarecrow with a post up its back so you can move it easily from one spot to another.
- Every week or so, give your scarecrow a flashy makeover by attaching dangling metal pie pans, CDs, or other shiny objects to its arms or head.
- When extra defenses are needed, give your scarecrow a helium-filled Mylar party balloon to hold in its hand.
- Use a small radio playing in the garden to keep crows from pecking into almost-ripe melons. You can turn it off at night, when crows roost in trees.

THE FORMATION OF FLOCKS

Many seabirds live in communal flocks year-round, but among backyard birds only swallows and martins typically breed while living in flocks. But in late summer, as adults of many other species recover from nesting and young birds become able to fend for themselves, they, too, assemble into groups or flocks. Fiercely territorial birds like buntings and kingbirds accept the company of only two or three companions, while several family groups of robins, cedar waxwings, or crows may merge into roving bands. In good weather, these late summer alliances may break apart during the day, with birds feeding and flitting wherever they like, and then reconvene at night, when birds roost together in shrubs and trees.

Bird experts point out that living in flocks provides birds with a safer, more relaxed lifestyle compared with going it alone or in pairs. Threats are easily detected when several pairs of eyes perceive them, and being in the group may ease worries about orientation and finding food. In exchange for this security, flock members must learn to get along within the flock's social structure, which is usually dominated by a mature male. Females have a pecking order, too, with young birds expected to be submissive followers. Mates of high-ranking males tend to enjoy high status within the flock.

Double Up on Feeders

Should a mixed flock show up in your yard during winter, you can guarantee many happy returns by offering sunflower seed for the chickadees and titmice and suet for the nuthatches and woodpeckers.

LIVING IN MIXED COMPANIES

Several birds that are likely to visit feeders year-round also tend to form off-season alliances with birds of other species. Chickadees, titmice, and nuthatches often live and feed together harmoniously and may be joined by kinglets or brown creepers. Whenever one of these mixed-species flocks passes through the territory of downy or hairy woodpeckers, the woodpeckers often stay with the flock for several days—or even weeks

Flying in Formation

Some flocks fly in noisy, chaotic groups, but birds with territory to cover—or those with heavy bodies that make flying difficult—often fly in a V formation. The physics behind this behavior are elegantly simple: As each bird flaps its wings, the one just behind it picks up a gentle updraft, increasing its flying efficiency. The formation can reduce energy needs by more than half, but it only works if each bird maintains precisely the right distance from its neighbor. Birds have a special talent for maintaining personal space, whether they're perched on a utility wire or flying in formation as part of a flock. In flight, they can sense a change in the way air flows through their wings if they drop away from the formation. And, in the case of talkative geese or ducks, leaving the formation might leave a honking conversation unfinished.

Take a Closer Look

Black-Billed Magpie *(Pica hudsonia)*

Large, rowdy, black-and-white birds with long tails, magpies often have bluish wing feathers and snow white patches on their shoulders. Males are slightly larger and heavier than females. Black-billed magpies range across the states of the western plains and mountains from northern Arizona and New Mexico to Canada's central and western provinces and throughout much of Alaska. Adult birds are 18 to 24 inches (45 to 60 cm) long. Magpies raise only one brood per year, but they often have large families. Some pairs manage to hatch and feed nine nestlings. To properly house their offspring, magpies may spend more than a month building an elaborate nest covered with a domed roof made of twigs. Usually located high in a tree, the nest may reach 19 inches (50 cm) wide and 29 inches (74 cm) tall before it's finished. Inside the twig walls, the parents make a sturdy mud bowl that's lined with moss, animal hair, and soft pieces of grass. When well-built, a magpie nest can be used for a second season. Nesting often takes place in loose colonies.

Feeder Favorites for Magpies

- Suet
- Meat scraps
- Peanuts
- Dry dog food
- Corn

Regional Relations

In the California mountains and along Canada's west coast, the yellow-billed magpie (*Pica nuttalli*) nests in orchards, parks, and neighborhoods that include oak trees. In late summer, these magpies with bright yellow bills and yellow streaks on their cheeks are often seen feeding in small flocks, and some groups nest in small colonies as well.

Tempting Features and Treats for Magpies

- When other nesting sites are rare, magpies may nest atop utility poles.
- Magpies are naturally curious and often pick up shiny objects such as keys, coins, or jewelry.
- Unmowed areas of tall grass attract magpies with their rich supply of grasshoppers.
- Provide coarse sand to supply the grit that magpies need to digest seeds from your feeder.

Did You Know?

- Magpies are omnivores that eat a huge range of foods, but they do have favorites. In summer, they eat mostly grasshoppers. In winter, they eat grains, berries, and even small mammals such as mice and voles.
- Moose and deer often benefit from magpies' taste for ticks. After picking them off of these docile animals, magpies may store ticks they don't eat in holes in the ground and return to get them within a few days.
- During the past 100 years, farmers have killed thousands of magpies in order to safeguard their seed grain, which is often eaten by these birds. Fortunately for magpies, this practice is no longer allowed.
- By the time they're 3 months old, young magpies leave their families and join flocks, where they often form relationships that lead to lifelong marriages.

Magpie Memorials

When a magpie encounters a fallen comrade, it immediately puts out an alarm call to others. Within minutes, a group of a dozen or more magpies may gather around the corpse, calling loudly from nearby perches. A few individuals may fly down in apparent attempt to rouse the dead. The ceremony usually lasts from 10 to 15 minutes.

Group Education

As you watch small flocks visit your feeders or food-bearing landscape plants, you may witness young birds being taught manners by their dominant parents and perhaps also see some flirtatious moves between young males and females. In some species such as robins, relationships formed between pairs during the fall flocking season can develop into mating bonds the following spring.

in yards with an assortment of well-stocked feeders.

Researchers have found that mixed-species flocks have a looser power structure compared with flocks of phoebes or finches, but they're still made up of leaders and followers. Chickadees often emerge as influential "nuclear" members, probably because of their communication skills. Chickadee calls are more easily understood by winter woodland birds than those of other species. Except for chickadees and titmice, most birds join mixed flocks in a half-hearted way from the start. They're content to follow where they're led.

BOLD BULLY BIRDS

The stealthy ways of magpies were noted by Lewis and Clark during their 1804 expedition, when they lost food to these sly birds. Magpies came into their tents and took meat from their plates, and sometimes harassed hunters as they skinned and cleaned deer and buffalo.

Magpies also steal food from other birds, coyotes, and other meat eaters by mobbing them. Irritated by magpies pulling at their tails or swooping at their heads, the larger animals typically take what they can carry and leave the rest to the birds.

Other birds are justifiably afraid of magpies, so they quickly leave feeders when magpies arrive on the scene. If no other food is available, the magpies may stick around until the last sunflower seed or bit of suet is gone. To make sure all the birds in your yard get a fair chance at the food you provide, consider setting up a magpie feeder away from your main feeding station. In a multiple-feeder yard, magpies may post a lookout to watch you fill empty feeders. If you stock their feeder first, they're more likely to ignore seed intended for smaller birds.

Avian Extraverts and Introverts

Social birds like swallows flock every chance they get, breaking away only for the weeks it takes to rear their young. Territorial birds strongly prefer to live in pairs or even singly, rarely forming lasting relationships outside the mate bond.

CHAPTER 11

LESS-WANTED GUESTS: "PEST" BIRDS AND OTHER WILDLIFE AT YOUR FEEDERS

The feeders and features that invite songbirds into your home landscape may also attract a few visitors that you find less appealing. "Pesty-ness" is in the eye of the beholder, of course—a squirrel may be cute when it's sitting on its haunches, nibbling an acorn, but your feelings of benevolence may fade when that same squirrel is gnawing through a feeder, the better to gobble up high-priced sunflower seed at an alarming rate. Other mammalian bird-feeder raiders also incur the wrath of humans who fill and maintain feeders meant for cheery songbirds. Hungry critters ranging in size from featherlight field mice to 300-pound bears think nothing of doing whatever it takes to get to seeds, suet, and other goodies inside a feeder. The devastation a determined raccoon, deer, or bear can wreak on a seemingly sturdy feeder is no laughing matter.

Some birds may be considered pests, as well: Starlings arrive en masse to noisily eat up every seed and suet cake in sight. House sparrows occupy housing intended for beloved bluebirds. Cowbirds lay their eggs in the nests of unsuspecting songbirds. These and other birds that we perceive to be messy, greedy, unattractive, or otherwise unworthy of our hospitality we dub pests, and we spend a good deal of time and energy trying to keep them from the food and shelter we offer to species we consider desirable.

WHAT MAKES A PEST A PEST?

Designating certain birds as pests and others as guests is an arbitrary practice, of course. Whether we thrill at the flock gathered at our feeders or curse them as intruders depends a great deal upon any expectations we had when we offered the food in the first place. When we serve up a feeder full of pricey nyjer seed in hopes of enjoying sunny goldfinches and bright raspberry-hued purple finches, only to have every seed gobbled up by a flock of house finches, we may feel disappointed. After all, we spent our money and filled our feeders expecting cute, colorful birds and got birds that were arguably less cute and definitely less colorful.

Viewed objectively, it's easy to see that what first needs adjusting is our expectation. Not everyone considers house finches to be pest birds, but their tendency to show up at feeders in large numbers and their association with outbreaks of avian conjunctivitis has tarnished their songbird status with some birdwatchers. In places where other songbirds are few and far between, however, most backyard birders are happy to host cheery house finches at their feeders.

As we've already discussed, several factors affect the types and numbers of birds that are likely to visit a feeder. Where you live, what other resources are available, what kind of food you put out and how you serve it, whether there are predators around, even the time of year will determine what flies in to partake.

DON'T BLAME THE BIRDS (OR THE BEASTS)

When you find yourself in a rage over squirrels that empty your feeders before birds even get a chance, over starlings that descend and devour everything in sight, or over any number of other misdeeds by pests that are ruining your enjoyment of birds and bird feeding—stop and take a breath. We may be too quick to ascribe human characteristics—good and bad—to the birds and mammals around us. Chickadees are pert and friendly when they perch nearby as we fill a feeder. Squirrels are malicious when they gnaw through that same feeder to get at its contents.

In our rush to judgment, we're equally quick to forget that these are wild creatures we're dealing with. Their needs (water, food, shelter) are both simple and all-encompassing, and meeting those needs is what prompts their every action. The jay that drives other birds away from a feeder is not greedy. The squirrel (or raccoon or deer or bear) that wrecks a feeder does not harbor a vendetta against you. The female cowbird that lays her eggs in a warbler's nest and the sharp-shinned hawk that nabs an unsuspecting sparrow from your feeder are not traitors against their own kind. All of these creatures are simply doing what instinct and need drive them to do. We're the ones who need to reexamine our motives and attitudes when we start to feel that nature is out to get us.

BEWARE OF THE "UNS"

Often the things we do to bring birds into our landscapes are the same things that prompt the arrival of pests. Offering table scraps and other people foods, for example, may attract noisy crows and jays or a flock of starlings—all omnivores that will readily take advantage of food other birds won't or can't eat. Stretching your bird feeding budget by supplementing seeds and suet with scraps

ACORN EFFORT, OAK TREE RESULT

Keep Feeding on a Higher Level

The benefits of feeding birds only in raised feeders are numerous. By serving seeds and other avian treats in feeders that are mounted on poles or posts or hung from trees or specialized pole systems, you gain significant control over what uses those feeders. You can use feeder placement and protective measures, such as baffles, to keep unwanted birds or critters from getting into them. You can remove and clean bird feeders when needed. And you keep food off the ground, where it attracts a host of unwanted visitors: high-volume flocking birds, squirrels, chipmunks, rats, mice, raccoons, and insects. Besides serving as a lure for problem diners, food on the ground can mix with droppings and dirt to create disease-ridden environments that affect birds, pets, and people.

from your kitchen also may draw unwanted visits from mice, rats, and raccoons.

Serving food on the ground is another practice that can welcome problems as well as desirable birds. From mixed flocks of starlings and blackbirds to large groups of game birds to four-legged visitors of all sizes, an array of less-than-desirable guests may turn up in your landscape if they discover you're providing an easy meal.

To a large extent, the arrival of problem birds and mammals is usually preceded by one or more of the "uns"—unrestricted food, unprotected feeders, unmanaged habitat, and unclean conditions. Using the right feeders; protecting feeder areas; restricting what, when and how you feed; and keeping things clean does a lot to prevent wildlife at your feeders from becoming pests.

Don't Be So Dense

One often overlooked bird exclusion method is simply the proper pruning of shade trees. Large trees with dense, round crowns provide protective roost sites for many pest birds. Prune overly dense trees to let in more air and light and to encourage a more open growth habit. This makes the trees less desirable for roosting, and most birds will seek shelter elsewhere.

Many trees chosen to line city streets are species and varieties that form roost-friendly dense growth. If roosting birds become a problem in your neighborhood because of municipal tree choices, you may need to appeal to your local parks department or other government bodies to get the situation corrected. Tree pruning is most effective in preventing mass roosting by starlings, common grackles, house sparrows, purple martins, and blackbirds.

ROOSTING AND FLOCKING BIRDS

The old saying, "Birds of a feather flock together" could easily end with ". . . and create a noisy, dangerous mess." Huge groups or flocks of birds can congregate seemingly out of nowhere and take over a neighborhood, farm, park, or tree canopy, driving away other birds and making problems for people.

A flock is a group of animals that travel, feed, or live together. Flocking birds include pigeons, European starlings, common grackles, Canada geese, house sparrows, various blackbirds, crows, gulls, and others. Notice anything in common? When these birds arrive in numbers, people take notice—there's often trouble brewing. So it's common to equate "flock" with "pest."

While we may take a liking to individual birds, nesting families, or small groups of birds, when their numbers increase to hundreds or thousands, it's usually too much of a good thing. And when a large flock chooses to roost nearby, potential trouble has arrived.

A roost is a place, usually elevated, where birds rest or sleep. Specifically, a bird roost is a perch or a site that offers many perching locations, where large numbers of birds congregate at day's end. Birds conserve energy, stay warm, and stay safe from predators by roosting together at night. A roost site may be the branches of a tree or a grove of trees, a utility line, the roof or ledges of a building, a barn or garage, a chimney, an attic, an ivy-covered wall, a hedgerow, or even an open space such as a lawn, a marsh, a field, a golf course, or a weedy vacant lot.

Birds were flocking and roosting long before people started plowing the land and building cities. Birds flock or roost to find mates (a kind of avian singles scene), to learn communication skills, to locate food, to keep warm and dry, to learn nesting behaviors, and to protect one another from predators by finding safety in numbers. Studies show that a flock of birds reacts to danger more quickly than individual birds do.

Offering food on the ground may encourage a flock of unruly guests to occupy your feeding station. Blackbirds, grackles, cowbirds, and crows often flock together in noisy, messy groups that may discourage other birds from visiting your feeders.

A flock of birds may consist of a single species, such as Canada geese, or it may include several species, such as the masses of congregating "blackbirds" that include grackles, starlings, blackbirds, cowbirds, and crows.

THE TROUBLE WITH ROOSTING AND FLOCKING

Forming flocks and gathering to roost at night are normal bird behaviors that are important to the health and survival of many bird species. From a human perspective, however, some birds are just too darned good at it. When the number of birds in a flock or at a roosting site grows too large, problems arise. Large numbers of birds in roosts or flocks threaten songbirds at feeders, the supply of food in feeders, our houses, buildings, and offices, and the health of other birds, pets, and people.

Flocks are noisy. The voice of a songbird as he advertises his qualities as a mate is a beautiful sound on a warm spring day. The caws and calls of a mob of roosting crows that start before dawn and interrupt our sleep is something else entirely. Roosting birds often begin stirring well before sunrise, singing, calling, and quarreling among themselves. If birds are roosting within earshot of your open bedroom window, you may find that enjoying a bit of fresh air comes at the cost of a peaceful night's sleep. In addition to serving as an unwanted alarm clock for you, the noise from a large flock also may drive away nonflocking songbirds that you want to attract to your feeders and landscape.

Flocks eat a lot. A hungry flock can empty out a bird feeding station in a few minutes, leaving nothing for the birds we hoped to attract. As long as a flock remains nearby, you have to either discontinue feeding the birds, which may cause songbirds to go elsewhere, or keep filling the trough, hoping that there's enough for everyone. (Trouble is, a flock will typically stick around as long as there's food handy.)

A flock of birds may not stop at cleaning out your feeders. They also can decimate fruit trees, berry patches, and garden plants. An entire season's crop can be gobbled up in a day.

Flocks don't always share. Some flocking birds, such as starlings, house sparrows, and common grackles, will attack, kill, or drive away song- and feeder birds from their nesting sites and feeding areas.

Flocks are messy. Water sources, such as birdbaths, fountains, and pools, get contaminated with droppings as flocks stake their claim on water rights to the exclusion of normal feeder birds.

Large numbers of birds carry a host of small insects and parasites that can spread to pester other birds, pets, and people. Mites, ticks, fleas, bedbugs, and carpet beetles are among the "wee beasties" that proliferate amid songbird populations and find their way onto our pets, and even into our homes.

Flocks and roosts create safety hazards. Massed nests may become fire hazards. The grasses and other dry materials they're made of can become tinder for fires, especially in or near electrical signs and power boxes.

Around airports and helipads, flocks are threats to airline safety. They may make runways slick with droppings, crash into cockpit windows, or be sucked into airplane engines, creating potential disaster.

Take a Closer Look

European Starling *(Sturnus vulgaris)*

European starlings, also called common starlings, are medium-size birds with glossy blackish feathers that have iridescent hints of blue, green, and purple during spring and summer months. New feathers in fall feature pale tips that wear away by spring; these give winter birds a speckled appearance. Starling bills change color, starting out yellow in spring and summer and turning to brown by winter. Adult birds of both sexes are 7½ to 8½ inches (19 to 22 cm) long.

Highly adaptable to a wide range of conditions and food sources, starlings are established throughout North America, from the edge of the Arctic Circle into northern Mexico, except in mountainous habitats. Wherever they're found, they compete aggressively with native birds for nest sites, territory, food, and survival in general. Starlings nest in holes and crevices in trees and buildings, including ledges, gaps, or holes in siding, on rooftops, as well as in nest boxes intended for native songbirds. They fill their chosen cavity with grass, leaves, evergreen needles, feathers, paper, string, and even bits of plastic, and lay four to six pale bluish eggs. Starlings typically raise two broods per year.

Relatives and Look-Alikes

Starlings often are confused with their flocking companions, which may include various blackbird species, brown-headed cowbirds, and common grackles. Despite these similar appearances, starlings are part of a separate family (Sturnidae), which also includes mynas. Blackbirds and cowbirds are typically slimmer than starlings, and have longer tails and thicker bills, and no blackbird has a yellow bill. Except for these differences, female and young brown-headed cowbirds resemble juvenile starlings. (Before you take any steps to control flocking birds, remember that all of these similar-looking birds, except starlings, are protected by federal law.)

European Starling: Pleasure?

+ The starling's voracious appetite includes many insects and small pests, including centipedes, moths, worms, and spiders. This bird also eats weed seeds.
+ If you like lively, gregarious birds and can overlook their aggressive and messy habits, European starlings provide lots of viewing action. They use their bills in a funny prying way when feeding, for example. They're among the birds that may be trained to hand-feed (but be sure you wear gloves).
+ Along with pigeons and house sparrows, starlings readily survive and thrive in urban conditions. For city-dwelling birders, starlings offer entertaining avian antics in environments that most other birds find inhospitable.

European Starling: Pest?

- Starlings aggressively plunder cavity nest sites that would be used by native songbirds, threatening populations of sapsuckers, wrens, swallows, and bluebirds, among others.
- Starlings are messy eaters, especially when they scavenge food wrappers, garbage scraps, and other debris. Keep trash containers covered when starlings are around and watch your food at picnics and cookouts.
- In the orchard and garden, starlings will eat apples, pears, plums, cherries, tomatoes, other fruits, all kinds of berries, and seeds.
- Starlings fight at nest sites and feeder areas over territory and food, driving away other birds and leaving carnage. An estimated 10 percent die in prolonged, bloody fights to the death over nest sites. Starlings will lock their legs in combat and peck at the face and body of an opponent until one of them dies.

Did You Know?

- Highly talented vocalists, starlings can mimic the barks of dogs and meows of cats, even frog calls and goat nags. In captivity, starlings have been trained to mimic the sounds of human voices.
- The starling's song consists of soft whistles, high-pitched squeaks, clicks, chirps, gurgles, and rattles. Starlings have a screaming call when threatened and a "chack-chack" call when showing aggression. They'll mimic other birds, such as the bobwhite and meadowlark.
- Starlings once were blamed for plant vandalism when they were seen plucking green leaves and carrying them to their nests. Further observation revealed that they selected leaves with pesticidal qualities, such as aromatic leaves in the mint family, possibly to control mites and other parasites in their nests. One study reported starlings using leaves of spearmint, lemon balm, catnip, and parsley in their nests.
- The European starling is one of only three birds (with pigeons and house sparrows) not included in the Migratory Bird Treaty Act (see "Know the Bird, Know the Law" on page 326). Although starlings are unprotected by federal law, be sure to check local ordinances before undertaking any control measures and be aware of protected birds that may be flocking along with starlings.
- Female starlings often parasitize their flock-mates by laying eggs in the nests of other starlings. Up to one-third of females that missed the first flush of breeding lay eggs in nests not their own, so later-breeding birds may hatch the eggs.
- When feeding, starlings pry open the tough skins or shells of seeds, fruits, and other foods by poking their bills into the food, then prying their bills apart to expose the treats within.

The Bird and the Bard

Before the early 1890s, North America did not know the European starling, a native of Eurasia and North Africa. Then, as legend says, along came a group of bird and literature enthusiasts led by one Eugene Scheffland, a New York industrialist. Scheffland had the desire to establish in America all the birds mentioned in the works of William Shakespeare. Not anticipating the effects of introducing nonnative birds, Scheffland's group obtained and released 100 European starlings in New York's Central Park between 1890 and 1891. Only 15 pairs survived, but that was enough. Soon their numbers exploded. Within 75 years, starlings had spread across the entire lower 48 states, throughout southern Canada to Alaska, and into northern Mexico. Today there are an estimated 200 million European starlings in North America.

The Scoop on Droppings

Massed bird droppings are a mess to see, smell, and deal with. They may damage our houses, walkways, lawns, cars, orchards, and plants. They stain surfaces, and with their acidic and corrosive qualities, they may eat away paint and coatings on gutters, roofs, siding, cars, outdoor furniture, fountains, birdbaths, and other property. Cleaning up bird droppings can be tedious, costly, and even health-threatening. If you've ever seen cluster droppings from berry-eating starlings or grackles, you know what a mess they are.

Droppings harbor diseases that affect birds, pets, livestock, and humans. Disease organisms such as histoplasmosis, salmonella, tuberculosis, internal parasites, forms of encephalitis, fowl poxes, and parasitic nematodes and flukes may be the consequence of large-scale, unchecked bird activity. As frequent visitors at picnic sites and outdoor restaurants as well as at bird feeders, house sparrows may carry the salmonella bacteria that cause food poisoning.

PREVENTING "PEST" BIRD PROBLEMS

When flocking or roosting birds threaten to take the pleasure out of bird feeding and watching, don't despair. There are things you can do to reclaim your home environment and your enjoyment of birds at your feeders and in your landscape. The first, and best, strategy is to stop problems before they get out of hand. An easy way to do this is to change things in the habitat that are attractive to flocking birds. By limiting access to food and/or nesting and roosting sites, you can discourage a flock from settling in around your home. Often just a few days of making it harder for birds to find food or shelter will make them move on.

RIGHT FOODS, RIGHT FEEDING

On a daily basis, choosing the right bird foods and controlling how you serve them are simple ways to help keep undesirable birds away.

- Many flocking and roosting pests like "junk" food. We don't mean Twinkies or pork rinds—although many a crow or starling would happily feast on those. In places where pest birds are a problem, avoid feeding bread crumbs and crusts, crackers, cake, cookies, breakfast cereals, cracked corn, fruit and vegetable scraps, and coarse or waste grain products, especially on the ground. If you choose to offer cracked corn or poultry "scratch" grains to pigeons, mourning doves, or other ground feeders, restrict the amount, timing, and duration of the feeding. Monitor the area during feeding time to watch for pest birds.
- Many song- and feeder birds eat early in the day. Place their foods out early, and put out only enough for the morning meal, if pest birds are on the scene. Refill feeders later in the day only if normal feeder birds, such as evening-feeding cardinals and juncos, show up then. If you leave feeders full all day, you'll attract nonresident birds, including flocking visitors. You'll also invite squirrels and other four-legged pests.
- Unless you're offering it as a carefully monitored treat for a favorite feeder guest, never put out meat, pet food, or dairy scraps to feed birds. Not only will you run the risk of attract-

ing larger scavenger birds and carrion eaters, but you also may get raccoons, skunks, stray cats, and dogs messing up your feeding area and driving away feeder birds.

- Many commercial birdseed mixes contain cracked corn, millet, wheat, and other "filler" seeds that few songbirds really like. If you put these mixes in your raised feeders, birds may sort through the mix and toss unwanted seeds onto the ground. The resulting layer of seeds beneath the feeder will attract ground-feeding pest birds and their flocks, plus four-legged critters. When in doubt, use sunflower seeds and hang nyjer feeders. If sunflower hulls become a problem on the ground below your feeders, try offering hulled black oil sunflower seed. You'll pay a little more, but will attract lots of feeder favorites, too.

MAKE YOUR HOME LANDSCAPE EXCLUSIVE

We're not talking about gates and bouncers here. Excluding pest birds is simply good home maintenance. Along with smart feeding strategies, exclusion is another way to keep pests from gaining a foothold around your house and yard.

- Make sure your house and any other buildings are tight. Screen your attic and soffit vents to keep critters out and check the screens and seals regularly to be sure they're tight. Caulk or fill any gaps around pipes, conduits, or wires entering the house. Place gutter mesh or guards over the tops of your gutters to let rain through but keep birds from nesting in the cavities. If house sparrows, starlings, or pigeons build nests where they're not wanted, in most cases you can move or destroy the nests because these three species are unprotected under federal law. It's important to be sure whose nest you're disturbing, though, and better to do everything you can to discourage unwanted nesting before construction gets too far along. Don't handle the nest or eggs of protected birds without checking with wildlife authorities for permit requirements.
- Use sticky repellents (polybutene gel or "bird glue"), metal prongs or spikes ("porcupine wire"), wire coils or springs, or taut strands of fishing line to deter birds from nesting or roosting on roofs, eaves, gutters, fences, ledges, walls, rafters, and similar sites. Monitor areas where you place bird glue to make sure that small birds or mammals don't become trapped by it. The sticky stuff wears out, so you need to replenish it for continued effectiveness. Coarse gravel, broken glass, or other tactile repellents may also discourage pigeons and other birds from comfortably roosting on horizontal surfaces.
- During construction or renovations, eliminate horizontal resting places. Design ledges and windowsills with at least a 45-degree angle. Do the same with new fences or walls. The sharp angle will make it difficult or impossible for nesting or roosting birds to occupy them.
- Cover fruit trees and berry bushes with plastic bird netting or spun-fabric row covers to keep flocks from flying in en masse to feed on the fruits. Do the same with tomato plants, peas, lettuce, and other garden seedlings that flocking birds find irresistible.
- Place shiny "scare" devices such as dangling reflective strips of Mylar, plastic, or vinyl; pie pans; or CDs in strategic locations where pest birds tend to congregate and cause problems. Use these to protect fruit and vegetable gardens or to make a roosting site unappealing.

TAKE A CLOSER LOOK

House Sparrow *(Passer domesticus)*

The house sparrow, also called the English sparrow, is the most widely distributed bird on Earth. Originally found in Eurasia and North Africa, today it's present everywhere but the regions of the North and South Pole. In North America its range includes almost all areas except northernmost Canada. House sparrows especially thrive in cities and other human-modified areas; if you see a sparrowlike bird in an urban setting, it's almost certainly a house sparrow—native sparrows tend to be shy and secretive and unlikely to linger in densely populated areas.

House sparrows are small and stocky; adult birds are 5½ to 6 inches (14 to 15 cm) long. Both males and females have thick bills, short legs, unstreaked chests, lighter bars on their wings, and brownish backs with streaks. The male has a red-brown back, a black chest and throat or "bib," grayish white cheeks, black bill, and grayish underparts. The female is dull brown all over with a yellowish bill, pale yellow eye stripe, and black and tan back stripes. Juveniles look like adult females. House sparrows are colony nesters that make ball-shaped, sometimes sizable nests of dried grasses and other vegetation, paper, string, feathers, and other lightweight materials in natural cavities, holes, or gaps. They often nest in man-made structures and nest boxes as well. Throughout their range they compete aggressively with native cavity-nesting species.

Relatives and Look-Alikes

Aside from the native or true sparrows that include the American tree sparrow, chipping sparrow, song sparrow, and white-throated sparrow—all of which generally have smaller bills than house sparrows—other familiar feeder birds bear a resemblance to house sparrows. Chickadees have black caps and bibs and white cheeks, but are more gray than brown. Female dickcissels look like female house sparrows at first glance, but the dickcissels have longer, thinner bills and sometimes truer yellow coloring on eye stripes and chests than house sparrows do. Don't mistakenly disturb the nests of all these look-alikes in your efforts to dislodge a colony of house sparrows; these other species are all protected songbirds.

House Sparrow: Pleasure?

- **+** In highly urban areas where few other birds are present, house sparrows, for all their faults, offer a welcome connection to the natural world.
- **+** House sparrows eat lots of weed and waste grain seeds. In their role in the food chain, they serve as food for raptors and other predators. On occasion they've controlled the spread of weevils and cutworms.
- **+** Populous and accepting of nearby human activity, house sparrows are useful subjects for biological studies that can further our understanding of all birds.
- **+** If you choose to try hand-feeding birds, you may find many of these little guys gorging themselves in your gloved palm.

House Sparrow: Pest?

- **–** House sparrows, like many other birds in this chapter, routinely and aggressively displace native songbirds from cavity nests, often killing them or destroying their eggs. Eastern bluebird populations, in particular, are threatened by this behavior.
- **–** In the garden, house sparrows sometimes eat flowers, buds, and young vegetable shoots, including peas and lettuce. Flocks can damage fruit crops, such as cherries, grapes, apples, pears, and peaches.
- **–** In urban habitats, house sparrows congregate in large numbers, make a sustained racket, mess up the ground around feeders, and leave unsightly, acidic, and damaging droppings on walkways, cars, and buildings.

- They can be persistent pests at picnics and outdoor eating areas, and have been known to carry disease organisms such as salmonella and tuberculosis, as well as pathogenic fungi, protozoa, and viruses.
- House sparrow nests, especially those made on or near houses, can be fire and health hazards. Nests may block gutters and downspouts.
- House sparrows are happy eating garbage, litter, and food debris, leaving a mess in their wake.

Did You Know?

- Like the English starling, the pigeon, and other widely distributed nonnatives, the house sparrow is an import from the Old World. The first 100 house sparrows were imported in 1851 from England and introduced in Brooklyn, with subsequent introductions in San Francisco and Salt Lake City.
- Despite its name, the house sparrow is actually not a sparrow but a member of the weaver finch family. House sparrows can swim to escape danger or predators.
- Like some other feeder birds, the house sparrow is a dust bather, usually on a daily basis. It will use dirt and dust to cover and penetrate its feather layers, possibly to relieve itself of lice, mites, and other irritating pests. Then it shakes loose the excess dust, leaving a ring on the ground.
- House sparrows aggressively fight intruders around the nest site. In these battles, females fight female intruders, and males fight only males.

Bad for Bluebirds

Bluebird lovers, in particular, try many tactics to keep burgeoning house sparrow populations from displacing less-populous bluebirds. In addition to taking over natural cavities and boxes and leaving bluebirds homeless, house sparrows will also kill bluebirds and destroy their eggs. In their efforts to give bluebirds an advantage in this uneven competition, birders may try everything from excluding to trapping and killing house sparrows. Even so, these strategies usually affect local sparrow populations only and often just temporarily.

One of the most effective ways of excluding house sparrows from birdhouses, especially those meant for eastern bluebirds, is to remove any perch placed near the birdhouse entrance. A perch helps give house sparrows access to a nest box; bluebirds don't need a perch to get into a box.

Unless you have specially-designed bluebird houses (see "Making a Birdhouse a Home," starting on page 149), don't try to attract bluebirds near farm buildings or—alas—in most urban areas. The presence of nearby food (from bird feeders or livestock feeds) will attract house sparrows, almost always to the detriment of the bluebirds.

Know the Bird, Know the Law

Before taking steps to control birds that are becoming pests around your home, you must positively identify any birds that you may affect. If you're not 100 percent sure—for example, so many "blackbirds" look alike—consult a good field guide and turn to local wildlife agencies, naturalist groups, Audubon chapters, raptor centers, or wildlife rehabilitators for help. You may avoid harming songbirds and other protected species.

Equally important is knowing the laws associated with wild birds. All birds except European starlings, pigeons, and house sparrows are protected by the federal Migratory Bird Treaty Act of 1918 and subsequent laws, which specifically prohibit trapping, killing, harassing, selling, or possessing protected birds, and their eggs and nests, without an authorized permit. State and local laws and ordinances may specify other protections and restrictions, such as prohibiting the use of firearms, including pellet and BB guns, inside municipal limits. Most states prohibit the use of poisons in dealing with birds. Check with your state's wildlife agency and any local authorities that hold jurisdiction in your area before attempting any active control methods. This caution also applies when hiring an exterminator or a wildlife relocator or rehabilitator. He or she must have all applicable permits and licenses to deal with unwanted birds, nests, and eggs. As a judge says, ignorance of the law is no excuse.

"SCARE" CONTROLS

Startling sights and sounds tend to produce limited results in terms of discouraging birds from flocking or roosting where they're not wanted. A small flock of birds roosting nearby might be spooked by loud hand claps or by your whacking sticks together. Or a shot of water from the hose might make them leave. Larger groups of birds might not even notice your efforts, or they might leave briefly and return when things quiet down.

Scarecrows and other effigies of humans and bird predators typically have a short effectiveness period. Birds quickly realize that an unmoving scare-thing is not a danger and so ignore it. Fake owls whose heads rotate in the breeze, helium balloons with menacing eyespots, and dangling hawk, snake, and predator replicas are a little more effective. Keep changing the kinds and locations of such devices for better results. To discourage flocks from cleaning out your vegetable garden or berry patch, the ScareCrow, a large motion-activated sprinkler that shoots water when a sensor is tripped, may be a worthwhile investment.

Other frightening tactics include recorded bird distress calls, firecrackers and small exploding devices (where legal), and spotlights. Remember your neighbors before using loud noises or bright lights—it's no good winning the battle against birds only to start a war with the folks next door. In level places where birds continually roost, electrically charged wires can be an effective deterrent. Ultrasound devices often miss targeted birds and can cause hearing loss in pets.

Take a Closer Look

Brown-Headed Cowbird *(Molothrus ater)*

The brown-headed cowbird is a medium-size bird, 7 to 9 inches (18 to 22.5 cm) long. The male is shiny black or glossy greenish black, except for his head, nape, and chest, which are a deep, dull brown. He has a large, conical, black bill. The female is grayish brown throughout with a whitish throat and a gray bill. The brown-headed cowbird does not build nests, tend its eggs, or raise its young, but leaves these tasks to birds of other species. Unlike other bird species, the female always lays its brown-dotted white eggs in a number of nests of other birds, leaving the foster parents to raise her young.

Relatives and Look-Alikes

Relatives in the blackbird family include the common grackle, red-winged blackbird, bobolink, western meadowlark, and Bullock's oriole. Similar-looking birds include the European starling, shiny cowbird (originally from South America, now appearing in the southern United States), bronzed cowbird (of the Southwest), and Brewer's blackbird. Brown-headed cowbirds often travel with these birds in flocks.

Brown-Headed Cowbird: Pleasure?

+ Around 75 percent of the brown-headed cowbird's diet consists of weed and other seeds, including the seeds of many pest plants such as dandelions and thistles.
+ Cowbirds also eat substantial numbers of insects, especially beetles and grasshoppers.

Brown-Headed Cowbird: Pest?

- Flocks of brown-headed cowbirds crowd bird feeders, driving away more desirable feeder visitors. Often the displaced birds must defend their territories against cowbirds, causing a ruckus around feeders and backyards.
- By parasitic egg laying and abandonment of their young to foster parents, brown-headed cowbirds may harm the reproduction rates and health of the hosts' babies. By this habit, cowbirds also endanger the entire population of host birds, including the Kirtland's warbler and the black-capped vireo.

Did You Know?

- The only "brood parasite" found widely across North America, the brown-headed cowbird uses no nest of its own. Instead, the female lays eggs in the nests of other birds, leaving them to be incubated and raised by other species. She may lay dozens of eggs, each in a different nest, in a single season.
- Studies show that 144 different bird species have been used as hosts for cowbird eggs. These species usually act as foster parents, rearing the young cowbirds as, and along with, their own. The cowbird eggs consistently hatch earlier than the host bird's eggs, and thus the young intruders out-compete host babies in the nest for food.
- Some host birds evict the cowbird eggs from the nest, or build a new nest layer over the cowbird eggs, which keep them from incubating. Yellow warblers have built as many as six new nest layers to avoid incubating cowbird eggs. Other birds sometimes choose to start an entirely new nest.
- Courting males sing a prolonged song and follow it with a head bow or "tip over" to impress the female—and to razz other courting males nearby. They keep a busy courtship routine, as genetic studies show that both male and female brown-headed cowbirds have many different mates throughout a single breeding season.
- Cowbirds are so named because they once followed herds of bison over the plains.

CHEMICAL CONTROLS

Most chemical methods of deterring bird pests are registered for use only by licensed applicators. Some success has been reported for bad-tasting chemical lawn treatments made from grape seed wastes and other bitter compounds that geese and other grazing birds find repulsive. (In the home landscape these may negatively affect robins and other desirable ground-feeding species.) Some taste aversion agents can be applied to fruit crops, but netting may be a more effective tool. Other agents make birds feel sick, so they leave the feeding area. However, unless the site itself is made uninviting through removal of food sources and exclusion techniques, other flocks may take their place. Taste aversion treatments must be reapplied when they wear out from rain and exposure. Always check local wildlife agencies and ordinances before trying any chemical treatment, and read and follow directions to the letter.

Foil Temporary Pests

Even desirable birds can become pesky when rising hormones and the resulting territorial and mate-attracting behaviors disturb our daily routines. Male woodpeckers, for example, like to advertise their whereabouts by drumming, especially in spring, and the louder the better. They sometimes use aluminum house gutters as drums, which may not be a welcome sound at sunrise on a Saturday morning. Gutter drummers often can be deterred by strips of aluminum foil attached to and waving from their favorite section of gutter, or by bird netting covering the gutter. Gutter drumming usually stops in midsummer, when nesting season draws to a close, allowing you a chance to take down your deterring devices and enjoy some uninterrupted rest, too.

CHOOSE TO COEXIST

If birds still roost nearby despite your efforts, try to coexist. They'll move on when another source of food and water or a better shelter site is discovered—usually in a short while.

Until they do, use tarps, plastic sheets, or painter's cloths to shield vehicles, walls, walkways, and other susceptible surfaces from droppings. At night, close windows against early morning serenades or try using a "white noise" machine indoors to mask the sound.

Discontinue feeding your usual birds for a few days (they'll come back when you resume). If handy feeder food isn't available, flocks get hungry and restless. Drain birdbaths, freshwater pools, and fountains so flocks can't find water in your area. Enlist the cooperation of your bird-feeding neighbors, since roosting flocks are a neighborhood problem.

Gradually resume feeding when pest birds leave, but don't fill feeders continuously. Put out only enough for your usual birds to use. Clean and refill your birdbaths, pools, and fountains. Enjoy the peace!

Don't Go There! Last-Resort Controls Rarely Succeed

If you've never experienced the problems created by a large number of flocking or roosting birds, you may find it hard to believe that you could be tempted to take drastic measures to drive birds away. Most of us are so delighted by the birds at our feeders and in our landscapes that we can't imagine wanting to evict them, let alone do them harm. But folks who've endured disturbed sleep and countless surfaces coated with messy droppings, who've watched as songbirds have been displaced—or killed—by invading hordes, certainly may feel strongly that anything they do to get rid of the invaders is justified.

The trouble is, control methods that go beyond those already described—choosing foods carefully, limiting access to foods, and excluding pest birds—are difficult, dangerous, and in many cases, illegal. And for all the difficulty involved, dramatic controls such as trapping, poisoning, or shooting rarely have a lasting impact on populations of pest birds.

Trapping

In extreme cases, trapping house sparrows, pigeons, and starlings may be an option. But you must be sure that no protected birds are harmed, and release any such birds immediately. Traps designed with funnels, drop-ins, triggers, decoys, and automatic closing devices are available for purchase or DIY construction. Consult a licensed wildlife- or pest-control company for best results when conditions warrant trapping, and check local ordinances regarding any permits or licenses that may be required. Also, you must have a sound plan to deal with the trapped birds.

Poisoning

Because of the risks that poisons pose to nontargeted birds and other wildlife, pets, and people, most states and localities prohibit the use of poisons on birds. In a few areas, pigeon poisons are registered for use by licensed applicators with special permits. Naphthalene mothballs have limited repellent effects, if any, and they stink up your yard and present a poisoning danger to any kids or pets that can make it past the smell.

Shooting

Shooting at pest birds typically causes more harm than good. Most municipalities ban the discharge of any firearm, including pellet and BB guns. In large part, such bans are because shot or bullets travel a greater distance than most people realize. A stray .22 bullet can hit an unintended target up to a mile away. Besides the obvious danger to people and animals in the area, errant shots can damage houses, windows, siding, or trees. Bullets and shot may pass through siding and walls, even endangering people indoors. Even if you're a great shot, the number of birds you may bag is tiny compared to the flock at large. In many areas, even starlings, house sparrows, and pigeons cannot be shot.

If you want to spook birds instead of killing them, use blanks for effect—but only if it's legal and your neighbors don't mind the noise. Again, you must check to see if any discharge of firearms is legal where you live. And you must be sure that no protected birds are affected.

Take a Closer Look

House Finch *(Carpodacus mexicanus)*

Although included in this chapter about pests, house finches are welcome at many feeders. House finch males are cheerful cherry-red birds with brown-striped wings. The females are grayish brown with a striped back and brown-spotted white breast, very dull compared to the males. Both have dark brown legs. Juveniles resemble the females. Colors are the same all year. Adult birds are 5 to 6 inches (13 to 15 cm) long. Females are cavity nesters and lay one to six very pale blue eggs with a few dark spots.

Relatives and Look-Alikes

House finches and purple finches often are mistaken for one another. The purple finch has a shorter and more notched tail, a pointier bill, and a brown ear patch. Male purple finches are darker red, have whiter abdomens, and do not have streaked backs compared with male house finches. (See "Take a Closer Look" on page 66 to learn more about the purple finch.) House finches also may be confused with Cassin's finches, female house sparrows, and pine siskins.

House Finch: Pleasure?

+ Colorful house finch males brighten the scene at feeding stations.
+ Their song is enjoyable, and has been described as an "ecstatic warble."
+ House finches eat weed seeds, including thistle and dandelion.

House Finch: Pest?

- House finches are often crop pests in orchards and on farms. House finches may damage or eat ripening fruit, especially cherries, plums, and peaches. In the garden, they have also been known to chew various flowers to bits for no apparent reason and eat flower buds. They spread lots of weed seeds in their droppings.
- At feeders, they may congregate in large numbers and scare away other feeder birds.
- House finches compete with hummingbirds for the sweet contents of nectar feeders.
- They may take over purple martin houses and other birds' nest boxes.

Feeder Favorites for House Finches

- Fruit
- Suet
- Peanut hearts
- Most seeds, including nyjer
- Hummingbird nectar
- Sunflower seed, especially black oil
- Millet
- Cracked corn

Tempting Features and Treats for House Finches

- House finches eat lots of weed seeds. If your dandelions go to flower, house finches will eat the seeds (but also may disperse them in droppings). The same is true of thistles. Cherry trees will attract house finches, too. These birds will also eat the occasional insect, plus flower buds and food scraps.
- Project FeederWatch participants report that house finches will also take safflower and even nyjer seed.
- Treat your house finches to their favorite, hulled sunflower seeds.
- House finches need a constant water supply—they can drink the equivalent of 40 percent of their body weight daily in hot weather.
- A saucer of rock salt will attract the attention of house finches.

Did You Know?

- As its Latin name implies, the house finch was originally found only in the Southwest and Mexico.

- Both house and purple finches were once sold as caged birds for their color and beautiful warbling song. It's because of this practice that house finches first came to the East in the 1940s. When pet dealers on Long Island were threatened with suits for illegally selling these "Hollywood finches," they freed the birds to spread and multiply in the wild.
- In the West where they originated, house finches were known as "linnets."
- Avian pox, which may appear as warty growths near birds' eyes or beak or on legs and feet, is another disease that has taken a toll on house finch populations.
- Trees in suburban landscapes in the Plains states probably helped populations of house finches expand from the West and the East until they met in the middle.
- Eastern house finches have developed bigger beaks than the western finches, enabling them to enjoy larger feeder seeds, such as sunflower seeds.
- Male house finches develop their bright plumage based on the foods they eat, so they may be yellow or orange in addition to red. The brightest red males seem to have the best luck attracting females in spring, perhaps because their vivid color implies that they're successful at finding food. In winter, the brownish juvenile and yearling males have the advantage, since unlike many species, male house finches let the duller-colored females eat first, and the youngsters can sneak in along with their mothers.
- If house finches are making it hard for hummers or orioles to get their rations, set out a saucer of sugar water just for them. They'll prefer it to the nectar feeders because the sweet drink is easier to get.

Keep an Eye on Bird Health

In addition to helping track of birds' migratory movement and the distribution of bird species, backyard birders have been instrumental in helping ornithologists monitor the spread and severity of diseases that affect wild bird populations. A notable example of this "citizen science" involves *mycoplasmal conjunctivitis*, also known as "house finch eye disease."

Previously identified in domestic turkeys and chickens, this bacterial infection that affects birds' eyes and respiratory tracts was reported in house finches in Maryland and Virginia in 1994, according to the Cornell Lab of Ornithology. Infected birds often have swollen, red, crusty eyes; as the disease progresses, it may cause complete blindness. Death may result because sick birds can't see to find food or shelter or to avoid predators.

In the East, house finch populations have suffered substantial reductions because of eye disease, possibly because of their flocking behavior during the winter months. If house finches visit your feeders, you can play a role in tracking mycoplasmal conjunctivitis by participating in the Cornell Lab's House Finch Disease Survey. Sign up at www.birds.cornell.edu/hofi/ or by calling 800-843-2473, and use the provided forms to report healthy and sick house finches at your feeders.

To protect the health of all feeder birds, clean feeders regularly—about once every 2 weeks—with soapy water followed by a rinse or soak in a 10-percent bleach solution. Dry feeders completely before refilling. Clean up seeds and hulls beneath feeders, too, and change the water in bird baths daily.

AVIAN ACTS OF AGGRESSION

Despite what you may have learned from watching old movies, birds don't often gang up on and attack people. On those occasions when a bird or flock of birds starts diving, chasing, or "buzzing" people or pets, it probably has a good reason. Survey the area and you'll likely determine the reason for the aggressive behaviors. In any case, never swipe at birds or counterattack with sticks or stones, or you may create a frenzy—or a misdemeanor (most birds are legally protected against attack or injury). Careful people don't whack at bees, wasps, or dogs for fear of retaliation; think of birds in the same way and you'll be safer.

Sometimes birds act aggressively when startled, but most likely a person has gotten too close to nests, mates, or young ones. Attacks are more frequent in spring and summer, when most birds establish mating and nesting territories. If a bird starts buzzing, chirping loudly and strenuously, or diving at you, retreat to a protected place and watch for a nearby nest or a baby bird that the parent is protecting. If there's a baby bird on the ground and parents are nearby, let Mom and Dad Bird handle it unless the young bird is in imminent danger.

The most common backyard birds to buzz humans are jays, mockingbirds, and blackbirds. Avoidance is the best solution—simply get away and stay away from the area the bird is protecting, and things should calm down. If a dog or cat is the cause of the ruckus, remove it from the area.

In most cases, birds' territorial behaviors are temporary. You may have to restrict your movements or your pets' for a few days or weeks until nesting season ends.

Sometimes an "attack" may be a case of wrong place, wrong time. Common backyard birds, such as woodpeckers, doves, or pigeons, may be returning to nearby nests when you get too close for their comfort. Again, make yourself scarce and the behavior should cease.

Sometimes tamed birds, such as ducks and geese that are accustomed to being fed by humans, will show aggressive behavior when a person approaches them but does not offer food. The birds expect to be fed, so they come closer without fear. When no food is offered, they start begging, or rather, demanding. This may take the form of hissing, pecking, and even chasing after the person. If you have some food with you, drop it and leave the area. If you don't have food, get away from the spoiled, aggressive bird. In a pinch, protect yourself with a kick or a stick; most ducks or geese will get the message. But leave the area anyway.

Because of the dangers presented by large, hungry geese and swans that are unafraid of people, and because of the mess created by their droppings, many municipalities now prohibit people from feeding waterfowl in public parks. We may miss taking the kids to feed the ducks, but we won't miss the monsters we were unwittingly creating when we did.

Aggressive bird behavior may also occur at the beach or seashore, where gulls, terns, or pelicans, used to food offerings or debris from picnickers and anglers, may get pushy. Keep food hidden and promptly pick up any food debris, wrappers, or other attractive items to keep these birds from getting too nosy. Bringing extra bird food with you and feeding shorebirds away from your site may help, but it may encourage the birds to continue seeking handouts from humans.

TAKE A CLOSER LOOK

Canada Goose *(Branta canadensis)*

One of our largest birds, the Canada (not Canadian) goose may be 2 to 3½ feet (0.6 to 1 m) long with a 5½-foot (1.65 m) wingspan and weigh 10 pounds (4.5 kg) or more. It has a black head with white cheeks, a long black neck, brown back, white chin area, and cream-colored breast. The rump is white, tail black, and bill, eyes, and legs all black. Some have a white neck collar. Males and females look alike, as do fully-fledged juveniles, which are grown by their first autumn. The Canada goose enjoys the widest range of any North American waterbird. It has recovered from the threat of extinction to establish itself as a year-round resident in many areas, and at least a part-timer in the rest of the continent. Canada geese nest near water, building substantial platforms of sticks, reeds, grasses, and down to hold 5 to 10 yellowish white eggs.

Relatives and Look-Alikes

There are 11 different kinds or races of Canada geese, with many variations in size. The cackling Canada goose is the smallest, at around 3 pounds (1.4 kg). The largest, the giant Canada goose, can reach 17 pounds (7.7 kg). Crossbreeding of Canada geese with domestic geese has resulted in a wide number of hybrids with unique markings. Some hybrid geese have red legs, red coloring on their bill, or more white on their head.

Canada Goose: Pleasure?

- ✚ Perhaps the most attractive aspect of having Canada geese nearby is watching them raise and protect their young. A family of geese is fun to watch, as long as you keep your distance.
- ✚ Geese are graceful on water and entertaining in their mating and feeding behaviors.
- ✚ If you want a large area of grassland or field kept down to size, a flock of Canada geese should do the job. They will eat most grasses and weedy plants such as sedges.

Canada Goose: Pest?

- ▬ The most common, and most evident, downside of resident Canada geese is the substantial, slimy mess of their droppings. A single goose produces about a pound of droppings each day. Goose droppings can kill grass and contaminate water supplies, encouraging harmful bacteria and creating buildups of phosphorus and nitrogen in freshwater sources.
- ▬ The Canada goose will take aggressive action against humans when it feels threatened, evidenced by honking, hissing, chasing, and even biting people to drive them away. This behavior may occur when overly tame urban geese expect food from unsuspecting humans.
- ▬ Flocks of roosting, feeding, or nesting geese will take over beaches, fields, parks, playgrounds, and bird feeders' yards and gardens, making them pretty much unusable. The geese will sometimes overwinter in these habitats and become a chronic nuisance. If unchecked, Canada geese will excessively graze on lawns, field grasses, and crops. Farmers growing wheat, corn, soybeans, oats, and other grain crops often must overplant to compensate for loss by grazing geese.

Did You Know?

- Besides their signature "honk," Canada geese have a dozen or more different calls, including clucks, murmurs, hisses, and loud alarm calls.
- Canada geese have excellent eyesight, which helps them fly so well. Their close-set eyes allow a visual range of 180 to 270 degrees. They also hear well.
- Newly hatched goslings are able to leave the nest, feed, and swim within a day of birth.
- Migrating couples or flocks often return to the same area and may even use the same nest year after year. Goslings stay with the family for at least a year and return to their birthplace after their first winter.

FOUR-LEGGED FEEDER RAIDERS

Pest birds aren't the only feeder hogs. In fact, most bird feeders are far more likely to be raided by critters dressed in fur rather than feathers. Rodents and other four-legged wildlife also enjoy dining on the seeds, suet, and other treats we serve up for the birds. As with problem birds, preventing animals from raiding your feeders usually is more successful than trying to keep them away once they've made the connection between your bird feeders and an easy meal.

SQUIRRELS AND DEER AND BEARS—OH MY!

Animals that make a habit of gobbling up the foods you put out for birds are not acting out of malice, even if they wreck your feeders in the process. To a squirrel or a raccoon or any wild animal, food is food, and the less energy it has to expend to get it, the better. To hungry mice, the fallen seed on the ground beneath a bird feeder represents countless easy meals, just as those same mice may represent easy meals to a hungry owl.

At night when the feeder regulars are sleeping, an entirely different crowd may drop by your feeding station. Mice and rats, opossums, deer, bears, flying squirrels, owls and other predators, raccoons, even skunks (usually digging for grubs and earthworms beneath the layer of seed shells and debris below the feeder) are possible nocturnal visitors. Unless you realize your feeders are emptying more rapidly than usual—and at night when songbirds are roosting—you may not notice the effects of four-legged feeder raiders. Or you may have the unpleasant surprise of discovering that something has ripped apart a feeder, the better to get at its contents. Here's a hint—it's not Goldilocks!

Before feeders turn up damaged or destroyed or just plain missing, before one or two mice turns into a full-scale infestation of vermin that moves into your shed, garage, or house, take the following steps to secure your feeders against these sorts of nonbirds:

- **Rodents.** Spilled seed, bread and doughnuts, peanut butter, cracked corn, suet: If these were lying around on the floor or counter of your kitchen, you'd expect to see mice (or at least signs that mice had been there), wouldn't you? The same is true outdoors. Squirrels aren't the only rodents that relish a free meal. Chipmunks, mice, and even rats may be drawn to feeder sites to clean up fallen seed—or simply clean up, period. Since mice and rats are more likely to feed under cover of darkness, you may not even see them—but fortunately, cats, owls, and other predators will. If you suspect that rodents are raiding your feeders, clean up spilled seed each evening and try to set out no more than the birds will eat each day.
- **Raccoons.** Raccoons are clever feeder raiders. Their dexterous hands, agility, and strength make them formidable opponents once they've discovered your feeders. Rather than watch helplessly as feeders are dismantled, removed, or simply breached and emptied of their contents, leave no bird food—or, for that matter,

pet food—outdoors at night when they're on the prowl. (They're especially likely to show up at your feeders when they're rearing young.) That also goes for suet feeders, one of their favorite targets. Take them down every night and bring them indoors, then hang them up again in the morning. Keeping seed, pet food, and other goodies cleaned up will also keep opossums, skunks, and other creatures of the night from taking up residence under your deck. Companies like Wild Birds Unlimited offer raccoon baffles for feeder poles, which work like pole-mounted squirrel baffles to keep raccoons from climbing up. Or hang your feeders from a wire or clothesline and make the raccoons walk the tightrope to reach them.

- **Deer.** You either love deer (if they're not in your yard eating your expensive landscape plants) or hate them (if they are). Deer enjoy birdseed, too, and can become a huge nuisance at platform and tray feeders. If they find your feeders, take tray feeders into the garage (after emptying them, of course) and allow platform feeders to empty out before dusk (when deer typically come out to feed), replenishing them the next morning when the deer have gone back to the woods for the day. If the deer in your area are so brazen that they march right up to your platform feeder in broad daylight, switch to tube feeders hung from high branches and strongly mounted metal hopper feeders, at least until the deer leave for greener pastures.
- **Bears.** You've probably read that bear populations are increasing in rural and suburban neighborhoods all over the United States. Unfortunately, this is no myth. And bears love bird feeders. It's hard to believe that a huge bear would eat tiny birdseed until you hear a commotion and see a bear upending a tube feeder in your yard and pouring the contents down its throat! Bears are strong enough to destroy any feeder they can reach, even squirrel-secure hopper feeders. You may even have seen a photo of a bear strolling off with a feeder slung over its shoulder, still on the pole, for all the world like a fisherman heading home with his catch. If you've seen or heard of a bear in your neighborhood, clean up any spilled seed at the end of the day, put out only what birds will consume during daylight hours, and bring your feeders into a closed garage at night. That includes suet feeders—a favorite of bears!
- **Predators.** Hawks, owls, cats, coyotes, dogs—any carnivore that can reach your feeder will consider visiting birds as fair game. Give your feeder birds a fighting chance by setting up your feeders or feeding station near dense cover like shrubs, hedges, brush piles, or evergreens, and roofing your tray and platform feeders. Hang tube feeders where they're out of reach of four-footed predators, or put a domed baffle below a tube feeder to make it harder to reach the birds from below. Bear in mind that it's easier for predators to catch rodents than it is to catch birds, and many predators prefer rodents, so if you take these precautions you'll be more likely to see a dismembered mouse or chipmunk at the feeder than a bird.

SQUIRRELS

Squirrels are the most common mammalian bird feeder raider. Not only will they eat bird food, they'll often damage feeders to get to it; the same teeth that enable them to feast on acorns also let them gnaw through wood and plastic with relative ease. Some people call squirrels "rats with fuzzy tails," while others think they're cute; these views tend to coincide with the number of feeders destroyed and/or the pounds of sunflower seed consumed. Whether you're inclined to fight squirrels or live with 'em, try to keep in mind that they're wild animals simply going after foods they need to survive. They're not out to get you nor do they damage your feeders just to enrage you. It only seems that way!

Preventing Squirrel Problems

The most effective way to thwart squirrels is to keep them away from feeders in the first place. Start with **feeder placement**: Install feeders as far away as possible from trees, overhead power lines, the house, and outbuildings—anything a squirrel can jump from to reach feeders. They can jump 10 feet (3 m) or more, and willingly drop from nosebleed heights just to get to feeder food.

Next, use **posts, baffles, cylinders, screens, cages, tumblers, spinners,** and **specialized feeders** to keep squirrels from getting into food. Smooth metal or rigid plastic posts at least 6 feet (1.8 m) tall make it hard for a squirrel to climb up to feeders. To further deter squirrels from climbing a post, use baffles. Also called squirrel guards, these are aluminum or galvanized metal devices, usually cone-shaped, that fit around poles and keep climbing squirrels from getting past them to feeders. A trash can lid cut to fit around a feeder pole can work the same way. However, if squirrels reach a baffle by jumping onto it, they can then reach the feeder. Some baffle models have a spring attached to their bottom, which tilts the baffle and (ideally) causes the squirrel to slide off. You can cover part of a pole with a cylindrical baffle of smooth metal to make it harder to climb up, too. Use an overhead baffle for hanging feeders. It attaches to the suspension wire and acts as a slippery roof or cover. It also helps protect feed from rain.

Screens or cages of many kinds fit around feeders to keep pests out but let birds in to reach their food. The mesh can be sized to admit smaller birds, but exclude squirrels or larger birds. Many feeders come with attached screens or cages to limit squirrels' access to their contents.

Another preventive method uses **tumblers or spinners**. You suspend a feeder from a strong horizontal wire or tight clothesline and string sewing-thread spools or 35mm film canisters (with the bottoms removed) onto the wire or line. When a critter tries to scurry along the line, the spools spin and down goes the squirrel. Some people use short lengths of hose for the same effect.

A number of **squirrel-proof feeders** are available, including models that lock up the food when a squirrel's weight trips a lever. Most entertaining

Pole System Accessories

If your feeding station is based on one of the elaborate feeder pole systems on the market, you can outfit it with a selection of field-tested baffles and guards. Choose squirrel baffles and protective domes to put both at the top of the pole and on the pole below the feeders. Besides the baffles and domes, there are sliding tubes that move on the poles when a squirrel tries to climb them from below. (Wild Birds Unlimited even offers a model for deterring raccoons.)

are those with metal or mesh bottom platforms that spin at high speed when activated by the weight of a squirrel, giving the raider a slippery heave-ho off the old merry-go-round. You can almost feel sorry for the dizzy, dumped squirrels. Almost.

Anti-Squirrel Actions

Treating your birdseeds with hot-pepper spray or powder may serve as a limited-time deterrent to squirrels without offending birds, which reportedly don't feel the heat of this particular hot stuff. However, you must replenish the spicy seasoning whenever you refill your feeders or else pay a bit more for seed mixes that have been pretreated with hot-pepper flavoring. Factor in the additional care you'll need to take when handling hot-pepper-laced seed to avoid getting it on your hands or in your eyes, and this seems less like an attack on squirrels and more like an attack on you.

Besides, reports indicate that the mouth-burning effect wears off shortly, at least with some picante-preferring squirrels, and they're right back eating bird food again. Wildlife experts will tell you that if a squirrel wants food badly enough, it will just ignore taste repellents.

Keeping a garden hose or a long-range squirt rifle handy is a good squirrel deterrent, if you're constantly on guard. Squirrels are quick to become blasé about loud sounds and any other efforts you may make to scare them away. If you run toward them as they perch on your feeder, they'll usually oblige you by scurrying away, but will be back within minutes after you've left the scene. Trust us when we say that your patience with this game will run out long before the squirrels'. Shooting them with anything other than water is not recommended and is probably illegal as well as dangerous. The same is true of poisoning.

Living with Squirrels

If you tire of doing battle and want to lay down your weapons, or if you choose to avoid "squirrel stress" from the start, try to coexist. Provide squirrels with their own source of food, in hopes that a well-fed squirrel will stay away from bird feeders. Some people even provide squirrels with nesting boxes, hoping to keep them out of attics and buildings.

Offer squirrels foods they like, but that also takes time to eat. These include hard-shelled nuts such as walnuts, pecans, hickory nuts, and peanuts in the shell, plus acorns. They like a fresh coconut cut in half and hung from a wire, too. Many people use spiky corn-on-the-cob feeders that provide lots of entertainment as squirrels sit, rotate, and chew on the kernels. Use dried field corn for this, which you can find with squirrel feeders at bird feeding and hardware stores; don't spend extra on tender sweet corn grown for people. Corn feeders may attract raccoons, however.

Avoid offering pet foods and table scraps unless you carefully monitor the area. Raccoons, opossums, and skunks will come around if there's surplus or strewn-about food. Clean up the area of edibles before nightfall to discourage these pests.

No matter what you use to feed squirrels, keep their special feeding area well away from bird feeders. Giving them ready access to food in their own particular spot will help them become accustomed to dining there and help to keep them away from your bird feeders. Expect a mess of hulls and debris beneath squirrel feeders—tidy they're not.

RACCOONS

Common in urban and suburban areas, raccoons are persistent and wily food raiders. Their intelligence, keen sense of smell, and climbing abilities bring them to feeders, where they love corn, fruit, nuts, and many other bird feeds. If raccoons raid your feeders, cages designed for squirrel-proofing may need upgrading. A raccoon can reach 10 or 11 inches (25 or 28 cm) into feeders and nest boxes.

Position feeders and birdhouses away from branches and structures that would allow raccoons to climb to food or nests. Use baffles on supporting posts or hangers and follow nest box specifications for features intended to block access by predators. Greasing the pole that supports a feeder or nest box may also deter these agile climbers, but avoid putting grease or other slippery or sticky substances on surfaces where birds will come in contact with the goo.

Keep raccoons away from bird foods by limiting feeding times and only filling feeders for immediate use. Avoid leaving feed on the ground—especially cracked corn. Don't leave pet food outdoors overnight or serve it to birds. Clean up the feeding area by nightfall, and make sure trash containers are tightly sealed.

Cute when viewed from a safe distance, raccoons carry ticks, lice, and fleas. Many die from rabies or canine distemper. Always keep kids and pets away and contact local health authorities if you see a raccoon acting disoriented, especially during the day. It may have distemper.

Healthy problem animals may be trapped alive and relocated, but check with wildlife agencies before attempting this—it's not as easy to trap a raccoon as you might think and dealing with a trapped animal can be difficult and dangerous. The same is true of hunting; check your local laws.

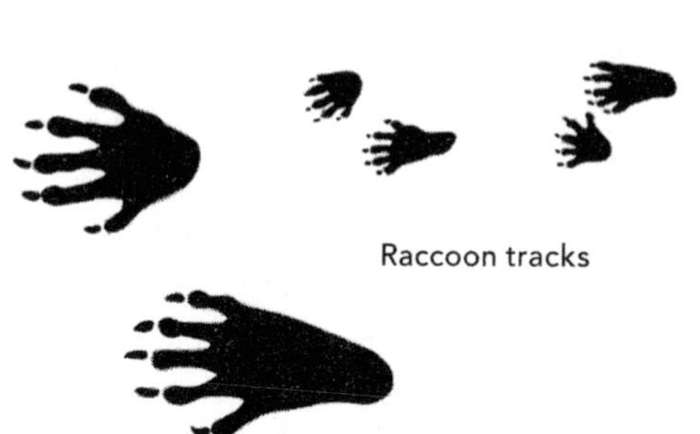

Raccoon tracks

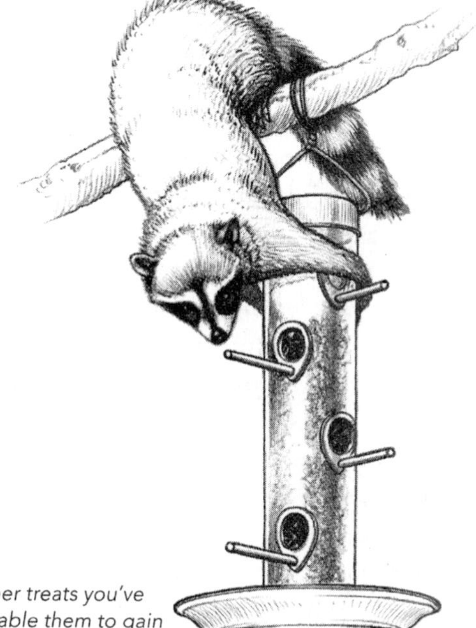

Omnivorous raccoons are happy to dine on seed, suet, and any other treats you've put out with birds in mind. Their dexterity and climbing abilities enable them to gain access to most feeders, even those designed to resist raids by squirrels.

DEER

A hungry deer will eat anything it likes—and even things it allegedly doesn't like. That includes food put out for birds, whether it's on the ground or in aboveground feeders. Common pests of gardens, trees, shrubs, and crops in rural areas, deer are seen more and more in suburban and urban areas these days, as their habitat becomes increasingly developed and crowded.

If deer are active in your neighborhood, you'll need to take some steps to keep them from feeders, fruit trees, and gardens. A tall, sturdy fence will work, but only if it's high or complicated enough to deter them. Most deer can jump at least 6 feet (1.8 m). A fence at least that tall—8 feet (2.4 m) is best—will be needed. Some people install a couple or series of fences, 4 to 6 feet (1.2 to 1.8 m) high and set far enough apart to keep deer from leaping across the gap. Others use double or triple rows of hedges spaced the same way to prevent deer from leaping into the area. Other tactics use regular-height fencing with sharp or electrified wires on top, or simply strands of electrified wire spaced close enough to prevent young and mature deer from going under, through, or over to get to food. With any deer fence, be sure that no gates or openings allow them to work their way through.

If fencing schemes are out of the question, place feeders at a height that deer can't reach. This may mean you have to install a pulley system to load feeders and then pull them up to a deer-proof height. Another tip is to feed birds only at times when deer are unlikely to be moving about, such as mid-morning and afternoon. An alert watchdog (the larger the better, in this case) will help keep deer away too, but it may spook birds as well. Using squirrel-proof screens and cages around feeders may slow down a hungry deer, but deer might damage feeders to get at food. Some people swear by devices like the ScareCrow, a motion-activated device that shoots an arc of water when a motion sensor is tripped by deer or other hungry critters.

Often deer whose habitat is lost move around until they find a safe place to call home. If your feeder gets raided, try stopping the feeding for a few days, and the deer will probably move on. Contact wildlife officials if deer become regular pests in incorporated areas.

OTHER FEEDER PESTS

Other four-legged and rodent pests around bird feeding areas include rats, mice, chipmunks, and opossums. The single best way to prevent problems with these pests is to avoid putting bird foods on the ground. Also, clean up outdoor pet dishes promptly after pets eat. If necessary, stop leaving food in bird feeders overnight until pest animals give up and go elsewhere. Trapping is an option for controlling small mammals, but traps need to be used with care to avoid catching birds. Check locally for regulations and the best types of traps and bait.

Mouse tracks Opossum tracks

RESOURCES FOR BACKYARD BIRDERS

Conservation and Education Organizations

American Bird Conservancy
PO Box 249
4249 Loudoun Avenue
The Plains, VA 20198-0249
540-253-5780
888-247-3624
www.abcbirds.org

American Birding Association
4945 N. 30th Street, Suite 200
Colorado Springs, CO 80919
800-850-2473
www.americanbirding.org

Birding.com
Hillclimb Media
710 Second Avenue, Suite 1130
Seattle, WA 98104
www.birding.com

Birdingonthe.net
www.birdingonthe.net

Cornell Lab of Ornithology
Attn: Communications
159 Sapsucker Woods Road
Ithaca, NY 14850
800-843-2473
www.birds.cornell.edu

eNature.com
1811 36th Street NW
Washington, DC 20007
www.enature.com

The Hummingbird Society
6560 Highway 179, Suite 204
Sedona, AZ 86351
800-529-3699
www.hummingbirdsociety.org

International Migratory Bird Day
2840 Iliff Street
Boulder, CO 80305
866-334-3330
www.birdday.org

National Audubon Society
700 Broadway
New York, NY 10003
212-979-3000
www.audubon.org

National Wildlife Federation
11100 Wildlife Center Drive
Reston, VA 20190-5362
800-822-9919
www.nwf.org

North American Bluebird Society (NABS)
PO Box 43
Miamiville, OH 45147
812-988-1876
www.nabluebirdsociety.org

Operation RubyThroat: The Hummingbird Project
Hilton Pond Center for Piedmont Natural History
York, SC
803-684-5852
www.rubythroat.org

The Purple Martin Conservation Association
301 Peninsula Drive, Suite 6
Erie, PA 16505
814-833-7656
www.purplemartin.org

Smithsonian Migratory Bird Center
National Zoological Park
Washington, DC 20008
www.nationalzoo.si.edu/ConservationandScience/MigratoryBirds/

U.S. Fish and Wildlife Service
1849 C Street, NW
Washington, DC 20240
800-344-WILD
www.fws.gov

Birding Supplies

Audubon Workshop
Customer Service
5200 Schenley Place
Lawrenceburg, IN 47025-2182
513-354-1485
www.audubonworkshop.com

The Bird House
2008 Stefko Boulevard
Bethlehem, PA 18017
610-691-8843
www.thebirdhousebethlehem.com

birdJam
670 Boulevard, SE
Atlanta, GA 30312
800-403-5524
www.birdjam.com

Droll Yankees, Inc.
27 Mill Road
Foster, RI 02825
800-352-9164
www.drollyankees.com

Duncraft, Inc.
102 Fisherville Road
Concord, NH 03303
888-879-5095
www.duncraft.com

eBirdseed.com
27823 86th Avenue S
Hawley, MN 56549-8982
866-324-7373
www.ebirdseed.com

For the Birds, Inc.
1209A Stamp Creek Road
Salem, SC 29676
877-261-6556
www.identiflyer.com

Garden Gate Enterprises, Inc.
6473 Ruch Road
Bethlehem, PA 18017
610-837-1114
www.gardengatebirdhouses.com

iFieldGuides
1219 Walnut Street
Newton, MA 02461
617-965-0354
www.ifieldguides.com

National Geographic's Handheld Birds
866-447-7696
www.handheldbirds.com

Optics4Birding
19 Hammond, Suite 506
Irvine, CA 92618
877-674-2473
www.Optics4Birding.com

Wild Bird Centers of America, Inc.
7370 MacArthur Boulevard
Glen Echo, MD 20812
800-945-3247
www.wildbirdcenter.com

WildBirdPlace.com
c/o epShops
350 Highway 7, Suite 14
Excelsior, MN 55331
877-271-2572
www.wildbirdplace.com

Wild Birds Unlimited, Inc.
11711 N. College Avenue, Suite 146
Carmel, IN 46032
800-326-4928
www.wbu.com

Organic Gardening Supplies, Seeds, and Plants

DirectGardening
Division of House of Wesley
1704 Morrissey Drive
Bloomington, IL 61704
309-662-7943
www.directgardening.com
Rugosa roses

Edible Landscaping
361 Spirit Ridge Lane
Afton, VA 22920
800-524-4156
www.ediblelandscaping.com
Self-pollinating sour cherries

Extremely Green Gardening Company
PO Box 2021
Abington, MA 02351
781-878-5397
www.extremelygreen.com

Forestfarm
9990 Tetherow Road
Williams, OR 97544-9599
541-846-7269
www.forestfarm.com

Gardener's Supply Company
128 Intervale Road
Burlington, VT 05401
888-833-1412
www.gardeners.com

Gardens Alive!
5100 Schenley Place
Lawrenceburg, IN 47025
513-354-1482
www.gardensalive.com

Heirloom Roses
161 Pockwock Road
Hammonds Plains, NS B4B 1N2
Canada
902-471-3364
www.oldheirloomroses.com
Rugosa roses

Johnny's Selected Seeds
955 Benton Avenue
Winslow, ME 04901
877-564-6697
www.johnnyseeds.com

Miller Nurseries
5060 West Lake Road
Canandaigua, NY 14424-8904
800-836-9630
www.millernurseries.com
Self-pollinating sour cherries

Peaceful Valley Farm & Garden Supply
PO Box 2209
125 Clydesdale Court
Grass Valley, CA 95945
888-784-1722
www.groworganic.com

Raintree Nursery
391 Butts Road
Morton, WA 98356
360-496-6400
www.raintreenursery.com
Self-pollinating sour cherries

Richters
357 Highway 47
Goodwood, ON L0C 1A0
Canada
905-640-6677
www.richters.com

Stark Bro's Nurseries & Orchards Co.
PO Box 1800
Louisiana, MO 63353
800-325-4180
www.starkbros.com
Self-pollinating sour cherries

Thompson & Morgan, Inc.
220 Faraday Avenue
Jackson, NJ 08527
800-274-7333
www.tmseeds.com

W. Atlee Burpee & Co.
300 Park Avenue
Warminster, PA 18974
800-333-5808
www.burpee.com

Worm's Way
7854 North State Road 37
Bloomington, IN 47404
800-274-9676
www.wormsway.com

Water Gardening Supplies

Arizona Aquatic Gardens
PO Box 68006
Oro Valley, AZ 85737
520-742-3777
www.azgardens.com

Lilypons Water Gardens
PO Box 10
6800 Lily Pons Road
Adamstown, MD 21710
800-999-5459
www.lilypons.com

Permaculture-Ponds.com
David W. Crimmins
13 Glen Oaks
Prescott, AZ 86305
928-273-5027
www.pond-doctor-dave.com

The Pond Doctor
119 N. Meridian Street
Sunman, IN 47041
812-623-2253
www.theponddoctors.com

Slocum Water Gardens
1101 Cypress Gardens Blvd.
Winter Haven, FL 33884
863-293-7151
www.slocumwatergardens.com

Tilley's Nursery/The Water Works
111 East Fairmount Street
Coopersburg, PA 18036
610-282-4784
www.tnwaterworks.com

William Tricker, Inc.
7125 Tanglewood Drive
Independence, OH 44131
800-524-3492
www.tricker.com

Van Ness Water Gardens
2460 N. Euclid Avenue
Upland, CA 91784
800-205-2425
www.vnwg.com

ABOUT THE WRITERS

Arlene Koch serves on the board of directors for the Pennsylvania Society for Ornithology and is a past president of the Lehigh Valley Audubon Society. Her "Nature Watch" column appears weekly in the Easton (Pennsylvania) *Express-Times*. When she's not tending her wildlife-welcoming home landscape or traveling in search of hummingbirds, Arlene often may be found counting raptors from one of the lookout posts at Hawk Mountain Sanctuary, in Kempton, Pennsylvania.

Deb Martin watches songbirds, game birds, and hawks (and listens to owls) from the windows of her home near Allentown, Pennsylvania. The most exotic birds to appear in her yard were a pair of (escaped domestic) peacocks but her favorites are the chickadees that "talk" to her while she fills her feeders. Deb has edited, written, and/or contributed to several bird books and gardening books and magazines; she enjoys a healthy compost heap every bit as much as she does a rose-breasted grosbeak.

Paul Peterson's native range includes the Midwest and North, where he was an award-winning gardening magazine editor. Currently a North Florida snowbird, Paul writes about birds and wildlife, native plants, herbs, and roses. He works with a native plant nursery that specializes in bird and butterfly gardens and tries to coexist with cats, squirrels, and other critters.

Ellen Phillips's college ornithology class kick-started a lifelong love of birds and backyard birding. She enjoys watching birds at the nine backyard feeders at her one-acre Eden, Hawk's Haven, in rural Pennsylvania, and at nearby Hawk Mountain Sanctuary. Ellen has authored, coauthored, and edited dozens of books on gardening, nature, pets, and home-related topics.

Barbara Pleasant lives in southwest Virginia, where she feeds dozens of phoebes and assorted finches through the winter and tries to outsmart robins and brown thrashers when her blueberries ripen in summer. The award-winning author of several gardening books, Barbara also grows sumac, elderberries, and sunflowers to help make her yard a haven for wild birds.

INDEX

Boldface page references indicate illustrations. Underscored references indicate boxed text and tables or charts.

C

G

H

I

J

K

L

M

N

Q

R

S

V

W

X

Y

Z

USDA PLANT HARDINESS ZONE MAP

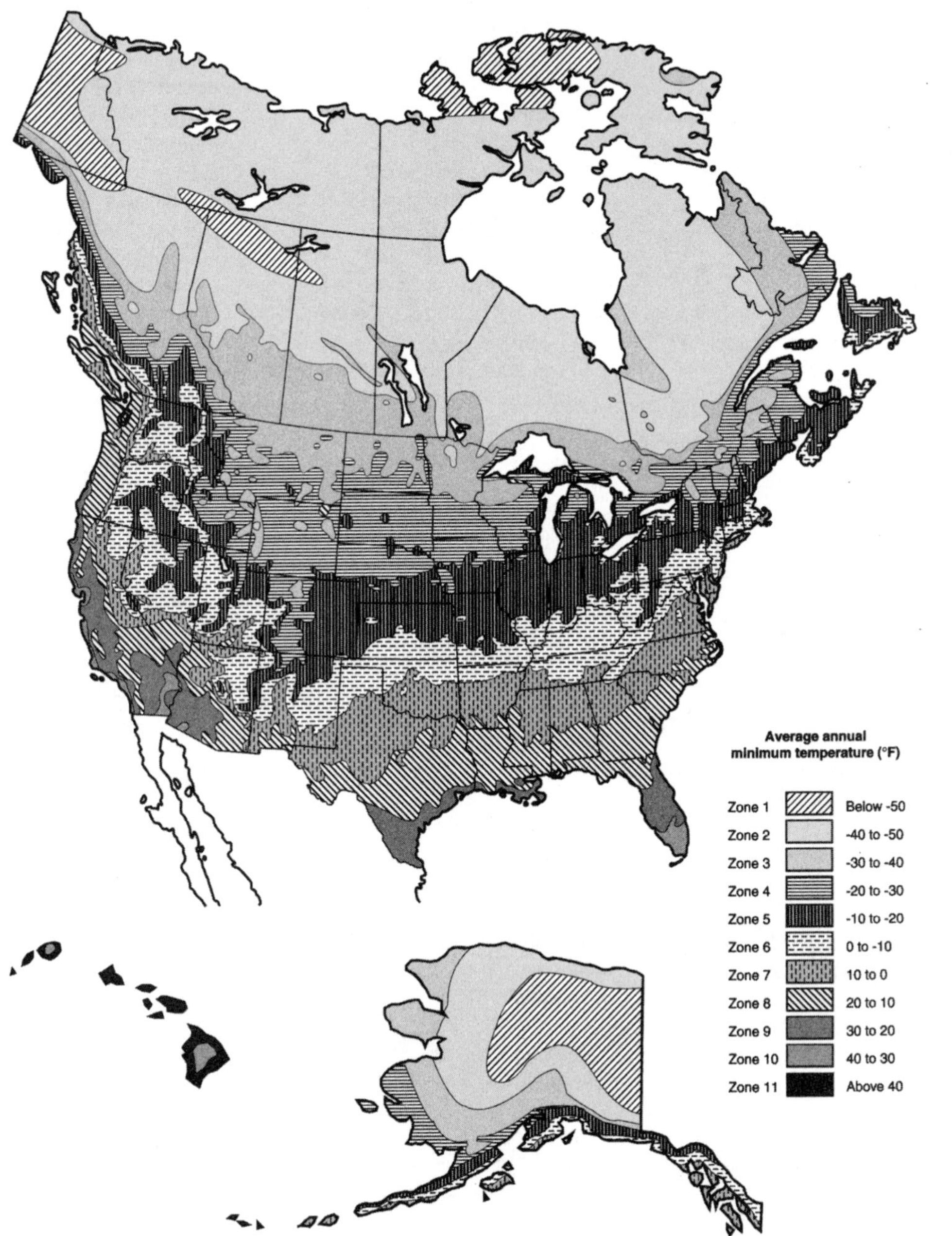

This map is recognized as the best indicator of minimum temperatures available. Look at the map to find your area, then match its pattern to the key at right. When you've found your pattern, the key will tell you what hardiness zone you live in. Remember that the map is a general guide; your particular conditions may vary.